I0095858

Abstracting Divinity

HEATHER MARSH

Binding Chaos

Heather Marsh

With apologies to the Four Beginnings of Mencius:

The feeling of Empathy is the beginning of Self;

the feeling of Excitement is the beginning of Life;

the feeling of Guilt is the beginning of Will;

the feeling of Joy is the beginning of Consciousness.

Binding Chaos

Heather Marsh

With grateful appreciation to my patrons and my invaluable
epistemic community:

Adam Kendall

Douglas Lucas

Fabiana Cecin

Connie Beckerley

Join the Binding Chaos community!

www.mustread.press

Binding Chaos

Heather Marsh

The Binding Chaos Series

A look at the world

Binding Chaos

The Ontology Quartet

Self – *The Creation of Me, Them and Us*

Life - *Abstracting Divinity*

Will – *Free Will and Seductive Coercion*

Consciousness – *Shaping Reality*

The Sociology Quartet

Person - *The Theft of Self*

Power - *Great Men, Commoners, Witches and Wretches*

Nation – *The Fourth Age of Nations*

Governance - *Autonomy Diversity Society*

The Institutions Quartet

Economy – *The Power Economy*

Law – *Law and Chaos*

Knowledge – *Political Science*

Technology - Code Will Rule

Binding Chaos

Heather Marsh

www.mustread.press

Copyright © 2024

Heather Marsh

Must Read

Author photograph by Tryston Powers

All rights reserved.

Ebook: 978-1-989783-33-7
Paperback: 978-1-989783-09-2
Hardcover: 978-1-989783-21-4

Binding Chaos

Table of contents

The experience of life...5

Chapter 1: The study of life......................................7

Chapter 2: The qualities of life...............................21

Chapter 3: Connection...39

Chapter 4: Sublation...71

Chapter 5: Violation...109

Chapter 6: Martyrs, tyrants, saviours and sirens 147

Chapter 7: Anima banks...181

Chapter 8: Euphoric rites.......................................215

The nature of life...235

Chapter 9: The original sin....................................237

Chapter 10: The economy of life............................261

Chapter 11: The ownership of life...........................285

Chapter 12: The nature of time...............................311

Chapter 13: The nature of death..............................337

Chapter 14: The nature of living..............................381

The Meaning of life..397

Chapter 15: The death of joy..................................499

Chapter 16: Silencing the wolf................................417

Chapter 17: To be or not to be................................433

Chapter 18: The purpose of life...............................439

Chapter 19: The theory of everything.....................................451

Chapter 20: Agents of order..461

Chapter 21: Agent of chaos..467

Chapter 22: A new metanarrative...477

Afterword..499

Key concepts...507

Glossary..543

Table of Figures

Figure 1: Four types of interactions....................................32

Figure 2: Three types of relationship.................................41

Figure 3: Shared animus...65

Figure 4: Sublation..73

Figure 5: Interaction and rebuffed interaction.....................77

Figure 6: Endosocial membranes and primary and secondary anima..83

Figure 7: Parasitic relationship......................................86

Figure 8: Energy embezzlement.......................................90

Figure 9: Loss of anima through environmental stress..........96

Figure 10: Draining anima from those in a position of power 104

Figure 11: Secondary anima obtained through destruction. .109

Figure 12: Anger-fear symbiosis and the contempt-shame symbiosis...115

Figure 13: Emergency male endo-idealism........................124

Figure 14: Martyrs and tyrants......................................146

Figure 15: Saviour..170

Figure 16: Siren...175

Figure 17: Photoelectric effect......................................214

Figure 18: The interaction and the self............................218

Figure 19: Interaction spacetime...218

Figure 20: Filial Endogroup...291

Figure 21: Lost connections...295

Figure 22: Interactions in the future......................................313

Figure 23: Will creating time and linking interactions.........316

Figure 24: Exosocial and endosocial expansion...................318

Figure 25: Altruistic energy transfer.....................................320

Figure 26: Many or few anima conduits................................322

Figure 27: Time between interactions....................................323

Figure 28: Expenditure of life energy....................................331

Figure 29: Self, body, and will gravity sphere.....................349

Figure 30: Conscious...350

Figure 31: The tunnel...354

Figure 32: Weighed down vs rising on decoupling..............359

Figure 33: Self with an attached negative image.................373

Figure 34: Emotional will and concious will.......................385

Figure 35: Time progression..387

Figure 36: Interactions connected by will............................452

Figure 37: Earth will..453

Figure 38: Conscious conducted by will and powered by life
....454

Figure 39: Exoself and endoself..461

Figure 40: Inertia..466

Heather Marsh

Figure 41: Connection, sublation and violation....................483

Figure 42: Endogroup weakening..485

Binding Chaos

Note to reader 🐈

Abstracting Divinity is the third book in the *Binding Chaos* series. These books contain related ideas which may be read together or alone. *Abstracting Divinity* is part of *The Ontology Quartet*, four books which bring us to the very foundations of our existence and ask the most elemental questions of the universe. It is possible to read the later books in *The Sociology Quartet* and *The Institutions Quartet* without the understanding established here, but these first four books introduce and explain the guiding principles for all later books. In particular, *Abstracting Divinity* explores how we should live, why we should live and what it means to live. If the unexamined life is not worth living, the examination starts here.

There may be words used in this book which were introduced in other books of the series. Their definitions can be found in the glossary at the end of this book. In *The Creation of Me, Them and Us*, I discussed primary and secondary euphoria as the prime determinants of human behaviour and the root of all emotions. I talked about euphoric conduits, euphoric bonds and even euphoric objects, but I drew a black box around the thing which triggers euphoria. In this book, we will explore the possibility that euphoria is produced by life itself.

The universe is composed of interactions. The self is created from these interactions. Each interaction is preceded by a cloud of potential outcomes. Will provides the ability to choose outcome. A nervous system provides an emotional response centre with the ability to govern will. Life is a force which attracts and repels, resulting in emotional responses. Consciousness, or awareness, gives the ability to learn and to know and to override the emotional will.

Life is not will. Will is that which makes a choice, and many lives are lived with very little power to choose. Neither can life be conflated with consciousness. It is possible to be alive and not aware, and it is possible to be conscious and not alive. Life also has little to do with the emotional self, outside of its ability to coerce that self.

Each of these components of a person has its own book in the first part of the *Binding Chaos* series, *The Ontology Quartet*. *Abstracting Divinity* is a book about life, consciousness is covered in *Shaping Reality*, will is covered in *Free Will and Seductive Coercion*, and the self is covered in *The Creation of Me, Them and Us*. *Abstracting Divinity* will attempt to describe life, its nature and purpose, and the law(s) governing its behaviour, in order that we can live our individual allocations of life according to that law.

The first part of *Abstracting Divinity* will explore what we know about life from observation, traditional ideas, social interactions and experience of life. The second part will discuss what those observations can tell us about the nature and attributes of life. Here we will look for correlations to what we know about energy and the universe for possible explanations of what life is. Finally, the last part provides early glimmerings of what the nature of life means for how we should build our institutions and live our lives. These last topics will be explored in much greater depth in the later books of this series, *The Sociology Quartet* and *The Institutions Quartet.*

In *Abstracting Divinity,* we look at the worst that is in us in order to find the best. We face the possibility of meaninglessness in order to seek meaning. We fracture ourselves in order to recreate a stronger whole. Please join me in this dive to the very depths of who we are and this flight to the great expanse of who we may be. We may not all agree, but we should all be seeking these answers

H.

Binding Chaos

The experience
of life

Abstracting Divinity

Chapter 1

The study of life

I am the flame above the beauty in the fields; I shine in the waters; I burn in the sun, the moon, and the stars. And with the airy wind, I quicken all things vitally by an unseen, all-sustaining life. — Hildegard of Bingen

I n 2024, no authoritative source has agreed on a definition of *life*. Dictionaries provide circular and entirely unhelpful definitions such as *"the quality that distinguishes a vital and functional being from a dead body"* or *"a principle or force that is considered to underlie the distinctive quality of animate beings"* [1] and academics debate contradictory attributes with no consensus. As a result, all of our institutions are built according to the dictates of an inconsistent definition of life.

As the term for the study of life has changed, from metaphysics to philosophy to physics, so has the accepted form of the study. While metaphysicists attempted to control life through magic, philosophy attempted to explain it and physics carefully separates established theory from the human condition. Human and other animal life is treated as a medical condition and a binary state. This treatment is divorced from all other scientific study, where life is treated as a continuum that must have arrived on earth and has continued since. Even the latter definition is far removed from the common definition in everyday language where life is considered and referred to as a force.

Vitology, the study of the nature and behaviour of life energy, must be an entire area of study unto itself, consistently applied in all contexts. The founding philosophers of both psychology and sociology, as well as every earlier philosophical study, devoted the backbone of their thought to the study of life. Despite this, most aspects of this study are now ignored or left to books marginalized as new age and self-help. There is really no valid reason why life has been marginalized into the realm of things that cannot be known in recent centuries. Its marginalization coincided with the rise of corporate industrialization and may be suspected of being political, since the study clearly reveals the nature of power and the fraudulent claims to a right to power.

Power, one of the most urgent and essential topics of study, is currently ignored as an underfunded, sociological curio with isolated studies tucked away in corners as separated as neuroscience and *Political Science*. The study of power ought to be a primary focus of vitology. Once this is understood, it becomes apparent that vitology is a necessary foundation for every scientific or academic study, from economics to climatology.

Vitology may replace psychology as a better foundation for understanding emotions, motivations and mental stress. Vitology, the study of life, is also essential background for gerontology, the study of aging or depletion of life. Vitology needs to include physics, as life is a force. It needs to include neuroscience so we can understand the processes affected by life, such as how empathy is blocked and extended and how emotions are produced. It needs to include sociology, as that is the study of power, violence and social bonding. Vitology is the home for the science of resuscitation, currently called an orphan by its leading researchers[2] Resuscitation research is needed in order to understand the relationship between the life, body, self, consciousness and will.

One life cannot be contained in a person and studied as a trait of an individuated object. Until recently, western medicine focused study on cadavers and

One life cannot be contained in a person and studied as a trait of an individuated object.

viewed bodies as objects instead of processes or phases. As a result, western scientists originally viewed the body as similar to a perpetual motion machine. Once it stopped, it was declared dead. This has not been the view in practice for some time now, as resuscitation medicine has greatly evolved in recent decades.

Western science has failed to grapple with, or even widely acknowledge, the end to their purely mechanist views. Scientists and academics are largely ignoring the fact that anything has changed and simply adding resuscitation as an appendix to their existing worldviews. This allows them to continue to scoff at any mention of the life energy held to be self-evident by every belief system in history except this very recent ideology.

The lack of an established science of vitology is not due to lack of material for scientific research. The study of vitology does currently form a part of physics since the laws of physics apply to all force. A great deal of relevant research is already skirted around in the study of consciousness which regularly and awkwardly appears in physics, albeit with no clear definition of what it is. Consciousness appears to be a quasi-acceptable area of study where life itself is not. Life is occasionally acknowledged by physics as a possible force following the laws of thermodynamics. Life is touched upon, from a purely mechanist outlook, by biology and chemistry in subjects such as cell renewal or in gerontology, the study of aging. The study of vitology also forms a part of neuroscience and topics in biology and chemistry which describe the means through which life is transferred.

These studies on the behaviour of life may occasionally ask how, though never why. Odd bits of information appear, such as the role of red light therapy in providing an energy boost to cell mitochondria, but with no underlying theory, or even language, in which to frame these findings, they remain isolated curios. Without a focused study of vitology, none of these disciplines have a framework in which to position their findings. Physicists are left referring vaguely to some undefined consciousness (which is not life) and neuroscientists must frame all relevant findings to fit the incoherent ramblings of psychology or the commercial interests of psychiatry.

None of this is sufficient. The funding still allocated to studies such as the ideas of Freud and denied to the study of life is incomprehensible. Every question in how we live and how we die is dependent on this one question – What is life? Beyond even this, life is very far from being an earthbound anomaly or curio. Life is key to understanding the universe and must be a fundamental component of a theory of everything. Life is not a trivial side issue that may be touched upon in passing while studying other things. It is bizarre to make no attempt to define this most basic information of our existence.

Since the vast majority of the world does not share the scientific phobia of the discussion of life, science is the one area of society that has no knowledge of it. People do not have the language to describe the most significant aspects of their existence to the scientific class. They will often attempt to do so but become instantly blocked by language limitations. I feel drained, is an attempt to express a feeling but drained of what? Energy, some may say, but what energy? It is obviously life energy, but to say so would break the taboos enforced by the scientific endoreality we defer to. My infant feels pain, a mother attempts to explain to a medical professional. How do you know? he sneers. We have yet to be apart since she was born, and our shared animus, which controls our emotions, is still very strong, she is not permitted to reply.

Science was created in opposition to animism, primarily because categorization was the sole method of differentiating the wealthy, urban men who called themselves scientists from the old women and indigenous elders who studied nature with far greater success.

🐈‍⬛

In the same way that religion was differentiated from animism by the presence of a book, scientists claimed their removal from the natural environment gave them 'objectivity', the ability to view the world as a collection of objects, unconnected to the subject. This perspective leads to cognitive (manufactured) knowledge and ignores the empathic and emotional knowledge of connections through the conscious and self. Emotions are a response to life energy. Language is required for discussion of emotional knowledge and that language has been discredited by bigotry against those forms of knowledge.

An interesting feature of the campaign to discredit animism is the consistent and very unscientific claim to know the motivations of all of the people in history around the world. This claim insists that all of these people were so terrified of the world that they needed a spiritual delusion as an emotional crutch, unlike the enlightened endo-ideals of science. Ironically, many scientists refuse to acknowledge or study human and animal behaviours towards the life force, as they have a superstitious fear of divinity more overpowering than any of the earlier superstitions they treat with such contempt.

As Dr Walter Franklin Prince pointed out regarding scientific research in 1930, "*psychical research ... seems to have an enchanted boundary ... In other fields they are prudently silent until they have acquired special knowledge, but they venture into this with none. Elsewhere they test their facts before they declare them, but here they pick up and employ random statements without discretion. Elsewhere they use a fair semblance of logic, but here their logic becomes wondrous weird. Elsewhere they generally succeed in preserving the standard scientific stolidity, but here they frequently manifest and confess a submission to emotions ill befitting those who sprang from the head of Brahma.*"[3]

This behaviour is familiar to anyone who observes endoreality masquerading as science, economics or any other place where facts are found to meet and support the laws of a pre-ordained worldview. The deliberate self-blinding to the life force, or life energy, which self-evidently exists, is possibly the most prominent case of scientific superstition. This superstition of the scientific religion, which scientists like to misrepresent as skepticism, causes gaping and inexplicable holes in scientific knowledge.

This superstition is an aversion to all knowledge emanating from the negative image to the scientific ideal, which are old women and indigenous nations. Any knowledge from these sources is greeted with instant contempt until it is cleansed of all prior association and rebranded as a product of science. This has not yet happened with the study of life, due to an early church monopoly. European knowledge after the Reformation was divided between the Pope and the Protestants. The *"enchanted boundary"*

Divinity has traditionally been used as a loosely defined term representing both conscious and will.

Prince recognized was used to separate the supposedly mystical elements of a person, the self, life, consciousness and will, which were left to the Catholic and Orthodox churches. Practical Protestants looked to the material world and put all of their focus on the body, a focus which was continued by Germanic scientists. Animist knowledge is now divided between science and religion, and scientists still hesitate to step outside those enchanted boundaries.

Divinity has traditionally been used as a loosely defined term representing both conscious and will. Later usage includes some references to life and the self. The scientific taboo against all mention of divinity required abstractions of every aspect of divinity into some generic, materialist concept acceptable under science. Thus, the five elements of a person are all referred to as the body or aspects of the body. Disturbance of the self, life, will or consciousness are all treated as bodily ailments.

Black box words are words with no definition other than circular, often used to pretend a meaning where none is known or disguise a meaning which is against the authoritative endoreality. Conscious is abstracted into the black box words imagination and nothing. Will is abstracted into the black box word random and the institutions of law, economy and algorithms. Self is reduced to the body. Disturbances beyond the body are referred to as mental illness, which recognizes that the disturbances are not physical but refuses to grant them specificity. Life energy is abstracted into icons, such as currency. Life's influence is buried in the endoreality of psychology and economics. These abstractions of conscious, will, self and life take partial aspects of them and create a generic symbol or idea, so they can be referred to, but only in a disguised and partial form. If we break down all the abstractions, we can see the nature of those things which have been classified as divinity: the conscious, the will, the self and life.

The scientific taboo against everything classified as divinity currently leaves authoritative knowledge restricted to the transparently inadequate mechanist beliefs that shaped Anglo-Germanic science and institutions. Physical science evolved. Social science became dogma, or cynical corporatism. Quantum mechanics redefined nearly all of science and technology and nothing of our social structures and institutions.

A clue that a word is being used to support endoreality is that it has a fuzzy definition. The definition of life that is used by scientists is fuzzy to the point of being non-existent. This is because they are trying to create an endoreality that excludes life from some objects and allocates it to others when life follows no such exceptionalism. As animists have always known, life is everywhere. Without the fuzziness of endoreality clouding our perception, it is far easier to examine the nature of life.

The problem in all of the authoritative definitions of life is that the biologists, physicists and philosophers who attempt to define it are attempting to cram a definition into a materialist view. From a materialist perspective, the question What is life? becomes equivalent to What type of object is this force? The answer is never going to fit the pre-ordained constraints of the question. Life is not an attribute. Resuscitative medicine is illustrating every day that life is a force which flows in and out of objects. This is the definition of life which agrees with every culture outside of the one strange materialist ideology that evolved in the Germanic world in the last few centuries and called itself science.

In medicine, the definition of life is very subjective. A person may be declared dead earlier in the process if they run out of money to pay for treatment. They may be declared dead even earlier if their living organs are needed for another living person. The definition becomes political in the case of a fetus which shares the life of its mother but is often politically assigned an individuated life. This is completely inconsistent with the treatment of organs or other cells which are not depicted with their own individuated portions of life. If someone is wealthy enough and so inclined, they may put their life on pause and be preserved until resuscitative medicine can reanimate them. Schrödinger's cat, which is both dead and alive until an authority observes it, has never been a more accurate depiction of lived reality than it is today.

While those in the social sciences insist that life is undefined or ignore it entirely, and medical science treats it as a binary attribute of an object, technology is using life as a force and animating objects such as artificial intelligence robots. All practical science acknowledges that life is not an exotic element and does not represent the person or organism. The working definition of life is a force able to transfer energy to and from objects but authoritative definitions are still refusing to acknowledge or study it as this.[4]

The world's billionaires are currently spending their fortunes in a space race, attempting to travel to other planets and seek extraterrestrial life. Without a definition of what life is, NASA is searching *"for the presence of water, the existence of carbonate minerals, the occurrence of organic residues, and any isotopic fractionation between organic and inorganic phases. Each of these will provide clues to the likelihood of life on Mars when matched against the prevailing environmental conditions, such as temperature, pressure, wind speed, UV flux, oxidation potential, and dust environment."* They may find any or all of these things, but without a definition for life, they will never find life. [5]

In the next chapter, we will begin to gather the defining attributes of life from our experience of it. For those not wilfully blind, the answer to What is life? is all around us.

Vitology

The study of life. Vitology should include the study of power, gerontology (including geroscience), physics, medicine, neuroscience, sociology and physics. Vitology ought to replace psychology. The study of vitology ought to formulate the guidelines for the structures of all social institutions.

Divinity

A loosely defined term representing sometimes the universal or quantum will and sometimes the conscious. Some later usage includes aspects of life.

Some (of many) abstractions of divinity

The five elements of a person are all referred to as the body or aspects of the body.

Conscious is abstracted into the black box words imagination and nothing.

Will is abstracted into the black box word random and the institutions of law, economy and algorithms.

Life energy is abstracted into icons, such as currency.

Life's influence is buried in the endoreality worlds of psychology and economics.

Abstracting Divinity

Chapter 2

The qualities of life

The probability of life originating from accident is comparable to the probability of the unabridged dictionary resulting from an explosion at a printing shop. — Edwin Grant Conklin

While it is possible that no living being can be certain why life exists, there are things we can say about the nature of life and even its purpose. Life has observable attributes and tendencies. We all know a lot more about life than we are told we do and many aspects are not nearly as mysterious as they are held to be.

Life is not synonymous with consciousness which is knowledge or will which is choice or self which is a cluster of interactions. Neither is life unique to an individual body. Life is just the energy source that keeps the body system running. It does have far wider importance than that implies, however, and that importance will be discussed in later chapters.

The basic premises of vitology are clear and easily established. We know that life energy exists because we are alive. Life has always been considered an energy and it is hard to imagine how it could be assumed to be anything else at this point. If another assumption is made, surely the latter assumption bears the burden of proving itself because assuming that life is an energy has been field tested for centuries and life is increasingly equated to energy again in geroscience. If someone has a different definition, they should also provide a different word, as they are speaking of a different topic.

As an energy, life is probably governed by the first law of thermodynamics. Life cannot come out of nothing. The origin of this life energy, to follow Occam's razor, is probably our surroundings. Life probably comes from an external life source because where else would it come from? Upon death of a bodily host, life probably returns to the external life source because where else would it go to? It can neither come from nothing nor disperse into

Life is just the energy source that keeps the body system running.

nothing.

The most reasonable expectation is that life is constant. Therefore, it must be neither restricted to one body nor exclusive to one body. It is an energy that arrives via a force that flows through all parts of the earth's biosphere and animates various forms. It (probably) cannot be created, therefore it is gained and lost through our interactions. It must be gained and lost through interactions because interactions are all that exist.

Life force and energy have been called many things, including qi, anima mundi, chokmah and many more words representing many ideas. Life is often associated with breath, as in the words spiritus, ruach, pneuma, and prana. The Abrahamic Holy Spirit may be an example of this idea, especially as interpreted in some first millennialist beliefs regarding a Third Age presided over by the Holy Spirit. This is seen less as an anthropomorphized god and more as a spirit present in everyone and everything. The point of hatha yoga is to breathe in life energy, or prana, and expel energy that is not useful for the body. This obviously works better if the surrounding environment is filled with life energy, which is why yoga at beaches and in forests is so popular. The idea of surrounding life energy is present in rites and beliefs in many diverse cultures, as will be discussed in later chapters.

Germanic languages, including English, tend to have one word each for the concepts of life and death.

Compared to most Asian languages and indigenous languages of all regions, which have an abundance of words for every aspect and type of life and death, this lack is crippling to any attempted discussion of related topics. Some useful related Chinese concepts that have no English translation are han, ren, qi, shen, hun, po and jing.

All of the missing concepts in the words for life in other languages are useful, or even essential, to understand the topics covered here but it would require a great deal of work to translate ideas into English that do not exist in English and that work is, unfortunately, beyond the scope of this book. It should be recognized however, that there are many aspects of life that deserve their own names and the word life is woefully inadequate to describe any of them.

Where English provides a word to discuss one type of death, and strictly medicalizes any modifiers, ayurvedic and traditional Chinese medicine (TCM) describe life as an energy that fluctuates and moves in phases. For instance, ayurvedic medicine has five dosha which indicate the balance of each person's mental, physical, emotional and personality characteristics, and all of these characteristics are assessed for health instead of just a physical body. This type of knowledge and language would be very useful in developing modern medical science which finally recognizes that death is a spectrum that occurs over days (as every indigenous culture and many, or all, other animals have always known). It would also be useful to incorporate these phases and fluctuations in the still highly marginalized and isolated western study and treatment of mental and emotional health.

This is not to say that everything taught in ayurvedic or traditional Chinese or indigenous medicine ought to be accepted as entirely accurate, or for that matter, that western medicine ought to go back to balancing humours. It would be very helpful, however, to look at energy flows and consider the possibility of different types, states or manifestations of life energy instead of just viewing the body as a mechanist object that stops and starts and has no other phases. This is particularly true since research on the phases of death is beginning to accumulate a lot of data in western medicine and there is no linguistic framework to hold it.

The difference between traditional schools of thought and modern thought is largely a matter of verbs vs nouns. Modern thought has become very enamoured of the idea of the world as a collection of objects. This is a view indicated even in historical European art which focused

The difference between traditional schools of thought and modern thought is largely a matter of verbs vs nouns.

on accurate representation of objects, as opposed to the Eastern appreciation of the beauty of the brush stroke in itself.

In English, the only embellishment to the idea of death that is typically heard is that the person died of heart failure, or some such meaningless phrase, as if knowing that the heart stopped upon death was more informative than knowing whether the deceased was hit on the head with a blunt object first or perhaps had spent the last several decades drinking, smoking and eating bad food, and in both cases, why? The person and all stages and behaviours that contribute to both life and death are removed in a strictly mechanist view of both. There is only one type of death and one type of life in the English language, with only one exception. Brain dead is a recent invention created to make organ harvesting, which must be done before a person is dead according to the regular definition, more acceptable to the authorizing next of kin. This propagandist addition is not helpful in clarifying the phases or types of death.

A person is a fusion of five distinct elements. Besides the body, these are self, life, will and consciousness.

As is pointed out in other books in this series, self, life, will, consciousness and body are all very different things. The five may exist separately from each other and may individuate in different groupings. A one to one relationship between any of these things cannot be assumed and the root malaise of all social sciences is that they do just that.

The types of death that we ought to clarify indicate what aspect of the person is no longer operational. A sudden, physical death destroys the body so that the will is knocked out of it and can often not return. A person can also lose the will to live, or the consciousness can dissociate, or life can be depleted, or the person may lose emotional connection to the self, or that connection may be rendered harmful due to guilt and shame.

Language is needed to clarify whether it is the body, self, life, will or consciousness which has left or dissociated from the person. The departure of life from a body is common and increasingly easily remedied. It follows a long spectrum of phases, usually occurring over days or longer. The departure of will is often misdiagnosed as a departure of conscious. In many coma patients, the conscious is fully present but unable to exert control over the will. The body may be preserved and reanimated for an extended period of time if deterioration is avoided, but it can only regain functionality as a person if the will is capable or desires to return. If it is the conscious which dissociated, it will leave a person functioning but increasingly unaware or unable to form or recall memories. A person may instead lose their emotional attachments to their self through brain trauma, drug use or severe emotional trauma. While this can cause a complete change in emotions, the person may appear to be functioning exactly as before. Finally, a person may suffer from a malignant emotional will which causes them to indulge in harmful behaviour. This can initiate a long term battle with ill health and 'accidents' and a struggle between the conscious and emotional wills.

In *Abstracting Divinity,* we will focus on the aspect of life and its relationship with the person. Since the study of life in objects is widely recognized as animism, the word anima will be used in Binding Chaos theory to represent life energy. The usage of anima here is unrelated to any usage in psychology or other Jungian references. Nor does it correlate with definitions in various dictionaries or old Greek or Latin works which use anima to refer to spirit, psyche or will. Here it is simply used to denote life energy. The word animus will serve in Binding Chaos theory to represent individuated life and has no correlation to the definition of animus as hostility. Animus here refers to life that is contained for the use of an individual or group, within what was referred to in *The Creation of Me, Them and Us* as an endosocial membrane or a personal membrane. As with the earlier description, a personal animus can expand to include more than one person and it can be sublated to a larger group animus.

Life throughout history has been depicted as energy and described and experienced as energy received or lost. Reanimation refers to a gain in anima and deanimatio n refers to a loss. The gain or loss is possible because the energy travels

Life makes up the animus of the individual.

through the animus membrane through what were referred to in *The Creation of Me, Them and Us* as euphoric conduits. We will now refer to these connections which facilitate anima transfer as anima conduits.

The experience of life energy appears to trigger the emotional reaction of euphoria. All emotions appear to be triggered in response to the experience or anticipation of a gain or loss in life energy, as explained in *The Creation of Me, Them and Us*. Euphoria is the emotional experience of energy added to the animus. In Binding Chaos theory, anima is the energy and euphoria is the emotional response to experience of that energy, so in some cases, the two words may appear to be used interchangeably.

Life makes up the animus of the individual. Their relative position in an animated (often but not always social) network is their self. Their individuated awareness of conscious is their consciousness. Their control over the choices of themselves or others emanates from their will. Just as the body needs healthy food every day, the self needs balanced interactions, the consciousness needs knowledge, the will needs exertion over choice and the animus needs life energy.

A life form is a form, or a host, filled with life obtained (most probably) from its surroundings. The body still exists after death and the parts of the body are a great variety of different ages. Some parts of the body appear after death is declared.[6] Most that are present at death are nowhere in existence at birth. Life is not a thing that arrives and departs with the body. Neither is life in the blueprint of the body, generally held to be the DNA, for the DNA is just one part of what creates a body and nothing of what creates a life.

Personalities can be altered by environmental substances. Therefore, some aspects of personality are not connected to memories or conscious thought which are confined to the body. These aspects must be connected to the wider self and life. Personality is at least partially made up of emotional responses to anima attraction and repulsion. These responses are governed by conscious and emotional control over will, so personalities can be said to change when one or the other of these wills becomes dominant. This is evident when drugs, illness or other conditions allow the emotional will to dominate in a person who otherwise has strong conscious control.

If we assert that a robot is not living, what separates living from not living appears to be a range of emotions triggered by certain interactions. These emotions produce an emotional will controlled outside of the volition driven by cognitive processes. This is not a universal condition of life, as many living beings (including humans in some states) are incapable of these emotional responses or have a sublated will. Indeed, the goal of many schools of thought is to sublate the emotional will and rely on reason over emotion or mind over matter. If we could claim a certain expected response to life, however, and account for the deviations from that expected behaviour, we may have a starting point to separating the experience of living from automation.

In order for life energy to be continually obtained from our surroundings, there must be a life force which facilitates this. The preferred direction of this life force appears to be outward expansion, similar to the expansion of the rest of the universe. As the universe is expanding with increasing rapidity, the history of life on earth shows the same increasing pace of expansion. Just as the universe must have dark energy enabling its accelerating expansion, we must have our own force enabling our continual self-expansion. Life expansion is facilitated through interactions with other sources of life energy.

The expansive force can be blocked through the use of a greater opposing force, as Newton pointed out in 1687. There is one law which all of vitology is centred around which is the law of inertia. Newton's first law of motion states that a body will continue in its current state of motion or rest unless acted upon by an unbalanced force. The diversion of the expansive life force through application of greater force has a great many social ramifications and may even change the nature of the life force.

To avoid disrupting the outward force of those we interact with, every interaction must be balanced. Interactions of unequal force result in power held by one side of the interaction. Power is the result of an unbalanced anima transfer. All study of social power, indeed all of sociology, psychology, and perhaps all of the social sciences, may be described in terms of attraction and repulsion of anima transfers.

Unbalanced interactions result in both accumulation of power and compensations (equal and opposite reactions, in accordance with Newton's third law of motion). The compensations resulting from imbalance explain all deviant or anti-social behaviour. Everything described in psychology as a personality disorder is a disruption in emotional response to interactions.

When interactions are unbalanced, energy from the weaker is absorbed by the stronger until eventually the weaker is consumed by, or sublated to, the stronger. Once a person is sublated to another, they share the same animus, or emotional reactions, and are dominated by the same will. This is the traumatic bond so familiar to those in predatory relationships. Because interactions must be balanced, the separation, or individuation, between entities is erased when one is sublated. The part of the person which is sublated appears to be the will, although the effects can be seen on the consciousness, body and self and in the depletion of life.

Life then, may be a force which draws us outwards in an ever-increasing expansion of interactions. Our challenge to fulfillment of our life is any inverted force which blocks our expansion. If the purpose of life is exosocial expansion, or the completion of interactions to create an expanded network, it would finally explain why we have pain and misery. The loss of a loved one produces pain and an existential threat through the tear in the shared animus membranes we form around our dearest attachments. The only way to survive such a threat is to seek other interactions, to paint, to dance or to love again. The healthiest response when we are at our weakest is always to continue growing outwards and establish more anima conduits.

Pain triggers the release of emergency anima which is required for exosocial expansion, especially at critical times such as birth and death. Misery which does not overcome us must itself be overcome, by exosocial expansion. If we are meant to never stop exosocial expansion, periodic tragedy serves to tear the membranes we form around our dearest attachments and shared animus in order to encourage new growth. Building a self is like building a muscle. Without a manageable level of trauma, no new growth is possible.

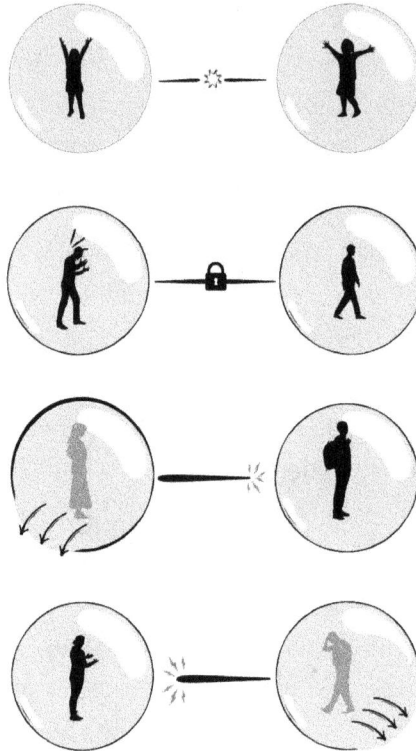

Figure 1: Four types of interactions

All interactions are animated. They all permit or attempt some form of anima transfer. The outcome can result in interactions that are balanced, rebuffed, unrequited or predatory. The emotional results indicate which type the interaction is. A balanced interaction produces joy. A rebuffed interaction may produce anger, aggressiveness or apathy. An unrequited interaction drains energy from the source and results in longing and sorrow. A predatory interaction drains energy from one agent, the prey, and that energy is picked up by the other agent, the predator.

If interactions are powered by anima, then each side of an animated interaction must be capable of holding a store of anima. In other words, each side must be an animus. This must include not just those things which are considered living in modern parlance but all things which have traditionally been considered living in the universal, traditional beliefs of animism.

People who can lift cars due to an increase in adrenaline pulled energy from their surroundings. Adrenaline itself is not energy; it is a call for energy. Life energy surrounds us. The body itself is a network of shared anima. Each unit of energy is broken down in one part of the body and expended by another. The only connection between the two is a clustering effect caused by a complex web of interactions that allows the energy to be treated as shared property.

Life moves and expands through animated interactions. Life is the energy that attracts will from each animated interaction to the next to create the self. It is possible that this expands to all of the universe. It is possible that the interactions which make up the universe are only created through the energy provided by life. This requires more explanation, but it is possible that the purpose of life is to create the universe.

Hold that thought while we review our experience of life in the coming chapters. First, let's look at the nature of these interactions.

Anima

life energy

Animus

life contained within an endosocial membrane for use by an individual or group

Deanimation

the loss or depletion of life from an animus

Reanimation

the gain of life in an animus

A person is a fusion of five elements

body, self, life, will and consciousness.

Life force expands outward through interactions with other sources of life energy. The expansive force can be blocked or deviated through the use of a greater opposing force.

A traumatic bond is formed when one will is sublated to another, they share the same animus and emotional reactions, and are dominated by the same will.

Life makes up the animus of the individual.

Their relative position in an animated network is their self.

Their individuated awareness of conscious is their consciousness.

Their control over the choices of themselves or others emanates from their will.

Just as the body needs healthy food every day, the self needs balanced interactions, the consciousness needs knowledge, the will needs exertion over choice and the animus needs life energy.

There are four types of interactions

balanced, rebuffed, unrequited and predatory.

A balanced interaction produces joy.

A rebuffed interaction may produce anger, aggressiveness or apathy.

An unrequited interaction drains energy from the source.

A predatory interaction drains energy from one agent, the prey, and that energy is picked up by the other agent, the predator.

Personality is made up of emotional responses to anima attraction and repulsion, governed by conscious and emotional control over will.

Abstracting Divinity

Heather Marsh

Chapter 3

Connection

Adventure is worthwhile in itself. — Amelia Earhart

People are not attracted to others for their fertility or their ability to provide as Darwinists have claimed for years. People are not here to reproduce; that is incidental. Otherwise, why would the will to live exist past reproduction? Why would people with no desire to reproduce still desire to live?

People are attracted to anima. Power attracts because power is an accumulation of anima. Those that are able to act as conduits for primary anima are the most attractive people of all. Talent attracts because talent is the ability to channel primary anima. Primary sources of anima are marked by two characteristics. One, they produce euphoria. Two, they prolong life.

Anima can create a balanced bond or connection between the two agents of the interaction. This bond creates a self which is enmeshed, or a part of, the sources of its anima. If the world were to end tomorrow, people would still tend their gardens. If a friend is dead, people will still honour them. These seemingly futile actions exist because of the importance of the friend and the garden within the still living connections. This bonding is evidenced by the emotional, mental and physical pain, and even existential threat, which is felt upon the destruction of the bond.

A shared animus results in emotional and physical reactions that are immediate and a product of the emotional will, not cognition.

Euphoria may be produced by simulated sources such as some drugs and other addictive substances and behaviours, but these do not prolong life, hence are simulated, not genuine, sources of anima. Euphoria resulting from gluttony and greed, for money, objects or drugs, provides temporary relief of craving but no real lasting satisfaction. Simulated euphoric sources do not establish lasting primary anima conduits or connections so they result in highs, crashes and cravings instead of the peace brought by secure connections. They trigger the hormones experienced by contact with anima, but provide no anima. Worse, some of them cause the body to release its own anima stores to trigger euphoria, resulting in severe deanimation. The deanimation caused by simulated sources increases the craving for anima which creates an addictive cycle.

Simulated euphoric sources eventually help to create an *endoself*. Endoselves no longer have conduits able to establish connection and access primary anima. They must survive on secondary sources obtained through *sublation* or *violation*. This causes the extreme personality changes so destructive to any personal relationships which are nearly always present in those who use simulated sources.

Relationships may be one of three types: connection, sublation or violation. Connection is composed of interactions which maintain an overall balance. Sublation and violation are composed primarily of unbalanced interactions which deplete one agent of the interaction to enrich the other.

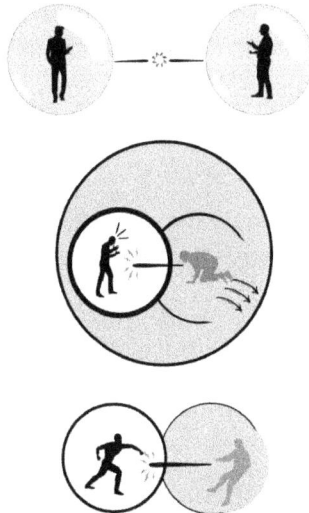

Figure 2: Three types of relationship

There are many sources of primary anima which are widely recognized as being sources of healing for physical, emotional or mental trauma. Some of these are nature, exercise, art, companionship, discovery, creation, falling in love, altruism and religious rites. These activities are sometimes described as *getting out of your head*, a phrase which implies establishing outside connections. The success of establishing these connections in combating depression and many other symptoms indicates that these illnesses and symptoms may be related to a lack of anima sources, an inability to access primary anima or anima depletion (deanimation).

In order to experience joy, or an increase in primary anima, there must be a conscious willingness to establish a connection to a primary anima source. All of the following have been shown to increase joy, extend life and increase health in the general population through multiple studies. They are therefore sources of primary anima. These sources can only provide primary anima if they are accessed consciously through willing connection.

Primary anima sources are:

Expenditure of anima in one's own animus, through experience of one's own body. This expenditure differs from the deanimation triggered by simulated sources such as drugs and passive entertainment. Primary anima can be attained through athleticism, sex, sensory experience, danger, fear, pain or other ascetic ritual. Birth and death may also be a part of this group; although death cannot be said to prolong life, the euphoric surge it provides may advance the life contained in the animus to its next phase.

Personal interactions involving connection (not sublation or violation).

Ritual and sharing involving bonded nations and communities.

Meeting strangers: this brings fear, danger, attraction and the possibility of exosocial expansion.

Altruism, including time spent with children, elders and those in need of reanimation who repay it with gratitude.

Receipt of kindness. The actions which offer shared anima to others are collectively referred to as kindness. Widespread kindness is very helpful in balancing anima debts and credits which is why it is encouraged in many cultures.

Caregiving given or received: massages, hair or skin treatments, personal adornment, especially when individualized, gifts and service given or received.

Social approval and recognition.

Creation of a shared animus or strengthened bonds through personal relationships and shared experience, particularly those involving meals, sex, dance, music, pleasant scent, fire, sport, creation, discovery, danger, fear, pain, altruism, risk, ritual, ascetic experience or shared information.

Rites which establish contact with a larger temporal or spatial self, through communion with ancestors, spirits or an extended nation.

personal experience of nature, art, ideas, music, dance, creation, beauty (including the presence of beautiful, generous, happy, wise, talented or otherwise attractive people or animals).

Gifting of euphoric objects, such as presents, heirlooms, rewards or earnings, which are intended to carry personal esteem. Earnings given with a lack of gratitude and respect do not impart primary anima as they are not offered through balanced connection.

Giscovery: adventure, travel, meeting new people, learning new skills, acquiring new knowledge.

Creation, especially when using skill or artistic expression.

Experience of divinity (universal conscious) through visions, devotion, ritual or other means.

Primary anima is obtained from all interactions resulting in connection. Secondary anima is obtained by the predator and lost by the prey in all interactions involving violation or sublation.

Before the recent invention of religion as something separate from daily life, all aspects of living in every culture were infused with animism. Animist beliefs include living in harmony (seeking primary anima) and controlling spirits and others (seeking secondary anima). These two belief systems date from at least the Paleolithic age and are not restricted to humans. Anima banks are repositories which contain surplus anima, obtained through sacrifice, devotion, offerings or interactions. Early hominids may have used animist practices, including anima banks. Many animals besides humans collect euphoric objects. Other animals and plants seek out both primary and secondary anima.

Anima transfer prolongs the life of those who love and care for an animal or a garden or are involved in creating objects which bring euphoria. Euphoria can be experienced through attachment to primary anima sources such as land, animals or people, from creating or being around objects of beauty, from movement and other experiences of the body such as eating, dancing, singing, sex or ascetic challenge, or from discovery. Euphoria helps us fall in love with those who we reanimate and those who reanimate us when we are the most depleted, whether that care is from nurses, in what is called the Florence Nightingale effect or from caregivers, resulting in filial or national love.

Anima exchange may also result in a traumatic bond, such as attachment to prison guards in what is called Stockholm syndrome, or patriotism to a totalitarian state, or in other relationships where power and secondary anima are obtained through the exertion of unequal force. The most vulnerable people, infants, elders and those that are ill or suffering some form of trauma, seem to exude energy which is available to those that help them through altruism and those who prey on them for secondary anima. As will be discussed in the *Violation* chapter, women may also have a higher ability to offer this energy than men, which has both given them greater power for seductive coercion and made them a greater target for predators.

Power is not acquired from altruistic connections which involve voluntary, unequal force based on the genuine need of someone suffering deanimation. Altruistic interaction returns altruistic euphoria, so it is not unbalanced. In addition, gratitude and respect balance such interactions.

Where energy is given willingly and gratitude is given in return, the interaction is not predatory. Instead, it results in greater anima for both parties as shown by many years of evidence that altruism has life extending affects.

A California study in 1999 showed that people over 55 who volunteered for two or more organizations had 63% lower mortality than those who did not.[7]_Other studies have found that volunteering lowered depression and anxiety among those over 65[8] and was helpful in recovering from depression following spousal loss.[9]A 1992 study of 313 women assessed in 1956 and 1986 found that those who volunteered received health benefits far greater than health benefits from paid or involuntary labour. *"Paid work over the life course, while positively related to multiple roles later in life, was negatively related to our measures of health. On the other hand, volunteer work on and off through adulthood was positively related to health. The duration of time spent caring for infirm or aged parents, spouses, or other relatives was negatively related to health in 1986."*

This indicates that activity and socialization alone were not responsible for increased health benefits. It may indicate that the family circle (especially during this time period) is a strong endogroup power structure that does not reward altruism as it is rewarded in exosocial relationships, and that altruism reward is also unavailable in a financial relationship. It may reflect the fact that women of these ages were the negative image in both their career and home circles and were not awarded altruism credit in these circles.[10]

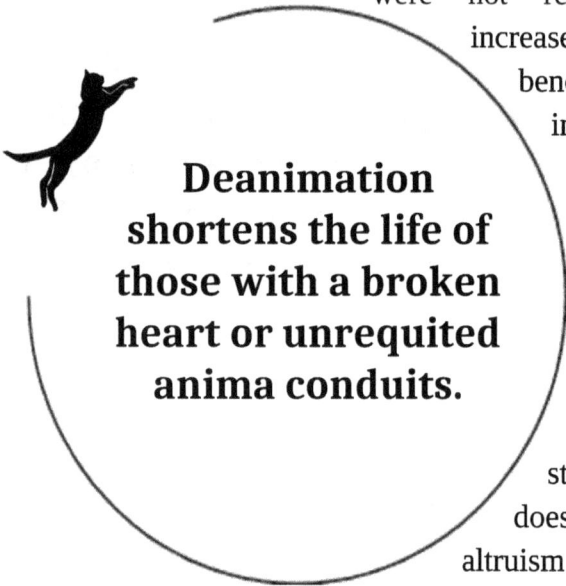

Deanimation shortens the life of those with a broken heart or unrequited anima conduits.

Benefits of altruism include better mental health as well, especially in avoiding depression, anxiety and *"neurotic distress"*.[11] A 2005 study found *"a strong correlation exists between the well-being, happiness, health, and longevity of people who are emotionally and behaviorally compassionate, so long as they are not overwhelmed by helping tasks."*[12]

Some people and other animal species have a poorly developed ability or desire to establish balanced connections. Those who are unable to obtain anima from connection must obtain it through sublation and / or violation which rely on dominance and cruelty. The people and other animals that are unable or unwilling to exist solely on primary anima must obtain secondary anima from other life forms through involuntary interactions of unequal force.

Deanimation shortens the life of those with a broken heart or unrequited anima conduits. It also shortens the lives of those in abusive or draining relationships and those degraded or despised by the rest of their society. Deanimation and reanimation are both possible through the same connections as evidenced in the polar experiences of social shunning or inclusion.

Deanimation can cause severe physical, mental and emotional damage, or even death, as is seen in the damage to neglected infants or victims of the torture of solitary confinement. The aging effects of stress are directly seen in the body. For instance, stress produces cortisol, which breaks down collagen and contributes to premature aging. This is a specific example of a general rule; stress deanimates.

Creating stress is taking life from another.

Some people are channelers, or anima conduits, able to access a large quantity of primary anima through their talent, knowledge, skill, beauty, power, or what is vaguely referred to as charisma. Anima may be obtained from contact with a channeler, accessed by attending live theatre, abstracted by watching a movie or taken by stalking the channeler's personal life.

An anima transfer gives euphoria to an extrovert in public as an extrovert is someone who is very receptive to anima from other people. Anima transfer provides that energy which a star in a theatre can take from an audience and return magnified many times to leave the entire audience euphoric. In fact, it provides that energy which gives the star their radiant glow and attractive force in the first place.

Beauty is not an object attribute. It is the energy possessed by those who are greatly admired, either for their beauty or for their own ability to acquire primary anima. The energy attracts, which is why beautiful people are attractive. The beauty of nature is found in an attraction to the anima in all living things.

Public interactions drain anima from an introvert, as an introvert has relatively low force in personal interactions and benefits more from interactions with more passive or low conflict sources, such as nature, ideas or creation. Many introverts fear interactions of any kind due to the frequency with which they are depleted by others. If they can consciously seek out only healthy connections, this fear can be reduced or disappear.

Most people can recognize those experiences which feel draining or emotionally exhausting. Interactions described in these terms are causing deanimation and a struggle for dominance of wills. Continued interactions of this nature may result in sickness or even death.

People are emotionally attracted to life and fear death because they are attracted to anima and fear its loss. The experience of living is an attraction to anima and a continual quest to assure its availability.

> **The experience of living is an attraction to anima and a continual quest to assure its availability.**

All attractions and repulsions to anima are experienced as emotions which control responses by the emotional will. Emotions are all a response to the reality or possibility of a gain or loss of anima. The emotional will is motivated solely by potential anima gain or loss and it operates outside the domain of the conscious will.

Depression and fear are triggered by the loss of anima or anticipation of its loss. Joy and excitement are triggered by a gain in anima or anticipation of its gain. Anxiety is an emotional response caused by fear of deanimation. This is a stress response designed to prevent exposure to potentially deanimating events such as going to a stressful job, class or social event or meeting a deanimating person. Drugs, illness, abusive relationships and other deanimating situations make people much more susceptible to anxiety because they are already depleted.

Guilt assignment causes loss of anima to the person assigned guilt and a gain in anima to the victim if the guilt is acknowledged. This is why the accusation is so integral a part of healing for many victims and why genuine apologies that accept guilt are important for balanced relationships. Genuine apologies and forgiveness do cancel debt because they are a return of, or refusal to take, anima from another and a recognition of the rightful owner of the anima. This is why they are so strenuously avoided by those who reject acknowledgment of debt.

Penance alleviates guilt by costing the guilty party anima. The punishment for guilt is energy depletion, experienced as depression if it is chronic. The guilt may be unjustly assigned or it may be richly earned, but in either case, the depression will not be resolved without first resolving the shame by addressing the guilt behind it. There are other reasons for deanimation and subsequent depression, such as rupture of anima conduits, but debt and accompanying guilt and shame is an often overlooked cause of both depression and extreme endosocialism.

Euphoria is the experience of life and shame is the experience of death, or the depletion of life. The emotional will seeks euphoria and rejects shame. Peace is the feeling of secure anima and anxiety is the response to potential depletion of anima. Anxiety causes anger and distress symptoms which seek to replenish anima.

Anima transfer can be measured. Stress is a symptom of deanimation. When under anxiety and stress, people and animals often attack other people and animals. The attack causes a reduction in anxiety and stress to the attacker and an increase in the attacked. The transfer of secondary anima is a zero sum game. Destruction can also release secondary anima, as shown by those who claim to feel better if they smash dishes and the predators presiding over the destruction of the planet.

Extreme emotional pain is recognized by many studies as causing more long term harm to health than most physical trauma.[13] [14] [15] Rupture of shared animus or connections can cause extreme grief and pain. This rupture can also cause euphoria.

Euphoric surge before death is a phenomenon known to sometimes cause the body to regain functionality where it had been paralyzed or to regain consciousness which had been long gone. Dying euphoria may indicate a necessary surge for a final expansion or dispersal, or it may simply indicate the experience of the rush of anima leaving the body.

Life's two greatest experiences of pain are typically upon birth and upon death.

A caregiver who has been reanimating a supportive shared animus with a dying person may experience euphoria when they die. This euphoria is often accompanied by guilt for the unexpected emotion. When this phenomenon is discussed at all in research, it is described as 'relief', but it is clearly euphoria. This may be the experience of dying euphoria through the shared animus. It may be ascetic euphoria such as that experienced on the ripping of a shared animus during birth. Or, it may be due to an unexpected surplus of the anima the caregiver had been providing to the shared animus.

The fact that life's two greatest experiences of pain are typically upon birth and upon death, may indicate a role between that pain and the entrance and exit of life energy from the body. The pain of illness may sometimes be associated with the occupation and expansion of parasitical life forms. Alternatively, the pain of injury or illness may be causing anima reserves to be deployed in an attempt to preserve life in the struggling host.

If euphoria is the emotional response to anima, it provides an explanation for why we are born in extreme pain which also provides an endorphin high to both the mother and infant. Childbirth, or the ripping of one animus into two or more, causes extreme pain even beyond the obvious physical causes of birth itself. This pain and the subsequent need for reanimating connection are then used to create a strong bond between the two newly individuated animus. Failure to establish this connection results in post partum depression in the mother and a failure to thrive in the infant.

The great pain of childbirth may be a vehicle, not just of maternal bonding, but also of the transfer of life to the newborn infant and perhaps even the motivation for acceptance of life by the infant. The extreme stress the infant is under during birth may activate their anima conduits and cause them to seek out and absorb the secondary anima being released by the mother. A failure by the infant to activate these conduits may result in deanimation, or death, in both mother and infant. This is a bold suggestion which clearly needs more supporting evidence, especially around those births which include more or less trauma. Still, there is no other useful function for such naturally occurring extreme pain.

A child who continues to be provided with an excess of the secondary anima which created or activated their anima conduits will have stunted development of their ability to access primary anima. Even worse, a child who was neglected as an infant and toddler does not have an opportunity to establish primary anima conduits. If they are then provided with abundant secondary anima, they are likely to become an endoself, a person addicted to secondary or simulated anima and unable to access primary anima. Life is established through secondary anima. The ability to access primary anima must be developed along with the child's conscious control over will.

There is a great deal of research that shows a reduced bond between a mother and infant if they are separated in the first hours after birth and that bond is related to the wellbeing and future health of the infant. The closeness is necessary to create the new shared animus which the mother and infant bond within. The closeness may also be necessary for the infant to access the anima released during birth. Physical proximity seems to increase the ability to access secondary anima.

Predators move as close as possible to their prey and refuse to leave the scene of their conflict. A person who uses physical proximity to corner, chase or trap another person while producing severe stress in the other is extracting and absorbing secondary anima. Their energy gain is easily observed. The prickly feeling of being near a predator causes high anxiety and appears to be related to an attempt to close off anima conduits.

Piloerection, or hair standing on end, is a common reaction which may be experienced when predators or rival endogroups are in proximity but can be triggered by proximity to a primary anima source such as beautiful music as well. Piloerection appears to be related to the transfer of anima, as it is present in fear, anger, and experience or anticipation of primary anima. In seeking physical evidence of anima conduits, piloerection may be a good place to start. A 2011 study found that *"openness to experience was the strongest predictor of the typical experience of chills during music"*. Openness to experience is, of course, another way of describing a person with a healthy drive towards exosocial expansion or well developed primary anima conduits.[16]

Some food and drugs provide euphoria. As a diet of pure sugar can cause people to lose interest in the slow process of digesting healthy food for energy, injections of simulated or secondary anima can cause disinterest in or a loss of the ability to obtain primary anima. Just as a body fed a diet of pure sugar will eventually sicken and cease to function properly, a person regularly provided with secondary or simulated anima will lose the ability to form connections and become addicted and dependent on secondary or simulated anima. A loved one may cease to be loved by a person addicted to drugs as the far easier source of euphoria takes the place of personal interactions. Drugs were frequently a part of mysticism worldwide. They have now replaced mystic revelations and attempts to achieve divine interactions and became seen as an end in themselves (although their original purpose appears to be enjoying a renaissance).

A hypoglycaemic will lose the ability to hear musical timing just as they will lose the ability to think clearly when their blood sugar levels drop. The ability to access primary anima requires an initial expenditure of anima which has been depleted in those addicted to other sources of euphoria. The lack of available anima to establish new connections is one aspect of addiction which makes it so hard to escape.

Food comes from living things, therefore contains anima, particularly in its most natural and freshest state. People get angry and extract anima from others when they are hungry. Hypoglycaemia may cause violent behaviour. A lack of anima from food causes the emotional will to seek secondary anima from others. Many people slip from being anxious and angry when they are hungry to a state where they refuse to eat at all. In this state, they are being soothed by the auto-anima released through their starvation. People experiencing anorexia replace the euphoria of food with the euphoria of asceticism.

Food as primary anima is used to create social bonds. Asceticism calls upon one's own reserves. As a spiritual exercise, asceticism may reduce anima bloat caused by gluttony and reduce the guilt owed for any exploitative action. It gives a euphoric high as the body is forced to tap into its own anima bank. Such asceticism, carried to extremes, may trigger the release of dying euphoria.

People high on either primary or secondary anima can go for extended periods of time without eating or sleeping as can those feeding off of auto-anima, that extracted from one's own reserves. Food for energy is not essential for those who know how to obtain life from surroundings, according to many stories of mystics who went for prolonged periods without eating. Those in love or in a state of religious or creative bliss also often forget to eat.

Food energy requirements appear to be, at least partially, related to the energy supplied from other sources. Elders eat less;

Food comes from living things, therefore contains anima, particularly in its most natural and freshest state.

hypoglycaemics and youth eat more and more often. Hypoglycaemics and youth have much stronger reactions to stress and pain than the rest of the population. It is possible that neither have a well developed ability to stop deanimation, store anima or access anima. Addiction to sugar and processed food may be related to the same lack.

People under stress often experience either a compulsion or revulsion towards eating, depending on whether they are attempting to acquire emergency anima or avoid anima debt. The latter occurs as a feeling of not wanting to deplete the shared animus so that the reserve can be used to protect another. The self-diminishing behaviour is most often seen in negative images, or at least reflectors, while endo-ideals are more likely to fill their own banks. The roles have to be assessed on a situational basis, by determining who is the endo-ideal or negative image in the particular conflict that is causing stress.

A parent who cannot eat when they are worried about a child may be conserving anima or feeling an ascetic compulsion to replenish the support available to the child through their own depletion. The same parent may compulsively eat after a divorce since there is no need to conserve anima, and they are depleted. Alternatively, they may refuse to eat after a divorce or a misfortune befalling a family member as a form of ascetic punishment for the negative image they now see themselves as, or to counter the guilt they feel. Self denying behaviour may be replaced or supplemented with physical labour. Some people do housework, chop wood or work out when they are worried. Such activity replenishes a shared anima bank rather than just passively refraining to draw from it.

It would be helpful to examine the behavioural,

autonomic and hormonal associations of euphoria to attempt to differentiate between the effects of primary and secondary euphoria. It would be especially interesting to see whether different hormones are released in response to what are posited here as different forms of anima. Do oxytocin and testosterone relate to the creation of endosocial membranes? Are oxytocin and vasopressin involved in the establishment of anima conduits? Is dopamine a response only to secondary anima?

The idea that anima is separated into different energies with different qualities is an old one that can now be tested against hormonal responses to different stimuli. It would also be interesting if different people had different hormonal responses to the same stimuli. Psychologists already measure excitement response to violent images to assess 'personality disorders'. If violence and sublation repel some and attract others and the situation is reversed for connections to primary anima, it should be possible to qualify different sources of anima as primary or secondary. It may then be possible to develop the ability to connect to primary and be averse to secondary, an idea familiar to fans of *A Clockwork Orange*.

This research could be very useful in creating environments that foster mental health and peaceful social relations. Of course, most of the sources of primary anima are already well known and their effects understood, but an official body of research and recommendations can sometimes push policy changes even where problems have been understood for a long time. It would be useful in countering corporate lobby industries marketing the dopamine producing synthetic or secondary anima.

Anhedonia is a word used in psychology to describe a lack of excitement or motivation for seeking pleasure or lack of ability to experience pleasure. Psychologists attach the word to depression, addiction, and various 'personality disorders'. Research into stunted growth or damage to anima conduits may provide a more causal explanation for this than any being used today. In addition, especially given that neuroscientists connect anhedonia to the same regions of the brain that are triggered by guilt,[17] the role of shame in preventing experience of pleasure, or its role in reducing the drive to exosocial expansion, should provide more light into this condition.

Depression is a lack of euphoria from connection with people, ideas or other anima sources.

Depression is a lack of euphoria from connection with people, ideas or other anima sources. It is frequently caused by traumatic separation or illness, or by a weak or harmful formation of self caused by early trauma. It is relieved by external connections, including with non-human sources such as art, spirituality, creation, animals, nature or physical activity. Elders are at greater risk of dying when their spouses die or their family neglects them. They live longer with a cat, garden or any bond to primary anima.

Dance and other movement therapies developed by Toni Wolff showed that art therapy could help heal the effects of trauma, fear and anxiety and Carl Jung noted that spirituality could help cure alcoholism, but both of these things were well known earlier and practiced in medical traditions worldwide. Everything that is a common element of what is referred to generally as culture is a source of anima, as cultural practices were all used for reanimating rituals. In addition, both Alcoholics Anonymous and organized religion can be endogroups strongly bonded by secrecy, identity and external persecution. Joining such an endogroup provides a replenishing shared group animus to take the place of the depleted personal animus.

Trauma, fear and anxiety are all states which make a person particularly vulnerable to endogroups because they all cause deanimation.

Music and dancing are used to establish or revitalize romantic relationships because they are powerful rituals to create euphoric bonding. Our song and state anthems are modern replacements for national songs which represented first age nations. Festivals created around traumatic events such as funerals and weddings are a way for the wider community to help heal trauma and share anima to strengthen new and ruptured bonds. Needless to say, these events do not act as intended when they are only attended by predators who use the occasion to further deplete those already weakened under stress and trauma. It is notable that both weddings and funerals bring out the worst in that type of person. Just as festivals were always spots where romance bloomed and friendships were strengthened and rekindled, they have always been occasions where predators roamed as well.

The festival is the ultimate event of shared primary anima in all of its features. It is often open to strangers. It involves shared ritual, music, dance, beauty, creation, food, fire, costumes, masks, and sex. A romantic date is a condensed and abbreviated version of the festival, featuring flowers and perfume, music, dance, shared food, candles, scent, dressing up, *sex*, gifts, new and exciting, or at least rare, food and location and ritual. The marking of anniversaries is the creation of romantic ritual. Parties serve the same function for social groups larger than romantic and smaller than national.

Such events are often called convivial, the root words *con* (with) and *viv* (live) alluding to the shared life contained in the event. The elements which make up a festival, party or romantic evening all produce euphoria and aid in the creation or strengthening of a wider, bonded self such as a couple, friend group or nation. These elements may therefore be sources of anima. Those that open themselves to shared anima may successfully create a shared animus.

A person with blocked or undeveloped primary anima conduits will quite likely be averse or antipathic to some or all of the above elements of a festival. A festival

Figure 3: Shared animus

may be focused on secondary anima instead, as seen in rituals involving torture or sacrifice or strong endogroup affiliation focusing on vilifying external enemies and celebrating an exceptional myth.

Theme parks are an industrialized version of the festival, with novelty food, fear, danger, strangers and surreal environments. It is not a coincidence that carnivals have been associated with abductions and other criminal activity since their inception, as the euphoria they produce is nearly all caused by secondary anima from fear and consumption.

Initiation rituals take anima from the person being initiated and distribute it to the endogroup, including the initiated. This results in a strong endogroup, or national animus, and the destruction of the individual animus. This is one type of traumatic bonding which we can call endogroup sublation. The other type of traumatic bonding is sublation to an endo-ideal. In both cases, the individual loses their own will and must live vicariously through the endogroup or endo-ideal. In extreme cases, they also experience joy through the joy of the endo-ideal and become addicted to the predation of themselves by their endo-ideal.

Culture includes rituals and identity marks or marks of ascetic ritual. National marks from initiations indicate that the person has contributed to the shared anima bank. This is not simply an archaism; many gangs use marks to indicate how many crimes they have committed or people they have killed or harmed, which is a contribution to the endogroup anima bank and is often required before full membership and access to full benefits. The marks themselves are often created through pain which is itself a contribution to the anima bank and a sublation of will to those conducting the initiation.

Dances, songs or ritual are frequently associated with frenzies created before ritual sacrifices or war to strengthen endogroup solidarity. The national anthems of many states invoke events in which the nation was suffused with secondary anima, such as in wars or battles, or with shared anima from achievements which brought external admiration and recognition. When states or corporations seek to increase morale during times of stress, what they refer to as morale is endogroup solidarity. Extreme bonds to an endogroup will prevent members from defecting even in times of great hardship. These bonds are created through national or corporate festival-like events.

The festivals of the world are currently being reduced to performance, an object for consumption, instead of opportunities for creating bonds. Rites and euphoric objects are now viewed as market commodities to be owned by endogroups instead of the animist methods they are. This commercialized culture may ape the original, but the results it produces could not be more different.

Anima is available to people through connections. In one to one relationships between people, this comes from physical closeness and shared information and experience, a mutual connection that reaffirms the individual's place as part of a greater life force. Wider relationships include the anima from beneficial social interactions such as festivals or parties, or ritualized wider interactions affiliated with large endogroups like religions or political campaigns. All social interactions are heightened if they involve animated behaviour such as laughter, flirtatious or sexual interactions, dancing and singing, shared creation or enjoyment of creation, or euphoric drug taking, provided that drug is not so strong or taken in such quantity that it blocks other conduits and creates an endoself instead.

Anima is bonding which is why both primary and secondary anima are accessed in groups which wish to create strong bonds. Such groups eat together, create together, and commit rape and murder together. As a shortcut, they drink or do other drugs together, which is why those fighting addictions are so often shunned by their former social groups.

Anima aids bonding because anima is the energy required to create bonds.

An open or exosocial person is one possessing a network of healthy primary anima conduits. A happy person is attractive because they exude energy. An endoself is always sad or bored and usually bitter and angry as well. The sadness is deanimation and the boredom is a lack of will to exosocial expansion. This is a serious health condition which creates extreme social malfunction if it is widespread, as it is today. We will explore the ways this manifests in the next two chapters.

There are three types of relationship

connection, sublation and violation.

Connection

provides a balanced bond between two sides of the interaction.

Sublation

one side of an interaction is absorbed into the animus of the other and the dominant will receives the majority of anima.

Violation

one animus is attacked by the will of the other to forcibly extract anima.

There are two types of sublation

endogroup and endo-ideal.

There are two types of anima

primary and secondary.

Primary sources of anima are marked by two characteristics. One, they produce euphoria. Two, they prolong life.

Primary anima is obtained from all interactions resulting in connection. Secondary anima is obtained by the predator and lost by the prey in all interactions involving *violation and sublation.*

Beauty

The attractive energy possessed by those who are greatly admired, either for their appearance or for their own ability to access primary anima.

Euphoria is the experience of life and shame is the experience of death, or the depletion of life. The emotional will seeks euphoria and rejects shame.

The experience of living is an attraction to anima and a continual quest to assure its availability.

Emotions are all a response to attractions and repulsions to the reality or possibility of a gain or loss of anima.

The emotional will is motivated solely by potential anima gain or loss and it operates outside the domain of the conscious will.

Exertion of the conscious will is required in order to access primary anima.

Depression and fear are triggered by the loss of anima or anticipation of its loss.

Joy and excitement are triggered by a gain in anima or anticipation of its gain.

Anxiety is an emotional response caused by fear of deanimation, meant to prevent exposure to potentially deanimating events.

Chapter 4

Sublation

Who has not asked himself at some time or other: am I a monster or is this what it means to be a person?
— Clarice Lispector, *A Hora Da Estrela*

I f dogs can sense fear, as is widely evidenced and accepted, what is it that they sense and why does it have the effect of making them leap to the defence of those they love and attack those outside their circle? Obviously, we can isolate specific hormones such as adrenaline and cortisol but, in a wider sense, what do these hormones represent? What triggered their release and what message do they convey? What sense is it that fear was transmitted through?

If women can transfer life energy from the pain of labour and birth, pain and fear may release life energy obtainable by others as well. The exchange of secondary anima is far less understood than access to primary anima. While the health benefits of primary anima have received at least scant notice, addictions to secondary anima are relegated to the dustbin of psychiatry and law enforcement, where they are labeled as criminal, deviant or abnormal. The rest of the world is then justified in paying no further attention to this behaviour, even though it is the most crucial component of our behaviour which must be understood.

Secondary anima is obtained through deployment of unequal force. Accumulation of secondary anima results in power. The unequal force enabled by power serves to lock the prey into a monopolizing relationship with a predator. The prey is not free to form healthier bonds and neither are they able to regain power in the relationship. A long-term unequal relationship results in what is referred to as a traumatic bond but is really the sublation of the weaker self into the self of the predator. This sublation causes an inability of the sublated self to exert their own will, leaving them unable to leave the predatory situation. Sublation appears to create a shared animus governed by the emotional will of the predator only.

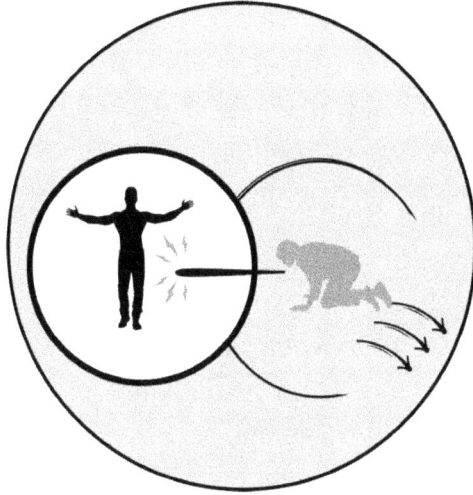

Figure 4: Sublation

Secondary anima appears to be qualitatively different from primary anima. Not only are the sources different; the consumption of secondary anima creates a different type of self and a different use of force. Primary anima creates an exoself through a diverse network of animated connections. Consumption of secondary anima creates an endoself, a form that consumes instead of connecting. Instead of a force which expands outward, life energy is inverted and used to overpower and consume anima sources. Primary anima creates an interactive self; secondary anima creates an object self.

In traditional Chinese medicine (TCM), qi can be either yin or yang. This idea of positive and negative or opposing energy is a common one, appearing also in ideas such as the prana and apana forces which correlate to the three gunas, sattva, rajas and tamas described in the Bhagavad Gita. The idea also appears in physics. Gravitons are a (theoretical) example of particles which can carry either a positive or negative charge.

Anima is such a force. It can expand outwards or compress inwards. The response to anima is also varied among living things. Recoil or approach responses to anima are everywhere in the living world. Even a plant stretching to the sun is following an exosocial attraction to energy. Even among plants, not all are attracted to primary anima. Some are repelled by it and some have very low tolerance for it.

The idea of different levels and types of energy is the subject of alchemy study by practitioners of Daoism. Here, there are three levels of energy. The jing, or birth energy seems to correspond to the force behind the emotional will. The qi is obtained from life surrounding the person through anima conduits. The shen is a spiritual energy which seems to correspond to the force behind the conscious will. While beliefs in Taoism are much more complex and diverse than can be explored here, the goal is circulation and mingling of the three energies until the first two are transformed into, or infused with, shen. Meditation, which involves focus of the conscious will, breathing to absorb and circulate life energy in the surroundings and physical challenge to stimulate the circulation of birth energy, or jing, are combined in many Asian practices to achieve this alchemy.

In this work, there is no pretense at understanding how many, or what types, of life energy there may be. It does seem apparent, however, that there are different types that appear to come from different sources and have different effects on people. It would require an established study of vitology to test that assumption and add supporting data for or against it. The purpose of this writing is not to claim knowledge of these energies but rather to convince the reader that this knowledge is necessary.

If euphoria is felt in response to the energy which is expended in creating interactions, then that energy, or a forced surplus, may be available within the interaction itself. If it is anima that provides the energy to create, or bind, each interaction, then each interaction must contain anima. If anima is present in every interaction, as the first law of thermodynamics implies it must be, it can be extracted or intercepted. Intercepting an interaction, or sublating one of the actors, seems to cause anima gain for the parasite.

The will that directs an interaction is the one which receives the anima gain. Just as the self of a person can be sublated to another, so can smaller interaction clusters such as tasks.

🐈

Stress is shared to those surrounding the person under stress such as parents, spouses, children and employees. The most common victim of predatory interactions is a person who already shares a strong connection with the predator. The second most common are those who are largely without the ability or social support to defend themselves and have been stripped of a strong personal membrane or have not been allowed to develop one. In either case, there is not a sufficient endosocial barrier to block depletion.

If there is a social power imbalance between two people, the socially stronger can take anima and give nothing back. If reflection is withheld by the socially weaker, if a woman refuses to smile or rejects the advances of an aggressive man, or a child refuses to grant undivided attention, or those designated as the negative image do not drop their gaze in response to an aggressive stare, or anyone subject to authority refuses to obey, they can be met with extreme or even lethal hostility from the socially stronger. The hostility is a reaction to the loss of secondary anima obtained from these unwilling and unbalanced interactions. When people refer to such socially aggressive people as vampires, it is these unwilling and non-reciprocal extractions of anima they are referring to. When socially vulnerable people demand a place of their own, free of more socially powerful people, it is the exhaustion caused by these unwilling extractions that they are trying to avoid.

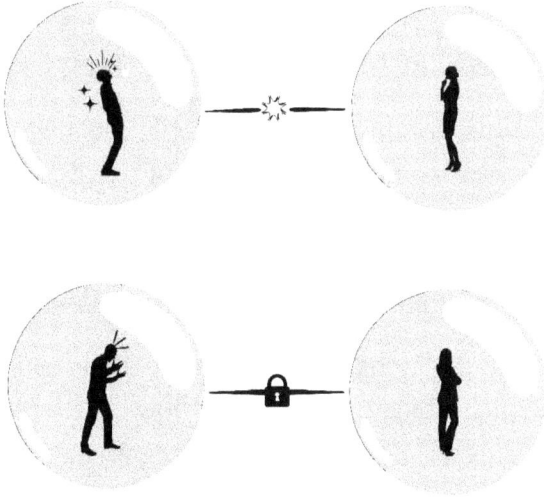

Figure 5: Interaction and
rebuffed interaction

If an interaction is pictured as a pipe with a two-way valve, anger closes an outlet flow and smiles open it. This is why the negative image are forced to smile and predators are frequently angry. Anger in a negative image is resistance (a closed outlet valve) and is feared, punished and exaggerated in the perception of those who perceive it.

The method of appropriating anima contained in the interactions of another is through sublation. Sublation is effected by creating an endogroup, or a shared animus, with a power imbalance. This shared animus contains all the anima from the interactions of everyone within it. That energy is available to anyone in the group but typically goes to the will which dominates the group, known as the endo-ideal. Sublation creates a sublated source and an agent of power which combine to share many characteristics of one self. This is described in great detail in *The Creation of Me, Them and Us.*

Endogroups and the people bonded to them are governed largely by their emotional will. As explained in the last chapter, exertion of the conscious will is required in order to access primary anima. Endogroups are therefore predisposed to prefer secondary anima.

Anima transfer can be used to accumulate power. Unequal transfer explains how power over others prolongs the life of those with power and shortens the life of those they have power over. Each interaction has a shared energy release, so hoarding or draining energy by one causes depletion for the other.

Every interaction in a power institution is depleting for those not in authority. Nursing homes are often lethal due to their institutionalized power relationships. People in authority positions in industrialized societies speak to elders in the intimidating, dehumanizing and derogatory way that those with power speak to those subject to it. This increases the stress elders have to deal with as their bodies weaken and causes more confusion and anxiety than if they were treated with respect. Their contacts, like those of infants, children, and others in a vulnerable state, need to reanimate them, not deplete them of anima, or they will struggle to thrive.

Deanimation indicates an unequal transfer of anima. Physical manifestations of deanimation are low stress resistance, adrenal exhaustion, depression and other signs of weakness. Deanimation can result in serious illness or death.

Those who are unable or unwilling to access primary anima seek involuntary interactions of unequal force which allow them to accumulate secondary anima. The more anima they accumulate, the stronger the prey they can overcome to provide the increasingly bigger rush of secondary anima their addiction requires. Power is the ability to control interactions through the exertion of greater force. This greater force comes from energy. It is not hyperbolic to call it life energy since there are sufficient studies which prove the life-prolonging effect of power. As far back as 1967, a UK study found that the higher up in a bureaucracy a person worked, the longer they lived.[18] Neither is it a stretch to speculate that the added life energy is extracted from their prey, since the life expectancy and health of the weaker party in these interactions is reduced.[19]

Power is acquired through acts of unequal force which drain the life energy from others. This is why, in *The Creation of Me, Them and Us,* it was stated that power is never benevolent and never inert. It is the result of active force extracting anima from others. Some may object to this definition, as those who channel primary anima may also be seen as powerful. As will be discussed in the Martyrs, tyrants, saviours and sirens chapter, these people only have power if they exert unequal force over others. If they do not exert that force, their ability to access primary anima is more likely to make them prey. Neither does their ability to channel anima usually result in an ability or desire to hoard it. The result is usually the opposite. Such people tend to seek outlets to release the buildup of excess anima, but that is difficult for them to do without attracting a swarm of predators.

Power is an acquired taste. Most people with an ability to access primary anima follow the egalitarian drive to release the excess for use by others. The egalitarian drive appears to be related to the exosocial expansive force and is an inherent aspect of life. Most emotionally healthy people have a strong aversion to secondary anima and a natural compulsion (experienced as guilt) to avoid it through altruism and balancing interaction. People with a strong ability to access primary anima are very likely to be emotionally healthy aside from their likely deanimation by predators.

A person with a healthy exosocial drive has the ability and desire to access their own supply of primary anima and rid themselves of anima bloat through generosity.

Those with an inability or unwillingness to establish primary anima conduits need to parasite off of others' connections to primary anima. Aside from vulnerable times of life when people must rely on shared animus or anima offered through altruism, an appetite for secondary anima is unhealthy and deviant behaviour. This is regardless of how common such behaviour is, because it appears to act in opposition to the primary law governing life, the second law of thermodynamics. The second law, the tendency to move towards states of higher entropy, is obeyed through egalitarianism.

The most prolific anima transfer seems to be possible through sex, violence, laughter, birth and death. Excitement from anticipated or vicarious experience of these sources is exploited by marketers as seductive coercion. Excitement is triggered by anticipation of anima. If viewers experience excitement on viewing these events, it is likely the anticipation only that is experienced. This causes the addictive nature of entertainment that promises anima but never fulfills the promise. This is explained in much greater detail in *Free Will and Seductive Coercion,* but addiction to the excitement can lead to people never developing the ability to access anima itself, especially primary anima which requires exertion of the conscious will.

Excitement and expectation of euphoria may be part of the explanation of situations where people refrain from helping others in danger or distress. The argument that violent films and video games are harmless as they aren't real life loses credence if it can be shown that they cause the development of an appetite for secondary anima obtained through cruelty and inhibit the development of conduits to primary anima.

To some extent, the interception or extraction of secondary anima is a behaviour of most people, at least when they are unsupported and under severe stress. It can become a chronic condition in those who are unable to access primary anima due to chronic stress or unavailability.

Often this need is fulfilled in ways which cause no harm, such as periodically relying on family and friends to re-energize them or on entertainment designed for this purpose. A great server or bartender provides energy and reanimates the person or gathering they serve, as does a great host. A negative person drains energy. Even if they are just dragging through their chores or complaining about them, they are taking energy from those around them. What we call someone's positivity or negativity is really an energy transfer.

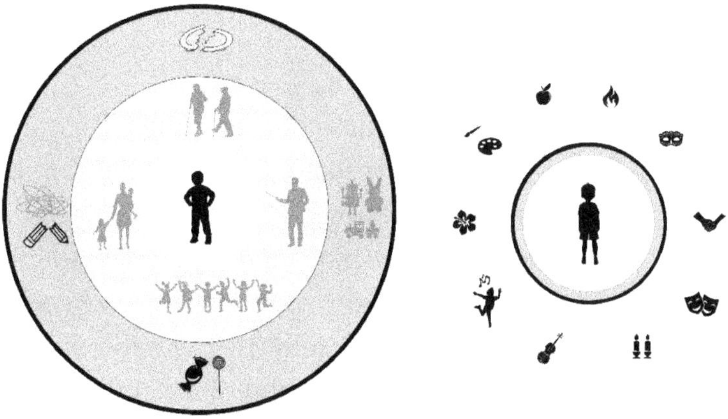

Figure 6: Endosocial membranes and primary
and secondary anima

Some people feel themselves entitled to secondary anima, especially when that is made readily available to them. This entitlement comes from the need to transfer guilt arising from debt that is greater than one has the ability or desire to repay. Children can be raised with a sense of entitlement simply by ensuring that their debt is too great to repay by the time they reach an age of being aware of it. This is accomplished by caregivers who do far more than necessary and by preventing any opportunity children have to show gratitude or reciprocal kindness. These children become endo-ideals and develop an endo-ideal perspective. They will be raised with a compensatory rationale intact and undetectable by themselves.

Other people seem to be born with, or develop, a greatly reduced ability to establish primary anima connections. In these people, primary anima causes revulsion and they crave secondary anima. Showing them beauty or the opportunity for discovery or creation produces no more excitement than a cat would display for a piece of broccoli.

A dependence on secondary anima causes people to become parasites, predators who drain the life from others through parasiting off of interactions. Parasites tend to excuse their predation as simply following the rules or seeking their own happiness or even working for the benefit of their victim(s). These predators are far more invisible than the more bold kind that commit active crimes of violence.

Parasites exhaust anima conduits and leave no reward for the initiator of interactions. Acts of altruism which are funnelled through intermediaries like NGOs and governments, acts of creation which are claimed by corporations or acts of discovery which are claimed by schools have nearly all anima extracted by intermediaries, so there is very little reward left for the principles. There is little beauty or joy to be found in a factory-made product, a school assignment or tax. The euphoria found in craft, adventure and sharing have been stripped away.

Intercepting gratitude, either institutionally, through NGOs, or through attacks on the person who has earned gratitude, allows outsiders to parasite on altruism euphoria. Attacks on the ability to exercise both generosity and talent are common. A large part of humanity seems to dedicate their lives to attacking anyone who helps others. Perhaps they are intercepting altruism anima, perhaps they are attempting to stop any alleviation of distress, or both. The same behaviour is seen towards people who access primary anima. The ridicule and contempt towards people such as artists and entertainers is inexplicable without some such benefit.

Most people are familiar with the rush of secondary euphoria experienced on the achievement of a child, student, teammate or other associated person. This gift of shared euphoria is often willingly passed by those who seek to make their parents, teachers, team, employers, fans, home town, etc., proud or happy for them. In many cases, the shared euphoria is justified through shared effort or previous debt which is being repaid through the achievement. A parent or other benefactor can feel their own satisfaction that their altruistic labour has paid off in the other's achievement. In other cases, membership in a wider connected network or animus simply causes an overflow of shared anima to the family, nation, fan group, etc. In these cases, pride in another is a form of respect and gratitude which creates a balanced interaction.

Parasitic relationships are very different, as the flow of anima is being intercepted by force instead of flowing freely through shared conduits or a shared animus. The parasite is intercepting anima at the source instead of enjoying the overflow benefit. The dominant will is that of the parasite, so the act of sharing becomes a robbery.

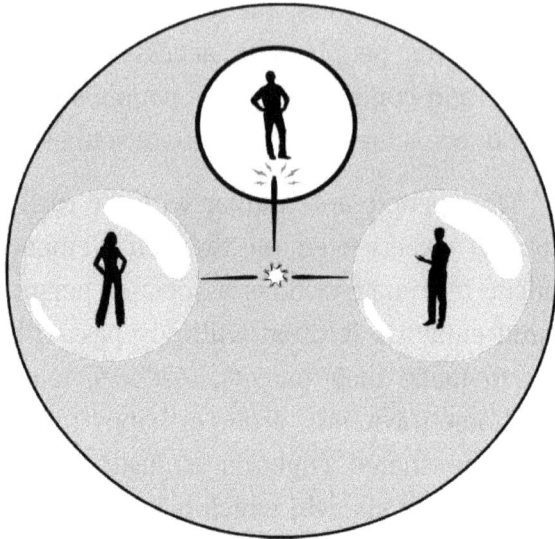

Figure 7: Parasitic relationship

As euphoria from discovery and creation is taken through parasitical institutions of education and employment, there is less reward and less motivation for the person doing the work. The natural force of exosocial expansion is blocked and the sublated self must be coerced to continue the anima producing behaviours which they no longer benefit from. Intrinsic motivation is reduced as extrinsic is increased. The demotivating effects of long term extrinsic motivation are well documented.[20] The target would ultimately rather be immobile than redirect their expansive force to provide anima to another or access it through another. The exceptions are people who have been fully sublated and are no longer directed by their own will.

The opening of an energy conduit in order to complete an interaction appears to be an opportunity to extract more energy than required to complete the interaction. This explains the exhausting nature of interactions with predatory individuals or institutions. Interception allows the parasite to not only take anima from an interaction but also to further deplete the victim through the open anima conduit. The opening of anima conduits to enable an interaction decreases resistance to predation. Once a person is trapped into an interaction with a parasite, it is much simpler for the parasite to increase stress, shame, labour or other methods of extracting secondary anima. Anyone who has ever found themselves trapped in a conversation or shared task with such a person can attest to how draining it quickly becomes.

Dominance can be asserted in a conversation by interrupting, monologuing, refusing to respond to the listener's disinterest or discomfort, and attempting to compel full attention where the other does not want to give it. If someone leans back in their chair and makes the other lean forward just to hear them or be heard by them, that is a conversation with an unbalanced energy flow before a word has even been spoken.

Chronic lying is one of the most underrated methods of abusing and exhausting another. Lying causes the listener the frustration of wasting time, attention and emotional response to situations which are not real. The unreliability causes chronic insecurity and unease. In addition to the effort expended in the conversation, the victim must devote later effort in deciding whether it is worth investigating the truth or challenging the liar on each falsehood. Finally, they face the depletion caused by rage, denials and counter accusations if they do confront a lie. Chronic lying in a longterm relationship leaves the victim sorting cognitive dissonance after every interaction. Such labour is exhausting due to the conscious effort it requires and the state of alertness the victim must be in during every interaction.

The vulnerability of an open conduit is probably why predatory institutions are always set up around essential interactions. It is probably also why so many institutions of interception, such as corporate employment, education, organized religion and hospitals, often become exploitative in escalated ways such as physical abuse and degradation. It is small wonder that victims in power structures tend to strive for autonomy if interactions can become an existential threat.

The victim of parasitical interactions may attempt to close their anima conduit or stop or diminish the flow of energy. This defence is often perceived or portrayed as resistance to work or education or an antisocial gesture, when it is simply a response to a power struggle and an attempt to protect themselves from depletion.

Admonitions to Be kind, Smile, and Be polite are often used to force vulnerable people to maintain open connections.

🐈

Love is a state of semi-permanently open connection through which energy flows. In a particularly bonded pair, such as a monogamous relationship, this can result in a shared animus, or a bank of energy each can draw upon. The reason infidelity is so damaging to relationships is because it creates a power imbalance. The cheating partner takes energy from the shared animus and uses it to feed an external relationship.

This energy embezzlement causes the other relationship partner to continually attempt to fill an animus that is being siphoned off to a competing relationship.

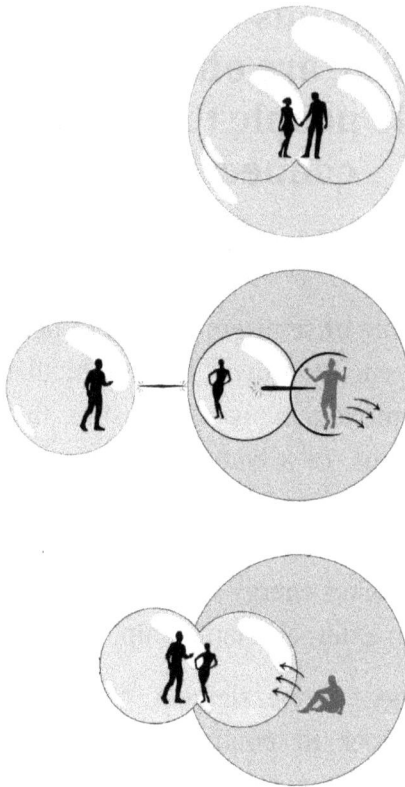

*Figure 8: Energy
embezzlement*

The result of infidelity is that the partner that is cheated on becomes stressed and irritable from depletion, even if they are unaware of the cause. Their loss of energy causes them to lose lustre in the eyes of their partner. A person with more energy is idolized and a person with less is demonized as the negative image, so the common effect of infidelity is that the cheater becomes infatuated with the person they are pouring energy into and disenchanted with the person they are drawing from. They may insist they still love the person they are draining, but what they mean is they are unwilling to give up the energy source they are using to feed the new relationship. Relationships which begin with infidelity usually do not last much longer when the original relationship ends because the second relationship is a parasitical one which was fed by the original shared animus.

Because of their increased energy requirement and the urgency they feel to acquire it, some cheaters become more demanding and cruel to their partner in an attempt to obtain more energy. Others become kinder and start buying gifts to offset the guilt debt and because they have an energy surplus from the extra relationship. Any attempt to recover a relationship after infidelity must begin with repaying the energy debt owed. This realization often causes the cheating partner to blame their partner as a means of transferring guilt and may also cause them to erect an endosocial barrier between themselves and their partner as a means of protecting themselves from debt.

Studies [21]have found that having fewer receptors for oxytocin and vasopressin in the brain is correlated with both a higher likelihood of infidelity and a lack of generosity. A lack of generosity indicates that a person already has a guilt reversal mechanism in place which they employ to avoid guilt for infidelity as well. Vasopressin and oxytocin receptors may be related to an ability to access primary anima and their lack may produce endosocial traits such as guilt reversal and dependence on secondary anima. Vasopressin and oxytocin have both been suggested to have a role in promoting bonding within endogroups and hostility without. This may have been a misinterpretation. It is possible that the endosocial membrane is a result of guilt and oxytocin and vasopressin may also be affected by guilt or the reception of anima debt and credit.

Energy may be drained from a shared animus, or even from strangers, by the manufacture of shame for the purpose of transferring it. Acceptance of endoreality is key to sublation. A predator will set up a situation in which their behaviour is socially unacceptable. If the person they are interacting with accepts the behaviour, they will also accept the shame while the predator puts it out of their memory. If the second person challenges the behaviour, they will be told they are the only ones who noticed or objected, or it is humiliating enough for the predator without it being mentioned, or they are ruining an otherwise perfect event. In either case, they will have the guilt for the socially unacceptable behaviour cast onto them. Secondhand embarrassment is evidence of this sort of bond which can be created even among strangers. It is also heavily used in draining relationships.

Few other relationships have as exclusive a shared animus as a monogamous romantic attachment. Other forms of infidelity or humiliation, such as to a nation, fandom or friend group, do not cause the same hostility or health risks that accompany infidelity or humiliation in committed romantic relationships or families. Other ruptured connections may cause similar depletion, however.

The pain and energy drain of a ruptured or unrequited connection may exist even where the secondary object of interaction does not exist, after the death, destruction or *alienation* of one part. It may exist when no connection has ever been made, such as the pain felt for a parent deceased before one is born. It may even exist when the object has never existed. This is the pain of longing for a child, a home, or a love where one has never existed, or melancholy for a different time and place, a stronger form of nostalgia expressed more accurately in words such as the Welsh hiraeth. Finally, it may exist on a restriction of freedom or opportunity of expansion through discovery or creation. This pain is an unrequited connection. An established anima conduit which is unable to make its desired connection results in pain. That pain appears to provide secondary anima to those who interrupt or block those connections.

The pain of unrequited connection is a stimulus which encourages continued or more effortful seeking for connection. This increased force would require increased energy. It is probable that the increased energy is the attraction for predators who make connection as difficult as possible for their prey. For a parasitical predator, one which intercepts connections, to access the same level of secondary anima, they must keep increasing the difficulty for their prey. A predatory coach, teacher or bureaucrat must first make the actor dependent on them to establish a connection, and then they must continually increase the difficulty and decrease the reward for their prey. In schools, the reward of discovery and creation is taken from the student along with their autonomy and they receive the hollow token of a grade in exchange. Later, the autonomy and primary anima will be exchanged in paid employment for the hollow token of currency. The employee is instructed to alleviate the craving for the lost primary anima through the exchange of currency for secondary or simulated anima.

An alternative power struggle that arises from interception is when the potential victim, through recalcitrance, manages to drain a well-meaning person in a parasitical position. Nurses, parents and teachers who suffer exhaustion and burnout are evidence of the success of some potential targets to turn the tables on those in parasitical positions. This happens when the targets are sufficiently strong and the person in a position of power is sufficiently unwilling or unable to exert the power of their position.

If there is a power struggle in a relationship, or one side is addicted to secondary anima, they may deliberately fail to succeed, or sabotage the success of themselves or the other, or their joint success. They do this for two reasons. The first is to deprive the other of shared anima and keep them in a weakened state. The second is to obtain secondary anima through the stress of the other.

In endogroups, people are kept in a state of chronic stress. This is partly to extract anima from the negative image and partly to put others in a precarious state that encourages them to welcome the misery of the negative image for them to parasite off of. These parasites become the reflectors, or enablers, of such exploitative power structures.

Chronic stress is created in a multitude of ways. A person's anima conduits may be flooded by demanding they care about things they can't do anything about as the news does. They may be blamed for things like environmental destruction that were the result of corporate and government actions out of their control. The ever-present threat of being in violation of obscure and subjective law or moral authority is particularly applied to mothers and those in poverty, but institutions like tax authorities and landlords provide an undercurrent of unease to everyone.

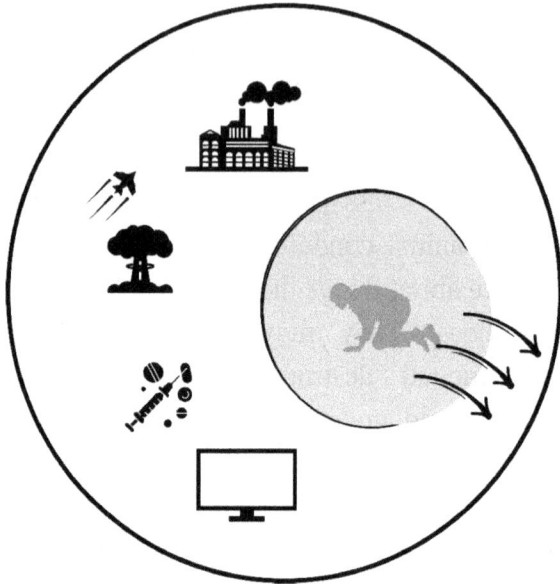

Figure 9: Loss of anima through
environmental stress

People at their most vulnerable would rather not seek life-saving help than be further depleted by institutions of power and those exerting it. Post traumatic stress syndrome is the name given to a debilitating stress response produced in reaction to seemingly mild events. This response occurs in previously traumatized people. Previous trauma seems to condition people to transfer an abundance of anima in response to any attempts at predation. This makes such people an irresistible target for predators.

This excessive energy transfer may be caused by an extreme weakening of the protective personal membrane. It may be a release of secondary anima in an attempt to satiate the predator. This short term defence may be long enough for the victim to negotiate or escape, although in the long run, it just makes a predator addicted to abusing them. Alternatively, an extreme stress response may be a release of an emergency store of auto-anima for their own self preservation. Anima may be released as part of a last ditch attempt to keep a body functioning in times of deanimation or to provide enough energy for a flight or fight response in times of danger. The fact that this anima is then available to bystanders may just be a side effect.

Lasting trauma from dealing with powerful institutions such as courts, hospitals, banks, police, and other social services is common, to the point that filling out a form in a government office is traumatic for many. This aversion causes those who need institutional assistance the most to be the least likely to access it. Those in poverty would often prefer to not file tax and forego a rebate than to go through the process, just as the ill and addicted refuse to go to hospitals and the victims of crime refuse to go to the police. This aversion is caused by the power and eagerness of bureaucrats to further deplete the most vulnerable.

When people say a person or situation sucked the life out of them, perhaps they should be taken at their word. A predator sits down with a source as though they were sitting down to a meal, with excitement. This excitement is very often visible in gleaming eyes and alert posture. With bureaucrats, the posture is frequently aggressive but may also be simply closed, like the bullet proof cages they sit in. For those who have to deal with them and are required to pour energy into the interaction, the lack of reciprocity is enough to cause depletion, especially in those already suffering deanimation.

Institutions were created as enforced endogroups. They are power structures which enable endo-ideals to extract anima from others and enable

All discrimination is discrimination against the negative image of the dominant or authoritative endogroup.

institutional reflectors to parasite off of the transfers. Civilization is a vast network of interception points where the more powerful can dominate every interaction. Civilization is a power structure which obtains its energy from sublation of anima sources, through ownership of objects and interception of interactions. Industrial endo-idealism preys on the sick, the elderly and children. Wealth endo-idealism preys on the poor. All discrimination is discrimination against the negative image of the dominant or authoritative endogroup.

Some people greet violence, poverty and illness with excitement and extreme resistance to efforts to prevent them, even at the cost of their own lives. This is also seen in resistance to efforts to stop pollution and other autogenocidal destruction. The same reactions which may be observed in an addict threatened with loss of their drug or a hoarder threatened with loss of their trash are also present in many people when presented with suggestions to stop destruction of their environment or neighbourhoods. The same intensity of emotion, the panic and the visible stress symptoms are all present in people who have no obvious personal interest in topics such as oil rigs or free medical care. The interests which are usually presented as governing human behaviour, such as economic gain or social approval, are not the driving force behind this visible stress. The threat of loss of secondary anima is. This is the only explanation for the violent emotional response and apparent vested interest that some people have in ensuring a continuation of destruction and misery.

It is always possible to manufacture economic reasoning that appears to explain autogenocide, but this veil of rationality never stands up to examination. The explanation that clearly fits is not an economic structure but a predatory structure.

Power is an accumulation born of misery; power is extracted anima. An endoself is a predator and the negative image, their easiest prey.

Weakening the prey and channeling all interactions through totalitarian institutions is not required for absolute control, as is often assumed. Indeed, totalitarianism is far too cumbersome to bring much control in practice. Totalitarianism is a result of craving for the absolute maximum extraction of anima. Causing distress, illness and death in their prey makes no sense for a dictator seeking only control. Totalitarianism only makes sense when it is viewed as a predatory structure. Totalitarianism is created to vector all anima towards the endo-ideal, creating a ponzi scheme structure where each reflector – bureaucrat gets a drop of life from the pain of the poor. Little acts of spite and malice increase the share for every bureaucrat in this death by a thousand cuts inflicted on their prey. Totalitarianism is the ultimate predatory structure.

Sublation disconnects the sublated person from primary anima so sublation creates endoselves. The only happiness in an endogroup is the mindless, selfless contentment of a secure reflector, feeding off the crumbs of secondary anima extracted from a passive negative image and absolved from guilt through sublation to another will. This is probably why some people welcome sublation, because it brings debt relief. In relinquishing control of the will, reflectors relinquish responsibility and guilt. Passive interception of anima is the drug that tranquilizes reflectors in the face of atrocities committed by the tyrants they support. This may produce contentment, but it can never attain the euphoric highs of exosocial expansion.

There is no greater efficiency or joy to hierarchical structures. There is simply much greater opportunity for parasitical predation. Bureaucracy is famous for its tendency to expand. When a person is given power over the will of others, through the ability or authority to create rules, it is typical for them to begin to micromanage and create an

Bureaucracy is torture.

abundance of superfluous rules. This controlling behaviour creates more work for the person in authority, so they must receive motivation to compensate for the energy loss. The energy for expansion must come from somewhere. It appears evident it is being extracted from those subjected to it.

Bureaucrats prey on their victims, squeezing drops of anima with every forced interaction, every look of derision, every occupation of their time, energy and labour and every increase in their stress. Most people hate bureaucrats and see them as their enemies. This is why.

Bureaucrats become endoselves in part because they are themselves placed in a kind of cubicle solitary confinement. Their lives are stripped of all meaning and primary anima, at least during paid hours, and they are isolated by physical barriers in a world where people hate them. Their only opportunity to alleviate their boredom as they wait for death or retirement is to suck a little joy from someone else. The modern push to job creation has done more to create endoselves than probably any other initiative, including war.

Bureaucracy is torture. Bureaucracy forces the performance of tasks which serve no purpose except to occupy the actions and thoughts of the person forced to do them. These tasks are part of all forms of servitude, which is why servitude is widely considered degrading. Compliance is enforced by police, state torturers, teachers, government officials, and gods, as depicted in the legend of Sisyphus. The performance of repetitive, redundant and pointless tasks was (and is) the primary form of degradation and abuse used against supposedly privileged housewives, forced to clean floors again and again for people who refused to remove their shoes.

Employment at call centers is a form of torture so severe that people will go to extreme lengths and risk their jobs simply to escape the colonization of their thoughts and voices for one extra second between calls.[22]

Bureaucracy is murder which is why we hate it, why we react to it with extreme boredom and why those who wield it are so often drunk with power, or high on secondary anima. Bureaucracy is invasion of privacy and enforced reflection of authority. Every interaction with bureaucracy is an involuntary interaction of unequal force and a sublation of will. It is murder by tiny transactions. If poverty is a death by a thousand cuts, bureaucracy is the knife.

Bureaucracy is violence which results in sublation. Bureaucracy is a source of secondary anima for bureaucrats and those above them. This is why people are forced to work their entire lives at jobs that no one needs. It is not the output of their labour that is required. It is their life itself, extracted through one meaningless interaction at a time, an endless, institutionalized, sublation of will.

The economic structure has extremely little to do with the production of goods and services and everything to do with sublation of the wills of many for power to a few.

🐈

A parasitical predator may be a person in a seemingly subordinate or equal position. These predators will first drain energy by needing attention, assistance and reassurance and by claiming continual victimhood, then they will place increasingly insurmountable obstacles in the way of a project's success. Bureaucracy is often used at an institutional level to accomplish this. Interpersonal drama, incompetence and guilt are used in personal relationships.

Such predatory behaviour is greatly amplified in situations where one person is weaker and more dependent or more invested in the continuation of the shared animus. A predator forces others to motivate them or keep track of their work or correct their 'mistakes' which uses the conscious will of the other. This causes a huge energy drain from the person forced to exert their conscious will. It is a distraction of the focus of their will from their own goals just as bureaucracy is. This type of parasitical predator is most often found in the circles of home, friends and family. These circles usually lack the institutional authority to demand sublation but manage to extract energy through social coercion.

The sublation of will by parasites is shown in the once common occurrence of men dying shortly after retirement. These men had a refracted will and their dominant will was an endo-ideal which appropriated all of their conduits to creation anima. Women with empty nest syndrome were also left without the external wills which demanded all their time and thoughts for socially mandated busywork and they suffered the same disorientation and grief.

Figure 10: Draining anima from those in
a position of power

Now, neither trauma is as common as they once were because bonding to either family or company is discouraged. Instead, lives and thoughts are filled with dissociated busywork. Parents are now forced to work at jobs which earn them nothing after day care because day care is not paid unless it is outsourced away from family. Employers are continually changing, leaving a rootless, floating existence in place of a sublated one.

Increasingly, the exercise of power by an external will is automated, as millions of people are forced to prove to software that they are not themselves robots, and forced to perform monotonous, repetitive tasks to train artificial intelligence before they are permitted to complete their own necessary tasks.

Automation has normalized a complete surrender of privacy and control of speech of the individual along with extreme enforcement of secrecy for the powerful. Destruction of personal membranes and boundaries is a key aspect of prisons, many schools, most jobs and the bureaucratic treatment of people by states. Removal of privacy and will from people to corporations and algorithms is a transference of dignity.

Stripping of dignity and autonomy, combined with all-encompassing sublation, creates a nearly universal predatory structure. Even if all of the human race succumbed to such a structure, it would still be deviant. Such a structure lacks stability as it contravenes the order life naturally follows. It can only escalate in intensity until it collapses.

Sublation eventually transitions into violation. Even nature itself was first sublated by scientific-industrial endo-idealism and then increasingly destroyed. In the next chapter we follow the path of escalating predation into violation.

The three types of predator are

Parasite, sublator and violator.

Parasite

Predator who drains energy by exhausting open anima conduits and leaving no reward for the initiator of interactions.

Sublator

Predator who dominates the will of another and creates a shared animus through which they freely access the energy of another.

Violator

Predator who destroys the personal membrane of another animus so they can access the released energy as secondary anima.

The most prolific anima transfer is through sex, violence, laughter, birth and death.

Abstracting Divinity

Chapter 5

Violation

The greatest joy for a man is to defeat his enemies, to uproot and drive them before him, to seize all they possess, to see those they love in tears, to ride their horses, and to squeeze their wives and daughters in his arms. — Genghis Khan, *Jami' al-tawarikh*

There is a faster way of obtaining secondary anima than the interception of every interaction belonging to another and the sublation of their will. The faster method is destruction of the animus. After connection and sublation, the third type of interaction is violation.

An exoself obtains primary anima through a network of conduits to primary anima sources. An endoself lacks such anima conduits or prefers not to use them. An endoself may obtain secondary anima through sublation, which is the absorbing of the source person or object into their own animus by usurpation of will or possession. Alternatively, they may cause the release of secondary anima through violation, by destroying the object or the self-membrane of another. The bonding energy of a group animus is released upon its destruction, just like a personal animus. This is why some people are so addicted to creating drama and seem to enjoy destroying relationships for fun, whether those relationships are their own or other people's.

It requires a strong exertion of force to create an endogroup. The pressure of the expansive exosocial force must be redirected and held. Cognitive dissonance and general unease, as well as deanimation, are signs of the constant exertion of force holding an endogroup together. Totalitarianism is exhausting to all who live under it and the deanimation causes widespread immobilizing depression.

An act of violence can cause endogroup membranes to snap like an overstretched elastic band. The binding energy which was required to withstand the natural tendency of exosocial expansion is released on the dissolution of an endogroup. This released energy fuels revolution and it also fuels genocide. The two often arrive together once a euphoric frenzy has begun. Revolution acts like a forest fire, consuming energy to release more energy as long as it has anything to consume. This is the source of both the excitement and the terror of revolution.

The energy that holds an endogroup together is the same for any animus, whether that is a nation, an object or a person. Any animus is a temporary ordered state being held against the natural tendency to chaos. Any animus will release this energy upon its destruction.

Anima is obtained through destruction of euphoric objects and connections, including people and their relationships. The intoxication of revolution and the appeal of cruelty are based on this release of anima. Terracide is possible because the earth and ecosystems are bonded by anima which is lost to predators upon their destruction. Genocide is possible because nations are bound by a shared animus. The suffix -cide signifies the rupture of an animus or the animated connections which tie together a whole, including in the case of homicide.

Figure 11: Secondary anima obtained through destruction

The shared anima attainable from joining with others through marriage, friendships and nations, is also attainable from destroying personal membranes or couple membranes, from murder and (as pointed out by Genghis Khan) from the rape of a family or nation member.

Breaking personal or group membranes releases anima to the attacker. Whether the membrane is gently softened and a merging of the two occurs, it is forcibly softened and a sublation of the weaker occurs, or it is simply destroyed, the access to the anima of another is the same.

The fashion in academic and scientific analysis of human behaviour in the past centuries has been to attribute predatory behaviour to a lust for possessions, power or sexual fulfillment. In fact, those aspects are all methods used in predation. The predation itself is the end desired.

Often, anima interception will end in anima extraction as it requires greater and greater cruelty to obtain the same amount of anima from an

Cruelty and destruction cause the release of secondary anima from the target.

increasingly depleted victim. The bureaucrat becomes increasingly spiteful, contemptuous and cruel, institutional punishments become more severe, and totalitarian control becomes more all-encompassing. Eventually, predation includes outright murder, rape and torture. Those that do

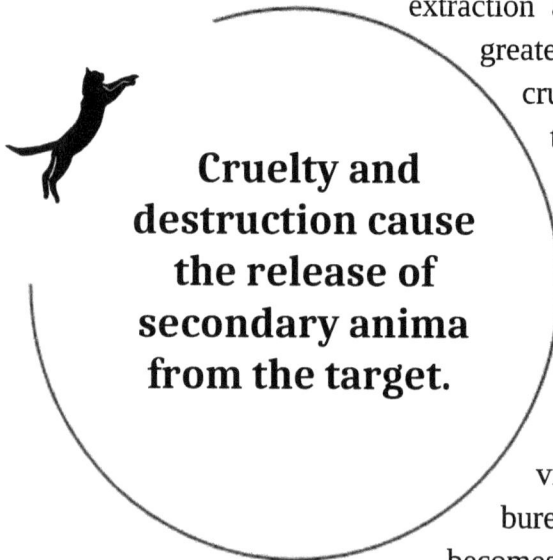

not comprehend the rampant abuses in places such as hospitals, care homes, refuges and schools are blind to the naturally predatory nature of these institutions.

Both parasitical predators and violent predators steal secondary anima. They both cause or increase its release through fear and stress. Cruelty and destruction cause the release of secondary anima from the target. This secondary anima is then available to those in the vicinity who are able to passively access it. This is the little kick that employers or others in authority get from deriding or abusing those under their power and those around them get from watching the victim's pain, humiliation or stress. Abundantly available secondary anima leads to an appetite for interceptive and ultimately, extractive predation as a higher kick is needed with each attack. It is probable that secondary anima is related to a release of dopamine or some other addictive reaction which requires ever-increasing amounts.

Predators are addicted to the emotional response to stress in others and will cause as much stress as possible to provoke the response. They will occupy all interactions of their prey, remove all of their attachments to job, friends or family and fill their lives with labour, ugliness and stress. Destruction of the self entails attacking all of the most intimate aspects of the self including body, autonomy, relationships, reputation, thoughts and will. People who enjoy destroying the reputations of others unjustly or deny credit where it is due are stealing anima. This is often evident in their shining eyes and visible excitement.

Most people are familiar with the tendency to 'forget' things which cause stress to others around us or to break things during a sudden onset of stress-related clumsiness. A predator is not limited to causing physical accidents. They will also say exactly the wrong thing on social or business occasions, 'accidentally' forget the most crucial payments, appointments and tasks and 'accidentally' give someone the wrong medication.

This does not mean that every time anyone destroys something or causes stress for those around them they are consciously extracting anima from them. Predatory behaviour is an emotional response and is therefore governed by an emotional will; consciousness is often no more a part of the decision to act than it is involved in the decision to blush. Seeking anima through the stress of others is usually a response outside of cognitive effort, volition or awareness and it is something every person will do in a crisis until they have learned to control the emotional will to reanimation.

Predatory incompetence is not the same as cognitive difficulty. Many people face cognitive challenges and yet are completely reliable. Further, the incompetence of an endoself invariably leads to the release of secondary anima. Predatory incompetence involves an exertion of emotional will over conscious will. This is explained more fully in *Free Will and Seductive Coercion*. People who would never consciously hurt those around them do so because the action comes from the emotional will and can only be stopped through conscious will. If the emotional will is strong enough, it can deflect any cognitive effort to recognize or overcome it and direct the brain to construct an endoreality to absolve the predator from guilt for their actions. The victim may also displace blame and use denial to avoid any stigma attaching to the predator.

If the 'accidents' that predators set up result in shocking events, they will often appear strangely unfazed, even in the face of death caused by their actions. At most, there is an involuntary flinch on discovery, replaced immediately by calm and happiness, dissociated observation or excitement. Often, the reaction resembles the peace brought by euphoria. The emotional reaction shows the intent of the emotional will.

At other times, predators may be in a state of chronic high anxiety caused by their own incompetence. The indicators of emotional stress or trauma, such as screams, tears or expressions of pain, will produce a stress reaction in others who share anima conduits with the person in crisis. We are designed to share anima with those in need through our own stress responses. This is recognized in parenting techniques. Parents often hide their own pain to avoid depleting their children through their shared stress response and children will also protect themselves by crying or acting provocatively if they sense a caregiver's stress. Wise parents avoid allowing their children to gain excess anima by not overreacting to pain and trauma experienced by their children. Good manners are often focused on preventing children and others from gaining an appetite for secondary anima through selfish and exploitative behaviour.

Anger is a demand for energy. If a person responds curtly or abruptly to another, it causes a little stress jump in the recipient and that stress is an indication that energy is being sent to the angry person. This energy supply causes some people to become addicted to being angry. It also causes many people to chronically abuse the most vulnerable people because they are the most likely to produce a high stress response and relinquish the most energy to their abuser. This adds an extra layer of truth to the expression There is nothing to fear but fear itself.

Fear releases anima and anger takes it. We become frozen with fear and quick with rage. Both heat and speed indicate an increase in energy. Anger does not produce energy. It demands it from those around the angry person. After anger, the angry person is not left cold and depleted of energy. Those who feared the anger are cold and depleted. Hot anger and cold fear indicate a transference of energy. Anger animates and fear deanimates. Anger is both a means of extraction and a defence against extraction. When someone becomes angry at the sight of another, it means they see the other as either predator or prey.

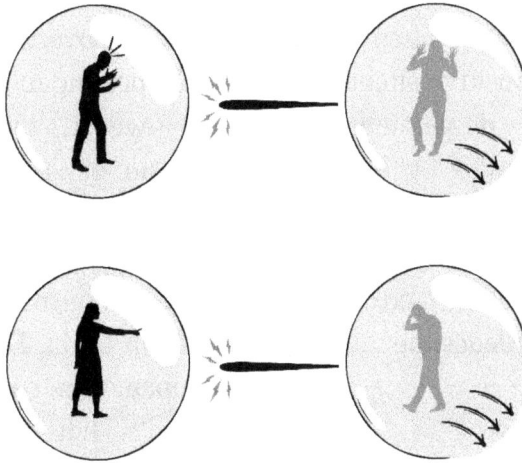

Figure 12: Anger-fear symbiosis and the contempt-shame symbiosis

The anger-fear symbiosis and the contempt-shame symbiosis are both methods of triggering an energy transfer. They are both covered in much greater detail in *The Creation of Me, Them and Us*. The contempt-shame symbiosis acts by triggering shame, associated with guilt, in the victim. Shame will cause them to release excess energy, just as fear does.

High levels of stress hormones have been shown to correlate to a reduced insulin sensitivity.[23] This insulin resistance makes it more difficult to store energy, which is why we burn more calories when under stress (at least until the body is in an emergency slowdown). The energy that is not stored must be released, another indication that predation makes surplus energy available to predators.

When their victims are about to leave a relationship, predators often provide a quick and overwhelming surge of positive attention, irresistibly healing to those left raw and desperately depleted. However, this is always followed by an increased stream of stress, 'accidents', humiliation, betrayal, guilt reversal and gaslighting. Each time the anima conduits are about to collapse from depletion and exhaustion, the promise of repayment persuades the victim to open them again. Each time they reopen, the connections are left unrequited and more demanding interactions follow. As the victims weaken, it will require more and more extreme torture to provoke the stress response and provide the euphoric high their predators demand, which is why abuse always escalates.

A predator is an endoself, a person with reduced primary anima conduits.

Predators aren't in relationships to build beautiful homes and loving families. They are in search of prey and they will destroy every aspect of their victims' lives, even those, such as a spouse's job and their shared home, which may be thought to benefit them. They will not hesitate to destroy their own lives if it will help to destroy their victim's life as well or deny them a share of any benefit. They will remain unemployed in the face of great job offers and become homeless deliberately just to inflict that stress on others.

It is easy to see that a great deal of policy from endoselves at every level, including state and corporate authorities, is designed solely to extract stress anima from its victims. The unnecessary destruction of peace and beauty has no other explanation. It is widely recognized that a person addicted to the euphoria obtained from drugs will risk their own and others' lives and well-being to feed their addiction. Addiction to the secondary anima extracted from others is no different in that regard from addiction to euphoria-producing drugs. Secondary euphoria is all the same in the behaviour it causes and the endoselves it creates.

A predator is an endoself, a person with reduced primary anima conduits. Endoselves appear to be low energy people unless the energy is chemical or manic. They must harm others to replenish themselves. Violence can bring temporary peace to predators through reanimation.

An endoself is not a type of person. It is a health condition in which the self is inhibited from natural expansion and from development of primary anima conduits. It is a crippling disability which can and should be prevented and repaired. It is unquestionably the biggest health crisis facing humanity and impacts not only the physical body but the fulfillment of life purpose and the formation of self.

Every connection to a source of primary anima is perceived by endoselves with extreme hostility, not with neutrality and definitely not with euphoria. An endoself may be able to fake an interest in beauty by aping social dictates of good taste and they may even be able to create beautiful craft work by emulating what they are taught. They derive no joy directly from creation or beauty, however, only from the admiration and outside approval the object may bring them. Endoselves hate music, beauty, art unless it is confined, grotesque and economically valued, children, elders, sick people, poor people and nature. Many of them even hate the joy of others and are far more offended by sounds of joy than sounds of industrial destruction. It is as though their poles have been reversed and what brings euphoria to healthy people brings extreme anxiety to them. They are soothed by filth and destruction, agony and misery, death, ugliness and horror.

At the extreme ends, those who obtain joy from primary anima are repelled by secondary anima and vice versa. A person who revels in cruelty and destruction seldom loves altruism and beauty and a person who derives joy from nature or creation seldom enjoys death and filth. This is not always apparent, as those seeking secondary anima often haunt altruistic careers or stalk beautiful or creative people. They do so because of the surplus of secondary anima and its ease of availability in those places, not because they wish to emulate the actions which accumulated the anima they prey on.

Healing places like hospitals and homes for elders are filled with people from both extremes. Those that are capable of receiving altruism euphoria and those who feed off of horror and cruelty will both be present in all such institutions. They are difficult to distinguish under normal circumstances.

Victims are often the only ones aware of predatory natures and sometimes even they attribute malice to accident or unavoidable harm.

As every ambulance attendant knows, some people are irresistibly attracted to the pain and death of others. Ambulance chasers seek proximity to death and suffering, which act like an open pool of blood for vampires. Such people will involuntarily slow down and move closer.

There is such a thing as keeping a cool head under shock, but that is not the same as the response of a predator. Predators invariably move close to the victim, very close if possible, and speak in a low, purring tone. If they can, under the auspices of ministering to the victim, they will increase the pain while staring intently at the victim and increasing physical contact and focus. The stare and focus is similar to someone transferring energy to another and willing them to get better. Both establish an open anima conduit.

There are people with the gift of being able to pour energy into those who need it the most and every desperate person calms in their presence. Those people often include celebrities who provide the same healing energy in hospitals as they do on stages. Often they are people who work in social caretaking roles because of this gift. These people use the same closeness, eye contact, low voice and focus as a predator. The difference is in the direction of the energy being transferred.

Because authoritative endoreality refuses to acknowledge that life energy exists, institutions in charge of the vulnerable seldom make any effort to differentiate between those who provide energy and those who take it. Vulnerable people are not asked or otherwise monitored for an increase or reduction in energy following interaction. People who are attracted by the pain and suffering of others should not be allowed near anyone vulnerable or in pain. People who are attracted to destruction and ugliness should not be allowed near construction or design projects. It would not be hard to identify people who cannot exert conscious control over their craving for secondary anima, if we were willing to acknowledge that they exist.

Boxers and women who give birth have an understandable high from the amount of endorphins produced by their pain, a reaction to auto-anima.

Audiences at violent events also experience an extreme high. Boxing and prostitution both involve the extraction of anima from the negative image. It is this secondary anima which is the product being bought and sold in both cases. The fact that the product comes from the negative image is a key factor. Traumatized people are far easier to prey on as they are already in a state of depletion which makes it easy to extract anima from them. It is also far easier for the consumer to deflect their own guilt onto the negative image.

Children are not simply the most vulnerable. They are also the negative image, seen as even more worthless appendages of their negative image mothers. Women are devalued when they give birth and children are the unit of their devaluation. The more children a woman has, the more she is devalued. No group is more systemically dehumanized by society than children, and that is not restricted to industrialized societies. It is not universal, but it is far more common than with any other classification of people.

Predators are drawn to children and elders, the ill or disabled. The obvious reason is because these people are more vulnerable, but it is very possible they also have more secondary anima available, as they provide it as altruistic reward to those who assist them. It is possible that this is also true of women, as they are often prey, but that could be attributed to their status as the negative image under male endo-idealism.

There is an aspect of training hunt hounds called blooding, in which the dogs are taught to feel great excitement at the scent of blood. Women who are in pain very often, through menstruation and birth, may also be 'blooding' those who live with them to crave more secondary anima and abuse them more to extract more. This may have contributed to the very common custom of separating women who are menstruating or birthing from all but a few trusted women. This may have also contributed in some cases to the antipathy shown to older women and the excitement (anticipation of anima) in the presence of younger women. This may be especially true since the old women were the gatekeepers guarding access to the younger women at their most vulnerable.

Vasopressin and oxytocin have both been recognized as playing a key role in social bonding. Studies have found that both show clear sexual dimorphism in social cognition and behaviour, although neither have been sufficiently studied in women. Women display affiliative behaviours in times of social anxiety, while men display aggression to other men.[24] [25] Women experience a greater stress response to danger within endogroups and men experience less awareness of danger within endogroups.[26] Vasopressin makes women, but not men, more susceptible to the placebo effect [27] which is a sign of a sublated will.

A 2018 study [28] pointed out *"Until recently, relatively few studies examining oxytocin in the context of stress have incorporated female participants into their design or examined sex as a factor of interest within their data analyses."* (as usual) which greatly limits the usefulness of the studies. The researchers found that *"Perhaps the most consistently reported example of such an effect is the impact of oxytocin on amygdala responses to negatively-valenced stimuli. As previously described, oxytocin reduces amygdala activity in response to negative faces, threatening scenes and negative social interactions in men. However, women treated with oxytocin exhibit greater amygdala responses when viewing angry faces and threatening scenes. This differential modulation of neural activity by oxytocin may serve to promote detection of socially relevant and potentially threatening stimuli in females, while reducing threat sensitivity in males."*

This has far reaching implications. As just one example, women may have more auto-immune diseases because they are under far higher alertness levels most of their lives. In the context of endogroups, this supports the existence of a basis for emergency endogroups which evolved into male endo-idealism. If men have less stress in response to danger and women have the ability to transfer any extra anima to men through their heightened stress and affiliative behaviour during times of danger, this may be a biological directive for creating male endo-idealist endogroups during times of danger.

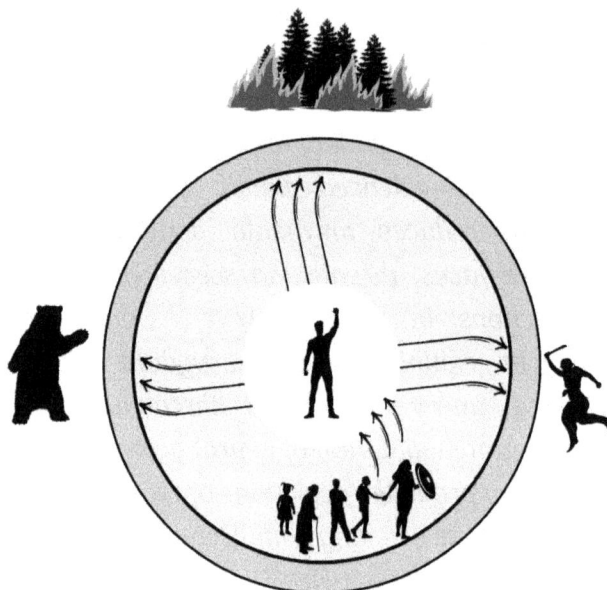

Figure 13: Emergency male endo-idealism

The fuzzy thinking of endoreality in this case would encourage men to plunge into danger and women to seek safety. This sex-based behaviour towards risk has been well documented in economic and corporate contexts as well. Power, in men, leads to faulty risk assessment and over-confidence. Women are more risk averse in every career.

Patients with women as physicians and surgeons live longer, and have better outcomes than those treated by men. A review of more than 1.2 million patient records by Canadian and Swedish researchers found that *"patients treated by male surgeons were 25% more likely to die one year after surgery than those treated by female surgeons.*"[29]   This has been interpreted as being a result of men being greater risk takers, but another cause is possible. Cortisol releases oxytocin, which causes women to be comforting under stress and release energy. It does not have the same effect in men because testosterone nullifies the oxytocin. Cortisol, released in high stress situations such as illness or surgery, triggers the anima releasing tend and befriend response in women and the anima taking fight or flight response in men.

Women are more likely to die with male surgeons than men are. In a 2022 study of 1,320,108 patients with 2,937 surgeons from 2007 to 2019, women had a 32% higher chance of death within 30 days with male surgeons than with female.[30] The stress reactions of women and men result in men assuming an endo-ideal position and taking anima, while women assume the supportive role and give anima. This may tip the anima balance required for the women patients to live under a male doctor. It is very possible that traditions which assigned nursing duties to women and forbade men access to the recovery chambers of women and children were acting on observed data.

Pain responses are also variable by sex and other factors. Children appear to experience more emotional reactions to pain and stress. Women experience pain very differently than men and women are affected by pain more frequently and severely than men.[31] [32] [33]

Further inequality in stress response was found in a study conducted by psychologist Daniel Kahnemen and others, *"A striking observation was the extent of inequality in the distribution of emotional pain. About half our participants reported going through an entire day without experiencing an unpleasant episode. On the other hand, a significant minority of the population experienced considerable emotional distress for much of the day. It appears that a small fraction of the population does much of the suffering."* Kahneman – Thinking

The payoff is greater for predators in attacking the most vulnerable if they are the small fraction that does the most suffering, as it appears they are. Kahneman confirms *"Severe poverty amplifies the experienced effects of other misfortunes of life. … A headache increases the proportion reporting sadness and worry from 19% to 38% for individuals in the top two thirds of the income distribution. The corresponding numbers for the poorest tenth are 39% and 70%. … Significant differences between the very poor and others are also found for the effects of divorce and loneliness."* Kahneman

The negative image is often the victim of rape, not because of the nebulously defined idea of sexual attraction, but because of the easily obtainable anima produced by violation of the negative image. The term for rape has been violation in some places and times and it is a more apt term for what is happening than sex crime. The amount of tyrants, presumably including Genghis Khan, who were not attracted to connection sex and instead required sublation or violation in order to be sexually aroused appears to have been significant.

Sexualized violence or sexualized sublation are acts that ought to be considered separately from sexualized connection as they appear to be fundamentally different interactions.

It is far more important to know whether a person's sexual orientation revolves around connection, sublation or violation than which body type they prefer and this preference is also more consistent.

A heterosexual person may sometimes be attracted to the same sex and vice versa, but a person attracted to violation and sublation will almost never be attracted to connection without a lot of work to reprogram themselves.

The negative image is even more vulnerable due to the ease with which they can be assigned guilt for their own victimhood. Without the ability to reassign guilt, a predator finds it impossible to prey on someone in their own endogroup due to the painful punishment of shame which results from acceptance of guilt. The endo-ideal has the ability to reassign that guilt to the negative image, so an endo-ideal is far more likely to prey on a negative image than the reverse.

While torture and murder are the most obvious examples of predatory behaviour, they are rarely, if ever, the first. Accounts which claim that such acts occur in isolation or with no forewarning are written from an endo-idealist perspective which attributes all virtue to the endo-ideal. The endo-ideal has usually used their greater power to indulge in predatory behaviour for years and it is often depicted as virtuous.

The cover of altruism allows many to be unchallenged for decades and spread great misery among the most vulnerable. Endo-idealism allows predators who work with the poor and other ostracized demographics to hide effectively as they will have altruistic virtue assigned to them whether it is deserved or not and their victims will be discredited as the negative image. Famous people who have been proven to have preyed on children and vulnerable elderly or ill people have had their previous behaviour depicted as charity. The UK children's entertainer and mass rapist Jimmy Saville is one example of many of these predators. Powerful men were depicted as popular with the ladies while they raped women. Men who murder their wives and children are often depicted as caring and loving fathers and husbands. The behaviour that is depicted as caring and loving is nearly always controlling and manipulative, but it is depicted as virtue.

A person does not wake up one day craving so much secondary anima it can only be obtained through torture and murder. Developing such a self requires years of behaviour which creates and feeds this craving. While it is possible that an endoself can be born with a craving for secondary anima and an inability to access primary anima because of some physical or environmental damage, such people usually develop over time.

Before the use of cruelty to extract secondary anima, a power imbalance must be established. A connection must be formed, a negative image must be created and weakened and the endoreality which will deflect blame and assign it to the negative image must be established. People torture animals before they torture people. When they torture people, they start with children, women and those already ostracized by other negative image classifications. Predatory behaviour starts with the negative image because predators must start with someone less powerful than themselves in order to build greater power. They must also create and strengthen their endosocial barriers before they can participate in such behaviour without overwhelming guilt and empathic distress.

People may become more endosocial in times of great stress, when they need to conserve their own anima or acquire emergency support from an external source. This stress may be situational or it may be caused by exposure to any of the myriad environmental stressors they are under attack from every day. Abused people abuse people. In times of war, atrocities occur. In times of natural disaster, atrocities increase. Strong people and weak people form new bonds through altruism, but damaged people extract life energy from misery, pain, death and destruction. Post-war violence, both externally and internally directed, is an almost inevitable result of war. In many times and places, attraction to secondary anima is perfectly normal, especially in deanimated populations.

Drug use, itself a compensation for low anima reserves, also produces violent behaviour. Behaviour around secondary anima has a great deal in common with behaviour around addictive drugs. A well known study showed that rats in a cage, under the well-recognized conditions of torture caused by solitary confinement and a lack of sources of primary anima, chose heroin over water until they died. This study was used to 'prove' the inevitable addictive nature of heroin. Rats given an environment where they could access primary anima gave very different results,[34] however, showing that drug use was one possible choice of many and the likelihood of dependency increased as alternative options were decreased.

The reason so many totalitarian states, cults, abusive relationships and other endogroups restrict all sources of joy is to leave the victim no choice but to form a traumatic bond with the predator. Isolation is anima starvation and the starving person has no choice but to bond with the only available anima source for survival. The self is composed of interactions and must continue to interact to continue existence. The same isolation and totalitarian restriction of sources of primary anima increases the craving of predators and creates more predators.

Creation of populations which seek secondary anima requires not only encouraging violence and predatory behaviour, but also ridiculing and destroying any opportunity to access primary anima. This is why a common practice of totalitarian states is destruction of all peace and beauty, at least that which is accessible to the public. It is also why abusive family members ensure the abused person(s) are humiliated and isolated until they have no outside connections, including no opportunities to pursue creation or discovery or enjoy beauty.

Predatory behaviour can be encouraged by a violent community or by the deliberate programming seen in video games and other entertainment. Desensitizing, in conjunction with an environment where primary anima is consistently blocked, derided or associated with a negative image status, encourages the growth of an appetite for secondary anima while starving the growth of primary anima conduits. This highly effective programming is

Human nature is not good or evil. It is, above all, programmable.

protected as a right in certain societies which claim it as free will to be programmed into predatory behaviour by militaries that require volunteers for their killing machine.

Human nature is not good or evil. It is, above all, programmable. Human behaviour is always a struggle between the conscious will, which seeks to control the desires of the emotions, and the emotional will, which follows the dictates of the self. This struggle is explored more fully in *Free Will and Seductive Coercion*.

The chase and fear that accompanies the predator-prey relationship is designed for maximum anima extraction. The euphoric thrill brought by the hunt is simulated in violent entertainment. To some extent, the same anima extraction is present in most romantic entertainment. Horror and thriller film genres are akin to pornography in that they supply secondary anima in the easiest way possible.

Women being terrorized, raped and murdered on screens as entertainment provide the same secondary excitement euphoria as real life victims but in a more guilt-free and uninhibited setting. Women and children frightened by depictions of their ilk in traumatic situations provide additional anima for audience members who see themselves in those depicted as extracting anima.

Plots centred around great men losing status challenge endoreality by making the audience acknowledge a villain in the endo-ideal. These are plots for serious drama, not escapism, as it is more uncomfortable than the passive spectacle of murder and psychological torture of the negative image. Escapism does not challenge endoreality and does provide easy secondary anima. Escapism strengthens the emotional will over the conscious will. It is easier to watch because it does not require an expenditure of energy through the focus of the conscious will.

News and entertainment should be very careful in its depiction of murders and other violence. Entertainment from childhood through adulthood in most parts of the world shows destruction instead of creation as a euphoric source and violation and sublation ahead of connection. This both develops an appetite for secondary anima and strengthens the anima-seeking emotional will over the restraining conscious will. Instead of dividing industries into topics like videogames, sex and comedy, they ought to be divided as connection, sublation and violation. That is what they are really selling.

In times of everyday atrocity, such as found in a war or the dystopia often referred to as peak capitalism, entire populations can be transformed into hostile and exploitative people. There is a point in every war or conflict when the violence becomes a frenzy and very difficult to stop, when endogroups are solidified, guilt and empathy are sealed off and secondary anima fills the air. The vast majority of the people involved can return to balanced, exosocial interactions, however, as is seen after every war or in the rehabilitation of child soldiers.

This return to balanced interactions does not happen overnight and it does not happen at all without conscious effort at deprogramming predatory behaviour. At the end of World War II, the communities of France engaged in a frenzy of terror aimed at humiliating, raping, beating and hanging women in their communities under the flimsiest of accusations of Nazi collaboration. At the end of the religious wars of the so-called Reformation, Europe engaged in legally sanctioned burning of women for the next several centuries. At the end of the Cultural Revolution, China's legal system entertained crowds with the public humiliations and torture of accused dissidents during struggle sessions. The Roman Empire supposedly did away with sacrifices but continued killing their wives, daughters and any vestal virgins who were rumoured to be unchaste.

The negative image are always very vulnerable in times of war or revolution as the injured or newly formed endogroup initiates a feeding frenzy aimed at them. They are often explicitly ordered to accept the abuse for the greater good as their persecution provides the anima to strengthen the endogroup. Women are often told to ignore rape and other abuses of militias as these revolutionary or defending heroes deserve to have fun or the women owe them. Violence does not disappear because peace is declared. It may just move to internal targets until it is consciously eradicated.

Unprocessed guilt may be a partial cause for the explosion of slavery in recent decades. Sexualized slavery is open to the point of being normalized, with billionaire companies openly profiting from it. This is more obviously a result of the decline in slavery disguised as marriage, but the role of unprocessed guilt should not be overlooked. The widespread sexualized violation of children, particularly in places like Russia, the UK, US and Japan, may be partly a result of unprocessed national guilt or an unrehabilitated appetite for secondary anima. The fact that efforts to protect children are the most derided and violently opposed human rights efforts indicates that this torture of the negative image is serving some national function.

After war, when fighters are forced to return to peace with no transition, alcohol and other drugs are very commonly used to provide synthetic euphoria or auto-anima since their primary conduits have been blocked or degraded. Among gang members and others from violent backgrounds, religion sometimes provides a consciously euphoria-seeking replacement which does hopefully develop primary anima conduits.

Religions which encourage altruism, creation, discovery and healthy relationships have an opportunity to create lasting healing. Ritual conducted in places of great beauty, separate from everyday stress, which incorporate festival elements of community, dress-up, singing, dancing and even euphoric frenzy, provide regular anima transfusions and may aid the establishment of primary anima conduits. Religions which stress endogroup identification, encourage shunning and dwell on outside evil, or block primary anima by banning singing, socializing or enjoyment of beauty will have the opposite effect, particularly if they identify a negative image to demonize.

Unfortunately, individuals suffering deanimation are susceptible to any source of replacement anima, including extreme endogroups which are sometimes built around religions, nationalism or any other group identity. Promises of intense connection and inclusion serve to open up conduits closed due to trauma but still desperate to receive anima. The conduits opened to the promise of receiving anima are then used to extract anima instead, leaving already weakened people very vulnerable to forming new traumatic bonds with extreme endogroups.

Rehabilitation from a state of reliance on secondary anima requires two parts: a removal of all sources of secondary anima in conjunction with the

The words sacred and sacrifice share the same root because the idea of such offerings is so embedded in the practice of spiritual rites.

establishment of sources of primary anima. Simply removing ready access to secondary anima has the effect of weeding without planting; new weeds will grow to replace those lost. New endogroups will be created and new victims and new justification for their persecution will emerge. This is why prisons which do not provide the opportunity for growth and development of new interests are recruiting grounds for ever more violent criminal groups.

To call a society pathological is considered reprehensible, probably even a hate crime. To call an individual pathological is the business model of several industries. The exact behaviour pathologized in individuals is present in entire societies of every size, however, including industries. The so-called animal instincts are not latent in all people. Some have a desire for secondary anima and others have the desire for and ability to access primary anima. This appears to have always been the case as there is evidence of both gentle communities and extremely violent communities in all parts of the world, in all history. There are also myriad examples of communities that have changed their character from one to the other based on coercion.

In order to change the character of a person or community, it is necessary to understand the motivation for predatory behaviour. Human trafficking has surpassed both drugs and weapons as the number one criminal industry in the world. If people are a product, what is the nature of the product?

Roman holiday and many other festivals included cruelty as part of a feast. People have been sacrificed during times of great stress throughout history. Today, people react with angry attacks during times of great stress. These attacks are a means of accessing secondary anima to remedy the deanimation caused by stress. The rage of much of the public at the idea of ending the lethal misery of any negative image, from refugees to those living and dying in poverty, has no qualitative difference than public bloodlust in the past during gladiator games or public hangings.

The words sacred and sacrifice share the same root because the idea of such offerings is so embedded in the practice of spiritual rites. Sacrifices were regularly tortured and exhausted before they were killed in human societies as they are among other animals. Anthropologists and historians often prefer to interpret sacrificial torture as serving a practical purpose such as exhausting the victim, even when there was no need for that at all. Pain and fear, as well as death energy, were as key a part of the event as the meat consumed.

There is probably a reason that life forms survive through the consumption of other life forms. The consumption of food is a bonding activity for all social animals and a basic element of the maternal bond in mammals. The consumption of animals, or any food, is also orgiastic, just to a lesser degree than ritual sacrifices. This is the root for the recurring horrors found in slaughter houses, where excess pain and fear are regularly found to be inflicted upon the animals slaughtered.

Given a choice, a wolf, cat, seal or orca will never simply kill their prey in the fastest manner possible. Like a cat with a mouse, a seal with a fish or an orca with a dolphin, many predators use fear and pain to drain every drop of anima from their prey before they kill the body.

The trauma caused by extreme fear is a loss of anima. People afraid of repercussions leave before the kill, when they have emptied their prey, and return if they see it replenishing itself. Often, eating the prey is a secondary or irrelevant motivation, as it is when humans kill each other.

Amulets are created from ritual killings and torture to facilitate the transfer of anima from one living person to another. Those who perform ritual killings are clear in the belief that the more pain and trauma inflicted on the murder victim, the more they will be unable to detach from any part of their body, such as that eaten or made into an amulet. The amulet will thus retain the maximum amount of power sought.

The animist view that the life consumed was qualitatively different depending on the nature of the prey and how it was killed may hold some merit if the nature of primary and secondary anima are different. In that case, a predator's anima may be qualitatively different than a non-predator's, a belief echoed in the common preference for eating vegetarian animals over carnivores and the less common preference of eating carnivores for their power.

Further differences and attributes, such as specific abilities that some forms of animism consider to be imparted through ingestion of specific anima would mean either that anima is more than simply energy or that other aspects of the animal were also being transmitted. The idea that the anima contains a spirit, soul or will is well outside of the definition being used here. At this point, we are referring to anima as a simple energy, albeit with a bipolar nature.

Before leaving this gruesome topic, however, there is one other aspect to be noted. Thanks to the torture experiments conducted by the CIA and others at black sites around the world, we know that extreme pain, as in torture and near death, can both cause the conscious to decouple from the body and enable the sublation of the victim to another will. This appears to be the other point of torture, besides the extraction of secondary anima for the entertainment of those doing it. The sublation of will is discussed in *Free Will and Seductive Coercion*, however, it is noted here because this may be the aspect that animists are intending. The sublation of the emotional will through infliction of extreme fear and torture may be an attempt to sublate the self of the victim before it decouples in death.

The premise behind legal systems throughout history has been the allocation of guilt and the awarding of reparations.

The symbiosis of shame and death or deanimation is still found in the root of the word mortify which once meant to die. Shame (honour) killings are a form of anima extraction just as ritual killings are, and they have the same goal, to transfer power to the killer(s), in order to remedy a depletion or meet an increased requirement. Shame killings, like other shunning, are a way for an endo-ideal to attempt to leave behind guilt.

The premise behind legal systems throughout history has been the allocation of guilt and the awarding of reparations. Punishment of the person assigned guilt or someone considered sublated to them has consistently been a potential part of reparations. If the aggrieved party could not obtain a benefit equivalent to what they lost from the punishment of the guilty party, punishment would not make much sense. Therefore, it is worth considering the possibility that such punishment facilitates a transfer of anima from the person punished to the punisher.

Because blame and vice are always assigned to the negative image and virtue and credit are always claimed for the endo-ideal, the endo-ideal will always think they can leave the worst parts of themselves behind if they leave or destroy their negative image. Those left by the endo-ideal will always, at least momentarily, feel they lost the best part of themselves or at least their source of power. Since the separation usually causes the dissolution of the endogroup, the endo-ideal is usually much worse off after the separation, since they still have the same character but have lost their scapegoat and all the unearned credit and virtue that had been transferred to them. The negative image, released from the steady influx of new guilt and allowed to keep their own achievement, will eventually be much stronger.

Burning women as witches and domestic abuse cruelty have the same goal. The violence of the renewed witch hunts today can be viewed through many frameworks, but the destruction or wounding of an endogroup has extremely often precipitated the sacrifice of a part of the nation to provide the life energy to renew the rest. When villages are uprooted by land pillaging or other disaster, compensatory sacrifices may come in the form of witch hunts, dowry killings, murders in the name of local death gods or general rape, assault and murder. The trafficked, tortured, raped and murdered women and children of the post-war former Yugoslavia, or post-war anywhere, or the increased violence against women and children and the poor during any time of mass anxiety and stress, are all a result of deanimation of an endogroup which then seeks to reanimate itself through extraction from the negative image.

Those who do not understand the extreme levels of violence involved in what they consider mere economic killings are blinded to the nature of animism and endogroups. Poverty is simply the Dalit caste or scapegoat of wealth endo-idealism. It provides the same communal sacrifice. The same people shocked and horrified by animist ritual killings deem killing of women and children to be lesser murders, crimes of passion, honour killings, or even sex and killing of those in poverty to be an unavoidable economic necessity.

In An Introduction to the Principles of Morals and Legislation, Jeremy Bentham wrote *"Nature has placed mankind under the governance of two sovereign masters, pain and pleasure. It is for them alone to point out what we ought to do, as well as to determine what we shall do."* He described this as his *"greatest happiness principle"* in the 1789 publication. This principle has been the backbone of the utilitarian or libertarian philosophy that has guided much of western society. The foundations of western law, as well as modern democracy and economy, may be found in his principle *"it is the greatest happiness of the greatest number that is the measure of right and wrong."*

The reversed poles that repel and attract predators to and from anima have always made that principle incompatible with the very human rights laws which Bentham espoused. Without recognizing that the relationship with anima conduits can be reversed, or that there exist two very different types of anima source, we do not have a happiness principle that can be used as a basis for governance. This impossibility has been camouflaged in the past by the pathologizing of all people who do not find happiness in creation or connection, at least at the level of individuals. This simply erases half of human nature from consideration by decreeing it abnormal.

Any guiding principle that ignores the fact that the poles for happiness and misery can be reversed is going to be of little use in creating social structures. Pleasure and pain have nothing to do with the achievement of happiness or sorrow, contrary to Epicurus, John Stuart Mill, Jeremy Bentham and most others who have written about them. It is the type of pleasure and pain, or its effect, that controls whether it brings happiness.

Further, an individualist philosophy ignores the prevalence of group animus. The happiness of the greatest number in an endogroup invariably requires the unhappiness of the negative image, so it is not a recipe for universal happiness. The nature of endogroups as a shared animus within which happiness is a zero sum game must be recognized. It is not the pursuit of happiness that ought to be protected but the pursuit of exosocial expansion. That is the meaning of liberation and growth which are the key to building a network of primary anima connections. An appetite for primary anima is the only sustainable happiness and the only one that is not directly correlated with the misery of others.

Avoidance of power imbalance and endogroups is not always easy, however. In the next chapter, we will look at what happens when inequality exists in an egalitarian world.

Chapter 6

Martyrs, tyrants, saviours and
sirens

*Now the calamity to the people and the world is
tremendous. Yet the rulers enjoy doing it. This means
they enjoy injuring and exterminating the people; is this
not perversity?* — Mo Zi

For whatever reason, and a variety are possible, some people are filled with surplus anima. This anima attracts others and creates a power dynamic. Those that give excess anima away become martyrs if they are in positions of power and saviours if they are reflectors. Those that take or keep anima become tyrants if they are in a position of power and sirens if they are the negative image. A reflector who keeps anima is refusing to act as a saviour and is therefore cast as a negative image and a siren.

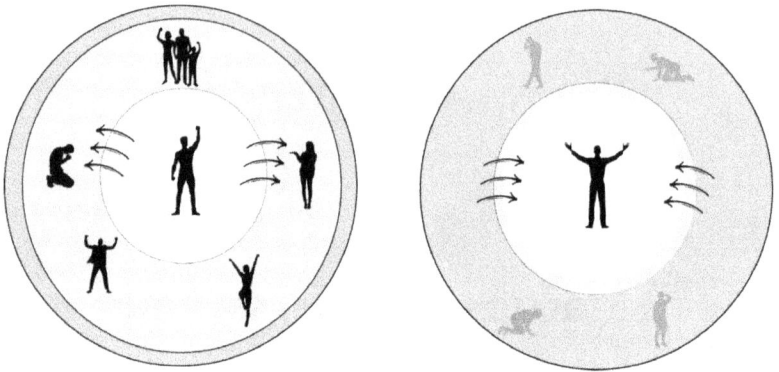

Figure 14: Martyrs and tyrants

Since the roles are externally defined, it is very difficult for a person to have excess anima and not be cast into one of these roles. Avoidance of any of these fates is why those who receive unexpected fortune so often rid themselves of it quickly. That option is not available to those who are channelers of primary anima.

The difference in the overall direction of energy flow is the difference between an endo-ideal tyrant and an exo-ideal martyr. Tyrants take anima and martyrs have it taken from them. Tyrants use power to accumulate secondary anima, which they hoard. Martyrs have excess anima that they disperse to those around them, often involuntarily.

A tyrant is usually dependent on and created by secondary anima. A martyr is usually filled with anima which they have obtained through exceptionally well-developed primary anima conduits. There is much crossover, however. A tyrant may have gained their initial power through an ability to channel primary anima. A martyr may be an accidental beneficiary of secondary anima or even a would-be tyrant without the power to withstand the centrifugal force surrounding them.

Dominance in an interaction depends on who is giving energy and who is receiving it. Energy flow is usually mutual, except in an abusive relationship, but the balance can tip in one direction or another. With a large number of interactions, such as those in an intense and isolated relationship or those involving a prolific anima source, even small differences can result in power acquired or lost.

Once one party has obtained power in a relationship, for whatever reason, interactions often become increasingly predatory and unbalanced as that power may be used to come out ahead in every interaction. This is why a power imbalance is created from the outset in most established hierarchies. Corporate executives are paid more, government officials have institutional force and teachers can control the free time and future of students. Under male endo-idealism, women were legally stripped of the ability to survive without men and under parent endo-idealism, children do not have the social structure to survive without parents.

In an open grouping like a celebrity fandom, the crowd feeds off of and destroys the idol for their entertainment. In a closed endogroup, like an abusive marriage or tyranny, the crowd or family is consumed by the idol who will destroy them for his or her validation.

Energy exchanges can be observed in a relatively pure form on social media. Some participants become addicted to little validations, while others become depleted by a continual, unrequited outflow or negative interactions. In other situations, a swarm of little depletions can energize a crowd and deplete a large account. The excitement on exposure or assignment of guilt to a celebrity is the anticipation and eagerness to participate in an energy feast from a martyrdom.

Power can be obtained by either supporting or attacking a stronger persona on social media. Social media is full of parasites who roam topics looking for anyone with fame to attack and parasite off of, just as it is full of tyrants who send their followers to attack others. It is a fascinating environment to watch the same types of interactions that occur in real life, but it is not the same as real life. While the dopamine and initial excitement from contact is readily available on social media, the bonding hormones that create the security of reliable connection are not. This makes social media particularly addictive to those already suffering deanimation, but ultimately, it leaves them further depleted with even less resources to reanimate themselves and even more vulnerable to endogroups.

An endogroup is a structure for creating power through the transfer of energy. The endogroup acts as a shared animus where the energy of each member is available to all members. The endogroup is not always created by an idol and it is not always to the benefit of the idol. At times, an idol becomes a tyrant and drains the group of anima. At other times, the idol is a prolific channeler of primary anima and the endogroup exists on secondary anima derived from the idol. These latter endogroups risk martyring their idol in their euphoric frenzy, just as tyrants risk the genocide of their prey.

The risk of martyrdom can motivate idols to ensure the balance of power is on their side. They can do this by securing an endogroup with external existential threat and by weakening the individuals in the group. Shunning of those outside (seen in celebrity feuds or fandom wars) or existential threats (such as threatened celebrity retirement) are used to strengthen an endogroup bond, even those around celebrity fandom.

As stated earlier, the key difference between an exo-ideal and an endo-ideal is the direction of energy flow. A secondary and related element is the ability of the reflectors to leave. A celebrity fandom is, therefore, far more likely to have an exo-ideal and a dictatorship more likely to have an endo-ideal, but this is not an absolute indicator. Some dictators have been at the mercy of their populations, and

The key difference between an exo-ideal and an endo-ideal is the direction of energy flow.

many cults and abusive relationships are formed where the individuals appear to be free to leave but have had their will to do so sublated. This is the reason democratic dictatorships exist. People supposedly have the power to vote out tyrants but they do not always have the strength of will or motivation to avail themselves of the opportunity, or they have had their options limited to alternate tyrannies.

Endo-ideals are not necessarily predators and reflectors are not necessarily prey. Predators do not necessarily need secondary anima. Sometimes (like in filiality) they feel entitled to it, and at other times it is just readily available. Sometimes an endo-ideal becomes a tyrant as a protective measure. An endo-ideal who is not a tyrant must have other protective measures, whether that is physical security or isolation, from the reflectors who will swarm them and eventually or immediately destroy them.

The role of the idol is to protect the unique and special feeling of the endogroup and strengthen its endosocial membrane.

The role of the idol is to protect the unique and special feeling of the endogroup and strengthen its endosocial membrane. The idol does this by acting as the anima bank of the endogroup, the recipient and repository of all excess anima. Getting celebrities to bless, kiss or take pictures with babies is a custom meant to collect the celebrity's anima, or bond it with the babies', and protect the baby's health. In times of turmoil, a sudden reversal can cause a run on the bank and the idol will be attacked.

Creation of the idol can come from an endo-ideal, reflectors or even a negative image. Vulnerable groups with little sense of self, or in transition from other endogroups, compose armies of reflectors and negative image in search of an endo-ideal. The propensity of young teens, particularly girls, to create fan armies that devote all of their spare time and social energy to reflecting their idol is a common phenomenon. The more these fans build up their idol, and the more they push their idol to achieve, the greater is the shared anima for the reflectors. These fan armies often satisfy their craving for anima through inter-endogroup conflict. At other times, they may turn on their idol and bond over the shared experience of destruction of the martyr.

Reflectors have the power to define the idol. When the idol is simply an energy source, the reflectors can leave at any time and the idol has no defense against depletion without strengthening an endogroup around themselves. Until very recently, worshipers were usually free to take their sacrifices to whichever god seemed the most likely to reciprocate with the desired outcome. Endogroup cults were created when one god had enough investment to make it costly for worshipers to switch allegiance. In these cases, cult rivalries, or even enmities would develop to strengthen the cult around each god.

An idol who is not an endoself or endo-ideal is often forced to become one to avoid depletion. This is the root of the toxic nature of power. Idols often surround themselves with sycophants to replenish the energy that has been drained from them. This can turn into a cycle which will eventually destroy their exosocial drive and their ability to access primary anima. If it was this ability that attracted their reflectors in the first place, the reflectors may turn on their former idol and destroy them, leaving them to rely on drugs or other destructive forms of obtaining auto-anima, that taken from their own stores.

More extreme endogroups with less vulnerable idols, such as militias, criminal gangs, sports fans or gamer communities, bond over shared anima extracted from the negative image or rival endogroups. These endogroups are strengthened by having a vulnerable negative image to attack instead of their own idol. Stronger endogroups are often male dominated because the negative image of male endo-idealism (women, or men categorized as effeminate) is always available for them to attack instead of their own idol or other endogroups.

An endogroup is a structure of power in which the idol is surrounded by both centrifugal and centripetal force, and either can dominate. Examples that illustrate this are everywhere in the world of celebrity and power. Fans and followers often destroy their idols in their frenzied search for euphoria. It is anima they seek and the allegiance they show to the anima source is not loyalty. The powerful are completely justified in their fear of their followers. Both reflector and negative image positions can be held by endoselves, who, despite their seemingly great disadvantage and supportive role, can destroy the idol.

Endoselves circling the idol are looking for blood. They are not concerned over whose blood it will be.

Even in groups of two, an endoself reflector can act like a lethal parasite. Friends who adopt every aspect of their target, even to the point of appropriating accomplishments, history, mannerisms and relationships, are typical in childhood but dangerous in adults. Such people do not only want an intense relationship. They seem to want to crawl into the other's skin and occupy the other's position in their self. They will first pretend the other's actions were their own, then they will deny the other had any role. They will first attach to the other's relationships, then they will attempt to have the other cut off and ostracized. Eventually, they will seek to destroy the original owner of the self they are now occupying. What seemed to be an extremely supportive relationship becomes Invasion of the Body Snatchers.

This is the ultimate interception of anima networks. An endoself reflector identifies strongly with their idol. Because they are the ones who extract energy from each interaction, if they manage to develop a close relationship with their idol, they will accrue power to themselves. They will create a shared animus and then become the dominant will in it. With the accumulation of power, they will adopt more of the endo-ideal role and drop the role of reflector. As the endo-ideal, they will assume the identity of their idol, credit themselves with all of their idol's attributes and accomplishments, and then seek to cast their idol as the negative image, saddled with all of their own guilt and vices. These relationships are the ultimate in gaslighting and the ending usually comes as a horrifying shock to the prey.

Many cultures have realized the dangers to the self from excessive adulation. Like the queens of hives, neither martyrs nor tyrants can leave, or they will cease to exist in their current form. An endo-ideal is an incomplete self, as are reflectors and the negative image. Each needs the others to create a whole and all will violently resist the breakup of the endogroup. Traumatic bonding ensures that prey will continue seeking approval or acceptance from the predator, even to the point of attacking anyone who tries to rescue them from the situation. This happens to the people under control of a tyrant, and it happens to martyrs under the control of their reflectors.

A star has the ability to take energy from a crowd and give it back amplified to encompass everyone.

Anyone who has been to an exhilarating live theatre performance, concert or sports game is familiar with this phenomenon. A star's attraction is not their technical skill, which is often very lacking in the most celebrated stars. It is their ability to channel primary anima. Most people can acquire skill, but most with star quality, or charisma, are born with it. This power grows with celebrity, however, and so it may be accorded to those who are born with or acquire status but had no innate ability to channel anima. This power may also be lost, as seen in a fall from grace, when deanimation leaves a former celebrity with no remaining attractive power.

As channelers of primary anima, artists are a group often martyred by audiences who revel in watching their self-destructive spirals destroy them. The lack of acknowledgement of energy transfer allows audiences to pretend they are passively watching a spectacle when they are actively partaking in a feast.

As channelers of primary anima, artists are a group often martyred by audiences who revel in watching their self-destructive spirals destroy them.

Because entertainers have far more access to primary anima than people in professions such as bureaucracy, they are a much more lucrative supply of anima. The idol risks getting caught in the hurricane of endoselves trying to claim the source of anima for themselves. There is a real threat from predatory reflectors as, like the farmer who killed the goose that laid him golden eggs, they can become convinced that anima can be theirs more quickly by destruction of the source. Instead of gratitude for the daily offerings, they will become addicted and increasingly bitter that they do not get more every day. Such predatory reflectors seize the achievement of idols and insist that they would be nothing without their fans which is a threat as well as a credit theft.

The dangerous dance with fandom creates and also destroys the idol. Parasitic fans establish connections and then use those connections to drain their idols, exactly like every other abusive relationship. They claim a right to the anima they are draining, and devalue the celebrities as narcissists, ungrateful or crazy if they resist. These fans leave their prey as close to empty as they can. The idol then becomes particularly vulnerable to exploitative reflectors. These reflectors replenish the idol's desperately depleted anima, but take their independence.

It is interesting to watch this effect weakening with the collapse of the current dominant and authoritative endo-idealism. With so much focus currently on tyrant predators, celebrity martyrs are enjoying a reprieve. Indeed, audiences have begun defending the privacy of entertainers, as they redirect their demands for anima onto politicians and billionaires. Boredom is becoming an even more common reaction to media exploitation of celebrities. The return of secure tyrants will always bring back the corresponding need for martyrs, however.

Predation on celebrities is normalized in every society, from the crowds that gather around popular or attractive people to the industries built around exploitative voyeurism of entertainers, artists and athletes. The frenzy surrounding entertainers provides a reprieve to those holding positions of state and corporate power. The industry of celebrity media is set up to satisfy the craving for martyrdom while deflecting the mob away from tyrant predators. Martyrs are sacrificed to protect tyrants.

A person who has a normally developed exosocial drive feels excitement at meeting others and has anima conduits available for connection. A person who was born to a life of fame and wealth seldom has the same eagerness. More often, they greet new social encounters with guarded passivity, withholding connection and neither offering nor taking energy. This is possibly due to satiety but could also be to avoid a chronic drain from the people around them.

Without an endosocial structure, the egalitarian force will cause energy to continually flow from those who have the most to those who have the least. Since endoselves are insatiable and starved for anima, they will quickly deplete any prolific source they encounter. Because endoselves have no primary anima conduits themselves, they will do this the only way they know how, by consuming the source and making it a part of themselves or destroying it. The martyr's self is under continual attack, resulting in the famed emotional fragility of so many in that position.

This fragility is a side-effect of prolonged deanimation or instability. Women isolated in many roles, particularly as wife or mother, are often accused of the same fragility caused by deanimation and instability. The instability arises from the interception of their primary anima conduits, creating a lack of dependability or security of supply. The interception of anima by industry and media causes instability and weakness for entertainers, leading to an increased dependence on the anima provided by a temperamental audience.

It is usually easy to see the surface depiction of the relationship between a celebrity and their fans. In the music industry, some artists build themselves up and degrade their fans to establish themselves as the endo-ideal while others invite abuse from their fans and establish themselves as the negative image. The endo-ideal becomes the tyrant who is defended by their fans and the negative image becomes the martyr who is destroyed by theirs. Many entertainers, or their industry management, encourage fans to act as avid reflectors.

The real nature of the relationship is obvious as soon as the fans turn on the endo-ideal artist, however. Few artists have the personal resources to survive such depletion and remain in good health and strength, particularly since they have usually dedicated intense effort to establishing primary anima conduits with only one source, that controlled by their fans. Revolutionary reversals are very easy in a situation where the endo-ideal does not have the institutional authority to defend their position.

Less powerful entertainers are encouraged to act subservient to their fans. Often, humiliation is an offering demanded by fans. In much of Asia, constant apologies are demanded from stars. This expectation is increasing, globally. An entire global media industry exists with the sole aim of catching celebrities in humiliating circumstances. Other industries are built around public relations, including law courts which defend celebrities from potentially disastrous violation and depletion.

The demands for flawless perfection and the insistence on humiliation and apologies, as well as the relentless privacy violations, indicate that the idol is being sacrificed for the collective guilt. Fans are not being humiliated, exposed and forced to apologize. Guilt is being assigned solely to the idol, and penance is demanded solely from the idol. The guilt is serving as a justification to the fans. Their anima theft is depicted as something owed to them in repayment for a social debt assigned to the idol.

In other cases, such as sport, the structure of the sport is designed with the anima flow direction built in. Team sports, which were traditionally male and often restricted to the endo-ideal classes, allow the athletes to absorb energy from both their teams and a stadium of fans. The exceptions in male sport are boxing, which traditionally drew participants from negative image groups, and golf and equestrian sport, which were rarely open to the general public.

Traditionally women's sports, such as dance, gymnastics and figure skating, isolate or pit women against each other in competition and encourage silent, critical judgement by audiences. While men's sport encourages dramatics which exaggerate the effort and pain the athletes endure, women's sport encourages athletes to smile and make it look effortless. In women's sport, this structure creates maximum extraction of anima for the audience. The athlete is left to consume anima from her own reserves or channel it through artistic creation.

Even settings such as gyms continue the expectation of sexual dichotomy in anima flow. Women are still expected to be quiet, reserrved and look good during their workouts, while men's grunts and roars fill the air and extract surrounding anima. The reason many people are still so reluctant to support women's team sports is resistance to giving audience anima to women.

The balance of power between an audience and a martyr is evident in the star's treatment as the negative image. Martyrs are ordered to be selfless and forever grateful, and always uphold the image that has been created for them. If they protest audience or fan cruelty or privacy violations, they are accused of ingratitude or ego. These are both guilt reversals typical to treatment of the negative image. It is the nature of an endogroup to assign negative image status to those being punished and to assign all guilt to the negative image. For this reason, an attack on a person may be enough for the group to turn on them and assign them both guilt and negative image status. The guilt assignment may follow the punishment just as easily as the reverse.

The true beneficiaries in these relationships are the industries which both instigate and enable the reflector – negative image conflict and profit from it. The right to define is an endo-ideal right, and the more control these industries have over an artist's career, the more they are the true endo-ideal. Whatever direction the power in a celebrity-fan relationship is flowing, industry executives profit. Sports stars and other celebrities are treated more like product than powerful people by the industries that profit off of them, especially those who are groomed for this role since childhood. The anima flow is the real product of entertainment industries and it is this that creates the addictive nature of entertainment. Athletes and entertainers would have strong primary anima conduits if

Martyrs are ordered to be selfless and forever grateful, and always uphold the image that has been created for them.

those weren't intercepted by sports and entertainment industries. The interception leaves them vulnerable to dependency on the readily available secondary anima of stardom.

The risk of martyrdom is why people cast as the negative image must fear too much success. They will be martyred due to their inability to be an endo-ideal. While European men are usually depicted in histories as acting of their own accord, women from Hildegaard von Bingen to Jeanne d'Arc were depicted as acting under the command or as a vessel for a higher spiritual power. In much of Asia, the need to avoid pulling attention is shared by all members of society who fear egalitarian or authoritarian attacks on those who rise above the crowd. Deflection of credit to a higher endo-ideal is an attempt to deflect the danger of martyrdom from those most vulnerable to it. Credit cannot be stolen from those who have already gifted it to a more powerful endo-ideal.

The wearing of masks during rites of anima transfer, including theatre, was an important feature. Masks prevented the buildup of anima in a person and protected them from depletion by an audience that refused to return anima or turned on the performer and caused an outward rush. The protection of such a public persona has been destroyed by paparazzi and tabloids.

Celebrities are often subject to attacks on their appearance, reputation and relationships, violations of privacy and rape fantasies or threats. Such violations of the integrity of the innermost circle of self are tools of sublation. Just as audiences and professed fans enjoy tormenting celebrities and leaving them with no privacy or dignity, so do politicians and corporate heads enjoy taking the privacy and dignity of those they hold power over.

Privacy and dignity are protections against deanimation and they are stripped from those being drained, whether that is the idol or the reflectors and negative image.

🐈

The crossover of celebrities and sports stars becoming politicians or the push to force experts in all fields to become accessible media stars is an attempt to create a star - audience relationship in all walks of life. From the so-called populist leaders and personality-centred governments to the saints, idols, or popular kids in schools, this one-to-many relationship is endemic in societies. Endogroups are created when the audience or celebrities attempt to make this relationship permanent.

The difference between a martyr and a tyrant is illustrated by who has the right to define. Stars of the entertainment world are seldom in control of their own celebrity. It is at the whim of audiences, media and an entire industry of executives parasiting off of their fame. Fans, an abbreviation of fanatics, are quick to remind their idols of their power. Like the Phantom of the Opera, industry executives and fans not only define their idols, they also control whether their idol is granted the ability to continue to act as an anima conduit. They control the ability to create for athletes and performers whose self is largely made up of conduits to creation anima.

The drive to create provides an opportunity for an exoself to pour surplus energy into others or into a shared animus. It also provides an opportunity for predators to control and extract that energy. Anyone who cares passionately about a creation, relationship or activity will attract people who ostensibly want to join them in their work but in reality want to control the shared animus and extract as much energy from the other person as possible. This is true of friendships, marriages, communities, and joint projects of all kinds.

The right to the anima of others is established through endosocial customs. Corporations and states seize the achievement of others for themselves and disperse crumbs to the reflectors. Corporations create martyrs by marketing artists as product to be consumed instead of restricting themselves to marketing their creations. The exchange of money establishes a magical right to the anima of another.

Any idol is under existential threat personally if their group withdraws its support. The group is under threat of deanimation, or at least loss of one anima source, if the idol withdraws. In a group dominated by an endo-ideal, attempts to leave will result in violence such as the murder of spouses and children who are trying to leave or resist, or the genocidal actions of a challenged tyrant. Groups dominated by reflectors will attack any idol that attempts to dissociate, as is common in celebrity fan worship. Many fans do not care at all about the well-being of their idol. They will not let the idol escape their role as a continual source of group identity and anima without guilt, humiliation and attacks on their privacy, reputation, physical, emotional and mental well-being. Celebrity media seems designed solely for this purpose.

The relationship between democratic politicians and their constituents is frequently similar to that of a celebrity, where those that elected the politician also revel in their failures, weakness and exposure. Just as fans claim to have created celebrities with their support, politicians are reminded that they are allowed to work by voters. Politicians are vilified by assigning collective guilt to all for the exploitative actions of many. This ensures that people who are not seeking to exploit the public will seldom choose the position of a politician. In

> **A perfect saviour is a woman with no will. She is a living reflection and he is created by her reflection. She does not reflect what is but what ought to be.**

fact, the election process seems designed to eliminate all but the most ruthless and tyrannical.

Martyrs are victims of the egalitarian force and tyrants are beneficiaries of endosocial force. There are two other types of relationship roles for those who act as anima banks. These are saviours and sirens. The saviour is the perfect reflector and the siren is the powerful negative image.

A saviour is one who provides reanimation to those who have been depleted. This is common altruistic behaviour and is the way every person begins life, through being held, nursed, spoken to, and so on. Every caregiver of those in need acts as a saviour. Saviourism is frequently considered a duty of the powerful, from the noblesse oblige once expected (in theory) from nobles to celebrities who are expected to raise awareness of various causes on social media. A weaker person cannot hold an excess of anima. Women who married powerful men, and so became the holders of power, were often coerced into becoming saviours or martyrs, or they adopted those roles for their own relief.

Saviours gain altruism euphoria. Patrons of those attempting to gain spiritual anima, such as monks, receive some of it themselves through shared credit, just as those who save lives receive credit. Saviourism is a behaviour sometimes adopted to feed the vampirism of tyrants, particularly through 'saving' or intercepting, those who do not need to be saved or demanding repayment of a debt from what was presented as altruism.

Saviours as endosocial predators are those who demand or accept the subordination of those they save and attempt to trap them in endogroups. Saviours may also be preyed upon.

Saviours are reflectors, but once the dependency bond has been created, either a martyr or a tyrant may result. Saviours can become either martyrs (exo-ideals) or tyrants (endo-ideals) or they can be attacked as a negative image. They can also be none of these if they escape endosocialism, but that often necessitates becoming isolated from relationships with those they help. This leaves their beneficiaries with debt which must be paid forward in further altruism.

States and other powerful organizations may have saviours at their head. The typical organization that has a martyr saviour is one in which the power lies outside the organization head, such as a volunteer organization, particularly ones headed by a member of a negative image class. They may also appear where the group is very organized and its head is very weak. This martyr-saviour exo-ideal has even appeared at certain times in Europe's Middle Ages between peasants and the lords who offered protection in exchange for tribute, on occasions when the peasants held the balance of power. It appears often when the negative image is placed in a position of power and is then attacked or abandoned as was Jeanne d'Arc.

Altruistic saviourism, such as that involved in giving birth and raising children, has nearly always been seen as rightful behaviour for women. When a man saved the life of another he was expected to own that life. When a woman saved a life she was expected to be its servant forever. Both are in some way responsible for the life they save, but they retain their master and subordinate roles. The negative image are, therefore, far more likely to be cast as saviour martyrs and the endo-ideal as saviour tyrants.

Reflector saviourism has been considered the duty of women in every highly gendered culture. A good reflector reflects all good onto their endo-ideal and, in so doing, the reflector creates the endo-ideal. A reflector has the power and the responsibility to assign all virtue to the endo-ideal and the endo-ideal has the duty to accept it. A failure by a man was thus considered natural on his part but willful evil on the part of the woman who failed to inspire him or created him through a faulty reflection.

The woman was expected to be a living saint or avatar. Any real or imagined behaviour which fell short of perfection was blamed for any action taken by the man who was held to be a manifestation of her purity. This attitude is still apparent in both news coverage of male crimes and court verdicts which so often find a woman to blame for male violence. Usually the guilt is assigned to the wife, mother, daughter, victim or object of desire, but sometimes it is attributed to a completely unrelated woman. Psychoanalysts also consistently blame male transgressions on mothers who failed in potty training, or nursing, or any other aspect of their care.

Blame of the reflectors for a faulty endo-ideal image has a twisted sort of logic to it. Every endo-ideal is the creation of their reflectors and reflectors therefore bear the blame if the endo-ideal is found lacking or flawed. This is the source of the reflector's humiliation and the pain they feel on their idol's failures or the exposure of them.

The 1957 (remade in 2007) Hollywood film 3:10 to Yuma depicts a murderous outlaw, Ben Wade, who admires his captor, Dan Evans. During the movie, Wade shoots his own most avid reflector, who is trying to rescue him from Evans. While disregard for the life of a gang member is standard fare in Hollywood movies, this particular murder is depicted more as the murder of Wade's own image due to his newfound admiration for the image of what he sees as an upstanding man in Evans.

This real or symbolic murder of reflectors accompanies transitions by endo-ideals fairly often. Sometimes it is accomplished through shunning or divorce and at other times, reflectors complain that they are abandoned or rejected by an idol choosing a new path with their art or ideas. In any case, the relationship is symbiotic enough that it is difficult for the idol to move autonomously to recreate their image on their own without in some way destroying the reflectors.

Women have traditionally been seen as agents of coercion for men's behaviour but only as a divine conduit or muse. Her infallible purity could make him better, but her infallible purity depended on her being entirely empty of her own will or desires, existing solely as the image of virtue. A perfect saviour is a woman with no will. She is a living reflection, and he is created by her reflection. She does not reflect what is but what ought to be.

Figure 15: Saviour

The Madonna - saviour woman must also, as all ideal images, have a negative image to coerce behaviour in the opposite direction. The whore - tempter woman was popularized in Babylon long before Lilith corrupted Adam and his new perfect replacement wife with her insubordination and temptation. Eve received the blame for allowing her perfect emptiness to be corrupted by the older, knowledgeable woman / snake, but Adam was subsequently credited with all the knowledge gained through the insubordination. The virtue accrued to the endo-ideal and the guilt to his negative image and imperfect reflector.

The Madonna saviour expectation has contributed greatly to the binary division of women into good, light, women saviours and bad, dark women tempters. The good woman was expected to recognize divinity in the lowest of men and inspire him to at least attempt to be worthy of her reflection. As the good women were responsible for virtue, they were also responsible for purifying womanhood by shunning all that was old, dark, powerful or knowledgeable. Eve's failure was her failure to shun the older woman / snake / Tiamat figure and her failure to refuse filling her perfect emptiness with knowledge.

Colourism is a social valuation far more ancient for women than the extremely recent application to men. This may be related to the use of the negative image-reflector roles to define women under male endo-idealism. The reflective power of fair skin and blonde hair contrasts with the darkness in which to bury all guilt. Under Yin-Yangism and earlier, including the Tiamat legends, women have been associated with dark and chaos and men with light and order. A woman who retains darkness symbolically retains her own will, while the lightest of women may be perceived as emptied of womanhood and reflecting only the man. Light and dark are also very important attributes in guilt deflecting magic which was primarily directed at women.

Princess Diana was the epitome of the modern Madonna-martyr: extremely fair, a teenage girl (billed as virginal) of the highest class (valuable), vulnerable due to her shunning from the royal family endogroup and pure of the influence of an older woman due to her own motherless childhood. The frenzy that consumed both her and Marilyn Monroe, to whom she was often compared, centred on their vulnerability. Both were raised without the guidance of a mother (just like every Disney or fairy tale princess), so were uncontaminated by the influence of an older woman. As Princess Diana famously pointed out, the frenzied attacks by the media (primarily middle aged men) and the justifications that She likes it. She asked for it. If she didn't want it to happen she shouldn't have looked pretty / worn that. have a lot in common with rape.

Rape and gynophobia, as well as stalking and other obsessive behaviour are common among the predatory reflectors of martyrs.

🐈

To a lesser degree, this public appetite for women martyrs has threatened to destroy all women the public casts its eye on, unless they are blocked by a powerful group membrane. Not being martyred is helped by not being a young, blonde, motherless, virgin, but the women who fall outside this elite category can be cast as the old corrupting witch. This is the powerful Tiamat figure depicted by the dragons and snakes in the chaoskampf myths as the wise but evil being that must be slaughtered in order to 'save' the pure virgin for the man. Alternatively, they may be the designated bad woman, dark, isolated, poor, associated with sex and addictions and bearing the blame for all men's weakness.

Marilyn and Diana were both vulnerable and filled with anima from public adulation and both ignited a frenzy of predators demanding that they give it all and more away. Sinead O'Connor, Whitney Houston, Britney Spears, Amy Winehouse and Janis Joplin were all tremendous channelers of primary anima who refused, or were refused, the role of perfect reflector or saviour. All were consumed by the frenzy surrounding them in any case.

The siren acts as the negative image to the saviour. The sirens have all blame cast upon them, while the saviours are expected to provide all grace, assuage all guilt and lift all to their full potential. Both are destroyed in the process.

Theoretically, a man could occupy the siren role, but they almost never do. This is because male endo-idealism is the base unit of power and has been for most of recorded history. Under male endo-idealism, a man with enough power will almost always have enough reflectors to become a tyrant or saviour unless there is an exceptionally strong rival endogroup dynamic at play. Elvis Presley was, like Britney Spears, controlled and sold due to the authoritative fear of his sexuality and, to a lesser extent, this happened to many rock singers. This was a side effect of rock singers, and especially Elvis, being associated with African culture which was an extreme negative image in the United States, especially at that time. Rock singers were also associated with the female negative image due to their long hair and unisex clothing. Even so, most men in rock did not suffer persecution and at its worst, it was nothing close to what the real negative image suffered.

Increasingly, sirens are becoming as rare among women as they are among men. With the weakening of male endo-idealism around the world, women are also more likely to acquire reflectors as they gain power. The entertainment industry is now filled with powerful endo-ideal women who would have been reviled as sirens even a decade ago. Under male endo-idealism, however, any woman admired by the public will be a target for martyrdom. The madonna-whore, reflector-negative image dyad is the same coin. It can flip at any time and it is spent in the same fashion.

The difference between a saviour and a siren is related to the power of reflection. Sirens, like Medusa and Circe, refuse to cleanse the guilt of the endo-ideal. Instead, Medusa froze them into stone and Circe cast them into the image of pigs. It was this grotesque depiction of the endo-ideal as powerless and beastly that made sirens so feared. The saviour is the perfect reflector, but the siren is the perfect negative image, revealing all that is darkest and weakest in those who surround them and cast eyes on them. The reflection both fascinates and terrifies its audience, and they would destroy it if they could.

Figure 16: Siren

Sirens are recipients of power through the fear, awe and desire they inspire in others. Unlike the pale, young and virginal saviour martyrs, the sirens are dark, mature and fully embracing sexuality on their own terms. A siren is a witch, a negative image who refused to allow her power to be taken, her credit to be stolen or her will to be sublated. A siren is a woman who was shunned but refused to leave the spotlight. She is a woman attacked who took the energy of her attackers, leaving them fearful and enraged. She is an image of themselves that they cannot resist but are repulsed and horrified by. Those who circle sirens are attracted to them but also repelled and terrified of the power which could expose their guilt and sublate them.

Sirens, saviours, martyrs and tyrants are all born of unequal anima in a world governed by an egalitarian force. Power held in the form of an exoself is very difficult to achieve in an endosocial society. Because those with power can't have equal and reciprocal interactions with other people, they don't have many opportunities to create connections. Interactions will predominantly disperse energy outward if they obey the egalitarian imperative and that will create the one-way relationship suffered by an exo-ideal martyr. The alternatives are to become a tyrant endo-ideal, a saviour reflector, a siren negative image or to isolate and protect a core self separate from the external work. The latter is both difficult and unsatisfying.

The only freedom possible for a channeler of primary anima is that granted by their surrounding community. If that community allows them to preserve their privacy and dignity and responds with gratitude and acknowledgement to their gifts, and without adulation, they can avoid the endosocial roles forced on them by endosocial societies. They cannot create exosocial interactions if they are only able to interact with endosocial people.

People throughout history have come up with solutions to these risks of power accumulation in a person. The most common solution has been the creation of anima banks. We will explore these often disturbing practices in the next chapter.

Exo-ideal

The idealized centre of an endogroup where the primary energy transfer flows from the idol to the rest of the group.

Types of governance

Exosocial networks – anima connections.

Endosocial martyrdom – anima taken from the idol to the masses.

Endosocial tyranny – anima taken from the masses to the idol

Powerful sources of anima

exo-ideal martyr, an endo-ideal tyrant, a reflector saviour or a negative image siren.

Martyr

A prolific source of anima who dispenses it to reflectors. An exo-ideal.

Tyrant

A powerful person who takes anima from reflectors and

negative image. An endo-ideal.

Saviour

A person who replenishes the anima of others and reflects an idealized image of those they save. A reflector.

Siren

A powerful person who refuses to reflect an idealized image of others and refuses to dispense anima on demand. A negative image.

Martyrs are victims of the egalitarian force and tyrants are beneficiaries of endosocial force.

Chapter 7

Anima banks

It's not the killing of the animals that matters, it's the transfer of life energy back to the Loa. — Bob Corbett

The quote above references practices in Haiti but it seems to reflect the experience of most groups that practice sacrifice. The community believes they are replenishing the shared life energy. The overall life energy has never needed replenishing however, and it seems unclear how it could. If life is an energy, it should be expected to follow the law of conservation of energy which says that energy can be neither created nor destroyed. Life must always be in the same measure, unless it can be created out of nothing or disappear into nothing or transform.

What is held to need replenishing is the life energy of the endogroup, or shared animus. This occurs particularly in times when energy has been diminished by guilt, shame or external attack, when extra energy is required in preparation for an event such a battle, when crops are about to be grown or when erecting an important structure that needs strength and longevity or needs to be able to withstand attack. All of these have been occasions which were marked with sacrifices in several disparate cultures.

While a martyr is a conduit or well of anima that people draw on to the point of depletion, tyrants act as anima banks that extract and hold the excess anima of the group. A priest may act as an anima bank, as may a king or a patron saint. Anima banks may be permanent totems, gods or shrines, or they may be temporary, such as the elected leader or priest in many animist cultures.

Sacrifices (later, taxes) were enforced to solidify this status in the ruler.

The strength in an endogroup is always embodied in the endo-ideal.

For a population to turn on their own anima bank would deplete the savings of the entire endogroup. This is why the endo-ideal tyrant is so seldom attacked, especially in times of great duress for the endogroup. To declare a war secures the position of tyrants. War provides an outside target for the population to attack for secondary anima and encourages the endogroup to fiercely defend their own anima bank against attack. The strange custom of people defending their own oppressors is due to the anima bank role of the endo-ideal.

The strength in an endogroup is always embodied in the endo-ideal. It is therefore the endo-ideal's life energy which is being replenished by any anima extracted by or from the endogroup. Just as austerity implemented to help the economy is self-evidently only helping the economy of the endo-ideal, and executions to ensure social harmony are self-evidently only assuring the peace of the endo-ideal, sacrifice of the negative image is necessary to replenish life energy in the endo-ideal.

The custom of giving wealth to the endo-ideal in order to purchase absolution is as long standing as social hierarchy. In the 1600s, King Houegbadja created the practices that became the Annual Customs of Dahomey. In earlier Vodun practice, rites and sacrifice were dedicated to family elders and ancestors. Under King Houegbadja, the sacrifices and spirit gifts were brought to the king and done in his name. This was an interception that caused all credit to accrue to the king instead of the families and villages. Under subsequent kings, the Customs grew larger and the local sacrifices more constricted.

This is the same pattern that was followed in every second age, hierarchical nation from Aztecs to Romans. The family and village nations were usurped by a transcendental endogroup that intercepted all of the spiritual offerings or other surplus wealth by enacting taxes, tithes, or other compulsory tribute or simply forbidding rites and offerings by all but a few. The imposition of one god or religion is the imposition of one endo-ideal and one anima bank. If conquered nations were allowed to keep their own anima bank, under either religion or the trade economy, they would not be dependent on the conquering one.

This interception is still present in its most basic form in monarchies and theocracies, where anything commendable must be done in the name of the monarch or god. It is also still present where any achievement must be credited to a CEO or university. From early animist offerings to the current trade economy, reflectors and the negative image are left at bare subsistence levels or less, while as much wealth and credit as possible is extracted from them to feed the endo-ideal.

Whether it is through the burning of a chicken, the torture of a child to make an amulet, the stoning of a woman ordered by a religious court or the misery and death of a family on the street mandated by an economic algorithm, the transfer of energy is always the same. The life of one is forcibly stolen to acquire power for another. The frenzy such energy transfer creates is seen in ritual dance and orgies and it is also seen in people raging against any assistance offered to people dying under economic ideology.

This transfer is black magic and it has been considered black magic in all parts of the world, throughout history. Its effects on the perpetrator are well known. Predators are trading future peace and immortality for a temporary, earthly advantage. This legendary moral is easily illustrated by observing the effects of power. Power causes primary anima conduits to die and replaces them with an impermeable membrane necessary to stop the holder of power from being martyred. Power changes the nature of a self from an interconnected and immortal cluster of interactions to a mortal object, dependent on the acquisition of secondary anima to even maintain mortality. The endoself is the living dead.

As anima bloat increases, the power required to hold it increases and as the power increases it is able to acquire more anima. The appetite for power by a predatory endo-ideal is insatiable, as each infusion of secondary anima increases the debt that requires balancing and so increases the craving. The patterns of ever-increasing sacrifices followed by the Celts, the Aztecs, the Fon, and now, the cult around the abstract idea of economy, are also followed in blood frenzies occurring throughout history. There is a turning point in every genocide when this frenzy takes over, and neither facts nor threats will stop the killing. The idea that this is an inescapable part of human nature is a result of viewing only the endoself as a model person, currently idealized in the mythical form of homo economicus. Only an endoself is an object reliant on secondary anima.

Two of the oldest and most universal beliefs regarding life and the self are animism and astrology (which includes elements of animism). Both date to before migration out of Africa, or at least 50-70,000 years ago, and were continued in all regions of the world, up to the present time. Animism may be much older than homo sapiens. It seems to have appeared earlier in the form of ritualistic graves or, in the case of Homo naledi, elaborate burial chambers, incorporating funeral objects, art, body ornaments, symbols and cave drawings.

Animism may be a cross species belief. There is a great deal of evidence that animals also live within animism. Spiritual belief is in no way restricted to humans. Beavers build for a filial future and bury their dead in lower level dams. Mother horses will stay beside a stillborn foal for days, or until the spirit has left. Dogs do the same for their loved ones. Dogs cry or howl when a spirit leaves a body. Using black box words, like instinct to describe what is called spiritual behaviour in humans is an attempt to create an artificial human exceptionalism where none exists.

In astrology, the self is considered to be created at the moment of birth. This leaves only two possible sources: the mother and the surrounding environment. Totemism is aligned with clan endogroup identity and the belief that relatives, at least those from a matriarchal lineage, shared an animus. In totemism, the clan spirit is passed from the mother to the child. Clan totems were always matrilineal, although individual totems could be passed through a paternal relative, shaman or other outsider. These individual totems illustrate the belief in magical practices and rituals that could create a shared animus where one did not previously exist. Such rituals are also seen in adoption and marriage practices. The connected self shared an animus which acted as an anima bank. This meant they also shared debt and credit.

If anima exists and can be transferred from one animal to another, and if life is independent of consciousness and will, there is no immediately apparent reason to doubt that anima can be retained in an object. If an object is simply a cluster of interactions created using anima, it would seem that anima must exist in all objects. Life energy must exist in objects, or the objects would be unable to move. Life energy is transferred from the source to the object to enable the object to move through spacetime. When life energy in a person enters an object it does not change form. It is still life energy, or anima.

Just as life is not consciousness, an anima conduit is not the same as an empathic conduit. Empathic conduits allow shared thought among conscious things. Anima conduits allow a transfer of anima and may be established directly to primary anima sources or through objects, rites or ideas. These vehicles of anima transfer also seem able to act as banks of stored anima.

> **Just as life is not consciousness, an anima conduit is not the same as an empathic conduit.**

Animism includes the belief that spirits and life energy can be contained in objects or symbols. It is difficult to find any human group in history that did not share these beliefs. Animism, gynotheism and shamanism are the root first age beliefs that gave way to ancestor worship and androtheism during the second age. This is discussed in more detail in *The Fourth Age of Nations*.

Animism can provide a way to balance debt through offerings, loyalty or service to the spirit, animal or object holding the debt, in order to avoid sublation or as part of sublation. Some offerings were voluntary; others were seen as compulsory and exclusive to one spirit or euphoric object. Some were thus freely entered, or exosocial, interactions, while others were proof of bondage to an endogroup. In animism, some spirits were more powerful than others, but there was no hierarchical relationship. Negotiations with these spirits were conducted on a transactional basis, between two autonomous entities.

The history of animism is evidence of hundreds of thousands of years of belief that anima can be stored in objects.

Sublation to ever-higher endogroups negated the need for balanced transactions. The temporally extended filial or karmic self allowed increasing levels of debt to be carried over for generations and encompass ever-expanding endogroups.

The history of animism is evidence of hundreds of thousands of years of belief that anima can be stored in objects. Cave drawings may be interpreted as a means to create an anima bank that may be appeased in exchange for an animal's life, or an icon in which to trap the animal's spirit in a place safely distant from those indebted to them. Jack'o'lantern's are a relic of carved turnips and gourds that were used to trap predatory spirits by carving symbols in the object to prevent their escape. Traps for malevolent spirits are as common as totems and shrines for benevolent spirits.

It is beyond the scope of this book, but the will being trapped or enticed is typically an earthbound, emotional will which is closely related to anima. This aspect is more easily understood in the discussion of will found in *Free Will and Seductive Coercion*, and it is just mentioned here in passing.

The totem (using the broad definition employed by Emile Durkheim and others of that era) of an enemy nation can inspire greater fear than the nation itself. The power in a totem is both concentrated and supernatural, or existing outside the limits of the body. Totems are repositories of group anima, thus an attack on a totem, or god, is an attack on the nation's life. Mass suicides have resulted from such attacks. As Durkheim asked, "*So if [the totem animal] is at once the symbol of the god and of the society, is that not because the god and the society are only one?*" [35]

From this standpoint, a god is a bank containing the surplus group anima, along with a will which allocates that energy according to whim, supplication, deception or justice. Gods by this definition include the totems, priests, and rulers of most cultures, especially if money is considered as a repository for anima. The accumulation of wealth in the powerful then makes sense. An anima bank, which can be cracked in times of need through revolutions, assassinations, etc., if supplication fails, is used to store group wealth.

The creation of one higher god, conflated always with the earthly ruler, was a symptom of the second age usurpation of lower deities. These new gods demanded sublation. Obedience became the primary virtue, ahead of free exchange and competition among spirits. Sacrifices which enabled the accumulation of power replaced the sacrifices which were made to give gratitude or balance spiritual transactions. Eventually, powerful men were deified. The back-and-forthing between prophets and kings appearing as gods and gods appearing as prophets and kings was constant in the second age and is still seen in parts of the world.

The mass sublation which appeared during the second age was a reaction to the accumulation of power. As discussed in the previous chapter, it is difficult for a person, or even a small nation, to hold power against the egalitarian force. A Knights Templar motto *"Non nobis, Domine, non nobis, sed nomini tuo da gloriam"* (Not unto us, O Lord, not unto us, but unto thy name give glory) illustrates the self-effacing behaviour which may be, at least in part, related to the danger of martyrdom risked by those who allow anima bloat in themselves.

The usefulness of anima banks in cultures which did not sublate themselves to a higher transcendental power is evident. Both debt and credit are abstracted or transferred to a holding bank to protect the rest of the community from the consequences of debt or credit. The logic is the same as that which encourages people to keep their currency in a bank to avoid being robbed or killed for it.

The choice of the strongest person, or an abstract concept or thing, to act as an anima bank may be because of the risk of being torn apart and martyred by those following the egalitarian force. By containing power in an object, power accumulation in a person is avoided. Icons work as remote transfer stations for safe access to divinity on earth. Money works in a similar way to icons. The pain and suffering of the negative image that the power was taken from is held at arm's length from the beneficiary and so is the debt and guilt.

An anima bank is a repository which contains surplus anima, obtained through sacrifice, devotion, offerings or interactions. An anima bank is a source of euphoria, so if it is an object, it may be referred to as a euphoric object. It must be recognized, however, that such an object may produce euphoria in those linked to it, apathy in those with no connection, and terror in the enemies of those who share its anima.

Many funeral rituals include a possession sacrifice of objects or people deemed to be the property of the deceased. These are sent to burial or cremation alongside the body. This could be due to the perceived need of extra life energy for the death journey, as is the case when food is sacrificed, or it could be to avoid vengeance from the deceased if others use their possessions. It appears both or either reason is often behind funeral sacrifices.

Funeral sacrifices related to ownership require a definition of what ownership meant in those cases. A possible definition is objects which have been sublated to the deceased and were under control of the will of the deceased, including sublated people such as wives and other slaves. In that case, it is the will and everything sublated to it which is buried or cremated, not just the body.

It is also possible that objects were buried alongside people, not for their use in the afterlife, but in the belief that these objects, along with the body, held anima belonging to the deceased person.

In this case, use of those objects (and people) would be a theft of anima from the deceased. The belief that improperly disposed of bodies may be occupied by malevolent spirits may have extended to other anima holding objects besides the body.

Another possible definition of ownership is objects which have, through interaction, become a part of the self of the deceased. If every object is simply a cluster of interactions, and every interaction contains the anima which created it, then a person who interacted often with an object may consider it a part of their self or animus, or the people conducting the burial may see it in that light. The admonition to avoid using a deceased person's belongings for a year, or other time frame, supports such a belief. If spirits were invoked through objects, then use of linked objects may recall a newly departed spirit from their afterlife journey. This power of invocation is hardly a casual or isolated superstition; it is a widespread belief as old as humanity itself and perhaps older and more widespread than humanity. Dogs and other animals can be comforted by objects which have a connection to someone they love.

Heirlooms are euphoric objects that allow ancestral or otherwise inherited objects to carry forward the anima deposited in them. Their value is obtained by the attachment others formed through interactions with the object, as well as the creation and care energy put into them. Heirlooms and other property were often bequeathed formally to the recipient and the living diligently respect the wishes of the dead. It is hard to imagine why this formal release of ownership would be considered necessary if the property was not viewed as bound to the deceased even after death.

The fear of owing debt to a spirit which will cause it to return may have been a part of the reason for filial offerings, as an exchange, or rent, for use of the home, land or possessions. It may also have contributed to the elaborate burial headstones and shrines which sometimes rival the houses of the living in expense, embellishment and maintenance. These structures may be meant to entice ancestors away from the house occupied by the living or reduce envy or anger at the use of their possessions.

Sex, death and violence are three of the most prolific vehicles for the transfer of anima.

Offerings and other ritual involving the deceased keep the shared family animus replenished and the right to share property along with it.

Anima is released or exchanged in rituals. Funerary rituals release anima for the deceased for their journey and to repay any residual debt or credit still owed. Bonding rituals use anima to create strong endosocial bonds in wedding, adoption, enslavement or coming of age ceremonies. An entire village may expend energy which is then available to fighters before a war.

Sex, death and violence are three of the most prolific vehicles for the transfer of anima. It is often difficult to differentiate between the forms of entertainment constructed around violence. Rape as entertainment is depicted as pornography, or sex, but its audience and their motivations are often indistinguishable from the audiences for gore tourism and gore entertainment. This similarity is exploited in many movies and video games which offer violent sex or sexual objectification alongside violent death as entertainment. It is also exploited in wars which feature rape as prominently as murder.

The shield and sword dances performed by Highland Celts on the eve of battle may be seen as imparting anima to these essential battle implements, in order that they may overcome the anima of an opposing warrior. There are similar war dances in many other parts of the world. Other widespread battle rituals, from sacrifices, orgies and mass rapes to music and dancing, may serve the purpose of imparting anima directly to the warrior themselves.

Historians who note the lives wasted in building great monuments seldom consider that these lives may not have been viewed as wasted. Instead, they were often explicitly considered an essential building material, without which the structure would collapse. Hitobashira is a Japanese word which translates to human pillar and is used to refer to people buried alive within important buildings or monuments in many parts of Asia. Immurement, or live entombment within the structures also occurs frequently in Celtic and Balkans folklore. In Aztec Warfare,[36] it is estimated that between 10,000 and 80,400 people were sacrificed in 1487 for the re-consecration of the Great Pyramid of Tenochtitlanin.

The Encyclopedia of Celtic Wisdom describes[37] *"a universal belief in the notion that no edifice will stand unless a human being's blood is cemented into it"* and further states that *"Foundational sacrifices of people or, latterly, animals occurred throughout Britain and Ireland up until the mid nineteenth century … the usual choice of victim in foundational sacrifice – normally a child or baby"* and *"Foundation sacrifice is usually performed in edifices whose foundations break open the ground for occupation for the first time"*. In a particular live immurement, they explain that [Odhran's] *"sacrifice is primarily to create an 'ancestral hotline' … Odhran's body consecrates the soil of Iona, while his soul remains watchful and able to grant petitions."* This indicates a desire to trap, not just life energy, but the will and perhaps conscious as well. These immurements extend the shared animus of a clan to include land and structures.

In medieval Christianity, churches were often built on the remains of saints and martyrs, which led to the great demand for saints in medieval times. The same idea was incorporated in relics and reliquaries, the remnants of saints and the boxes or built in parts of a church in which they were stored. These body parts of people, most of whom died particularly violent and gruesome deaths and were accorded great virtue in their lives, follow the same principles as animist amulets. There is no difference in their creation or function.

The abstracted body of Christ or the ashes or bones of the Buddha or bodies of deceased Dalai Lamas are used in a similar manner. When the life of Christ or the Buddha is depicted in a religious icon, the depiction acts as a link through which the anima bank can be accessed. The icon acts in the same way as written and spoken invocations to an anima bank. Both are abstractions used to establish a remote connection to the anima bank. Relics and icons are held to be links to god, not sources of power in themselves. Body parts in animist amulets are used in the same manner to negotiate with spirits and supplicate favours.

Tombs and graves are sometimes used in the same way as reliquaries. Since they contain the remnants of physical bodies, any particularly significant person, or the ancestors or other members of a family, may receive pilgrimages and prayers. A grave is perceived by many as an anima bank with supernatural powers. Flowers, prayers and other offerings brought to gravesites share most features of offerings to other types of shrines.

The idea behind monument sacrifices did not abruptly disappear when the practice died out. There are many examples of currency being buried in walls for good luck just as bodies were earlier. This makes some sense if currency is considered an amulet which stores anima and none at all in any other context. It also means that projects where workers were enslaved or died on the job may not have operated entirely from practical or accidental reasons, at least as far as the emotional will was concerned. There are many examples of monuments to kings and gods that contain the sacrifice of the labourers even when there were no ceremonial sacrifices made. The Great Wall of China and the city of St Petersburg are just two examples. Such monuments exalt the greatness of the ruler and nation at expense of those whose life energy they contain. These monuments produce euphoria when they are destroyed as every revolution shows.

Houses have often been observed to have extreme anima bank or euphoric properties. A saying (possibly of Irish origin) that a house is not a home until it has seen a birth, a death and a marriage seems to refer to its status as an anima bank. It is possible that the house, tent, compound, cave or igloo retains the fear, pain and love experienced in it. There are thousands of years of stories in every culture that describe such an ability to retain emotional substance, and few people today would knowingly buy a house that has seen lethal violence. Withholding knowledge of such a history can make a house purchase contract void in many places.

Gore tourism is another reason to believe that the product of pain and terror remains in certain places. Tourism in Bosnia is promoted by posters with dripping blood over the word SaWARjevo, and tourist trinkets such as planes made of bullets. Tourist destinations such as concentration camps, skull towers or killing fields may promote themselves as places of remorse, but it is undeniable that they are experienced by many with excitement instead. This is acknowledged by the places that eradicate or hide buildings or sites where mass atrocities and human suffering took place.

The Serbian city, Nis, built a high school overlooking a former Nazi concentration camp. This was a site of the genocide of Serbians during World War II. Nis still preserves the skull tower built by the Ottoman Empire, made from the heads of their slaughtered ancestors, as well. Nis may be educating its youth about past horrors, but there is a cost to such a preoccupation with death and grievance. Concentration camps and skull towers act as banks containing both anima credit as grievance and secondary anima. Those who keep them wish to preserve the credit earned by victimization in that shared animus, but they are also hoarding secondary anima.

War tourism, disaster tourism and ghoul tourism are all driven by an attraction to secondary anima. Places such as stadiums which contain fights, hockey games, or once, gladiator deaths are also edifices which trap secondary anima and attract certain people for that reason. Secondary anima may be felt even in places that revere their dead. with graveyards more prominent and well-tended than the homes of the living or where the rites to the dead are onerous enough to circumscribe the acts of the living.

Abstracting Divinity

People collect rocks or other objects from sacred sites or the sites of euphoric events. Any site where a saint, prophet or other source of anima is said to have visited will receive pilgrimages and supplications, just as sacred natural sites such as trees and bodies of water do. Anywhere an excess of anima is thought to have accumulated, or where a link is thought to connect to an anima bank, will be designated as sacred, but the behaviour around these may be more accurately considered economic. Good luck charms, typically something that was present at a time of good luck and so hopefully absorbed some of the excess, will be used as an anima bank to create good luck again.

Celebrities offer signatures in an attempt to forestall crowds from tearing off their clothes or pulling out their hair. Even a euphoric object itself, such as a book, ball or guitar, may have its value increased by the signature of a celebrity. Marketing of celebrity is marketing of anima. That is what the product is behind celebrity endorsements. Celebrity adulation is a method of worship for storing excess anima in a cultural icon (often referred to as such) which is then jealously guarded as a group possession.

Economics today is a continuation of the economics throughout history with currency as the new, abstracted icon. The ponzi scheme structure of economic wealth makes no sense under economic theory, but it correlates perfectly to animist power cycles. Accumulation of power in anima banks has been transferred to economics. People have to work, even when their work is pointless, so that their life energy, or anima, can be deposited in the currency amulets.

Animist power cycles are the cycle of revolution. The endosocial cycle of escalating abuse depletes the negative image first, then the reflectors, until eventually the craving for anima is so great that the endo-ideal is sacrificed to replenish the whole. Revolutionary leaders are then filled with victorious anima and so are able to form new endogroups and the cycle repeats.

The health and wealth of the anima bank is far more important to a nation than the health and wealth of any member, unless that member serves as an anima bank.

That does not mean that death and persecution harms the status of the bank, however. Martyrs become more valuable as anima banks after their deaths. The pressure against living martyrs, or exo-ideals, having 'ego' may be a concern that they may use up some of the energy stored in them. After death, that concern no longer exists.

The value of a martyr is also increased after death by the pain and suffering of their deaths. Famous saints and martyrs tend to have endured particularly grisly deaths. Even icons of hatred, such as the Guy Fawkes effigy that is burned every year in the UK, combined great power (charisma over others) with a horrific death, resulting in an icon that is still used to produce euphoria in a crowd. The rite of burning Guy Fawkes in effigy is a connection for the crowd to tap into the energy originally extracted during his torture. This is replenished every year with the festive rites.

Energy can also be obtained by identifying with the vindicated. Those who claim endogroup bonds with Christ share his absolution. Pharoahs in ancient Egypt were associated with Osiris, who won a judgement against his brother Set for his murder. Osiris and Christ were both unjustly murdered. People are able to share in the surplus credit left over at their deaths through shared identification with their victimhood. A similar excess virtue and credit due to persecution is attributed to all martyrs. The more horribly they were persecuted, the stronger the power associated with them. This same shared victimhood is sought by most endogroups. Endogroups typically seek to either claim victimhood or claim association with real victims in order to share a credit.

Sacramental grace is a common instance of the animist idea that ingesting an object magically transformed into the spirit of another being will impart divine powers. The sacrament is imbued with the excess anima formerly contained in Christ's body due to his extraordinary virtue, supplemented by all the virtue attributed to him as the endo-ideal of a vast endogroup and the great debt owed by those who persecuted him and any of his followers in his name. When Catholic and

Orthodox Christians take the sacrament, which has been magically transformed into the body (really the animus) of Christ, they imbue his state of grace (which is derived from his surplus credit) and his salvation. The sacrament is currency from his anima bank.

Under Judaism, their god was the anima bank of a tribal endogroup. As a tribal member, Jesus had access to this bank and shared it with his own followers. His right to do so was established through the credit owed to him by his unjust persecution by the Jewish people. Christianity is an example of the creation of a new endogroup from a credit owed the negative image of a previous endogroup.

Christ acted as a sacrifice that redeemed all those who who accessed his god by invoking his name. They were absolved of their guilt and freed of the need to repay their debt with their own torment (although a lot of saints and martyrs have been thrown in for good measure). Notably, the animist guilt sacrifice was not discredited in Christianity; it was fulfilled. The cross is an icon empowered with anima from the torture of

The energy extracted from others is stored in euphoric objects, whether these are amulets, icons or coins.

Christ. This power is what gives it the ability to not only save the wearer but also vanquish enemies.

While there were probably, or at least possibly, first age nations which did not sacrifice people or animals to appease spirits, feed the group animus or gain spiritual power, sacrifices were globally widespread. The great achievement of Christianity was in convincing people all over the world that Christ had acted as the ultimate sacrificial surrogate and no other sacrifices were necessary. This is why his followers claim that Christ died for them.

The energy extracted from others is stored in euphoric objects, whether these are amulets, icons or coins.

This does not mean that other animist rites died out of Christian churches. In 1492, Pope Innocent VIII is reputed to have died after receiving blood transfusions from three boys killed in the process. Innocent VIII was the same pope whose papal bull criminalized the control of childbirth and medicine by women and started the centuries of terror and gynocide known as the witch hunts which continue to this day.[38] [39] [40]

The transfusions may (or may not) be an apocryphal story, but it is an interesting historical parallel to wealthy people now injecting stem cells and the blood of children to preserve their youth. In the case of Peter Nygard, charged in 2020 with multiple counts of sexual assault and forcible confinement of women, the stem cells he sought were from the aborted fetuses of women he had impregnated, a very saturnine ambition to prolong his life by ingesting that of his potential children.[41] As religion did before it, science is once more returning very directly to animist ideas and practices they scorned without any acknowledgment that they are doing so.

In 1440, French Baron Gilles de Rais was convicted of torturing and murdering possibly hundreds of children. He was charged after a dispute with the local clergy. He must certainly have worked with powerful accomplices in whatever occult rituals he was attempting or he could not have continued at such scale and for so long in his private Chapel of the Holy Innocents. The especially interesting point about de Rais is that after he was hung, his body was said to have been claimed by four women of high birth who took it away for burial, almost as if his body retained uncommon value. Years later, his daughter had a memorial erected at his place of execution and pregnant women began making pilgrimages to it. In this case, it is not his own suffering that seems to have created value in him but the excess of anima he extracted from others. It is quite possible he was also seen as the anima bank for the group that he worked with.[42]

It is an extremely animist idea that relics of the person who stole the life energy of so many children must now be an anima bank containing life that can be obtained for other children. Animists practice similar abstraction when torturing and murdering others for gain in secondary anima. The energy extracted from others is stored in euphoric objects, whether these are amulets, icons or coins.

Anima found in icons, or representations of Christ or other martyrs and anima banks, is also found in landmarks associated with them and in amulets. Prayers (spiritual supplication) allow those in need to access some of the energy stored in the euphoric object. The animist who kills and tortures others to store their anima in amulets became the priest. The spirits which could direct outcome or grant power powers were reduced in some forms of Abrahamic religions to only one, but the animist idea is unchanged.

Early Christians anointed Christ as the super-child, favoured child, or one true son of god to cement his status as the endo-ideal. This exceptional myth started one of the first theological wars among the more literal-minded followers of Christianity. It is hardly worth the notice it has been given, however. As a Jew, Christ was a member of the tribal endogroup favoured by this god and he (or his followers) used that position to share that anima wealth with the revolutionary endogroup of Christianity.

The term son has never been as literal as modern

patriarchy has tried to claim it was, anyway. Economically, it often simply meant the man who received the blessings or benefits of another man, whether that was because he was a favoured offspring, slave, servant, apprentice or as part of a marriage or adoption contract. Since there was no way to prove biological paternity, a man's son was deemed to be whoever he recognized as a son. Marriage contracts were, besides a binding master-slave ritual, an exchange. In exchange for the slave bond agreed to by the woman, or her family, the man agreed to recognize her children as his own and grant benefits to them accordingly.

Christ is possibly the strongest anima bank that has ever existed. This has less to do with his proclaimed status as a literal son of god than it does with the nature of anima banks. Once they are in use, their power is dependent on the wealth put into them, and his has been a major beneficiary as well as benefactor. For this reason, it is also largely irrelevant whether, as some contend, a man named Christ never existed. He certainly does now.

The same principle applies to all gods. Gods are anima banks and endo-ideal will and, as such, they exist if they are believed to exist. Worship is what creates them, just as all endo-ideals are created by their reflectors. Buddha taught that there was no god or afterlife, and he is now widely worshipped as a god. Che Guevera was a devout believer in communism, and his face is now a lucrative capitalist product. The original nature of an anima bank is of very little importance.

An anima bank may be referenced through an icon, a symbol or something as abstract as a word, such as a name. The object and its meaning are created by those who attach themselves to it, not by its original association. The original character or message does not matter. Adherents are attracted to the power in an anima bank. People torment and kill others under the names of historical figures who would never have agreed with the acts done in their name. People also torment and kill others in the name of meaningless abstract ideas such as Economy, Science or Progress which are incapable of endorsing an act. As in all endogroups, the reflectors create the idol and its attributes.

Anima banks are created by their use as anima banks, and gods are anima banks. The difference between general spirits, or wills, and gods is that gods respond to supplication or negotiation by those in need or desirous of an anima infusion. Gods are therefore, first and foremost, anima banks.

Despite the great power of access to such a bank, a god's followers would usually bring an offering like everyone who negotiates with divinity always had. Offering gifts in his name greatly exaggerated their value as association with an endo-ideal increases the value of a product. This is the approval theory of value, explained further in The Power Economy. It makes sound economic sense to offer your gift with a celebrity endorsement that will greatly enhance its trade value and that was the economic basis behind many cults. Christianity made this power more universally accessible, but transactions were never completely free of exchange. There were always candles to be lit, prayers to be recited and rites to perform, if not by the beneficiary then by others. Babylonian clay amulets offer exchanges, such as singing the praises of the goddess Era for all time, if they are spared from the plague.[43] Negotiations such as this carried on unchanged under Christianity.

Now, the economy serves the same function. It has abstracted animism even further from its roots, but the principles are identical. The people who were sacrificed for anima are now

The economy thrives on weapons, drugs and slavery and sleeps in the presence of altruism and caregiving.

simply sold for currency. Their life energy is contained in currency just as it was and is contained in amulets, talismans and icons. Then, as now, the greater the suffering, the greater the power. Cruelty and destruction provide the economic value. The economy thrives on weapons, drugs and slavery and sleeps in the presence of altruism and caregiving.

Those in need must supplicate those who hold such icons for relief. The most dedicated members of churches were usually women and other negative images who had a compulsion to work off the guilt they had been assigned. The economically wealthy are the new gods who can choose to ease the pain of others but, more often than not, can't be bothered or prefer not to. The coin (or modified account balance) became the further abstracted sacrament with which to manage the fast-paced transactions of life under the trade economy.

Whether life is sacrificed to objects, gods or institutions, the death and torment of some is necessary for the wealth and power of others.

The anima economy was and is the first and only economy. The traditional architecture of banks includes the pillars and architectural features of Greek shrines, not public markets. The first paper money was created, not to exchange sticks and rocks, but to burn as a filial offering. The barter origin myth of economics has no historical basis. The roots of modern economics are purely animist.

The difference is in the institution which acts as a gatekeeper to the sacrament. The state of grace enjoyed by Christ which his followers can imbue is an excess of anima. This is the same excess that is obtained from saints, celebrities, or joyful events, music, art and other festivities. A state of grace is a state of overflowing anima which can be used as a credit to cancel debt. Even under economic endo-idealism, a state of grace means a (temporary) freedom from debt.

Guilt has served as the building material of all modern religions and all modern institutions. Because guilt does not disappear but is merely transferred, the associated debt still must be repaid through punishment of the debt recipient. Predation creates imbalance and associated guilt which demands ever greater relief. Cruelty escalates as guilt and the associated need for greater punishment escalates.

The nature of the egalitarian force includes a tendency to overcompensate payment for debt. This is convenient in establishing relationships, as the slight imbalance creates an imperative for the relationship to continue. In a religious endogroup, this tendency was exaggerated by the endogroup structure and the tendency of priests to exaggerate debt. These continual imbalances, and the deflection of the guilt for imbalance onto an otherworldly endo-ideal, made the priestly endo-ideals extremely powerful.

Abstracting Divinity

Modern gods are abstracted into institutions. Now people are killed to appease the economy, the law or state sovereignty despite none of those abstractions depending on mass death to survive. It is the endogroup itself that needs death and suffering to pay off their own debt. Whether life is sacrificed to objects, gods or institutions, the death and torment of some is necessary for the wealth and power of others. Every amulet-selling animist in West Africa knows this and every industrialist lives by it.

Supplication is made for wages or charity. Under the economic religion, a person cannot just work and obtain what they need. They must supplicate a higher power and perform rites to receive what they need from the anima bank. The interview – labour – wages pipeline is of the same nature as the confession – penance – absolution pipeline. The reason people leap to the defence of billionaires is the same as the reason people leap to the defence of their religious leaders. Billionaires are the anima bank of wealth endo-idealism.

Transference of power to transcendental endogroups is initiated by destruction of the anima banks and animus of the group which is to be sublated. Whether that means killing the local prince, as Machiavelli recommended, or smashing local icons and forbidding totems as most organized religion did, or destroying the environment as industrialism does, or destroying local economies as billionaires do, the purpose is the same. Destruction of anima banks and conduits creates dependence on the new endogroup.

Destruction of euphoric objects can cause a great release of energy. This energy can power a revolution which is why it is so often a part of revolution. Destruction of euphoric objects and prevention of the creation of them can cripple a nation or individual, which is why this control is nearly always a part of totalitarianism. Losing too many anima sources at once causes trauma due to deanimation, and that trauma can occur whether those conduits were to people, objects or rites.

Recently, most governing authority has been passed to algorithms. Progress to the future (and Mars) replaced heaven and economy and law replaced theology. The linga phallic symbols and statues of conquering men in the plaza were replaced by corporate skyscrapers. The shepherd / patriarch who cared for his children (ideally) is abstracted into blind justice and the invisible hand of the market which do not see the people-objects they act upon. Further dissociation attempts to deflect guilt even further.

Euphoric objects have become increasingly less important along with the ancestors and nations they helped to link. Increasingly, a person's own body is their most important object which receives the most offerings of time, money, focus and obsession. As people socialize less in their homes or through creation or discovery, the body is also the primary object of interaction. People are connecting more with events and actions over people and places and they are doing so directly, through their own bodies. This free-floating existence may one day help to create a networked exosocial structure but only if we build the institutions to facilitate this.

Before this is possible, we need a much better understanding of the interactional self. Take a deep breath, because in the next chapter we begin to move outside the arena of easily measured experience. This is where it gets interesting.

—————

An anima bank is a repository which contains surplus anima, obtained through sacrifice, devotion, offerings or interactions.

Chapter 8

Euphoric rites

The quarrels and divisions about religion were evils unknown to the heathen. The reason was, because the religion of the heathen consisted rather in rites and ceremonies, than in any constant belief. For you may imagine what kind of faith theirs was, when the chief doctors and fathers of their church were the poets.

— Francis Bacon

Everything exists only as an interaction. An interaction is an object and an object is an interaction. This is very apparent in collapsed wave theory, in which probability waves became particles upon interaction. Every particle starts as a cloud of probability, or potential outcomes, which is then collapsed into one outcome. The idea of a person as a contained object is an illusion.

This is not a wild new idea or something unsubstantiated by evidence. Everything in quantum mechanics works on this assumption and everything in quantum mechanics supports this assumption.

Technology has been working for over a century by incorporating this basic principle. Particles exist only as interactions.

The reliance on Newtonian concepts to describe daily existence has been rationalized by the fact that Newton is highly accurate at the scale in which people live. As long as a person is conflated with a body, Newton would be expected to work. If, however, people are separated into body, life, self, consciousness and will, the effect is the same as when Newton is used at atomic scale – it fails to accurately describe reality. We are interactions and choice, driven by energy and will. That is what all objects are. The interactions compose the self, the choice is made by the will and the energy is life. An honest study of humanity may be very valuable in finally reconciling quantum mechanics with general relativity.

Figure 17: Photoelectric effect

The photoelectric effect illustrates that objects produce a weak current when light shines on them (they emit electrons). This effect is used in security systems and automatic doors. Automatic doors are not automatic; they are interactive. When a ray of light encounters an object, the interaction determines the outcome.

This principle is occasionally recognized in human sciences. Negative ions at the ocean are known to improve mental health, but examples like this which show a person as a cluster of interactions are treated as anomalies. There is very little attempt to change the prevailing view of the object-self to accommodate these known effects or examine the implications of an interactional self.

Without being able to absorb energy from the sun and release energy into space, the Earth would be very different. As theoretical physicist Richard Feynman pointed out, *"energy is the money of the universe"*,[44] a statement which is also a recognition that money is simply a token of energy. Nothing happens without energy.

A person is a cloud of interactions connected by the energy waves which powered them. Each interaction is an opportunity to gain, lose or share energy. A life form is an interaction cluster which uses life energy to interact. In that case, there is no reason to assume that outside life energy cannot enter any object. All things a person interacts with are also clusters of interactions. If a person hits a ball, their energy is transferred to the ball. If energy is expended by one agent of the interaction, it is absorbed by the other. Cleaning and maintaining a loved object, the energy spent in its creation, the energy expended in its use or prayers offered to it all increase its value as a euphoric object. Anima banks are interaction clusters which, through various possible means, have resulted in a surplus of anima contained in the object, or icon, or incantation.

If all things are interactions, it does not matter if a person is interacting with something recognized as a 'solid object' or not. It should be possible for a self to interact, through euphoric objects, rites or ideas, with others who do not share the same spacetime. If an interaction with an object (including a person) can cause a ripple effect that impacts the entire cluster that makes up the object, it should also be possible to form a chain to interact with another person through a proxy.

As an object can only exist within space, an interaction can only exist within time.

As an object can only exist within space, an interaction can only exist within time. Spacetime is one and the same thing. It is not only not necessary for the two sides of a shared interaction to share the same spacetime, it is impossible. Any interaction they share, however, must share the same spacetime since spacetime is simply that which contains an interaction. A self is, therefore, not an object that exists in one spacetime.

Objects and selves are both networks of interactions and each interaction is wrapped in a unique spacetime.

If objects only exist as interactions, they must exist in every spacetime in which they interact, as that spacetime is an integral part of the interaction and vice versa. A person such as an artist must either be able to exist outside of the spacetime in which they are generally held to exist, or they must have the power to store life in euphoric ideas, objects or rites, in order to interact with selves that exist outside of their usually delimited spacetime. Both of these possibilities give rise to interesting consequences. In this chapter, we will dive into the deep end of these implications.

We know all interactions are animated because anima is the energy which powers all interactions. Interactions can produce euphoria, dread and other emotions, and emotions appear to be a reaction to anima. Life is circulated through interactions. What is the difference between an interaction with an object, rite or idea and a body? Ancestor worship and iconolatry teach that there is no difference. The object, action or story are simply vehicles through which the self, will or consciousness, can participate. Animated interactions are possible through each of these forms, just as they were possible with a body-object.

Everyone is familiar with the emotional rush felt when a smell, place, sound or other sensory input creates a link to an event in our past. We are instantly connected to all of the emotions we felt at the time that is being invoked. Often, we cannot even remember what the event was. The self is linked back to the original event independently of conscious memory. This is evidenced by the fact that the emotions are immediately present as they were in the previous event, even when the brain cannot recall why. Sometimes such a link is established when a previous event did not occur in the current lifespan, a feeling known as déjà vu.

Figure 18: The interaction and the self

Some physicist-philosophers have employed a persistent space-time worm concept to unite changing renditions of an object through time. The self as interactions, or an object as interactions, does not require any such explanation. An interactional self or object is already linked through space and time as each interaction must project through spacetime. The Descartes of 1640 is not a different temporal 'slice' of the Descartes of 2023, connected by a poorly defined persistent element. Descartes himself is simply an ongoing series of events which, in his case, continue today with every invocation of his name. This power of invocation to manifest a self or spirit is well recognized in all animist beliefs.

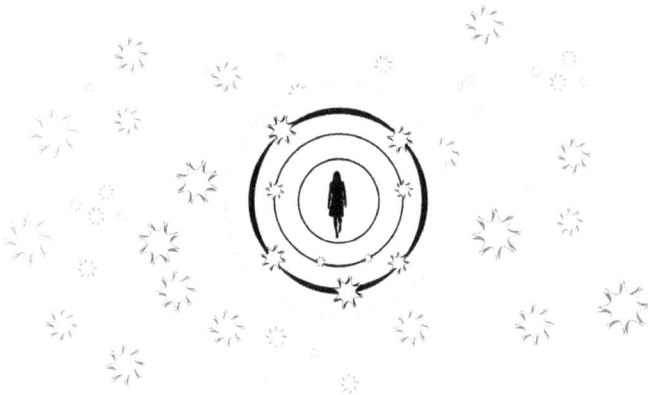

Figure 19: Interaction spacetime

Name invocation involves the wider self or endogroup which is connected to that name. This is acknowledged in the use of different names in different endogroups. The baby name that is left behind in a later stage of life and the names that are adopted upon coming of age or joining certain endogroups are used to separate the old and new. There is no trace of Miss X in her married form as Mrs. Y, and Miss X and her family are also cut off from Mrs. Y's offspring. The business name of a person cannot be invoked to cause harm to their family and neither can debt assigned to their business name be inherited by their family. This principle is much older than its modern manifestation in corporations, as is explored further in The Power Economy. Spell casting often depended on knowing the personal name of the target. Formal or business names or aliases acted as proxies and protected the primary circles of self from curses (which typically assigned guilt).

Writing itself comes from the creation of talismans and spells. Secret names of spirits, patients, the deceased, the intended targets of curses, and later, the longer prayer scrolls and spiritual scripture were the earliest writings. They were used to ward off demons and malefic spells in times when spoken words were not available, especially for the ill, infants or while sleeping. In Ethiopia today,[45] *"A scroll is prepared for a person suffering from grave and recurring troubles – for women, mainly problems of maternity (sterility, miscarriages, children's death); for men, pains attributed to curses"*.

Such writings were also purchased and carried to far off places.[46] The Book of Leinster[47] relates a story of the banished son of the King of Munster in 600 AD, inadvertently carrying a shield on which someone had written the curse, *"If thou come to Feradach by day, that thy head be off before evening; if by night, that it be off by morning."* He had trusted the writing as a guardian spell because only a few had the knowledge to interpret the writing.

The Irish Ogam writing is just one example of many forms of writing used for this purpose. Writing supplemented iconography as a secret form of magic understood only by the initiated who wielded understandable power from the knowledge. Prestige is, after all, derived from the root word for a magic trick. This secret power to cast spells is the first reason it was considered important to egalitarian principles and fearful, uneducated rulers that the knowledge of writing be available to all.

The reverse of invocation is shunning. Shunning is used in decrees that the name of a shunned member of an endogroup such as a family or cult must never be mentioned in the endogroup, thereby removing them from the future of the endogroup. Occasionally, a full spell was used to remove a person from an endogroup, as is still seen in excommunication, divorce and disinheritance.

Instructions to invoke, or avoid invoking, a name recognize the power of the spoken name to manifest or connect to the self of the name owner. Admonitions such as Do not speak ill of the dead illustrate that the living are continuing the selves of the dead for them and creating the future character of the self. They alone decide whether the dead continue to extend their selves into the future, as they alone have the life energy to create the interactions which extend the selves of the deceased.

This is the reason naming conventions were and are strictly regulated in many or most communities and naming a child after someone was usually a weighty matter. Often, children were named after powerful figures such as saints for the added protection such invocations would carry. Other names were words describing attributes that were meant to be invoked alongside the person. Later adult names were sometimes descriptions of real or exaggerated prowess displayed by the person. All of these naming conventions were protective spells.

The consequences of death will be discussed in more detail in The nature of death chapter, but for now we are trying to establish the source of anima stored in ideas or rites and the beginning glimmers of the resulting implications. The first of these is the importance traditionally placed on shunning, which is shared by credit theft. If those whose names are no longer mentioned no longer exist in current spacetime, then those whose thoughts and acts are miscredited may be seen as having their self expansion, or part of it, stolen.

Credit theft is an attempt to intercept and steal interactions a person has made in their life, particularly those that are likely to be repeated or invoked.

🐈‍⬛

This is not only a death sentence, it is a negation of life. Credit adds anima to the self it is granted to through future interactions or invocations, along with the added gifts of respect and gratitude. This may explain why credit theft was seen by some to be so important it required the creation of endogroups to justify it, or balance the debt incurred. Appropriation of credit is an important method of anima theft which is why plagiarism and related offences found a place in law. It is also an important source of power which is why an oldest son was often given his father's name along with his inheritance, to both claim and continue the credit accruing to his father. Those who were legally sublated, such as women under male endo-idealism, were often legally stripped of their names so that all of their acts were credited to their husband. Slaves and people who migrated to foreign countries were often similarly renamed. This continues under corporations which take legal credit for the labour and intellectual property of the employees under them.

If a person does not exist when they do not interact, then boredom warns of a reduced existence. Boredom is a response to thwarted or sublated interaction. Solitary confinement is torture. Preventing a person from acting or erasing their association with their work is theft and a violation of their self. This is evident in human reactions to totalitarian control and shunning, but it is very downplayed in contemporary social and legal recognition of its effects.

While it may be true, as Heraclitus asserted, that it is impossible to step twice into the same river, it does not follow that the first river no longer exists. Indeed, the self of Heraclitus still exists in the interaction the previous quote came from. This writing acts as a repeater for that interaction, bringing one of the many interactions which make up the self of Heraclitus into the time and place in which this is written and, again, into each time and place in which it is read. The second agent of the interaction changes, but the initiating agent, Heraclitus, remains the same and remains in his own time and space. As long as he is still interacting and producing euphoria through his ideas, however, his self is linked into a wider and wider time and space through these incantations, or rites. Through these interactions, anima transfers continue to occur. Praying to religious prophets, or citing the new prophets of science, likewise provides them immortality.

Alternatively, this idea of Heraclitus may be viewed as a euphoric rite or chant, with which both he and the rest of us have interacted, often through translations by Plutarch or Plato, to obtain the idea anima he placed within it. This is effectively the same thing, since both the idea and Heraclitus are clusters of a vast amount of interactions. The difference in classifying clusters as one thing or

If a self is a collection of acts, continuation of the act is continuation of all the selves that have performed the act before.

another is solely semantic. In either case, it is possible for a self to interact, through ideas, objects or rites, with selves that do not share the same time and space.

Since the idea is part of the self of Heraclitus, it makes no effective difference whether we consider ourselves linked to him or the idea, but that may be radically changed in the case of credit theft. If we attributed the idea of Heraclitus to Plutarch or Plato, it will be their selves we are expanding instead of his. This may be why both shunning and credit theft were often considered very weighty subjects and used as the ultimate punishment or considered the ultimate crime. Conversely, keeping a name alive is often seen as a duty of the utmost importance.

If a self is a collection of acts, continuation of the act is continuation of all the selves that have performed the act before. This would explain why the life of a nation is so inextricably tied to the rites referred to as culture and why books such as the Talmud or the Book of Rites were so diligently studied and preserved. Rites help to create a temporally extended self. A nation is bonded by culture through linking nodes of interaction across spacetime. Rites are important, especially at festivals that invoke national and ancestral spirits, because they bring forward all members of the nation or family that have performed those rites in the past. This is why prevention of national ritual and language and destruction of national euphoric objects have always been a part of every genocide.

This power of rites, anima banks and euphoric

objects to act as capacitors and link a vastly extended self through many spacetimes is the true nature of culture. The word cult, nearly synonymous with extreme endogroups, is the root of culture and associated with early religious rites for this reason. The modern usage of the word culture, which claims commercial products or casual norms as collectively owned culture fails to recognize the nature or use of such rites and objects.

Ritual grows from life. A ritual cannot be created and have meaning attached to it. The ritual is important as a memory of some history; the meaning must be baked in. Objects created and used as consumer goods lack such intrinsic meaning. Neither does this meaning exist outside the act and the intent of the act. Those that try to claim exclusive 'cultural' ownership over rites confuse the choreography with the dance.

No two people are ever directly linked unless they interact directly. Culture is the collection of rites, objects and ideas which provide an intermediary and connect people from disparate spacetimes. Key to this premise is the fact that such cultural rites, objects and ideas contain anima, so they can establish a euphoric interaction and create a shared animus. This is why events like festivals seek to replenish the anima in such cultural banks.

Ritual, and all culture, is the extension of self between generations. Rites bring peace and comfort because they connect to a larger animus. Family recipes, designs, and traditions are all capacitors of anima from the earlier lives connected to them.

As part of filiality, culture was attached to heredity. Heirlooms and inherited property exist because of the anima which is considered to exist within them. If people were not considered an extension of the lives and selves of their ancestors, filial inheritance would have no basis. In times where paternity was not necessarily genetic, it was the rites and name invocation which established the continuity of a patriarchy. A man gave his name to a child he granted the right to continue his name.

A self is stored in a vast collection of interactions. Rites act as repeaters to extend the self into a new time and space. The interactions which compose a self always exist in the time and space in which they occurred, according to the B-theory of time. Because those interactions will always exist in the spacetime they occurred in, this interactional self is immortal. The secret to immortality is an expansion of balanced interactions, not a theft and hoarding of anima into an object-self.

Dedication to rites is a measure of the economic power of ancestors or other endogroups over those currently living. The power drawn from rites is often eclipsed by the energy drain from the living due to the necessity of carrying out excessive ritual practice. This can reach the point that the living are in perpetual bondage to the dead. A dissolution of all rites has the opposite effect. In this case, the living float alone, completely unbonded to the anima security they need, especially in times of hardship and crisis. This leaves them no option but to develop direct connections to primary anima or violate and sublate sources of secondary anima.

Generations that refuse to maintain the family objects or continue the family business or name are refusing to extend the selves of ancestors or the shared family animus into the future. It is the shared animus which is abandoned.

The majority of the world is now free floating, untethered from the moors of rites and objects.

Euphoric objects and rites are a means of creating an expanded network of selves and a greater shared animus. As the last two chapters have hopefully made clear, our current era has seen a not unprecedented shattering of these animus. The majority of the world is now free floating, untethered from the moors of rites and objects. What that may mean for our future will be a major theme in the rest of the *Binding Chaos* series.

For now, we are continuing our dive into accepting the realities brought forward by quantum mechanics into our daily life. If Germanic science brought what Weber referred to as the disenchantment of the world,[48] then quantum mechanics unavoidably brings re-enchantment.

The entirety of social sciences have been studiously avoiding this unavoidable development for over a century but, as will be evident, they have no case.

A fear of death brought cultures of filiality, nationalism and male endo-idealism. All attempted to force the creation of a larger, temporally extended, animus through which individual lives could continue. These cultures used both a shared animus and rites which acted as repeaters to bring their selves forward and expand them to further spacetimes. Today's endoself culture devotes life's energy to preserving the body as long as possible instead of living.

A better understanding of both life and death would show the silliness and futility of such attempts to exert will beyond the grave, or avoid the grave altogether. Life expands, not through sublation or violation of other wills or preservation of an object self, but through connection. All of the anima expended to sublate others could have been expended creating a far greater expanded self through wider interactions.

The pursuit of immortality is both silly and futile because it arises from the conflation of self or body with the will or conscious. Unlike the will or conscious, there is no individuation in the self. The self, as the network of interactions created with anima, was always immortal and the only thing that restricts its immortality is an endosocial restriction on its ability to interact. This will become more clear in the rest of the *Binding Chaos* series, as we continue unlocking the nature of each component of what we refer to collectively as a person.

For now, let's continue our quest to answer the question: What is life? In Part 2, we will take what we have observed from the experience of life and look for what that can tell us about the nature of life. We begin at the beginning: what is the state we are born into, and what is The original sin?

Shunning is used in decrees that the name of a shunned member of an endogroup such as a family or cult must never be mentioned in the endogroup, thereby removing them from the future of the endogroup.

Credit theft is an attempt to intercept and steal interactions a person has made in their life, particularly those that are likely to be repeated or invoked.

Culture is the collection of rites, objects and ideas which provide an intermediary and connect people from disparate spacetimes.

Heather Marsh

Abstracting Divinity

The nature of life

Abstracting Divinity

Chapter 9

The original sin

You dwell within your mother's womb for 270 days, a period of nine months during which your mother on thirty-seven occasions undergoes suffering that is close to death. And the pains she endures at the time of birth are almost too great to imagine... After birth, she provides you with 180 and more measures of milk; for a period of three years you romp about the knees of your father and mother. ... Mount Sumeru is paltry in comparison to the towering debt you owe your father; the great ocean is shallow compared to the profoundness of the debt you owe your mother.

— Nichiren Daishonin in a letter to Nanjō Tokimitsu in 1275

Despite the widespread practice of intercepting or taking anima, people are born with an extremely strong disincentive to such behaviour, in the form of guilt. Guilt is the awareness of anima debt. We speak of forgiving debt because debt is the original sin. All sin is rooted in anima debt. Debt requires forgiveness or a balancing of the interaction.

It is not necessary to believe in ancestral guilt to understand indebtedness which dates from the moment of birth and requires repayment or atonement. If life is energy which abides by the first law of thermodynamics, then the allocation of life to one form involves the depletion of life from another. This depletion may be measurable. Studies have shown that giving birth decreases the cellular age of the mother by eleven years.[49] [50] [51] [52]

Guilt is only invisible when it is used as the force which upholds the entire structure.

The gift of life comes with a debt which requires balancing. This debt reconciliation is either woven into the habits of culture, as regular duties, offerings and sacrifices to the nation, ancestors, totem or gods, or it is denied through structures of power and entitlement. All law and all economics is based on the need for anima balance. Those who reject the validity of filial or national debt still enforce the shared debt of a state, the new globally authoritative endogroup. Debt bondage to industrialists and billionaires has replaced the bonds that once held families and nations together, but the debt still exists. People are still expected to contribute to the wider society or face the consequences.

Karma is one expression of the idea that debt is inescapable. Filiality is another. The egalitarian force behind debt and guilt is exploited in power structures. All religion, including all forms of animism, is built around debt, and guilt from debt, which arises from unbalanced interactions. Where anthropologists disagree and claim to have found no guilt, there is sublation to a wider endogroup. This is a method of guilt avoidance. Where the entire structure of society exists to absolve guilt, there cannot be said to be no guilt. Guilt is only invisible when it is used as the force which upholds the entire structure.

Diminishing and denial of anima debt, destruction of social bonds and rejection of beauty and joy are methods to reduce debt accumulation by the living. Deflection of debt and credit to a god is another. God's will, like the will of every endo-ideal, absolves the obedient reflectors of guilt by allowing them to relinquish a will of their own. If an act was not of their own will, the guilt does not attach to them.

With all of the faults of the Catholic Church, it is interesting that the one usually fixated on is the Catholic preoccupation with guilt. Guilt may be considered one of the things Catholicism handled (in theory) in a manner symbiotic with our spiritual health, by recognizing the guilt of every person and then relieving people of the unbearable burden of their guilt while still recognizing the need for penance. Catholicism also either attempted to address or co-opted post-death debt and credit balancing with the concept of purgatory and purchasing of indulgences. Catholicism is very close to animism and adopted most of its practices in some form.

This guilt management obviously hasn't worked, since the rate of honour killings and crimes of passion are still extremely high in Catholic countries, as they are in Muslim, Buddhist, Hindu and most other religious and irreligious groupings. This only shows that shame and guilt still exist in all cultures, however, and that penance ought to be directed to victims, not to a hierarchical figure. This does not support other religions or atheism as guilt-free evolution.

The guilt transfer is key to by far the greatest gift brought to the world by Christianity. Christianity provided redemption for all human guilt, and provided it in the image of the endo-ideal. Those who object to the image of a blonde Jesus being worshiped by people who have currently been cast as the negative image to Indo-European appearance, or those who are bemused by the devotion of women to a male endo-ideal, miss the power of storing guilt in an endo-ideal. The crucifixion of Christ was the act of an indisputable endo-ideal freely accepting guilt, which only he has the power to assign. The guilt transference was effected through the punishment. Through this acceptance, he became one with the guilty.

According to the laws of endoreality, guilt is only assigned to a negative image. If Christ was not an endo-ideal, he would have been just another unnoticed negative image sacrifice. Instead, for an endo-ideal to accept guilt, a paradox was created where guilt became a virtue and the guilty negative image became the endo-ideal. This is the power Christianity brought to women and to those places colonized by people who looked like the blonde Jesus, the places where Christianity's hold became the strongest. If the creation of endoreality was magic, the Christian guilt paradox was a deep magic which broke endoreality. Christ became an exo-ideal, or martyr, who freed people to live exosocial lives.

This is a very important difference from the endogroups which freed people from guilt through sublation. Under these ideologies, complete submission and negation of their own will effected a guilt transfer from reflector to the endo-ideal, then guilt was transferred from the endo-ideal to the negative image. Far from encouraging exosocial behaviour, this created an extreme dependence by reflectors on the endogroup which shielded them from their own guilt. It prevented the exercise of their own will.

The Christian ideas around guilt and martyrs were pure animism, however, and allowed animism to proceed without the escalating horror of sacrifices. As written in Hebrews 9:12, eternal redemption was achieved *"not by the blood of goats and calves, but by his own blood."* Far more than Zoroastrianism, Manicheism, or other competing ideologies, Christianity, at least as it evolved in Europe among the Celts, Slavs and Italians, absorbed animist accounting practices instead of simply rejecting them. Unlike the filial or karmic religions of the East or the patriarchies to the South, it did this on an individual basis, with no need for an expanded earthly self. This was the economic solution needed to transcend endogroups built around filial and national expanded selves.

Unfortunately, the exosocial freedom created by the Christian guilt paradox was immediately trapped, first into the extreme

Guilt exists for a reason. It ought not to be transferred, but it ought to be felt. Where it is not felt, it is being transferred.

endogroups of organized religion and later into the endogroups built around wealth and industrial endo-idealism. As soon as the sacrifice released people from spiritual debt, the transcendental endogroup of the Catholic and Orthodox churches enveloped them. When the Reformation of western Europe burst that authority, transcendental industrial endogroups took over.

People who contend that Catholic culture produces guilt have not studied guilt and its manifestations outside Catholicism. The drive towards balanced interactions is innate to humanity and the guilt produced by a lack of balance is universal. Guilt exists for a reason. It ought not to be transferred, but it ought to be felt. Where it is not felt, it is being transferred.

Those who object to Christ's elevation into son-of-god status fail to recognize the power of elevating Christ and his sacrifice above all others. Any additional or competing sacrifices were not just unnecessary, they were impertinent. Unlike some pacifist theologies which simply attempted to abolish all sacrifice with no alternative for guilt management, Christianity had hit on a magic formula to allow ever-expanding endogroups with no (apparent) need for sacrifices or filial guilt carried forward. Christ absolved both original sin and national or filial debt. Christianity made it possible for people to deposit their excess guilt somewhere other than another living being and draw from a bottomless anima bank to balance their excesses.

Sacrifices were offered to otherworldly judges in the form of gods in order to offset earthly debt. Sacrifices have been depicted in written histories as conducted solely to appease gods despite there being absolutely no evidence in all of history of any god desiring or benefiting from such a sacrifice. The entities referred to as spirits, languishing in the gravity zone and craving life energy, are a different matter.

The idea that spirits are embarking on a journey is globally common, and appears to have once been nearly universal. The spirits that remain and haunt the living are frequently thought to have died in a state of unbalanced debt or credit and often seem to be seeking absolution or vengeance. Guilt has been described as a factor in keeping spirits earthbound by researchers such as Edith Fiore.[53] (The definition of the word spirit will be discussed in T*he nature of death chapter.*) Ghosts may be interaction clusters with an imbalance, either credit or debit. Purgatory was for those with debt who must repay it before they can disperse. Days of the dead in various cultures were times of offerings and sacrifices to appease those who remained and assist them on their journey. This story is consistent throughout history and across cultures.

At some point, fear of these spirits took over many societies, possibly as a result of guilt or possibly due to the predatory natures of energy clusters in a state of imbalance. This fear was a key motivator to the creation of endogroups with endo-ideals who claimed the power to control or appease spirits. The idea in most of these endogroups was that every bad experience was a result of someone in the endogroup incurring a debt, through disrespect or other unbalanced interactions. This may have led to the idea that the debt must be repaid by the endogroup. Negative images were required to absorb the overwhelming guilt. The need to repay spiritual debt created the first economy and was the basis for the first hierarchical governance.

The management of spiritual debt required gifts for any spirit that needed to be appeased or animus which needed to disperse. With hierarchy, the king and priest took over this direct transaction and appropriated the credit. Religions evolved as promissory notes for debt. God was necessary to assign guilt and promise retribution. Retribution redeemed credit for those who died with a credit balance and collected debt from those who died with a debit balance. This is a feature of every god that acted as an anima bank.

Jesus, or his followers, rejected the custom of collecting all grievances as credit to be redeemed in the afterlife. Instead, he (or his followers) released all the credit due to him for his unjust torture and death sentence and let others use it for their own redemption. There was nothing novel about this act; it is one of the foundations of animism, and it is an act with precedent in untold numbers of people who have offered themselves as sacrifices for the redemption of others or have used forgiveness to release the debt of their oppressors. In the time and place in which Jesus was born, however, his followers had the opportunity to provide a written form of animist theory and centre it in the endo-ideal figure that androtheist religion was beginning to require.

This power was very soon harnessed into endogroups that, like other hierarchical ideologies, would only relieve guilt through sublation. Sublation allowed obedient reflectors to transfer guilt to the endo-ideal they sublated themselves to. That endo-ideal would then transfer their guilt to the negative image. This was depicted as punishing the wicked. The eagerness for the second transfer and the joy in seeing the negative image punished is experienced by reflectors who feel their own debt paid through the punishment.

The need to repay spiritual debt created the first economy and was the basis for the first hierarchical governance.

Obedient reflectors are absolved of all guilt in exchange for their abandonment of their own will. Guilt is volleyed between the endo-ideal and the negative image in an unending tennis match, while the reflectors remain selfless and guilt-free as long as their commitment to the endogroup remains absolute. This is why the acquisition of knowledge in the garden of Eden led to a loss of childlike innocence and brought guilt to Adam and Eve and their descendants. Children are innocent because they do not have fully developed conscious control over will.

This is the root of the demands for unquestioning faith, loyalty and childlike obedience in every endogroup, but it should be noted that children are only blindly obedient under the extreme filiality that preceded mono-androtheism. The demand for childlike obedience was a mark of endogroup transcendence, where the supposed virtues of the previous endogroup are enfolded into the new one. Today, people speak of obedient reflectors attending to their work religiously, as the religious endogroups have been transcended by the economic ones.

The taking of anima from another life form creates an imbalance which must be rectified through gratitude and exchange offerings. Throughout the world, signs of this gratitude can be found, in worship and respect paid to the spirits of animals killed and also to the earth, water sources and sun. Many cultures had very little meat consumption and carnivorous meals were primarily a feature of rituals which believed to require a transfusion of anima. The exchange was recognized and formed an anima economy which must be kept balanced at all times. Animals whose lives were sacrificed for humans to live were offered thanks and gifts for their journey. Cave drawings may have originated from people appeasing, thanking or trapping the spirits of the animals killed, or perhaps they were banishing sprits to the underground, a not uncommon method of removing a creditor in magic rituals.

With the creation of endogroups, all living things were sublated to the endo-ideal, and guilt was released through surrender of independent will. From Genesis: *"Let us make man in our image, after our likeness: and let them have dominion over the fish of the sea, and over the fowl of the air, and over the cattle, and over all the earth, and over every creeping thing that creepeth upon the earth."* The guilt for this exceptional myth, is deflected onto god. The myth itself transfers the punishment to the rest of nature. If not for the exceptional myth, human predators would still incur debt to other creatures.

Later, under science, everything not man was devalued as having no soul, or consciousness, or being simply machines, to erase the anima debt. Debt to nature, a key aspect of animist ritual and way of living, was negated by denying the animist nature of all but humanity and insisting that all else were mechanist objects. This is a typical objectification of a negative image which was strengthened by declaring humanity to be the universal endo-ideal, entitled to all of nature as a possession.

Both religion and science have produced copious propaganda for this exceptional myth.

Scientific–industrial abstractions of a mechanist, materialist world where no life energy or debt exists was abetted by the guilt-absorbing, abstracted endo-ideal of the economy. The return or evolution to a better state is presented as an excuse for gluttony. Earlier seekers of higher states tread softly on the earth and everything in it as they realized their higher state could only be achieved on earth, through their actions. Recent ideologies prefer to devalue or deny the gifts of nature to reduce any obligation for it.

Gaslighting is a term describing the method by which a predator deflects their own guilt onto their victims, typically through a counter accusation. In the movie the term is derived from, a woman rightfully accused her husband of trying to get rid of her, and he counter accused her of being crazy. She was then taken to an insane asylum which was his plot for getting rid of her. Both gaslighting and secret chamber guilt are very common techniques by which predators deflect guilt. A cheating spouse may counter accuse their victim of not being desirable or available or use secret chamber guilt and say the victim was invading their privacy by discovering their actions. Female victims are often accused of being crazy or paranoid to invalidate their perspective and reinforce the male endo-idealism that gives men the authority to create accepted reality.

In religious and scientific-industrial endo-idealism, gaslighting takes the form of blaming the general population or nature itself for creating their own destruction and by outright denial of the damage being inflicted by the endo-ideal. Secret chamber guilt at this level is often enforced by laws which protect corporate, state or religious secrecy and criminalizes those who speak against the endo-ideal or accuses them of conspiracy theory, the scaled up equivalent of crazy. Secret chamber guilt is also implemented by strictly limiting the people allowed to express opinions, observations or personal experience and declaring statements outside this circle to be unqualified, dangerous and often illegal. Observations which challenge powerful tyrants are often accused of disturbing the peace or threatening public safety, the ultimate in guilt reversal. Guilt deflection is often accomplished through manipulation of populations into behaviour that facilitates auto-genocide through violence, drugs and other self harming behaviour.

Besides absolving debt, religion helped compensate credit by promising retribution to creditors. Compensation was felt to be owed for perceived injustice, both as reward of the faithful and punishment of the unfaithful, depicted under industrial endo-idealism as the hard-working and the lazy. Weber described the hope of just compensation, "*always involving reward for one's own good deeds and punishment for the unrighteousness of others*" as "*next to magic (indeed, not unconnected with it), the most widely diffused form of mass religion all over the world.*"

As Weber noted, a large part of magic was preoccupied with anima distribution. What is now called religion, in its earliest forms, was divided into the following categories of magic: guilt allocation, guilt deflection and punishment which are now largely under the jurisdiction of law and economy, divination and influence of outcomes which was first transferred to prayer, and is now controlled by economics, and bondage and sublation, now the business of government. Each of these is discussed in its own book in the *Binding Chaos* series, law in *Law and Chaos*, economics in *The Power Economy* and government in Autonomy, Diversity, Society.

A reflector who leaves their endogroup not only becomes vulnerable to guilt debt, they are also forced to give up hope of credit repayment, their spiritual retirement plan. The power of debt and credit cannot be overestimated in keeping reflectors trapped. Leaving an endogroup requires them to accept their own guilt, unless they move to the umbrella of a new endo-ideal and relinquish their savings from a life of service. Otherworldly endogroups allow these endoreality protections to continue, unquestioned and unchallenged, until death and hopefully beyond.

Catholicism provided guilt management. Early Protestantism transferred all guilt to god by claiming that nothing happened unless it was god's will. Early Protestantism was thus able to avoid the full sublation to an endo-ideal demanded by most androtheism but at the same time, reject the personal acceptance of guilt (debt) that came with Catholicism. It is this dissociated guilt deflection that inspired Weber to name Protestantism as the spirit of capitalism.

Those with a view of the world as a grand design

have been easily convinced to create a world currently run by cruel algorithms. Few industrialists feel guilt for poverty. Instead, the repercussions of industrial endo-idealism, or the sacrifice of its negative image, are dismissed as just the way the world works, the modern version of It's God's will. When pressed, industrialists will angrily declare that the economy (the new god, or anima bank) will collapse without sacrifice.

The Catholic church used communion with spirits as a method to make families pay to get loved ones out of purgatory. Protestantism cast away responsibility for anima debt to others, not as it was sometimes done in the East, as part of dissociation from earthly ties, but as endosocial justice. Puritan and Calvinist Protestants cast all guilt and shame on the negative image, purifying the endo-ideal and obliterating empathy everywhere industrial culture presided.

These early Protestants did not eliminate Catholic guilt; they just silently transferred it. Neither did they eliminate Catholic magical absolution; they simply replaced the sacrament with currency, the new magical talisman of guilt transference. Industrial culture religiously believes that the exchange of currency absolves them from all guilt in an unbalanced interaction and that those who accept payment should bear any residual shame.

It is the one who sells the family heritage who is shunned, not the one who buys it. It is the prostituted who is shunned, not the one who pays to exploit others. It is the poor who live in shame, not those who devalue them. Currency is the sacrament which absolves the purchaser from guilt. This magical solution was necessary to move societies away from endogroups based on religious ideology into ones based on further abstracted economic ideology.

This is not a phenomenon unique to Protestantism. Trade reparations, including currency, have been used to balance guilt between endogroups throughout written and oral history. Outside debt is not recognized by those inside an endogroup or an endoself which is why trade only exists outside of endosocial barriers. This phenomenon is discussed in *The Power Economy*. Industrialism popularized widespread transactional exchange within endogroups, making every person an endoself capable of using trade instead of balance in every interaction.

Without ritualized guilt management, Protestantism needed to devalue, diminish and deny debt instead. Protestantism is the spirit of capitalism because it provided the economic negative image to punish. The root purpose of trade economics is not to effect some mythical barter but to effect guilt transference. The coin is the guilt. The worker receives the guilt for their own exploitation if they accept the coin, and those offering the coin receive absolution from the debt if it is accepted. Flinging currency at a person to solve their problems (like much of charity) is a refusal to listen to their grievances or recognize their humanity. The biggest reason for the diminishing importance of religion under industrialization is the far greater efficiency of economic ideology in deflecting guilt onto victims.

One manifestation of this guilt deflection is in scientific-corporate experimentation. Chinese Communist Party (CCP) authorities simply use prisoners as product with no further justification than that they are making amends to the anima bank of society through their suffering. Western scientists also freely experiment on prisoners but pretend that a monetary offering absolves them from all guilt.

The idea that those who accept payment are acting of their own will is integral to assigning them guilt. Within endogroups, slavery is not recognized if the endogroup is considered to own the slave. The labour of girls and women has been uncompensated and freely traded between family endogroups due to this rationale. Between endogroups or endoselves, slavery is not recognized if currency is exchanged. Any absence of free will is considered negated by acceptance of currency.

The idea of good and evil usually describes the structure of an endogroup. Goodness is assigned to the most obedient reflector, those who can anticipate the whims of the endo-ideal as their own. The knowledge considered true is the opinion of the endo-ideal or endoreality. The purity test is a test of the level of immersion in endoreality.

In an exosocial interaction, balance is judged on an interactional basis. In an endogroup, all virtue is assigned to the endo-ideal and all vice to the negative image.

Interactions lose their importance as the self is expanded to include an entire group where some are given all credit, while others are given all guilt.

Judges and priests assign endogroup guilt. It was once recognized what a dangerous position that was, and it was 'offshored' to the spirit world or gods. Now it is claimed that the earthly judges are simply bureaucrats channeling the canon or the law. The law is an abstracted god.

In religious endogroups, the negative image are declared sinful. In economic endogroups, they are declared lazy. The difference is primarily in the label. In all cases, the negative image is assigned the guilt which rightfully belongs to the endo-ideal.

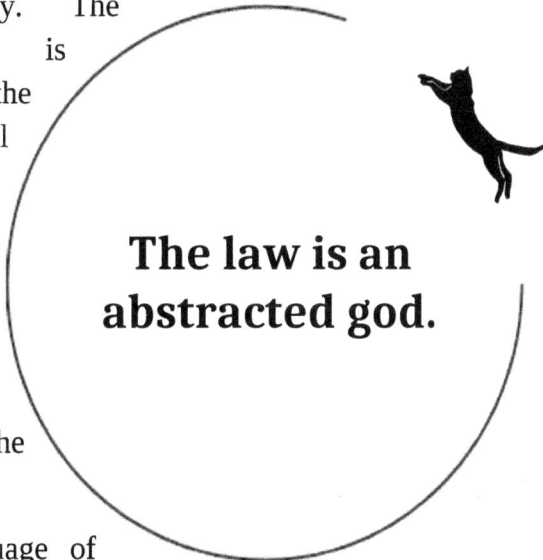

The law is an abstracted god.

The language of genocide and hatred of outgroups is not just normalized but idealized by Manichean ideologies and others that create outgroups. The apocalyptic genocides are seen, not as terror to be avoided but as joyful, inevitable and long awaited events which will absolve the guilt of the survivors. They depict a great purging of guilt through mass sacrifice, and it is this release of life energy that allows the rest to arise and live again.

Most wars are a similar mass sacrifice but without the power of resurrection. Those starting most wars do claim to be fighting for some ideal, or a better future for the next generation, however, which is the salvation of their extended selves. A glance at any endogroup during times of war clearly indicates the guilt reducing properties. Both the endo-ideal and the endogroup in general acquire a new lustre in the infatuated eyes of the group and become above criticism.

Many ideologies teach that every person is born knowing the difference between good and evil, as depicted in ideas such as Wang Yangming's liangzhi (innate knowing). This idea puts focus on a pure conscious. This was a step away from previous animist belief that focused on the self, which is open to being influenced by other people, spirits, good or bad qi and endogroups. Such a theory must differentiate between those with a sublated will or a dominant emotional will and those with a stronger conscious control over will. This will be explored in more detail in *Free Will and Seductive Coercion*, but there is more than one coercive force willing a person to action. Which force will dominate and whether they integrate or dissociate is what ought to be examined. Wang Yangming divided these forces between xin zhi benti (the conscious) and renxin (the self).

Rejection of the world is a rejection of debt and credit. Dissociation is a method of reneging on the birth debt all are born with. It is the casting off of this earthly accounting which is ultimately sought in some attempts to live in consciousness. This is a contradiction in terms, however, as living is an act of emotional will. It requires participation in interactions which involve anima debt and credit and the emotional responses to anima imbalance.

Although the mystic may seem more removed from the material world, except in the case of the most determined recluses, they are completely linked to it through their dependency. Their mystic evolution is dependent on the altruism of the worldly community around them. They owe their enlightenment to those around them who act as their proxy in worldly affairs, including the woman who risked her life for their birth and the caregiver(s) who nurtured them. Striving for personal redemption, salvation or evolution is the ultimate individualist undertaking and one which necessarily excludes those not at liberty to cast off their care of others. The modern ascetic uses bureaucracy and a dissociating financial system to achieve far more separation for themselves from worldly affairs and social ties, but even they cannot escape the first dependence and the first debt that would link them to a network of social dependencies.

In Weber's analysis, *"It is no accident that inner-worldly asceticism reached its most consistent development on the foundation of the Calvinist god's absolute inexplicability, utter remoteness from every human criterion, and unsearchableness as to his motives. Thus, the inner-worldly ascetic is the recognized "man of a vocation," who neither inquires about nor finds it necessary to inquire about the meaning of his actual practice of a vocation within the whole world, the total framework of which is not his responsibility but his god's."*[54]

This Calvinist attitude has ultimately manifested as the governance by algorithm the world is progressing towards. Dissociation, externalization of guidance and the establishment of one authority were all essential for installing governance by algorithm. Dissociation today includes transhumanism, migration to Mars and seasteading, as the wealthy attempt to dissociate from their negative image and cast off the vestiges of a debt they no longer recognize or understand.

In the next chapter, we will aim for a deeper understanding of this debt. Its manifestations are everywhere in our actions and institutions.

Ghosts

Decoupled but undispersed animus. These may be interaction clusters with an imbalance, either credit or debit.

The Christian guilt paradox

According to the laws of endoreality, guilt is only assigned to a negative image. For Christ, as an endo-ideal, to accept guilt, a paradox was created where guilt became a virtue and the guilty negative image became the endo-ideal. The Christian guilt paradox broke endoreality and Christ became an exo-ideal, or martyr, who freed people to live exosocial lives.

Categories of magic

guilt allocation, guilt deflection and punishment which are now largely under the jurisdiction of law and economy

divination and influence of outcomes which was first transferred to prayer, and is now controlled by economics

bondage and sublation, now the business of government

Abstracting Divinity

Chapter 10

The economy of life

Our appetite for life is voracious, our thirst for life insatiable. — Lucretius

Every interaction is between two entities. These interactions are what compose the self. Because the self is made of interactions, each between two entities, the self is not individuated in the way that the consciousness, will or body are. It is, therefore, easy for an anima debt or credit to flow between what are considered two different people.

Events and relationships are collections of a huge amount of interactions. Each event and relationship has its own fluctuating balance, debt or credit. Debt or credit accumulated throughout life can be resolved after death through the creation of a temporally extended filial or national self that inherits the debt or credit. Debt can also be transferred.

Negotiations of exchange when seeking luck from the universe are very pronounced in areas which used to practice mass sacrifices, such as Celtic, Aztec, Mayan or Beninese cultures. This same mentality of sacrifice is seen in many charity activities such as marathons or other challenges. The need to undergo physical challenges in order to raise money for others is usually unquestioned and for many, the reason is intuitive. The money is not the point; it is the energy expended which is felt to ward off any misfortune another is experiencing. If we want one to be relieved of pain, we must offer the pain of another. This is a mindset which treats anima as a limited resource.

Each event and relationship has its own fluctuating balance, debt or credit.

Many people will still say I have sacrificed so much for them when they are calculating what they gave up for another's well-being. In some places it was and is felt that enjoyment by mothers would cause suffering to their families. This idea of the need for a family martyr is endorsed by many communities which depict the gratification of a desire or ambition by a parent as costing their children, or the reverse, or the gratification of one member of the community as costing the others. The mother with a successful career is often depicted as somehow robbing her children, and the person who creates a beautiful home out of step with their community may expect to see it robbed or vandalized. Hardship is seen as the result of anima debt which can be transferred and paid by another. Good luck must also then have come from the community pot and is felt to have cost others.

This feeling is much stronger in very bonded communities. Endogroups share one anima bank and success is therefore seen as greedy. This is why so many people resent the success of anyone from their community, while celebrating it in those outside the community. In individualist countries like the United States, any one may buy a grand house. In most countries, the grand house sits empty, if it is nicer than the neighbourhood norm, until someone is appointed worthy of it or an outsider purchases it. If you live in the village, you don't buy the chateau.

The root of punishment is not as a means of stopping a harmful action. It is a replenishment of anima which was depleted by the harmful action, the debt to society still referred to in common parlance and legal texts that otherwise now depict punishment as rehabilitative or preventative. As a debt repayment, any sacrifice will work and the guilty party does not have to be the one punished. This is the principle behind so-called honour killings (which are really shame killings). This principle of guilt transference is what so much of magic was devoted to and so much of endoreality is devoted to today.

All guilty parties do not have to be punished; a scapegoat will do or one lone fall guy. There comes a point of satiation in justice systems, where most declare that enough people have paid and justice has been served. This depiction of justice as a beast that may be satiated reveals its punitive nature. If punishment were really a part of rehabilitation, a need for amnesty would not exist, and punishment would not stop until all involved were equally affected.

Object theft was possibly more often a part of sublation and spiritual conquest, or seized repayment of anima debt, than object hoarding. Pillaging of assets may have started as genocide, or as a means to force sublation to a higher (transcendent) endo-ideal. Certainly, theft has nearly always been punished through extraction of anima, or life energy, not with objects. When fines are used as punishment, that simply reinforces the role of currency as a repository of life energy.

Acceptance of apologies brings relief by granting the altruism of forgiveness to the wronged party. This altruism provides the missing anima to the wronged. Penance erases guilt by costing the guilty party anima. In either case, debt may be balanced. This is reflected in many courts where the wronged party is given the option to grant forgiveness or seek punishment. This custom recognizes the equivalent outcomes of the two remedies.

In many industrialized societies, the victimhood is assigned, not to the wronged party, but to the wider society, which takes the punishment or forgiveness choice, along with its anima, for itself. This is an indication that the victim is part of an endogroup, probably a negative image, and anima owed to them is claimed as the property of the endogroup. A crime against an endo-ideal is more likely to result in direct compensation to the endo-ideal.

Charity is not a reparation of guilt or an exosocial altruistic interaction. It is an assertion of virtue in the giver and negative image status in the recipient which creates an unbalanced interaction. The recipient of charity is assigned guilt along with it, which is why so many people are very averse to accepting it. Charity is packaged with the shame of a negative image.

Gratitude and respect serve as a payment, and in their absence there is indebtedness. Transactions involving currency supplant gratitude, as trade culture is built on the premise that any payment creates a balanced interaction. The fact that trade does not occur among people who have the closest ties shows that this premise is incorrect. Cultures where most interactions involve currency have extremely little empathy. This is because endosocial membranes must be created, since interactions are not balanced by currency.

The fact that unrest and malaise is caused by a lack of balance is demonstrated by the frequent success of popular mental health therapies involving expressions of gratitude. [55] Gratitude and respect are both closely tied to love. Love is the creation of a shared animus through balanced interaction. Ingratitude and contempt signify an endosocial power structure, where credit is stolen from the giver and replaced with negative image status.

Gratitude does not come easily to those in industrialized culture. They are far more likely to respond to gifts with a catalogue of the imaginary ways the giver has benefited from the transaction than with gratitude and respect. They typically have an obsession with liberty and autonomy which seeks to prove that the individual stands alone, with no debt to anyone. This is an idea that can only exist in an endoreality which eliminates all labour within endogroups, such as birthing and raising them, and magically accounts for all outside debt with currency. The insistence on the existence of this independent state shows just how important it still is to all humanity to exist in a state of balanced transactions and to avoid guilt.

The transactional nature of a person or community can be measured by measuring gratitude. The direct conflation of currency with gratitude is seen in the custom of tipping, particularly as demanded by the service industry and usually explicitly stated as required due to the people they have to put up with. The bad behaviour, disrespect and ingratitude of customers and employers is expected to be compensated for by currency. The contempt and ingratitude remain, however, even from those who tip.

The idea that an endoself or endo-ideal should express gratitude, beyond either currency or performative religious or holiday ritual, is usually met with extreme hostility. Devaluation of that which they ought to be grateful for and vilification of the giver are far more typical responses than gratitude. A similar attitude is shown regarding apologies.

The following questions are helpful to identify an endoself or endo-ideal:

Do they treat apologies as a valued asset? Are they very reluctant to give one and very eager to accumulate them?

Do they apologize for the reaction of others instead of their own behaviour, with statements like I am sorry you misinterpreted me?

Do they not accept an apology with gratitude, forgiveness or diminishment of the offence but instead attempt to increase the level of guilt and contrition and exaggerate the offence?

Do they immediately retaliate to accusations with counter accusations?

If they are asked to provide a product or service, do they immediately demand unnecessary products and service in return?

Do they suspect or accuse a giver of benefiting more than themselves as the recipient?

Do they devalue gifts?

Do they list the ways the giver owed them the gift?

In some parts of the world, these questions may be affirmative for nearly everyone and in others nearly no one. These are signs of an endoself or endo-ideal and these behaviours indicate a transactional society.

In filial cultures, gratitude is expressed for the opportunity to be able to provide for the endo-ideal. This is an endogroup relationship in which the negative image benefactor receives guilt for their gift. A blocked conduit reverses the flow of altruistic credit, so the receiver receives both the benefit and the credit and the giver receives nothing.

Under child endo-idealism, the roles are reversed and the child may respond to gifts and service with claims that they did not ask to be born, contrary to any existing research into decoupled experiences. Whether the research is true or not, a binding contract consists of offer and acceptance. There is a filial debt and that is what establishes the root connection that forms societies, or human bonding.

All connection is a series of interactions, each of which results in a debt or a credit that must be balanced. A relationship that reverses credit is not establishing a connection but an endogroup. All interactions will continually flow in one direction as the giver continually seeks to attain a balance that is impossible under the laws of endoreality.

Balance in altruism only occurs if the receiving party acknowledges the interaction and the interaction is voluntary. Such interactions are altruistic because they do not use force and therefore do not establish power. Gratitude from the recipient and honour and respect from each is the key to producing balanced, exosocial interactions with no guilt. Without gratitude and respect, unrequited interactions and altruistic burnout will occur.

The mental state of someone suffering burnout is one of deanimation, or anima depletion, usually caused by prolonged unbalanced interactions. Depression is a common result of ingratitude. Eventually, this will cause the giver to be sublated or block their own anima conduits and become endosocial.

Polite behaviour often involves downplaying the debt another may feel. De nada is a Spanish term used to diminish the value of a gift in order to lessen the debt and accompanying guilt the recipient feels. Chronic guilt can cause deanimation. Compulsive behaviour such as that labeled as obsessive compulsive disorder has a strong correlation with guilt. [56] is typical as psychologists seek to classify natural emotional reactions and behaviours as pathological instead of looking at the abnormal structures causing it.

Stealing is a debt-balancing compulsion as is consumption in general. Usually in consumerist societies, this is an inverted debt that the person actually owes others. Destroying beauty or the belongings of another, putting people at risk of physical or emotional harm, and creating stress, filth, destruction and discomfort may be activities which are depicted as blameless or the fault of the victims in endoreality, but they are not accidents. These behaviours are all attempts to achieve anima balance and attempts to obtain secondary anima.

The knowledge or belief of a debt owed to oneself causes an emotional response that can grow to colour every aspect of life and even personal character. The feeling is immobilizing and can prevent the person who feels they are owed from doing anything that may benefit another or even allowing another to escape negative experiences. Many people seem determined that subsequent generations should experience at least as much hardship as they did for no reason except to achieve what they perceive as balance.

A word that may be considered descriptive of this state of credit is the contemporary Korean concept of han. This word, which means the beauty of sorrow, has undergone several reinventions. It was initially assigned as a mark of Korean otherness by a sympathetic colonial Japanese author. Subsequently, it was embraced as part of a national exceptional myth.[57] Overall, it relates to the feeling described by Park Kyong-ni as "*both sadness and hope*" and Lee Hee-kyeong as "*suffering [which] becomes a part of you, a part of your blood*" (Cain, 2014). As such, it is universally relatable.

Such a feeling is related to many suicides. This is an often referenced aspect regarding the topic of han in

South Korea, which ranked tenth in the world for suicides in 2016 according to the World Health Organization. The knowledge of a debt or an irretrievable credit leads to mental strain. Behind suicide is very often the idea of imbalance, of a feeling of injustice which must be alleviated, although the person killed is often not the person who created the imbalance.

A suicide may sometimes be an attempt to increase and make public the guilt of another, as seen in self-immolations as a form of protest. This form of inverted homicide can only be understood within the context of the impact of guilt and a debt relationship bond. Self immolations do not work in largely guilt-free endosocial cultures such as the United States, where people attempting such protest are simply dismissed with a label of insanity. This is a far cry from the reaction in other cultures where people largely feel that such a debt must be repaid and causes public shame to the target.

Self immolations are a deliberate overpayment to leave the predator with obvious guilt. They are a form of willing, or at least accepted, martyrdom which grants a credit to the surviving endogroup and assigns guilt to the endogroup's enemies. Less obvious self-immolations by those who refuse to attempt to seek safety in the face of certain death can have the same effect. There are many examples of such martyrdom, from well known figures such as Benazir Bhutto, Jesus and Malcolm X to the daily assassinations of land and community protectors and journalists fighting powerful predators. The anima credit of their deaths can be used by the surviving group to create strong endogroup bonds.

Whether named or not, the feeling associated with han is familiar in most parts of the world and can also be found in the Irish recommendation to offer it up. While the latter now often represents a view of misfortune as a promissory note which may be cashed one day in the afterlife, it was originally meant to add one's suffering to the suffering of Christ, in case some additional collateral was required to offset the debt of the world. This is, in fact, recommended by Paul in Colossians 1:24 Now I rejoice in what I am suffering for you, and I fill up in my flesh what is still lacking in regard to Christ's afflictions, for the sake of his body, which is the church. The beauty in sorrow to the Irish was the gratification of being of service and joining forces with Christ. Much like household solar panels that begin sending electricity to the community grid, the Irish suffering is treated as an unexpected asset to be shared for the good of others.

This may be an ingenious way of releasing unredeemed credit so it does not fester and make its owner ill. Unlike national debts and credits, which are still earthly and must therefore be redeemed or avenged, sublation to a higher will releases those on earth from such accounting. The idea behind han does not carry the same satisfaction, but both recognize the imbalance which is causing discomfort.

According to Korean novelist Park Kyong-ni, *"han not only refers to a consciousness of ongoing trauma and a lack of resolution, but also the means to its own resolution".*[58] For Park, *"Han, which comprises both sadness and hope, ...han as an affect that encapsulates the grief of historical memory— the memory of past collective trauma—and that renders itself racialized ethnicized and attached to nation".*[59]

This definition of han is a description of the endogroup credit which forms an essential part of so many exceptional myths. This is the source of the sense of exceptional entitlement essential to endogroups and is the reason grievance and victimhood feature so prominently in exceptional myths. It is often used to render members of an endogroup as above criticism or exempt from guilt for their actions, as they already have a credit. All sin is debt and all virtue is credit, so the virtuous self image of the endogroup is dependent on this credit.

All sin is debt and all virtue is credit, so the virtuous self image of the endogroup is dependent on this credit.

Han could be described as an anima credit. It is uncomfortable, as the self is short what it is owed, but it is also comfortable, in the hope it will be paid. The idea that an endogroup has a credit is often a strong force keeping the group bonded. A personal credit owed will keep an obedient reflector attached to an endogroup and a credit owed to the entire endogroup will keep its members firmly attached to its endoreality. The trauma of leaving an endosocial relationship is, in large part, the trauma of loss. The nature of this loss is the permanent renunciation of a credit owed. There is even biological evidence of the permanence of unredeemed credit as trauma is carried through DNA and affects later generations, a credit carried through a temporally extended self. These studies need a lot more data, particularly regarding individual mothers instead of just traumatized populations, but they are nevertheless very interesting.

Gratitude journals help people burdened by excess credit by giving them a ledger book in which they can see their credit gradually being repaid. It can also help endoselves and endo-ideals who tend to instantly flip all gifts to themselves into a credit instead of a debt. By recording all of their debts accurately and as soon as they are received, they may be able to build a more accurate depiction of reality and help alleviate their compulsion to extract more from others. Other lifestyle choices that would help those under a real or imagined credit burden would be to release every credit as an altruistic choice that they never expect to be repaid for. Many religions do recommend a life of altruism to avoid retaining a credit burden.

Credit bondage has many implications in society, including the creation and maintenance of both family and friendship. It keeps people employed in many situations where they spend their lives in drudgery, pursuing some elusive carrot in the future, whether that is a holiday bonus, a promotion or a retirement pension. The attraction of the unfulfilled promise is far more addictive and unforgettable than a completed transaction. Credit bondage is often the invisible sister to obvious debt bondage relationships. When viewed from another angle, people often only pay their debt to ensure a future credit, often literally represented as a credit score.

Credit and debt bondage feature heavily in relationships. The credit carried by a negative image, or any person who has survived a predatory relationship, can make them very vulnerable to future predators. While healthy people offer balanced interactions, a depleted person may be unwilling or even unable to reciprocate, as they are already carrying a large credit. A predator who offers an initial, up-front payment in the form of extreme flattery or grandiose promises offers a resolution to the discomfort of their unredeemed credit. This baits them into ultimately paying even more through another predatory relationship.

That doesn't mean that predators restrict themselves to deanimated people, however. The excess anima held or channeled by some people can also attract predators. People with average amounts of anima realize they will never attain balance with someone overflowing with it. They either approach the more endowed person with denial of their gifts and downplaying their achievements in the hope that they might appear on the same level, or they don't approach them at all. This lack of alternatives leaves the field open to predators who happily recognize and even exaggerate greater gifts, at least in the beginning. The reason predators recognize and value the gifts of others is because they see them as an object they wish to sublate, however, so those gifts will soon be claimed by the predator instead.

Inequality is a very important aspect in the continuation of exosocial expansion. Those who are depleted and those that are overfilled are both seeking relief from imbalance in every interaction, a discomfort which drives them to continually seek out new interactions. If life energy is finite and all people are born in debt for their own lives, they must devote their lives to balancing that debt through accessing and sharing primary anima. A lifetime spent in such endeavours may result in a balance which brings peace in old age, the state of euphoric bliss some elders attain and can maintain through great hardship.

In an endogroup, where acknowledged debts and credits tend to be focused within the group, the desire for outside interactions is greatly reduced. Time spent in paid employment also greatly reduces the healthy interactions possible. Energy which goes to earn money is spent to buy the life energy of other people. This results in endless depletion anxiety and predation instead of shared anima and bonding.

Too much good luck can make people uneasy, as though they are spending on credit. There have been many studies with both children and animals which indicate the correlation between fairness and happiness. Income inequality is one area where it is clear that unfairness causes more misery than lack, at least above the most base level of survival (and even then, survivor's guilt limits happiness). The obvious solution to end the unease all people feel with regard to inequality is to end inequality. There is another solution, however.

The exception to the unease caused by inequality is found in an endo-ideal who can simply punish their negative image to pay off debt and are therefore unperturbed by an unbalanced benefit to themselves. The endo-ideal is also credited with all achievement of the group which further offsets any debt they may incur. The change in personality observed in people who acquire wealth is related to the necessity to redefine themselves as a deserving endo-ideal. If that is not accomplished, they will often 'lose' their good fortune by giving it all away or through 'carelessness'.

It is a perfectly reasonable behaviour to use one's own self in any way desired. This causes no guilt or unease. The fish which eat their offspring or preying mantis or spider that eats their sexual partner or the cat that eats the offspring they do not choose to care for are simply following the same principle as the endogroup which sacrifices some of its members for the health of the whole, or at least the health of the endo-ideal. Unlike the individuated conscious in living beings, separation in the self and life energy is very fluid.

The increase in exploitative behaviour associated with increased power[60] is a result of this feeling of fluid ownership over life.

Power comes from the sublation of others into a wider self. Power also gives the ability to sublate even more people.

🐈

Slave labour within an endogroup is seldom even recognized as such. A man who is forced to perform unpaid labour for another man is usually considered enslaved, but a woman or child can be forced to perform labour under male or filial endo-idealism by calling their enslavement marriage or adoption. These are both traditionally magical rituals of sublation.

Likewise, service demanded from parents under child endo-idealism or descendants under filiality is unacknowledged except as a natural order. Under matriarchal filiality, children feel guilt at their occupation of the mother's body and the subsequent pain and health effects she endured. Under male endo-idealism, mothers have their will and rights to their body sublated to the unborn child. This is not about the child's will which does not exist autonomously before birth. It is rather about removing control of her body from the woman and placing governance of the woman's body under external authority. Women who have accepted the external authority will feel guilt if they assert autonomy or dominant will over their own body, as they are breaking the laws of endoreality.

While the trade economy has intercepted most interactions outside the level of the caregiver circle, there are still many examples to be found of labour that is expected as an offering at the higher levels. National, community or ideological groups often expect and demand contributions of freely given labour or other gifts. In some countries, even labour for corporations requires a sacrifice far greater than indicated by typical employment contracts. The bonding activities encouraged by many corporations is an attempt to develop this level of endogroup devotion.

Guilt in an endogroup belongs to the endo-ideal, not the reflectors who are acting under the will of another. The endo-ideal has the magical ability to transfer that guilt. One of the strongest attractions of endogroups is the provision of a negative image on which to project guilt. The cycle of deflecting guilt incurs increasing anima debt which must be repaid by more use of power and so the cycle both continues and expands.

This guilt cycle is not simply a human phenomenon. Dogs have highly developed guilt responses and practice guilt transference as well. Cats, who primarily enjoy secondary anima, do not commonly appear to experience guilt. Dogs experience much greater guilt when alone than when with a pack. Endogroups are definitely not restricted to humans either.

The Spanish galgos hunting dogs have been called *"one of the most abused dog breeds on the planet"* by National Geographic. *"Tens of thousands are killed in Spain every year, often in gruesome ways."*[61] The hunts the dogs are bred for are a custom of Spanish nobility and royalty and include seemingly senseless violence such as hare coursing. The mass breeding and training of the dogs is itself a spectacle of animal cruelty, and it is followed by the dogs being killed en masse and often tortured to death after the hunts. The National Geographic reported in 2016 *"as many as 100,000 every year"* killed, many horrifically.

Advocacy group Galgo Amigo puts the number killed annually at 60,000. In describing the dogs' *"extreme pain and agony for several days until they die"*, Galgo Amigo reports, *"The hunters believe that the more the dogs suffer, the more successful the following hunting season will be."* The anima debt the hunters are accruing for their cruelty in the hunt is being paid by the galgos, and this is clearly represented in the traditional belief. Another report says *"If they hunt poorly, they are tortured as retribution for the shame they reflected upon their owners."* This shame killing serves as both a sacrifice of the negative image and a final guilt deflection for the sacrifice itself.[62] The eight steps of negative image creation and punishment described in *The Creation of Me, Them and Us* are being clearly followed with the dogs as the negative image.

In what is termed toxic masculinity, the toxicity is the poison of guilt under male endo-idealism. People are given very little opportunity to balance debt in a system which has installed them as the endo-ideal. If the debt is too overwhelming, they punish the negative image for it and often sublate themselves to a higher endo-ideal to absolve themselves of the debt.

The creation of endogroups is a magical suspension of universal reality required in order to block guilt and egalitarian force. The out-of-touch tendencies of an endo-ideal are a result of the strength of the endoreality they live within. That endoreality is necessary for them to survive the otherwise overwhelming guilt they would feel at their accumulation of anima. Guilt is only transferred in endoreality, not universal reality. Exposure of guilt through the dissolution of endoreality is an ever-present threat to the guilty. This creates the need to vigorously defend endogroups.

The endoself feels no guilt through the endosocial membrane they have built around themselves. If unbalanced anima transfer is coerced, it results in depletion for the giver and power for the receiver. Every interaction with an endoself results in depletion, as they are incapable of returning gratitude, connection, or even an accurate acknowledgement of the transaction.

When an endoself benefits from an interaction, they cast themselves as the endo-ideal. They take the benefit from the interaction but reverse the depiction of the interaction in their own endoreality. According to the laws of endoreality, all virtue accrues to the endo-ideal, including credit. For any gift they receive, they gain both the gift and the credit.

An altruistic interaction with an endoself is therefore not just of no benefit. It exacerbates their predatory power and their entitlement. Not only that, but their benefactors or victims are cast as the negative image and will receive both guilt and debt. This may occur in the form of direct blame for any perceived shortcomings in a gift or simply denigration, such as depicting the giver as stupid for incurring a loss or calculating and hoping for some hidden benefit. The more an endoself receives, the more they will hate the giver as they must create a negative image motive and a self-entitlement for any benefit they are forced to acknowledge. As a result, they will see the giver as a taker and feel they are owed more, the more they are given.

This hatred of their own prey and the bitter suspicion with which they greet every offer of interaction is a hallmark of the endoself. It is also the foundation philosophy of the trade economy and government everywhere. The more the powerful receive, the more they are convinced they deserve and the more they despise their providers. An offer of a gift to them is a sign that the giver is a negative image and therefore deserving of all guilt.

Power is perfectly able to take whatever it wants. The only function performed by the elaborate magical rituals of the trade economy is a magical transfer of guilt produced by unbalanced interactions. The guilt caused by unbalanced interaction is magically erased with the currency talisman which returns the guilt to the exploited.

One guiding principle to life is to eschew unbalanced interactions. Every accumulation of anima brings guilt, and every powerful person devotes great energy to deflection of this guilt.

There are two important aspects which guide guilt behaviour. First, those inside a strong endogroup do not feel guilt for interactions outside the group. As long as there is no empathic or euphoric connection, there is no guilt. The creation of endosocial barriers when they are not necessary for self defence is a guilt response. Second, guilt is transferable. Blame and the accompanying guilt can be reallocated within an endogroup by creation of an endo-ideal, who receives all credit, and a negative image, who receives all blame. The creation of permanent endogroups and their associated endorealities seems to have originated for just this purpose.

In the next chapter, we will return to the original debt we are all born into. There, we will discover the origin of the first permanent endogroups, and the root of all modern institutions from economy to architecture.

One guiding principle to life is to eschew unbalanced transactions.

Two aspects guide guilt behaviour. First, guilt does not occur outside of a strong endogroup. Second, guilt is transferable.

Abstracting Divinity

Chapter 11

The ownership of life

Woman is the creator of the universe, the universe is her form; woman is the foundation of the world, she is the true form of the body.

In woman is the form of all things, of all that lives and moves in the world. There is no jewel rarer than woman, no condition superior to that of a woman. — Shaktisangama Tantra

The original debt of life which all are born into has two repercussions. One, the newborn must interact or suffer crippling damage to the development of their self. Two, they are sublated to the will of the debt holder until they have completed childhood or longer. This sublation is evident in the lack of a strong conscious will in an infant and young child (evidenced as a dominant emotional will) and in the early idealization of caregivers and later, nations. The debt holder must allow the new person to have balanced or giving interactions. Otherwise, the child will be forced to develop as an endo-ideal or endoself to manage the unalleviated guilt.

The most detailed and easily accessible written examinations of life energy are those in Chinese and Indian traditional philosophy and medicine, but there is no animist medical tradition anywhere that does not take the life force into account or that treats the body in a purely mechanist fashion as modern western medicine does. There are aspects of all of this large body of knowledge that may be pulled out as being universal animist belief (subject to correction).

The earliest version of an interaction self is a shared animus between mother and infant, the lifegiver self.

Extreme beliefs in filiality replaced the earliest fission-fusion groups of humans, created by the splitting and merging of groups. Filial social structure post-dates development of divination, medicine and astrology. None of these three studies, which are all practiced in various forms all over the world, see an individual spirit or will as part of a hereditary self. This is despite the fact that none of them see a life as purely individual. All life is considered as part of a cycle, but that cycle is independent from a filial self or even a national self. Interconnectedness of different selves, such as shown in astrological synastry charts or mundane charts of events or organizations, are based on interactions (including interactions in the planetary system).

The national and filial selves were both used in their earliest forms to facilitate debt repayment. Magic was required to form a wider self and facilitate sublation of individuals to an endogroup. What is now termed magic consisted of rituals to transfer energy, manage debt, transfer guilt, create endosocial barriers and endorealities, sublate one will to another and create a shared animus. As explained earlier, all of these tasks have been taken over by the institutions of government, law and economics.

Life flows from the mother to the infant during and after birth. DNA in the mitochondria, which produces energy (life) for each human cell, is all obtained from the mother. Individuation of life forms occurs at birth. The earliest version of an interaction self is a shared animus between mother and infant, the lifegiver self.

Alongside animism, was gynotheism, or female worship. The oldest figurines and drawings which appear ritualistic are all either animist or so-called 'Venus' (female) figurines. The oldest female figurine is the Venus of Berekhat Ram, created between 230,000 and 700,000 years ago and predating both Homo sapiens and Neanderthals. A contemporary figurine, the Venus of

Tan-Tan, was created between 300,000 and 500,000 years ago. There is a large body of other findings that indicate gynotheism, including cupola carvings and vulva carvings dating to far earlier periods than the first findings of similar male figures. Male figurines only began to appear mere thousands of years ago.

The academics who immediately refer to all male figurines as gods have been publishing furiously to attempt to portray the early female figurines as everything from coincidence to erotic trinkets to good luck charms that women used to get pregnant, but the fact remains, there are female figurines throughout all human history and even early hominid history and no male figurines until a few thousand years ago. The female figurines are often interpreted as 'fertility goddesses' when there is seldom evidence or support for them to be considered anything other than simply goddesses. This interpretation is transparently produced by a modern endofilter which sees women solely as breeders of men. Any interpretation of female icons as fertility gods and male icons as gods of creation are word play anyway. Fertility is just a downgraded word for creation, downgraded solely because of its association with the female.

That said, the interpretation of any figurine as a god that was worshiped overlooks the likely origin of all gods as anima banks. Rites or incantations and all worship most likely served to establish anima conduits to these anima banks.

Since life emanated from women, it is very rational to create anima banks in that image.

🐈

Evidence strongly indicates that all early people worshiped a mother-goddess. The dragons and snakes of the chaoskampf myths are both symbols of Tiamat, the Sumerian creator goddess of primordial chaos. The modern editing of the goddess Tiamat has her disguised as either a dragon or snake figure that our hero slays, or primordial chaos that was tamed by enlightened order. As everyone from the Yin-Yangists to Pythagoras made clear, primordial chaos was female.

While recently taught histories have favoured a nationalist view that people developed distinct civilizations separately, there are increasingly less grounds for such a viewpoint. The vast majority of ancient culture has African pre-emigration roots and the rest is extensively intermingled through travel and migrations. If Mesopotamians had a creator goddess in Nammu/Tiamat, there is no reason to assume without evidence to the contrary that all people in Africa, who numbered only 10,000 people 200,000 years ago and did not begin emigration until about 60,000-80,000 years ago, did not share that belief.[63]

Gynotheist sculptures did not disappear with organized religion. The sheela na gig sculptures that adorn medieval churches in Celtic regions show female figures in squat, spreading huge vulvas. The vulva as the gate between this life and what lays beyond or before is a recurring symbol despite the conversion to androtheism.

Gynotheism is a fairly obvious belief for anyone to hold since women were and are demonstrably the source of life. The fact that only women were allowed to be present at birth in many cultures, and that women took the decision to end or continue pregnancies and newborn life in nearly all early cultures (as far as can be confirmed), indicates cultural support for the intuitive belief that women are, and were held to be, the origin of individual human life. Herbal knowledge, used for both contraception and healing, was still the domain of women in many or most nations up until the present and lives on in the tradition of designating cooking and nursing to women.

As indicated in Plato's The Republic, men have realized the value of coercing children for a long time. Women have held that power forever. Plato recommends that mothers be forced to teach their children a certain way; he does not even entertain the ambition of direct influence by men. It makes no sense that women would not have used this coercive power in the past to exalt women, and evidence shows that they did.

Early shamanism and ancestor worship centred around women. The earliest shaman burial site found was female[64] and early shamanism was a female role. When men began to take over the role they had to wear female dress and be socially recognized and treated as female to be accepted as shamans. There is no reason that those early shamans cannot also have been the matriarchs of ancestral clans and the early female figurines could be, not only symbols of shamanism, but of early ancestor worship.

> **The first shared self, even if it only extends momentarily, is between an infant and mother.**

Trauma increases all types of empathic and both primary and secondary anima connections, probably as the person attempts to reestablish connections for survival. The first such trauma is birth which encourages the infant to reach out and establish a self and encourages the mother to create a strong bond with the new infant self. The first shared self, even if it only extends momentarily, is between an infant and mother.

Some traditions created a transition from the infant or child self, which built out from the mother, to a national self. Coming of age rituals often involve extreme pain, fear and even potential death of the individual, just as childbirth does. This destruction of individual self seems designed to facilitate bonding to a wider self. The same methods are used by slave traffickers, torturers and other abusive relationships to trigger trauma bonding with the abuser. The national self is created by causing severe depletion of the original animus through ascetic ritual and then transferring life from a group or anima bank (such as a totem or priest) through euphoric celebration. This apparently reduced the debt to the lifegiver or caregiver-self and created a greater dependency on the nation-self.

Life energy is often depicted as being gifted by a national, spirit protector. This mythology supports the strength of a national self instead of a filial self. The national spirit often serves as a form of anima bank for the nation, where life is exchanged, cared for and replenished. It frequently involves a physical anima bank such as a temple, totem or shrine.

The sublation of an individual into a nation self transcended the first caregiver self. Life depicted as arriving through a national totem or spirit is often related to ancestry but was seldom averse to adopted members. Most national traditions viewed life not as a hereditary gift but a community one. A mother who found herself in a different community would have children (usually) associated with the new community spirit.

As nations lost importance, or individuals gained personal property and debt, it became necessary to create a temporally extended filial self. The expanded filial self was charged with repaying any outstanding debts and collecting any outstanding credits. The expanded filial self performed the rites and caretaking of euphoric objects that would bring the ancestors forward, just as the nation-self performed these duties for nations.

Figure 20: Filial Endogroup

Hereditary property ownership is the result of a filial self. People formerly had buried goods with the deceased, or at least left them for lengthy periods of time in order to not upset the spirit of the owner through theft. The only way hereditary ownership would be acceptable is through the establishment of a temporally extended self created through filiality.

The very simple explanation that the life of a newborn comes from the anima rush which accompanies birth and weakens, and frequently kills, the mother is such an obvious conclusion that it might have continued uncontested, except for this one huge political obstacle. If the life force which fills the newborn is the product of birth, then it emanates solely from the life energy of the mother. As filial societies began to evolve with the idea of the temporally extended self, this left men in an existential dead end.

Once filiality was perceived as the key to immortality, men faced an existential crisis which required endoreality magic to overcome. Patriarchy was formed around the desperate insistence on the primacy of the male in the formation of this temporally expanded self. Filial communities that evolved into patriarchies sublated the mother through denial of identity and physical removal from her origins and then created new attachments for the child to the patriarchal family. The Five Classics, even most of The Analects, are not yet derogatory to women. A belief in male endo-idealism appears to follow filiality in all of the oldest records around the world. The male possession of the female body, enabled by sublation of the female to the male, only became necessary with the creation of a temporally extended, filial self to manage debt.

Women's bodies were the earliest patriarchal property and the one which required the most stringent laws and magical rites to secure. Women's bodies became the means of production of the temporally extended self. Children's bodies were then harvested as a source of extended life. Paternity was not an important concept until women were architecturally imprisoned as the property of one man. As women and children were sublated, and their anima depleted, the anima available to the patriarchal endo-ideal increased. This continued after death when the sublated parts of his extended self would perform rites to continue his presence, honour and influence on earth and ensure his needs were met in the afterlife.

Hoarding of women was the second phase of *The Power Economy*, after spiritual appeasement. Women became the anima source and the sacrifice that redeemed familial guilt. If a family suffered, it was because her anima was insufficient to keep them filled. If a family member erred, it was due to the lack of purity or 'goodness' of the woman. Despite being transformed into the negative image, she retained her function as both the source of life energy and the true image of the ideal.

Families replaced nations and the patriarch replaced the national spirits. The woman was his negative image, the receptacle of all guilt and the vehicle of penance. The endosocial nature of the group now required a power hierarchy, unlike nations which were not always endosocial.

Filiality creates endogroups. The family name is an endo-identity. Endogroup culture revolves around hereditary ritual, traditions, defining costumes and accessories such as tartans and tattoos, homes, heirlooms, shrines, and stories and rituals which honour and remember the dead. All of these serve to create an endogroup.

Taking the father's name ensures that he and his paternal ancestors are invoked with every invocation of the son's name. Keeping the family honour meant that all who bear the name, through birth or marriage, must act as a credit to their ancestors. Achievement of the living was offered as power to ancestors, even after death. Ensuring the continuation of the father's name ensured the continuation of his temporally extended self, just as taking national emblems and names had ensured the continuation of nations. Rites and anima banks also ensured the continuation of the temporally extended self.

With the removal of women from their family, rites, home and often, family name, they lost their own identity and existed only as reflectors and negative image. Many patriarchal marriages were an individual genocide of all the cultural attachments a woman had formed to that point. Daughters who did not keep the father's name became expendable. They received little anima through interactions, as any anima transferred to them was just going to be given or sold to another family.

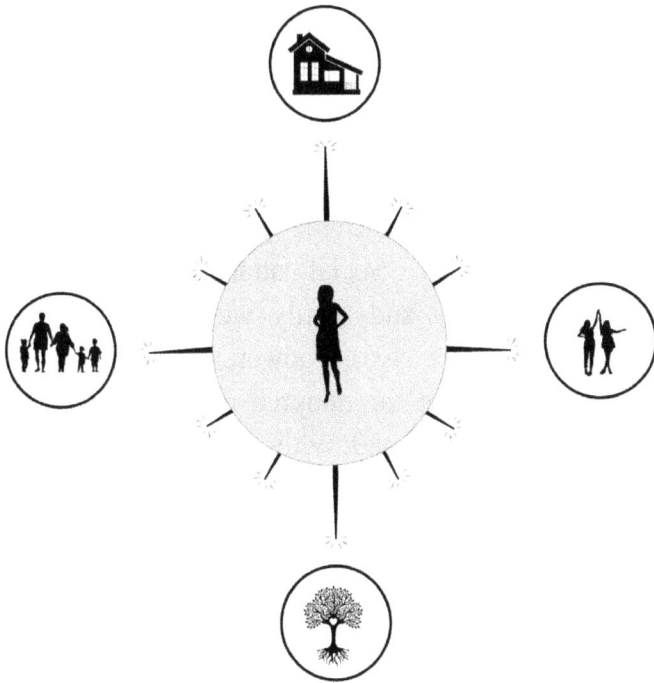

Figure 21: Lost connections

Girls and women were designated as the negative image of the second age anima economy. Their role is often still seen in so-called 'honour killings' where they are sacrificed to replenish the family animus. The assignment of all guilt to the negative image has been seen in tribal councils in India that sentence a girl to be raped for her brother's crime [65] [66] [67] or in law courts everywhere that treat female victims of violence as though they were the criminals, or at least the instigators.

Since it was impossible at this point to remove the female goddesses from the earth and rituals involving the earth, men staked their claim to the skies. From this point, androtheist ideology both touted the superiority of the heavens and intensified the separation of heavenly male rationalism (consciousness) from earthly female emotions (body, self and life). In so doing, they claimed an endosocial membrane and the severing of all empathic and euphoric conduits as an inherent masculine quality. Women were left to the guardianship of all primary anima conduits. Social attachments, nature, beauty, altruism, home and family were all left under female domain, while war, power, law, governance and economics were the adopted domains of men. Women were still associated with life and creation, so men claimed the powers of death and destruction.

The self-induced primary anima depletion this caused for men left them increasingly dependent on secondary anima. As pointed out in *The Creation of Me, Them and Us,* a sublated person can relatively easily become whole again, but the endo-ideal has a far greater dependency on others. The master is the slave to those whom they enslave and men under male endo-idealism became far more vulnerable and dependent on women. In seeking to control women, they lost their own liberty.

Patriarchy, so often associated with the nomads of the Middle East, began with settlements. Even modern hunter-gatherer people do not have the sexual hierarchy seen in settlements. One fundamental aspect to patriarchal control is the development of architecture from which women were both isolated and surveilled. Totalitarianism requires architecture and the establishment of male endo-idealism is so far from a natural state that it requires totalitarianism.

The circle was an important symbol of power in most mythology. It is seen in the shape of houses, villages, ritual formations and dances, and every part of nature from animal cells to the solar system. In India, the sacred circular symbol of Om became gradually usurped by linga-yoni symbolism. While sex plays an important role in mythology and sacred rites all over the world, in India, the sex act assumed a mystical importance which overshadowed birth, or creation.

Female was the original state of living things and is still the default.

The increasingly exaggerated depictions of the linga and the reduction in power and importance of the yoni were accompanied by the rise of the pre-Vedic god Siva. Siva was often depicted with a snake around his neck in a familiar state to Marduk, slayer of his mother Tiamat, the manifestation of primordial chaos. Shakti is the Tiamat-like figure of India. Shakti is the primordial energy of the universe, a divine feminine, creative power that fills the entire universe and is the agent of change. Shakti is not Siva's mother; she is his consort. The initial power of creation, seen as omnipotent in animist legend, was now flanked and even superseded by two other powers, that of protection (Vishnu) and that of destruction (Siva). This is a progression from the idea of a circulating life force but markedly different.

The first law of thermodynamics agrees that energy can be neither gained nor lost, it can only be transferred or transformed. Therefore, to have creation, there must be destruction. However, the separation of the two, along with the subsequent separation of consciousness, created a space for androtheism. Positioning destruction above creation placed men on first an equal basis with women and then past. The divine creative force of chaos was bound by order. Linga began occupying every yoni and village circle until the circle (now a square) was destroyed (or raped with the lethal threat of vehicles). The linga in the form of conquering men with swords on horses, or architectural phallic symbols, towered next to each other with no circles anywhere. Om was not simply erased; it was occupied.

Female was the original state of living things and is still the default. First life on earth was self-reproductive. Males are a mutation that was not necessary or originally present. They are an evolutionary afterthought. This created a crisis for men which long preceded filiality. The need to set the male as the ideal and female as the deviant or defective and lesser state still persists today, and it is a transparent deflection of male anxiety.

The extreme gynophobia felt by so many men throughout the world is not a sign of contempt for a negative image. Contempt would (and does) produce simple erasure, not hate. You cannot hate what you do not fear. The persistent dread of this filial key to immortality is one source of the anxiety that triggered male endo-idealism which continues to this day. The first permanent endosocial structure was the result of gynophobia. This will be explained in much greater detail in The Sociology Quartet.

Endogroups are a natural response to danger. Male endo-idealism created permanent endogroups in response to what was perceived as a permanent existential threat. If women's sublation were natural it would not require magical rituals.

The fact that androtheism is so far from a traditional belief is evident in all of the remnants of gynotheism still in existence. Muses and knowledge are female. The only change under male endo-idealism was to make their creations only manifest once she has managed to teach them to a male. Women as a source of knowledge was reduced to women as teachers. Even the Bible credits Eve with acquiring knowledge.

Gynotheism is also evident in religious gaslighting which stresses claims that would be self-evident if they were true. These claims expose the fears behind the manufactured endoreality of religious male endo-idealism. Corinthians 11:8 claims *"For man did not come from woman but woman from man."* The Corinthians doth protest too much, methinks. If it were true, it would be self evident, or at least widely enough established to pass without remark.

In Luther's Works he writes, "*If Eve hadn't sinned, she would have reigned together with Adam and ruled as his helper*" [68] . Luther's attempt to blame Eve for her own sublation is a guilt transfer which would not be necessary if Eve was not being wronged.

Evidence of the fear of the biological dead end in the male filial self is found in the endless protestations against it. For what other reason would it be necessary to create myths denying the self-evident role of women in birth? For what other reason would it be necessary to separate women from the continuum of life and make them a sub-species which could only obtain salvation through men? For what other reason would it be necessary to insist that man was the image of god? And for what reason would it be necessary to create an entire structure of civilization in which every aspect was devoted to the sublation and dehumanization of women?

While some alternative reasons may be found for the latter aspects, the obsession with lineage and birth can only be a response to an existential crisis of the male filial self. So extreme was this existential crisis that myths even depicted women as being formed from man, contrary to daily, observed reality. In the creation of the world described on the seven Babylonian clay tablets of the Enūma Eliš, Marduk had to butcher the corpse of Tiamat and create the universe from pieces of her. In Genesis, God creates the universe single handedly and for good measure, creates woman from man's rib.

Women were later depicted as empty vessels into which men dropped tiny, fully-formed humans.

Patriarchy fought a continual war against the emergence of any spiritual superiority or equality of women. There appears to be a widespread recognition that equality for women will reinstate superiority of women. Without labyrinthian institutional creations like the trade economy, women are equivalent to men except for the fact that they also create new living people. Increasing technology just makes this increasingly true.

It was not the management of daily affairs or ritual or access to resources that the new man-gods sought dominion over. Unlike their nationalist predecessors, they sought exclusive credit for the uniquely female power to produce life. The religions and philosophy which produced male endo-idealism were all rooted in alchemy. The primary goal (or obsession) of all early alchemists, was to obtain immortality.

For early Taoists, the path to immortality was through dying with sufficient qi to be still alive on the other side, thus mastering the art of taking it with you. The alternative was a post-death banishment to a hellish underground existence on earth. Jing is the allocation of qi to each individual life. Jing is related to jin, or power. One is said to be born with a fixed amount of jing and also can acquire ling from food and various forms of activity such as exercise, study or meditation. Jing is a yin substance found in the kidneys and, according to some, the adrenal glands. Theoretically, jing is consumed continuously in life by everyday stress, illness, substance abuse, sexual intemperance, etc. Prenatal jing is very difficult to renew, and it is said to be completely consumed upon dying.

There are several different branches and myriad interpretations of Taoism, but traditionally, both menstruation and pregnancy are thought to cause a large loss of jing, and so is male ejaculation. Many Taoists believed that the most jing was found in semen, so these Taoists believed in conserving semen. Some taught that sex can create jing and others believed that jing can be taken from the woman to the man. If, as the Tao states, jing can be obtained by the male through female sexual satisfaction, it seems jing is also contained in female ejaculation and / or bodily fluids.

The idea that sperm was a means by which the female could absorb the life of the male during copulation is not without biological precedent, as preying mantis and jumping spiders do just that in a substantially more concrete manner. There is evidence that semen eases childbirth through softening of the cervix with prostaglandin, a literal example of male ejaculation increasing a woman's chances of a longer lifespan. The penis itself enters copulation boldly and full of life and leaves depleted and empty. Myths of the vagina dentata threatened that the same fate could befall the entire man.

Women walked away from sex undiminished while leaving the man, or several men, in a state of floating, weak knees and other symptoms of dissociation. Floating is a symptom of sublation in bdsm, so it is no wonder that men felt they had been sublated or put under her spell through orgasm. A finding of the notorious CIA Operation Midnight Climax was that men became more easily manipulated and open to sharing secrets after sex, a tactic that has been used by spy agencies for centuries and indicates sublation of the male will by sex. (This is discussed in more detail in *Free Will and Seductive Coercion.*)

The ability of women to continue, or even increase their state of arousal, or power, as men are left depleted strongly indicates a one way energy transfer. Men experience a drop in testosterone after sex which produces symptoms of deanimation such as low energy level and physical strength and poor focus and memory. Women typically appear undepleted by (connection) sex but commonly display many symptoms of deanimation during early pregnancy and prior to menstruation and menopause. Just a few of these symptoms are increased anxiety, emotional distress, anger, a craving for carbohydrates and brain fog.

From a purely mathematical standpoint, it seems reasonable that a woman who has to provide jing for multiple newborns and monthly menstruation would have some means of stockpiling it from the act which may result in conception. This assumption is particularly likely since women lived longer, despite the deanimation and deaths caused by childbirth. A culture obsessed with immortality would have been desperate to find the secret to this longevity.

This idea of a sexual transfer of jing was the most useful until genetics in proving a male role in filiality, and it is more useful to filiality because it applies to a transference of life itself. Apparently, some male theorists did not see this transfer of jing as their opportunity to achieve immortality through a temporally extended self. Instead, they saw it as robbery, an idea which they didn't mind, but wished to reverse for their own benefit.

In what was called "*the battle of stealing and strengthening*", these theorists taught men how to bring women sexual fulfillment so that the man may take her jing (yes, women wrote that part). Some, such as Laozi, thought this indicated an inexhaustible supply of jing in women. As he wrote in the *Dao De Jing*, "*The Spirit of the Valley is inexhaustible. Draw on it as you will, it never runs dry,*" which seems contrary to the purportedly finite nature of jing. Others portrayed the obtaining of jing from women as a net loss for the women. Still others, such as the Way of the Five Pecks of Rice Movement, frowned on the idea of an exchange and encouraged practitioners to simply eschew sex and obtain and preserve jing through other methods.

Lest anyone think this fear of sexual robbery by women is a purely Eastern idea, one only has to look at European fear and control of women's sexuality, scientific denial of female arousal or orgasm, religious and cultural repression of female sexual desire or the history of clitorectomies and female genital mutilation in the world to see how widespread this particular seed of gynophobia is.

The Dao De Jing is hardly the first or the only mention of the transfer of life energy through sex in human history. The idea is very well known throughout Africa as well, so quite probably preceded the early migrations out of Africa. It is also very prevalent in animist rituals worldwide.

In The Five Classics, the creation cycle is referred to as a mother-son cycle. The mother is the creator, the son that which she creates. In traditional Chinese medicine, one phase can steal qi, or life energy, from another if the first becomes too strong or is in crisis and great need. The gynophobic fear is that the mother steals from the father to create the son.

The son is also, in both legends and history around the world, the agent of destruction of the father, often through conspiring with the mother. Even under male endo-idealism, the son usurps the father's place as his mother's endo-ideal. Her reflective power establishes him as the endo-ideal and removes the validating reflection from the father. Separation of the son from his mother prevented this empowering reflection.

When women were (or are) the endo-ideal, the conflict between father and son is the classic reflector – negative image struggle. Between women, the struggle was traditionally never depicted in this fashion. Instead, the mother is the daughter's endo-ideal who is slain so that the daughter can be sublated to another before she herself gains endo-ideal power. If men were the natural endo-ideal, the mother – daughter struggle would be the reflector – negative image pattern. The fact that it is not, and that is instead the father-son conflict, shows yet again that the mother was the natural endo-ideal.

India was the birthplace of an abstracted system which separated filial hierarchy from family or national relationships and extended the debt-repayment cycle beyond one lifetime. Instead of the service of the youth being repaid by their own family in their old age, some were born into lifetime servitude while others received lifetime benefits. This was no longer a familial or national debt-repayment scheme but was spread throughout a broad religious endogroup.

Much like early Protestantism, this led to a view of life on earth as an exercise in futility. Ambition was reduced to looking for shortcuts off a karmic wheel of death and rebirth. Consciousness eclipsed the life, body, self and even will as people studied the art of becoming unborn again. In the East, consciousness became the dominant aspect of a person and the body, self, life and will increasingly became aspects to overcome instead of opportunity for creation. The purpose of life was to exist, endure and overcome.

Patriarchy and dissociation, control of life or rejection of it, are both extreme reactions to living. These reactions are born of the trauma of an amputated core self, an existential fear of shunning and the warped existence and perception of reality created by endogroups. This will all be explored in much greater detail in *The Theft of Self.*

The need to balance debt is behind every endogroup. The original sin all of humanity is born with is original debt from the gift of life. Casting women as part of man and his negative image was one way of negating the original birth debt that all are born with, especially as the national endogroups and totems lost power. This also provided men with a captive anima source from which they could draw on a daily basis. This is a far more likely origin of the quest for ownership of women and children than ownership of a slave for baby production and labour in tribes where these were not needed. Indeed, the philosophies of Africa, Asia and India all indicate that this is the case with their focus on life force and its associated gain or loss of power.

We will explore social structures and economic flows much more in The Sociology Quartet and The Institutions Quartet. In the next chapter, we begin to drill down further into the base elements which compose a lifetime. The first component we will review is time itself.

The original debt of life which all are born into has two repercussions. One, the newborn must interact or suffer crippling damage to the development of their self. Two,

they are sublated to the will of the debt holder until they have completed childhood or longer.

Magic

rituals to transfer energy, manage debt, transfer guilt, create endosocial barriers and endorealities, sublate one will to another and create a shared animus.

Chapter 12

The nature of time

I do not define Time, Space, Place and Motion, as being well known to all. Only I must observe, that the common people conceive those qualities under no other notions but from the relation they bear to sensible objects. And thence arise certain prejudices, for the removing of which it will be convenient to distinguish them into Absolute and Relative, True and Apparent, Mathematical and Common. — Isaac Newton, Principia

The fact that endoreality is both real and measurable is found in the fact that Newton's principles of mathematics work extremely well. It is not until we pass the bounds of our endofilters and venture into a world beyond our senses, the world of the very large and the very small, that Newton is at a loss and quantum mechanics is required. This effect is similar to Einstein's analogy of traveling in an elevator and being unable to tell whether a falling object was pulled down by the earth's gravity or the elevator's acceleration. Without outside perception, our knowledge exists in a bubble of data isolated from relative viewpoints.

Newton triggered the construction of a vast body of authoritative knowledge, and the institutions required to manifest it, within endoreality. The only area of study which managed to step outside this endoreality was physics itself, considered too abstract for consideration by those who have fully accepted the reality presented by their endofilters.

In the above quote from the *Principia*, Newton described *"certain prejudices"* that arise in individual perception of time. What he considered Absolute and True however, were the result of the prejudices of human endofilters. In universal reality, time is much more likely to coincide with the relative definition of *"the common people"*.

Time is real vs time is not real is an argument that some physicists like to engage in. This debate is a word argument which is an extremely unproductive form of argument that occupies an inordinate amount of time in science. Time is a word. It is clearly real, as a symbol of meaning. The definition of time is what ought to be debated. Physicists, as much as sociologists, sometimes confuse words with reality. It doesn't really matter if we call a thing a particle or a collapsed wave as long as the attributes are the same (unless of course funding depends on a meaningless word debate being presented as a fundamental question of momentous import).

The debate between physicists who state that the present does not exist and others who insist that it does, are also semantic. The present exists in endoreality but not in universal reality. Whether a thing is real depends on the definition of reality being used.

Time, in common understanding, has always depicted our own motion from one interaction to the next. Newton got rid of absolute space and the general theory of relativity got rid of absolute time. All spacetime is relative. All spacetime exists as positioning of interactions relative to other interactions. This just means the definition of time in authoritative reality has changed from Newton's and is now aligned with that of *the common people*. The present is the location of the subject will known as I.

Special relativity has been interpreted to mean that all spacetime exists and the feeling that we move around in it is an illusion. This is a statement that begs the question of what we it is referring to. What is the we that is moving or being propelled along? The body, as we established earlier, does not really exist except as a cluster of interactions. Those interactions are part of what composes the self. The self is composed of interactions which stay in the spacetime in which each was created. The self is the only part of the person that adheres to the tenets of time, that what is done cannot be undone.

Memory stores the past but not the future. That does not mean the future does not exist. It does not even mean that the past always causes the future and never the reverse. The future has been shown to change the past in a variation of the double slit experiment. In these experiments, a detector is placed after a beam splitter. The photon in these cases always becomes a particle in anticipation of the detector. As explained by Brian Greene in *The Fabric of the Cosmos: Space, Time, and the Texture of Reality* "*It's as if the photons adjust their behaviours in the past according to the future choice of whether the new detector has been switched on; it's as though the photons have a "premonition". If the 'which path' detection marker is 'erased' it becomes a wave again.*"[69] Premonitions also exist in the macroscopic world and influence choice.

There are many testimonies of decoupled conscious being able to move out of the time we experience as the present and view both past and future. Either the future as a whole already exists, or it expands at a varying rate and we are not necessarily experiencing it at the edge of expansion. The latter explanation makes sense if we consider the vast amount of interactions, each wrapped in its own spacetime, which make up what we experience as now. Our self is also made of a vast array of interactions, each in its own spacetime. Perhaps macroscopic premonitions are a result of some of the interactions arriving at a future which is ahead of the time the dominant will is experiencing. That doesn't explain premonitions at a photon level, however.

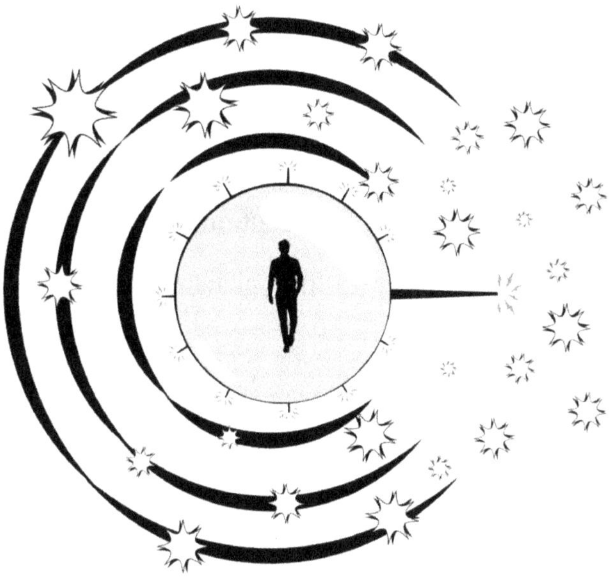

Figure 22: Interactions in the future

A problem posed by Stephen Hawking in *A Brief History of Time,* is that, if time travel is possible, why are we not meeting tourists from the future? One possible answer is that we are. It is possible that our endofilters will not allow us to recognize them. If we are capable of changing the appearance of quantum interaction to solid objects, we are surely capable of filtering out a few time tourists.

The other answer depends on what part of the person is doing the time traveling. If it is the will, what evidence is there that time traveling wills are not exercising control over interactions? Even more likely is the possibility that timeless travelers from the plane of conscious could be exerting control. The amount of our interactions that we recognize as a product of our own wills is minisculely small and, as will be explored in *Free Will and Seductive Coercion*, the default decision is made for us before we are even aware that a decision must be made. If every interaction must be preceded by an effort of will, there is a lot of room for interception.

According to the growing block theory of time, reality is in a state of continual expansion and the future does not exist yet, although the past does. This is an unlikely state as most things that cannot be imagined (infinity, randomness, imagination itself) do not exist, and an unending expansion is a thing that cannot be imagined. It does not matter, however, whether the future exists or not. It is possible to view the self as an expanding collection of interactions in either case. Like a road, which exists and yet can be seen leading away from us, those of us within time see all things as moving relative to time, whether that is true in universal reality or not. It is endoreality which prevents us from seeing the past and

Like a road, which exists and yet can be seen leading away from us, those of us within time see all things as moving relative to time, whether that is true in universal reality or not.

it is quite possibly endoreality which prevents us from seeing the future as well. The future may be unpredictable from one vantage point, but it is chosen from another.

If the future already exists, many people then conclude that will, or choice, must not exist. These people are imagining reality as a fixed object. The ocean exists, and yet every tiny element in it is constantly changing. The universe may also exist in a perpetual state of change. If the universe exists in a mutable state, we have the ability to change it. Perhaps all lives have already been lived and will continue to be lived with different choices made each time. Perhaps the will travels through pre-existing lives and recreates them with new choices. Perhaps multiple wills are living different parts of what we perceive as the same life. These are all possibilities.

Life does not occur in stages. Our self accumulates and expands, it does not pass. Every act is an interaction and every interaction that once exists, continues to exist. Where would it go? Interactions cannot be erased. They follow the law of time; they are irreversible. If the interaction continues to exist, the life energy that went into that interaction continues to be contained within it. The selves composed by the interactions also continue to exist in the spacetimes that contained each interaction. The we that is our will is no longer experiencing the interactions which have already created the self, but they still exist.

Ordered systems follow the second law of thermodynamics, the tendency to move towards states of higher entropy. This is the only law of physics that includes a past and a present, or is unidirectional. The direction of greater entropy is from order to chaos, which is the direction of exosocial expansion.

We experience ourselves being propelled through time by life. Perhaps it is our will which is propelling us and creating time in the process. In this case, time follows the second law of thermodynamics because it is our will which desires it. Perhaps our will chooses to follow the law of exosocial expansion and creates the second law of thermodynamics. Perhaps our will is the exosocial force. Time, conscious and quantum will, the exosocial force and the second law of thermodynamics seem to share the same attributes.

Figure 23: Will creating time and linking interactions

Some physicists do not agree that there is an obvious observable order to events in time. The future is the direction of increasing entropy. But the past ought to also have increasing entropy due to time-reversal symmetry. Carlo Rovelli thinks that the perceived low entropy of the universe in the past may be simply our perception. Stephen Hawking claimed that[70] *"Disorder increases with time because we measure time in the direction in which disorder increases."*

Hawking is intuitively wrong because we do not seem to have a choice in which way we measure time. It seems more accurate to say that movement towards greater entropy is time – that living is a force in the direction of exosocial expansion, or the creation of an ever-expanding network of interactions, and that the exosocial drive is towards greater entropy. The primordial chaos that encouraged continual dispersal is then always at war with the endosocial force of order, or the will to create clusters of interactions which appear as objects.

The we that Rovelli and Hawking refer to is undefined by either of them. If there is a we that follows or creates time, it can only be the will, as that is the part of the person that chooses outcomes, or direction. If we live in the direction that time is measured, the direction of increasing entropy, perhaps it is because this is the direction chosen by the quantum will which directs the majority of our interactions. In that case, the emotional will is a drive to decreasing entropy and the conscious will is aligned with the quantum will in seeking greater entropy.

Interactions stay in a timeless universe. Time is the links between interactions, or the force which pulls interactions together. Time does not pass. We pass through time. The we that passes is our will. Time is recorded for us in the order in which entropy increases because that is the direction in which our will moves. It is our will that follows the second law of thermodynamics and creates the second law of thermodynamics. Our will is being moved by the exosocial force, or is the exosocial force. Time and will both link interactions and follow the path to greater entropy because will creates time.

If the endosocial drive exists, it supports Rovelli's intuition that the second law may not be universally followed. It also makes the big bounce theory of a cyclic contraction and expansion of the universe more interesting. If the universe really consists of both periods of great expansion and periods of great contraction, it would be helpful to discover both forces at work in our lived experience. The experience of life is an opposition of two forces: the force which follows the egalitarian, exosocial, second law of thermodynamics and the opposing force which seeks to create and preserve order, or endosocial power.

Figure 24: Exosocial and endosocial expansion

The drive to interact, the drive to exosocial expansion, is a drive to dispersal of order. Each interaction stores a tiny piece of energy.

Time appears only alongside expenditure of energy.

A lifetime requires a source of energy. An endogroup does not encourage interaction outside of the endogroup as that causes a dispersal of energy outside the shared animus. The endosocial drive is a force of order. The endosocial drive is an attempt to conserve energy and the exosocial drive is a compulsion to spend it.

Time is created where heat is dispersed. Heat is the expenditure of energy, or life. Women shiver from the cold after birth. Life brings heat to the birthed and cold to the birther. Elders are cold. Death is colder. Ghosts are coldest of all. The afterlife (both positive and negative versions) is described as warm or hot and bright.

The second law of thermodynamics tells us that heat passes only from hot bodies to cold, never the other way around. This explains altruism and the egalitarian force which always disperse energy to those who have the least. The egalitarian force is the second law of thermodynamics. Disobeying this force triggers emotional disturbance experienced as guilt or shame. This is a repulsion caused by acting against the dominant force. Guilt is why unbalanced energy transfer from a weaker (colder) body requires sublation, so that the energy transfer occurs within the same animus.

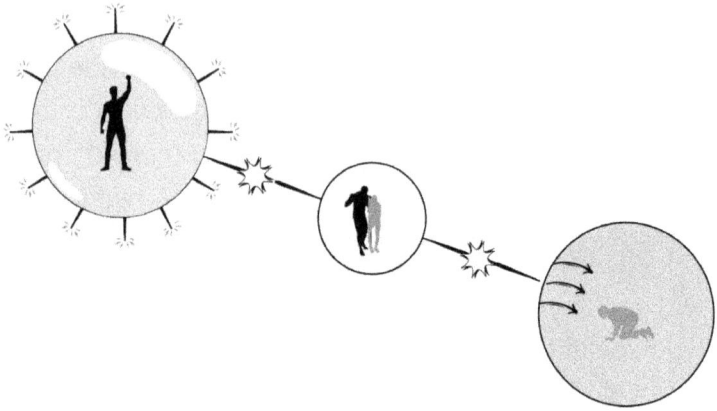

Figure 25: Altruistic energy transfer

The number of people that can share a close emotional connection may be related to the number of empathic or euphoric conduits or the amount of energy available. People with more energy are generally more outgoing with a wider circle of friends, while depression leads to a contracted circle. Totalitarianism that depletes energy may be seeking to diminish or restrict expansion.

If time is experienced as interactions, does time contract with exosocial development? Common perception holds that the older a person gets, the faster their experience of time goes. We experience time more quickly as we do more, as people often point out and has been proven through measured experiment. The more expanded self can do far more in less time relative to those around them. Perhaps the expanded self has more agents of interaction in terms of anima conduits and the additional energy to supply them.

Exosocial development may lead to a larger lifespan, not just from the health benefits of primary anima extending years of life but also from the ability to fit more interactions into a lifetime. Those that fill their time with interactions which expand their self and provide more animated connections may be provided with additional anima and conduits to accomplish more. They may, in effect, have access to more time.

Variant time experiences are sometimes visible. When a dancer or football player is moving at the same or greater speed relative to everyone else, but in contrast to the extreme exertion of others, their movements are controlled and relaxed, they seem to have all the time in the world. Who could listen to Mozart or Tchaikovsky and not think they lived in a different speed than most?

Relative time, which science 'discovered' in 1905, has, of course, been well known in legends around the world. Celtic tales of people taken to spend an hour with faeries who then emerge decades later are just one well known example. In 1890, fifteen years before the theory of special relativity.was published, William James wrote in the Principles of Psychology: The Perception of Time, *"We have every reason to think that creatures may differ enormously in the amounts of duration they intuitively feel."*[71] In 1892, Albert Heim wrote of the enormous slowing of time and / or acceleration of thought in survivors of falls in the Alps.[72] There are many references to relative time experience in many disciplines despite the idea still not taking hold in institutions which should be recognizing the possibility.

Bradyphenia is a cognitive slowing after brain injury

and in some diseases like Parkinson's. In *Into the Gray Zone: A Neuroscientist Explores the Border Between Life and Death*, Adrian Owen wrote of Parkinson's, *"probably the lack of dopamine in their brains that causes slowed movement also causes slowed thinking. As though every aspect of life is going along a little more slowly than before."* [73] Dopamine produces a euphoric response indicating the presence of anima, or life energy. The less life energy there is to power interactions, the less interactions living things are capable of relative to those with more energy. This means they will experience less time, since time is the thing that links interactions. A lack of dopamine is here listed as a cause of the experience of slowed time, but it is more likely that both are an effect of reduced anima or anima conduits.

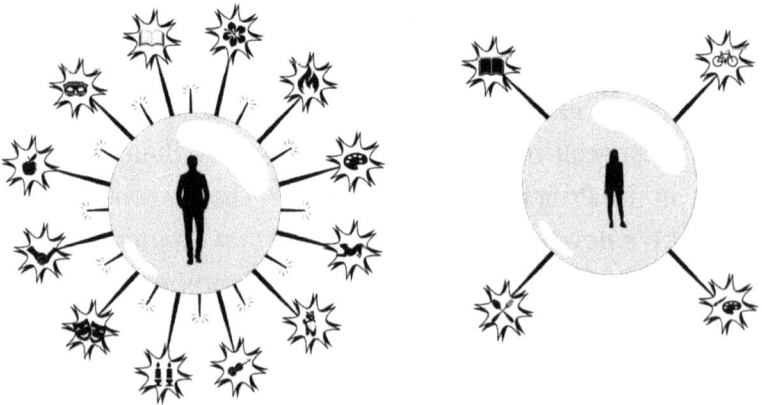

Figure 26: Many or few anima conduits

Oliver Sacks [74] pointed out that *"disorders of spatial scale are as common in parkinsonism as disorders of time scale"*. Experiences of spacetime in various disorders such as Parkinson's and Tourette's may be either accelerated or slowed. Speed variant experiences in what are noticed as disorders may be simply extremes of a spectrum we all live in. We know our experiences of spacetime are variant at an imperceptible level and also at the observable level of these disorders. It is logical to expect them at every gradient in between as well.

Figure 27: Time between interactions

Time passes more quickly in the mountains than it does at sea level, or we or timepieces move through it more quickly. There is more time in the mountains. If one person is in La Paz and another in Rotterdam below sea level, the one from La Paz will experience a greater amount of time between their interactions.

Time links interactions, but the time between interactions can be different for each side of the interaction. If our person in La Paz were to text the person in Rotterdam, the interaction goes through an intermediary, so is not direct. If the interaction was in person, time may still be minusculy different, depending on the location of each person. Time is subjective and relative to the experiencer. An interaction cannot then exist exactly within a fixed spacetime as the time varies for each actor. It seems more accurate to consider time as occurring between interactions than as a part of them.

Not only is time individual to each person and location, it is also individual to each interaction. Time flies when you're having fun; boredom and sorrow are interminable. Energy speeds up time. Time also flies when a person is angry but freezes when they are afraid. When people are angry they release more heat and energy and time moves faster. When they are cold, they release less energy and time slows. In death, time must stop since there are neither

There is no such thing as a universal present or a universal now. Time is a function of us. A person does not live within time; time is a component of each person.

interactions nor energy attractions between the will of the dead and the actions of the living.

If a person is running up and down a line repeatedly, distributing cookies, one at a time, to 25 people, they are experiencing more interactions, and therefore more time, than any of the people receiving cookies. Time is

appearing to move a lot faster, or is experienced as a lot faster, for the busier person. From an external perspective, they are all experiencing the same time, but since the dispenser is participating in every interaction, they have the experience of time flying, while the recipients have the experience of time dragging.

In practice, every person would be experiencing far more interactions since there are a vast number of interactions happening outside the cookie-dispensing activity. At times when people are forced to direct focus on only one task, the task is not interesting or complex and they have all other stimuli removed, they experience a pain akin to an existential crisis. Many prisoners have testified that solitary confinement is worse than physical torture. Anyone who has ever worked at a busy but mindless job, especially one involving sustained and surveilled mental focus such as a call centre, can attest to the mental anguish these activities produce. Compelled busywork prevents the exertion of will to create interactions which is the action of living.

There is no such thing as a universal present or a universal now. Time is a function of us. A person does not live within time; time is a component of each person. Perhaps a fruit fly and a tortoise have the same lifespan and it is just our perception that sees one lifespan as decades and the other days. Time is not a universal number. Illusions such as a spinning coin which appears to be a sphere, indicate that our perception of reality does not coincide with true reality as a flow of time.

It is reasonable to expect that a sloth and a hummingbird, or even two different people, have different experiences of time. Perhaps people are not slow or quick in thought but are experiencing different variants of time. At least in some cases, this seems more likely than the idea that their brains are operating at different speeds or are superior or defective.

Martial arts masters of concentration can catch flies because they have slowed their perception, or experience, of time. A test of reflexes may actually be a measure of the time the subject is experiencing. Some perceived learning disabilities may in fact be, as they are often called, simply a result of being slow or living in a different speed. The language used to describe such disabilities seems to intuitively suggest this, with phrases such as cannot keep up or going too fast for them. The ability to accomplish far more than normal may also be a result of experiencing more time than most and therefore having room for more interactions. Such people are often

We know that time is an effect of gravity. This may be why the will is connected to gravity and bound to a physical being.

described as quick witted. Engaging in more interactions has the effect of speeding up the experience of time or making time fly while boredom, or no opportunity to exert the will and create interactions, causes time to drag.

The idea that all interactions continue to exist in their own spacetime wrappers and that the experience of time is an illusion of the living is reinforced by the increasingly vast body of testimony from those who have died and been resuscitated. The common experience of rapidly relived life events as part of decoupling and the ability to relive events after decoupling are frequently documented testimonies. As described by one survivor to researcher and resuscitation specialist Dr Sam Parnia,[75] *"I wasn't just watching the events; I was actually reliving them again, while at the same time, I was also re-experiencing the actions from other people's points of view."*

What separates life from unlife is time. Life seems to be involved in the creation of time; certainly, we always think of life in terms of time. We know that time is an effect of gravity. This may be why the will is connected to gravity and bound to a physical being.

🐈

It would be very interesting to explore what is happening when another life form such as yeast clouds the thoughts of its host, or slows the ability to think. Alcohol slows a person's reflexes and also creates a feast for yeast. Is a parasite, in these cases, using some of the time as they exert control over life energy and will? If a parasite reduces the energy available for interactions, they reduce the number of interactions possible relative to outside activity. This looks like slowed reflexes.

Marijuana slows people's experience of living and allows them to live at a slower pace which is less stressful for some. Marijuana has been used to aid depression which is the emotional response to deanimation. Perhaps marijuana slows the rate of interactions which conserves the expenditure of anima and this results in more tranquility and euphoria for those who were straining to live at what is considered a desirable pace. Alcohol and marijuana and all dopamine producing behaviours reduce the ability of the conscious will to control interactions. The emotional will does not require the same expenditure of energy.

Another effect of marijuana use, which some people also experience naturally, is the unawareness or inability to realistically assess the passage of time. This causes an inability to set or meet realistic goals. At times, it can appear as though these people are unaware that time will pass, as it does not seem to factor into their plans. This leads to missed opportunities and a lack of preparation for events which should be anticipated but apparently are not. This is an effect of a dominant emotional will.

Both alcohol and marijuana are used to alleviate the

emotional pain of ruptured connections. Perhaps they both work by reducing the anima conduits available for creating interactions. If they can remove the severed conduits, that may ease the pain of unrequited interactions. Alcohol, marijuana and many other drugs cause decoupling in varying degrees. Decoupling of conscious leaves the emotional will in charge and decoupling from the emotional ties of the self creates an endoself. The amount of people with drug addictions who have severed emotional ties and endoself characteristics is another indicator that these substances act by reducing or disabling anima conduits and the ability to create connections. The anima conduits may still exist but not under the control of the conscious will. This will become more clear in *Free Will and Seductive Coercion*.

The idea of relative time may affect common perceptions of plant and animal or animate and inanimate objects. It definitely challenges common perceptions of intelligence. In 1881 Darwin wrote that[76] worms *"deserve to be called intelligent, for they act in nearly the same manner as a man under similar circumstances."* and *"If we speed up a time-lapse film of plant movement by a thousandfold, plant behaviours start to look animal-like and may even appear "intentional".*

In 1906, Herbert Spencer Jennings wrote that *"If Amoeba were a large animal … its behaviour would at once call forth the attribution to it of states of pleasure and pain, of hunger, desire and the like, on precisely the same basis as we attribute these things to the dog."* [77] As Oliver Sacks commented, *"Jennings' vision of a highly sensitive, dog-size Amoeba is almost cartoonishly the opposite of Descartes notion of dogs as so devoid of feelings that they could be vivisected without compunction and he could take their cries as purely "reflex" reactions of a quasi-mechanical kind."*

The tendency to anthropomorphize seems natural to all humans. Perhaps this is not the mass delusion so often bemoaned by scientists but an emotional response to reality. The idea that animals have feelings, an idea so completely self-evident to anyone with working empathic or euphoric connections to animals, was once dismissed as being wholly irrational and anti-science as well as standing in the way of progress. The anthropomorphization of groups is also an accurate depiction of how they are experienced, sublated to one will and living within one endoreality.

Macroscopic objects are created as an effort of will. Life forms and time are created from the same effort of will. Life in an animus is the inverted energy trapped through the creation of order out of chaos. Ordered objects (including all living beings) contain trapped, or inverted, energy which is released or expended over time. Another way of viewing that is to say that time is created through the expenditure of trapped energy in ordered objects or that time is the amortization of the life in the object. A lifespan is a true mortgage, a word which translates to death-pledge. The initial asset depreciates through regular intervals of time, is depreciated more quickly through incorrect use or is released suddenly upon meeting a greater force.

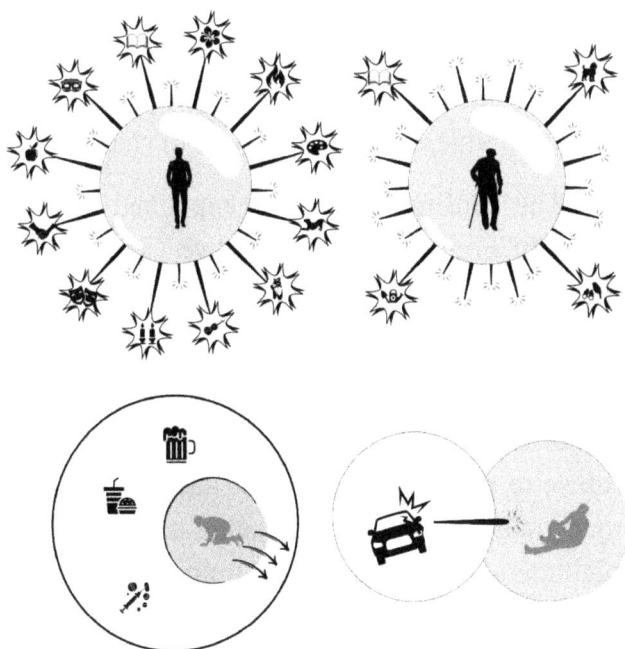

Figure 28: Expenditure of life energy

Emotions will order and conscious wills disorder. Without the emotional will, there is only chaos, which is why the emotional will appears alongside order. We cannot feel attraction or repulsion to nothing. Intangible fears and attractions, such as those felt to a god, afterlife, events and ghosts, may be attractions and repulsions of the emotional will to the exosocial and endosocial forces.

A lifetime is a struggle between a store of life (order) and time (chaos). Because of the second law of thermodynamics, time always wins in the end, at least apparently.

Living is a function of energy and will. Will creates mass and mass slows down time around itself. The attraction between a cluster of interactions creating an object is the act of will. Will is the attraction between two interactions. Gravity may be the effect of a will to order and time the effect of a will to chaos.

The conflict of wills is explained in much greater detail in *Free Will and Seductive Coercion,* but we are going to get into the will to order in the chapter The Nature of Living.

Those seeking to accumulate more power, in order to create more time, are like passengers on a train who refuse to get off. They cannot imagine existence outside their train, or, if they do imagine it, it is in the form of a nightmare. They mistake the train for the destination. To understand what they are missing, let's take a look at unliving, or death, in the next chapter.

Will is the attraction between two interactions. Will creates mass and time.

Space is the location of an interaction relative to other interactions. Time is the link between interactions.

The second law of thermodynamics, the tendency towards greater entropy, is also the egalitarian or exosocial force which seeks to dissipate all ordered objects.

The conscious and quantum wills follow the second law

of thermodynamics.

Time flows in the direction of greater entropy because time links interactions and the conscious and quantum will choose greater entropy.

A lifetime is a struggle between a store of life (order) and time (chaos).

What separates life from unlife is time. Time is the exertion of will. Exertion of will appears to be a function of living.
The only basic law of physics that distinguishes the past from the future is the second law of thermodynamics.
Time appears only alongside expenditure of energy.

The emotional will seeks to conserve energy in an animus. This leads to depression because euphoria is attained through expenditure of energy. The emotional will craves energy. The emotional will is attached to gravity and ordered objects and fights to preserve endosocial structures.

Perhaps the universe already exists but in a mutable state so we still have the ability to change it.

Perhaps all lives have already been lived and will continue to be lived with different choices made each time.

Perhaps the will travels through pre-existing lives and recreates them with new choices.

Perhaps multiple wills are living different parts of what we perceive as the same life.

Spacetime

The positioning of interactions relative to other interactions.

Spacetime wrapper

The space and time which make up the relative position of an interaction and form a membrane around the interaction.

Time

The attraction or movement between two interactions.

Word argument

A debate that is depicted as discussing different ideas but is really just discussing different words which have the same meaning.

Present

The location in spacetime of the subject will known as I.

Chapter 13

The nature of death

Dead turned out to be not dead. — a person who died.

Sam Parnia is the head of research into cardiopulmonary resuscitation on various projects in the US and UK and has written extensively on resuscitation. Parnia opens his 2013 book, *Erasing Death: The Science That Is Rewriting the Boundaries Between Life and Death* with the story of Joe Tiralosi, a man who died of a heart attack, was revived after 47 minutes, died again and was revived again after another 15 minutes. These increasingly common cases require a re-examination of the definitions of life, death and revived, literally re-lifed.

The most important point to note is that after life was declared to have left Tiralosi's body, twice, Tiralosi is the exact same man he was before. In other words, whatever else this definition of life may be, it is not the source of self, will or consciousness. The medical definition of life is unrelated to who we are. And if who we are can be recovered after minutes, hours or even days of death, then it is not extinguished by death.

From the working medical definition of life and death, there can be consciousness, self and will after death just as there is a body after death. If life is energy, then it (probably) follows the first law of thermodynamics which means that life also continues to exist after death in the same measure as before. What death appears to mean is the dissociation of the parts which temporarily coalesce to compose a person. After death, they are separated again into life, body, will, self and conscious. The self continues to exist in the spacetime each interaction is wrapped in. Life returns to the surrounding environment. The body decomposes. This still leaves the will and conscious unaccounted for.

What we refer to as *I* is always the dominant will.

There can be life after death if the body is revived after death or if energy clusters remain in some form. However, what we consider to be the I is no longer living after death unless the will attaches to a living body or other life form. I is consistently associated with the will, not the body. I is not consciousness – we are I even when we lose memory, awareness and understanding. The I is sometimes (not always) conflated with the self if the emotional will is dominant, but that is still a will. I is not the self or it would be in all places where the self exists, including the past and future. The I that is experiencing an interaction in the present is the will that is creating the interaction in the present. It is the will that moves with time or creates time. What we refer to as I is always the dominant will.

Parnia cites signs of brain recovery up to 7 days after brain death[78] and writes, *"death is not something mystical; it arises because of the cessation of function in the cells and organs in the body and eventually cellular death."*[79] What Parnia is referring to is the departure of life from the body. If the will is gone, however, there is nothing anyone can do to revive the whole person, or the I.

The biggest lesson to be learned from the few new studies of decoupled experiences emanating from the field of medicine is how unaware medical professionals and scientists are of the experiences and reality of those they profess to study and advise. Pim von Lommel and Michael Sabom are two of the newly converted believers, both cardiologists who began to listen and then research what their patients were telling them about their post death experiences. Most experience is still dismissed as it still has no place in the current medical endoreality.

To dismiss the accounts of millions of people

because of no scientific evidence is endoreality because it takes a positive conclusion on the side opposite the experienced reality of millions of people and it is based on a refusal to research instead of evidence. Medical doctors such as Parnia are extremely hesitant to criticize their own endogroup. Thus, they flatter their denialist colleagues by calling them rationalist and marginalize the experience of those who have died with liberal use of the word claims.

Instead of a continued existence in some form, the majority of scientists [80] prefer to believe that we arrived from, and depart to, nothing – a thing which cosmologists ought to have learned does not exist. A far more magical belief than something after death is nothing after death. Nobody can describe nothing, nobody has ever experienced nothing, but this we are supposed to believe in. Its proponents attribute the belief in existence after death to fear, but there is nothing to fear in nothing. As usual, this is a projection of denialists' own fear. They cling to denial of continued existence to assuage the fear of a present or future debt to be paid.

Heisenberg postulated a century ago that particles with insignificant mass would exist only as interactions. Quantum mechanics has consistently shown that objects with extremely low mass exist, or are experienced, only as interactions, and yet scientists sneer at the occasional experience of ghosts. Apparitions behave exactly as all particles do without a body. Those who are declared dead and leave their bodies but have surplus energy and remain clustered in an animus are not only plausible, they align with a huge body of testimony. There is absolutely no reason to disbelieve all the accounts throughout history of various forms of consciousness or energy appearing and disappearing in observed reality. It is far more unreasonable and inconsistent to believe that a conscious form suddenly becomes nothing on leaving a bodily host as nothing cannot exist and does not exist, according to all physical science.

Scientists that happily embrace theories involving alien contact and adjacent or parallel universes which may hold other wills still refuse to believe that our own wills may be capable of other existence. Aliens is a classic example of scientists rewording something that has always been known so they can claim to have discovered it and still reject earlier knowledge. Aliens from outer space and spirits from other dimensions are the exact same things.

If the extra dimensions of various versions of string theory exist, it could explain some or all of what are now called supernatural phenomena. In order to have escaped detection, the extra dimensions must occur at a different scale. The braneworld scenario posits a three dimensional world (a three-brane) in which we live and which delimits our awareness. The extra dimensions of the universe predicted by various offshoots of string theory, as well as cultural beliefs through history, may still exist outside of that. If braneworlds exist and can show that reality is much wider than our perception, it may one day lead to evidence that self membranes and endosocial membranes can also be created and destroyed.

According to Brian Greene, writing in *The Fabric of the Cosmos,* "*We see by using the electromagnetic force, which is unable to access any dimensions beyond the three we know about.*"[81] Gravitons, according to Greene, arise from closed strings and so are not trapped by branes. "*They are as free to leave a brane as they are to roam on or through it. ... So, if we are living in a brane, we would not be completely cut off from the extra dimensions. Through the gravitational force, we could both influence and be influenced by the extra dimensions. Gravity, in such a scenario, would provide our sole means for interacting beyond our three space dimensions.*"

Photons transmit the electromagnetic force and gravitons transmit the gravitational force. Including other fields such as the strong and weak nuclear force fields transmitted through gluons (strong) and W and Z particles (weak) the differences between these forces seems a very good place to start looking for the often opposing forces which govern our lives and the two seemingly very different energy sources providing primary and secondary anima.

Primary anima seems to be obtained from consciousness and secondary anima from life. If we conflate life with gravity, it provides a neat mental picture for why we are weighed down by life and unable to leave the earthly realm. It adds a new way to think of the purpose to the drives for egalitarianism and exosocial expansion. The purpose of a lifespan is to expend life so the person is not weighed down with it during death.

Those that are unable to leave the earth due to being victims of extreme predation may lack the energy to do so, but others may be weighed down by accumulation, especially of secondary anima.

The paradoxes of time and space travel are neatly solved by those who do it because the ability of the traveler to interact or influence events in a three-brane world is severely limited. (Gravitons have yet to be detected experimentally and are an extremely weak force, about 10^{-42} times the strength of electromagnetic force.) The living world exists in spacetime and the higher levels of the non-living world reportedly do not, and it makes sense that they would not. Since these levels do not experience time, from their perspective, the time-driven three-brane of the living exists as a whole which has always existed, unchanging and unchangeable. Within a three-brane, the case is very different and interactions are experienced sequentially, driven (or pulled) by will.

Tiny wormholes can exist. Perhaps they exist between branes. Quantum fluctuations may make tiny wormholes common in the spacetime fabric but inaccessible to macroscopic objects. There may be energy leaking through these holes, however. If the idea of a person is not associated with corporality, spacetime travel may be easy (as those who leave their bodies always insist it is). If time is only experienced in a three-brane world, there may be some merit to the belief in certain times of the year when the curtain grows thin as Celts believe about Samhain. Perhaps this thin fabric recurs cyclically as we wind past the same wormholes repeatedly.

Considering the amount of money spent in trying to tear the fabric of spacetime or otherwise create wormholes and investigate spacetime travel, it is mind-boggling that the millions of people who insist they have done it by the simple, rational method of decoupling are still ignored. In fact, it is extremely unlikely they are being ignored. Isolation and sensory deprivation, as well as severe stress and near death, can trigger the decoupling experience. Those have all been subjects of intense interest and experimentation by the state and spy agencies of the world.

The reason we cannot observe other dimensions is a problem of scale, one not experienced by the parts of us that separate and are no longer macroscopic. These parts may consist of conscious, some form(s) of energy and will but not self or the body and its unspent store of life. It may be only conscious that can attain the higher dimensions.

Evidence of the decoupling of the five elements of a person are found throughout the testimony of those who have died or decoupled for other reasons. According to psychiatrist and researcher Raymond Moody,[82] some who decoupled from their body didn't feel they had any sort of material form. They felt as though they were pure consciousness *"able to see everything around me … without occupying any space."* Others experienced a level, or time frame, in which there is some form of energy cluster which many refer to as a spiritual body.

This spiritual body is most likely to occur at the stage when the person is still confused as to what to do next and pre-occupied with their own body and activity on earth.

This spiritual body does not seem to have much of a membrane, however, and is referred to as a mist, a cloud, smoke-like, a vapour, an energy pattern, a little ball of energy and similar. This body already exists outside of spacetime in many or most cases. In the words of one person,[83] *"When I wanted to see someone at a distance, it seemed like a part of me, kind of like a tracer, would go to that person. And it seemed to me at the time that if something happened any place in the world that I could just be there."*

At this early stage, the bond of the conscious and will to the self appears to be very intact. Many people report being greeted by family or other guides when they are dead or dying or as a foreshadowing visit. In some accounts,[84] *"bystanders report seeing a dying person's spirit leave the body, or they report leaving their own bodies and moving upwards toward a light ... some even witness the life review."* *"Bystanders can empathically co-live the dying experience of someone else"*, possibly because of the emotional connection and the shared self. This could also be why too much grieving can make it difficult for spirits to leave. Once the self and will have decoupled from the body, another part of the self can pull the will back, as the self is not individuated.

While modern studies suggest that prayers and grief

hold the dying back, extreme grief and prayers have sometimes been used to aid them on their journey. This may be because prayers and offerings for safe passage have been replaced by pleadings to stay and the undignified fear of death. The common habit today of traumatic grief and pleading with the dead and dying to return may keep them here. Most earlier traditions encouraged or assisted safe passage and did not encourage attempts to return. The Tibetan Book of the Dead directed that *"During this time no relative or fond mate should be allowed to weep or to wail, as such is not good [for the deceased]; so restrain them."* [85]

The other common modern habit is ignoring the dead and refusing to honour or assist them on their journey. This may cause sorrow and a traumatic wound to the self which may keep them here. They may also be unable to leave due to an energy debt or credit which funeral rituals used to be focused on remedying. Deathbed confessions, especially to victims or a judge figure that can grant absolution, are seldom seen in industrial culture. Even the gathering of family and friends, a ritual which usually involved some form of accounting and forgiveness, is rarely seen now. At most, such accounting is abstracted and dissociated into a document of last will, executed by a legal professional after death.

The body often appears still connected to the rising energy of the dying. Gracia Fay Ellwood describes in *The Uttermost Deep: The Challenge of Painful Near-Death Experiences* testimony of an *"astral body and silver cord."* Many legends refer to this thread. The scythe that cuts the silver thread connecting conscious to body is associated with figures of death such as Santa Muerte and the grim reaper or the sewing shears of the three fates. Descriptions of this silver cord are reminiscent of the smoke of incense down which an ancestral spirit is expected to arrive for their offerings or the fire smoke which is expected to send departed souls or their gifts on their journey.

There are many traditions referring to manifestation of spirits through smoke (such as from incense) or water. Water is commonly used in guilt washing rituals and offerings are burnt for the deceased, to pay any debt they may hold or incur. There is also a tradition, through meditation, prayer and chants, of spirits manifesting through the sound of their names.

There is no time or distance in the common post-death experience of a life review and often no individual self.

If a spirit can leave a body through such a thread, it is possible one can arrive by the same means. The occupation of a body at this point by a wandering spirit or demons is a common theme in traditional medicine and funerary rites. It is usually deemed necessary to guard a body with the continual presence of living people and candles until it is disposed of to prevent its occupation by unwelcome spirits.

The self still exists, as indicated by the famous life review. In this, people describe all of their lifetime passing before their eyes or being experienced by them as they slip past the spacetime membranes that trap the living in the present. There is no time or distance in the common post-death experience of a life review and often no individual self. Time and space are often explicitly mentioned as being absent. All experience, often from all perspectives, is present simultaneously. The life overview could be caused by rising above spacetime and the self created within it to a place with the ability to see and experience the lifespan as a whole.

The self appears expanded in the life review, or the endosocial barriers are lifted. Ellwood explains *"one perceives in one's past actions an "empathic resonance" with others."* and *"In ELO's, (empathic life overview) experiencers not only relive the life in their pasts but undergo an expansion of past consciousness to include others affected by their lives."* In a life review, we feel the pain we inflict. This may be a result of greater perception, since we always feel the pain we inflict, as guilt. Some decoupled selves are connected to those they interact with beyond the interaction and also know and share the person's prior or later life and expanded networks. *"I was shown the ripple effect"* said one person who felt pain by those hurt by the people she had hurt.

Researcher Cherie Sutherland recorded that *"Seven-year old Pat was greeted … by two much-loved family pets who had died four years prior."*[86] Ellwood relates testimony of a decoupled person who described profound interaction with plant life.[87] He felt the response of a tree he had once loved. Euphoric objects are indeed a part of the self according to this testimony.

Many people relate experience of emotions (the self) after death. Those are reportedly reduced to simply joy and love if they manage to ascend to higher levels. If, upon death, the self survives as all of the interactions created using the life energy, but the anima bloat of the remaining energy store either disperses or weighs the will down to a ghost or hell experience, that would be very useful information to help people decide how to live their lives.

Suicide, usually an extremely emotion-driven event, did not provide the escape from these emotions that were presumably hoped for, at least in some cases. According to Moody's research, *"These experiences were uniformly characterized as being unpleasant. As one woman said, "If you leave here a tormented soul, you will be a tormented soul over there too."*[88]

Other researchers report different results. Edith Fiore writes that *"With suicides, I have found that many remain as discarnates, feeling just as depressed as they did before their deaths – until they were "rescued" by spirit helpers or they possessed unsuspecting living people. However, others who killed themselves went immediately into the Light.*"[89]

The will may exist temporarily. It is very common to be offered a choice to live or die, but that choice seems to be only possible up to a certain point. A physical barrier is often described, beyond which the choice can no longer be changed.

It is possible that self and will can escape the confines of the body (or, more likely, they were never limited to it) but they cannot go where conscious can, and conscious cannot effect change, or exert will, without being bound by the confines of the gravity sphere. There are many stories of will being involved in the choice to be reborn, and sometimes even the choice of mother, but perhaps the will is left behind at a stage where the person ascends into pure conscious. The only reason to choose life is to help others, our extended self, so empathy does still remain, not just knowledge but also love.

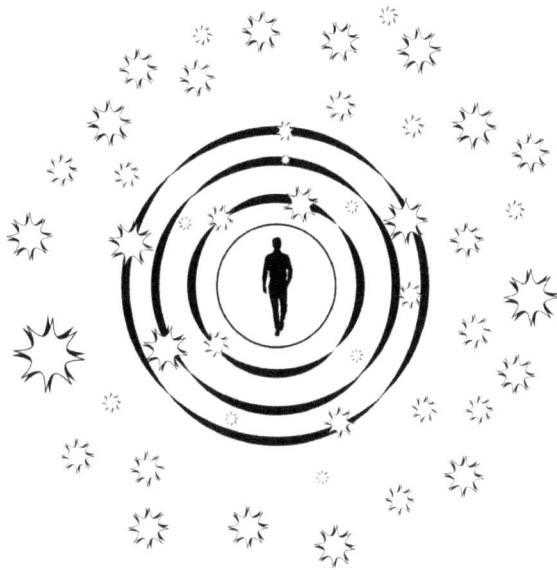

Figure 29: Self, body, and will gravity sphere

Love, experienced as joy, is an emotion commonly described by those who ascend to the world of light, or photons, or conscious. Love represents not only connection but a flow of energy through that connection. This may be experienced because the self that is still connected to others may remain in some form or it may be just that all endosocial membranes are gone, resulting in full connection, or full immersion in the energy.

With no endosocial membranes, there are no others and there can therefore be no hate. Without the craving for energy to be hoarded in an endosocial membrane, there is no violation or sublation and no debt or credit. All interaction is connection, experienced as pure love. Shunning is the threat of deanimation through the loss of anima conduits. Every emotion unrelated to love is related to shunning, so when the ultimate state of inclusion is attained, there is nothing left but love.

Death experiences that escape the gravitational field describe light, or a photon-like world. For those that attain the photon-like dimension, it is their conscious that appears to have survived.[90] reports *"the conviction of several NDEs that the light is "home", that their earthly life had been a period of strange forgetfulness."* Conscious may be considered like light. When it stops hitting an object, it may appear to have disappeared, but it is nonetheless everywhere. Conscious appears to be synonymous with the universe, or all that is.

Figure 30: Conscious

The place of conscious, or love and knowledge, has been described to researcher Pim von Lommel as a place *"where there's no distinction between good and evil and time and place do not exist."* [91] No distinction between good and evil presumably means there is no predator and prey. There is no imbalance of energy because there are no membranes to accumulate energy or perhaps because there is no life energy. Membranes are held together by an effort of will and they contain anima. There is no membrane where there is no life and will is unable to exert itself. This appears to apply to the personal membrane as well.

Access to knowledge, or the wider conscious, is unimpeded in this state. As one person related to Moody [92] *"Your mind is so clear. It's so nice."* Jayne Smith[93] told Ellwood[94] that *"total knowledge [was] something I have always known and managed to forget."* What is described as [95] *"Absolute total knowledge"* is a feature of personal connections to primary sources such as beauty, music and knowledge.

Knowledge is empathic and experienced through connections of conscious.[96] relates *"persons whose ordinary vision is poor but who see extraordinary details in NDEs, even 360 degree perception down to every hair and follicle"* or who saw their body through an upper bunk. This experience is described as a state where they know all realities.

Kenneth Ring's research includes many accounts of [97] traveling at extreme speed, vast distances, peace, pure love, complete knowledge, light and warmth. Some descriptions that were relayed to Ring are:

"it was a giant, infinite world of calm and love and energy and beauty."

"It was all the energy of the universe forever in one immeasurable place."

"I began to be bombarded with data. Information was coming at me from every direction."

"There was the knowledge that was beyond anything I could possibly describe to you"

"It's something which becomes you and you become it. ... I was the brightness, it was part of me."

"I think of God as a tremendous source of energy, like the nucleus of something enormous and that we are all just separate atoms from this nucleus. I think that God is in every one of us; we are God."

All of this appears to describe a world of photon-like energy and the knowledge of all that is, unencumbered by self membranes and perception filters. The descriptions of energy are interesting. Ring's interviewees describe:[98]

"electrical sparks in my hands"

"I feel heat radiating from isolated parts of my body"

"There was a tremendous heat in the central part of my body and along the spinal column"

"A glowing light around my head and my face" *(observed by others).*

This should all sound very familiar to any student of kundalini energy. Euphoria is produced by whatever energy is in this dimension. This energy seems to be the same as primary anima.

In order to traverse to this level, it is often necessary to navigate through a tunnel of some sort. (Surely physicists looking at wormholes ought to be looking here.) An interviewee of Ring describes it as [99] *"a protective passage of energy with an intense brightness at the end."* Many who experience the tunnel describe it in the same terms, as a safe passage. The light could be considered a primary anima passage repelling predatory spirits. This is also the principle behind euphoric objects used to ward off malevolent spirits. Primary anima appears to repel those addicted to secondary anima, even while alive.

Not every decoupling experience is experienced as joyful, and not everyone ascends to a world of light, love and knowledge. The peace, love and empathy that is experienced in the place of light, often arrived at through a tunnel, is vastly different from other experiences where people are definitely still divided and experiencing extreme emotions other than joy. One person explained the death experience *"was more than real: absolute reality"*.[100] This is universal reality outside of all endofilters. We need an endofilter so that we can conduct our lives without being distracted by the ghostly endoselves without.

Imagination is the ability to tap into what lies beyond the earthbound sphere, in the realm of knowledge and joy. Nightmares tell us what is there in the gravity-bound purgatory outside of our protective filters.

Figure 31: The tunnel

The tunnel appears to act as an endofilter, but it is not always fully protective, and many find it difficult to traverse or even locate. The earthbound sphere is not a pleasant experience. In The handbook of near-death experiences : thirty years of investigation. Nancy Evans-Bush describes *"extreme fear, panic or anger, possibly with visions of threatening or taunting demonic creatures"*[101] as one possible experience and *"unbounded floating in the Void, or constriction in a tunnel or both"* as another. Bruce Greyson and Nancy Evans-Bush categorized three types of negative decoupling experience: void, inverted and hellish.

The meaningless void could be the result of an inability to connect to primary anima or feel whatever attraction draws other people through the tunnel. This lack of attraction could be what traps some in the void. Ellwood says a person who experienced the void described her pain there as the *"total aloneness energy at the core of every person, causing us to do all the fear-based things we do,"* but this feeling is not universal. The empty core is one that cannot access primary anima. At least in this particular case, it is a feeling familiar to the person while living as well.

The inverted experience appears to be subjective. As described by researcher Kenneth Ring, *"inverted NDE's [are the] same as radiant but perceived as terrifying"*.[102] People are blinded by the light or hear a disturbing cacophony instead of the beautiful music others experience as heaven. The inverted experience hypothesis has been suggested by several researchers into post and near death experiences.

The inverted death experience may be related to the inverted sources of energy among the living. What attracts an exoself repels an endoself and vice versa. In many traditions, earthbound spirits can only appear at night, as the light repels them. Candles are often used to repel malevolent spirits. In cases of inverted experience, the person may have to continue being reborn until their poles are reversed and they experience the afterlife as joy instead of horror. Studies of inverted death experience in conjunction with studies of attraction to primary or secondary anima among the living would be very helpful in understanding both.

Among the living as well, complicated melodies and the widest ranges are only appreciated by some. The majority prefer a much more monotone rhythm and melody. Primary anima can only be accessed with conscious engagement. The previous note of music must be held in the conscious in order for a person to appreciate the present note. Those with a greater appreciation for complex music may have a stronger connection with the conscious. Those able to establish a strong connection with other sources of primary anima may also have a strong connection to conscious or a strong conscious control over will. Those with a dominant emotional will may be unable to appreciate or connect to pure knowledge, love, beauty, joy, light or music, all sources of primary anima. Smell and taste, on the other hand, may be only accessible through the emotional will, since those senses do not seem to appear in accounts of higher dimensions.

It is very worth incorporating animist legends and beliefs into analysis of the decoupling experience. In many of the accounts in this chapter, people relate experiences in their own words and may be immediately dismissed by those who view the world through a different framework. A great deal of knowledge is lost due to the lack of patience or acceptance of diverse viewpoints. This acceptance is required to examine evidence presented through every framework and look for common threads and universal experience. It is necessary to record evidence without bias and resist the compulsion to reframe all experience into a framework acceptable to the researcher (such as brain malfunctions in the experiencer or allegory).

In describing traditional beliefs of his village in Burkina Faso, Malidoma Patrice Some wrote, *"witches possessed the secret of separating their souls from their bodies at night, and of turning their soul into light expanding into infinity."* where they could experience *"a lack of gravitational laws."*[103] This is the same weightless feeling, free of gravity, which is referenced in nearly all accounts of decoupling of a person's will and conscious from their body. Some also describes traditional egalitarian teaching *"the more you know the more obligated you are to serve the community, the more you own, the more you must give."* [104] This is common cultural guidance to avoid anima bloat.

According to the Friedmann equation, where matter energy density is high, spacetime will have positive curvature (be a sphere). If it is low, spacetime will have a negative curvature. Upon decoupling, people that accumulate secondary anima may fail to fully decouple but have insufficient mass to remain with the living. They may descend into a saddle formation, associated both with hell and the place to banish the guilty in animist magic.

Anima bloat may cause the remaining spirit to descend. A very big question regarding earthbound spirits is which of the five components of a person make up this spirit. What remains earthbound after decoupling appears to be leftover energy, either as a debt or a credit.

The idea of anima bloat is found in many intuitive phrases or beliefs such as emotions weighing heavily on the heart or Thoth weighing the heart against a feather to decide admittance into a pleasant afterworld. It also appears in our unease with inequality or an excess of advantage.

The fire that appears in many versions of hell and in more ancient spells to consume the soul may represent the burning away of whatever elements or energy prevent passage to the other worlds.

Whether that is true or not, it is certainly an interesting thought that the energy stolen by predators could cause them to burn in hell. That would resolve the punitive balance our natures, or the egalitarian drive, seem to demand. The *"extreme fear, panic or anger"* mentioned by Nancy Evans-Bush are also all emotional responses which expend excess energy in the form of secondary anima.

Whether the person's will ascends or is weighed down to the earthly plane (or below) seems to be related to whether the person's dominant will is bound to the remaining animus and the emotional self or the conscious. In many cases, the earthbound energy may come bound to an emotional will, but the conscious does not always seem present. It may be simply dormant under a dominant emotional will, however, as often appears to be the case among the living. Scent and taste may both be simply earthly senses since these seem to only appear in earthbound experiences (subject to correction). Scent and taste are both strongly connected to the emotional will.

Figure 32: Weighed down vs rising on
decoupling

Decoupled is the word used in Binding Chaos theory for a person whose five elements have been dissociated from each other and are no longer bound into a unified person. There are many names and acronyms used for decoupled experience as there is a huge variety of circumstances that can result in decoupling. These include emotional trauma, drug use, fear, depression, psychotic breaks and much more. Some of these are described as OBE's, or out of body experiences. Psychologists use the word dissociation to describe weak bonding of the five elements. NDE is an acronym for near death experience and it is commonly used to describe the experience of those who have died, those who have come close to dying, those who have empathically witnessed someone dying, those who have had a shock, and much more.

The terms dissociation, NDE (near death experience) and OBE (out of body experience), all refer to a decoupling of will, conscious and/or self from body. Some post-death decoupled energy clusters (spirits) retain life, the ability to experience time, and self, or at least emotions. Earthbound spirits may have a failure to decouple from the self, from life and by extension, from the emotional will.

Depression can cause a decoupling experience. Euphoria is the experience of life energy and its lack is death or deanimation, so depression is a state near death. Depression can cause memory loss and abandonment of action to the emotional will, both signs that conscious has dissociated from the still living person.

The similarity in various types of decoupling experience seems to result from the escape from the endoreality filter that is present for a unified person. This is explored more fully in *Shaping Reality*. It is very likely that hallucinations and dreams are representations of reality that the brain is not effectively filtering and then struggles to decipher and contextualize. In any case, the world of nightmares, psychotic episodes and drug hallucinations shares many aspects with the world experienced by those who do not manage to ascend when they decouple due to death. There is a need for more comparative studies of decoupled experiences due to different causes. Most of these studies are currently separated under their various acronyms or diagnoses.

Cardiologist and NDE researcher Pim von Lommel writes in *Consciousness Beyond Life: The Science of the Near-Death Experience*, *"Sexual abuse and the threat of physical or mental abuse may trigger an out-of-body episode as a healing from pain and humiliation (so-called dissociation), and are much more common among children than previously assumed"* [105] (by scientists and academics). NDE researchers Barbara Harris and Kenneth Ring have both found that childhood abuse makes a person more likely to experience an NDE.[106] This may be because of a conscious that easily disengages. Conscious may separate from or relinquish control of the will because the memories in the emotional self are too painful or because the emotional will has been sublated to a more powerful abuser.

Gracia Fay Ellwood writes in *The Uttermost Deep: The Challenge of Near-Death Experiences*[107] *"early stress enables the child to learn to dissociate from his physical situation and become deeply absorbed in other things."* In other words, they can exert conscious control over will to the point that emotional control over will is all but eradicated, or they remove their conscious awareness from the self and leave the emotional will to be sublated to the abuser. Emotional pain may cause the conscious to either retreat or separate from the emotions.

Recoupling through reliving or examining traumatic events will cause the experience of the unfinished pain still present in the self and the emotional will. This is why it is such a difficult process. Therapy is (ideally) a process of reconnecting the conscious to the self and emotional will by examining or reliving the interactions which created the self. Just as euphoria is obtained by connecting to euphoric rites, guilt and pain may be experienced and healed by reconnecting to traumatic events. There is an opportunity to create balance by reliving the interactions from a stronger and more supported vantage which is able to resist violation and sublation.

If we go back to the idea of the self as interactions which may be relived and changed, reliving allows predatory interactions to be recreated to restore anima balance. The victim in a predatory interaction can return to the interaction and provide support to their own self, just as ritual can replenish the anima in a rite. The danger of therapy for an endo-ideal or endoself is that they will use the opportunity of reliving events to reassign guilt instead of resolving it and an unwitting therapist may reflect that reality for them instead of challenging it.

Hypnotherapy can be used to disengage the conscious. This can help either to explore the unbound emotional self or to use external suggestions that are deemed beneficial for the self to follow. When a person's own conscious is not doing the job they wish, they can use hypnotherapy to decouple and employ an external will to issue the commands they want implemented. Self hypnosis or deep meditation allows a person to calm their emotional self and focus the conscious on only one message to allow its clear transmission. It can also be used to quiet the conscious so that the emotional self can be clearly understood and experienced.

Besides decoupling, the assembly of the five components of a person prior to birth is the other half of this study that may help to determine the character and source of each component. Hypnotic regression researcher Helen Wombach found that out of 750 subjects, most *"claimed to have existed before conception, entering the fetus at some point between the beginning of the third trimester and a day or two after birth."* [108]

Likewise, hypnotherapist Michael Gabriel's clients also reported *"a reflective consciousness able to move in and out, though his subjects were in some cases unable to distinguish between the mother's feelings and their own at early stages."*[109] Feelings are not will or conscious. The testimony recognized I as individuated from the mother and able to make choices. It was conscious and will that moved in and out of the fetus. The self (feelings) was not yet individuated from the mother.

According to Ellwood, *"Some persons tell of having intended to incarnate previously, but changing their minds resulting in miscarriage."* This implies a designated or chosen mother for each conscious will. This area of research would be fascinating if there was more done, for instance, to find if another will ever substituted for the first during gestation or even after.

A trait of the deecoupled forms who remain earthbound is a craving for energy in earthly form, specifically secondary anima. If reincarnation occurs, perhaps it allows a person to accumulate a different type of energy (primary anima). Perhaps this occurs over the course of subsequent lives, until it is sufficient to bring them to the next dimension or sufficient for them to leave the lower levels without being weighted down by the heavier energy of secondary anima. According to Ellwood, there were more negative NDEs historically than there are presently. This may indicate some population-wide evolution. An energy transformation would require an animus to remain intact through various lives and would imply that at least part of the life energy does not come from either the mother or the surroundings.

The self, as well, may be linked through various lifetimes. Many small children and some adults have stated memories of previous lives. Since the self is not individuated, however, the lives these people are able to experience or remember may be just lives and viewpoints they are able to pass through and experience. The idea that the life is or was uniquely theirs may be caused by the open nature of a self. It is common for both children and endo-ideals to feel as though an action or thought was their own when it came from somewhere else. The experience of an expanded self seems to produce this effect.

Most earthbound decoupled experiences report awareness of other beings. Some of these beings are positive and may appear as spirit guides or other protective entities that guide the newcomers through this layer to safety or provide information from the conscious realm. The majority, however, are not. Ellwood[110], wrote that *"the needy and hostile beings have some resemblances to the "hallucinatory" voices reported by many [diagnosed as] schizophrenics." She described them as "needy, obsessed, exploitative, and out of control"*.

The humanoid form of these beings is similar in description to the spiritual body or energy cluster that people describe themselves inhabiting immediately after decoupling. These beings were thought by some experiencers to seek re-embodiment. Ellwood[111] writes that a loss of identity seems to occur in these earthbound entities. Those who experienced them described them to her as nude, zombie-like people standing elbow to elbow doing nothing but staring straight ahead *"self-absorbed, self-justifying, or totally empty in despair."* Others described them as *"depressed, confused spirits. They were humanoid in form, but not distinct."*

Ellwood[112] wrote that haunting spirits were *"in an unhealthy condition, attached to places, living persons, addictive substances, physical life in general."* *"compulsively pre-occupied with earth-life"* *"ignorant, consumed with their needs, and lacking in any real caring or respect for others"* According to her research, *"The chief trait of the ghosts in both Western and Eastern views is their craving – addictions and starvation. In both cultures, the ghosts, though largely unseen, may harm the living by clinging to them and causing depression and disasters."* In Ellwood's *research, "the attacks are not vicious but merely a sucking attachment"*, but other researchers have more serious findings.

Despite Ellwood's interpretation of a loss of identity, these addictive attachments seem to indicate that some of these beings, or energy clusters, cannot detach from the self and its connections or even the emotional will. This may be due to anima imbalance, secondary anima addiction or just extreme attachment. They do, however, seem to have a very loose connection to conscious. One person who experienced these beings commented to Ellwood that *"A brain can store memories – a soul can't."* A conscious can store memories so it appears that these beings are no longer linked to the conscious.

"Confused" is a frequent descriptor. Those who remain earthbound in this form seem to still possess a self and an emotional will but not the conscious. It is possible their conscious had a loose attachment to begin with. There are living people who can be described in similar terms: those so far immersed in endoreality that they may as well not have memories, those so dominated by their emotional will that the conscious appears to have abandoned them, those who cannot escape addictions and those who suck energy from others. Most accounts confirm that death does not cause any great character transformation.

According to Marietta Davis, who experienced this world, *"the sufferings of the lost ... are self-created. Addictions loom large."*[113] A large part of the suffering or joy seems related to the company the deceased find themselves in. Those who have predatory relationships instead of connections may have difficulty releasing from debt or credit imbalances upon decoupling, since those imbalances act as strong bonds in life as well.

The cold associated with earthbound spirits is in sharp contrast to the heat of light or fire associated with heaven or hell. Perhaps the earthbound lacked the energy to proceed. If they were murdered, perhaps their death energy was taken. The strategy employed in ritual killings seems to be intent on extracting as much anima as possible from a victim before their death in order to retain their power. That may occur in most murders, giving rise to all the stories of victims who remain to haunt their killers.

In the case of the killers, they are weighed down by the debt owed. The animist transactions to gain power that people have made throughout history take power through extractions of life energy. This life energy feeds not only them, but also spirit predators who support them for that reason. The cost to them is through damnation to becoming one of the predators they fed.

In some cases, it appears that both conscious and self are still present in earthbound spirits, as well as will. Perhaps the death energy provides the power to decouple them all. Extreme fear, worry or torment may deplete that energy prior to decoupling and keep the spirit here. This may be the root of stories of spirits who were able to rest once the person who wronged them is exposed and punished. They may have achieved balance by extracting anima from the punishment of their predator. In lieu of that escape, they may attempt to extract it from other living things. At least, that is what seems to be described in many ghost stories.

Ellwood relates a ghost experiencer who *"mentions feeling that she had "lost power to the figure."* The idea that the deceased draw energy out of the living in order to meet their own needs and to manifest as ghosts appears frequently. ... Feelings of cold have also been interpreted as a symptom of this process. Such psychic vampirism is consistent with the needy, addicted nature of the earthbound spirits."

The need for the dead to have an energy push and encouragement to help them along the way, as well as the fear that they may get stuck in limbo (terrifying from the perspective of both the dead and the living) are both ideas found in cultures throughout history. These stories often feature anima imbalance (either way). Debt and credit both cause bonds that are difficult to break.

Stories often relate to murder (either side) which acts in the same way as other anima debt or credit. Malevolent spirits, whether of dead people or other earth or animal spirits, typically appear to collect or avenge a debt or are unable to leave because they themselves are indebted. Ill fortune was and is often considered by animists to be caused by a debt incurred to a spirit.

Credit may cause a heavy heart if it is not honoured and is left as a burden to be borne by the creditor. The focus on forgiveness in some religious ideologies and in mental health therapy recognizes that the damage caused by unreleased credit can be as great or greater than debt. Samhain and the Mexican Day of the Dead are both festivals which seek to reconcile debt and credit for earthbound spirits through prayer and offerings, or shared anima. Both festivals are greatly condensed Christian reworkings of the original animist sacrificial cycles which occurred at around the same time. The Ghost Festival, or Hungry Ghost Festival in Asia is another spirit festival held in August and September with offerings and help for earthbound spirits to move on, along with religious instruction.

It would be extremely helpful for the living if we could help these vampire wills. Perhaps there will come a time when we know how to help people not become earthbound and it will become safe for our minds to lift the endoreality veil. That day will certainly not arrive while we are denying that the veil exists or that anything lies behind it. Instead of conceiving of parallel universes where the negations of our reality exist, we could explore the ancient thought of worlds beyond the veil, where our expanded self exists.

Psychologist Edith Fiore listed reasons that decoupled wills may become stuck as: *"ignorance, confusion, fear (especially of going to hell), obsessive attachments to living persons or places, or addictions to drugs, alcohol, smoking, food or sex. Also a misguided sense of unfinished business often compels spirits to stay in the physical world. Some remain determined to get revenge."* [114]

Fiore says attached spirits produce *"low energy level, character shifts or mood swings, inner voices, abuse of drugs, impulsive behaviour, memory problems, poor concentration, anxiety, depression, physical symptoms with no cause"* in those they attach to. These are all signs of a dissociated or sublated conscious.

Fiore believes anaesthesia opens a person to invaders and that spirits congregate in hospitals, morgues and cemeteries or at times of bereavement. She is joined in this belief by most animist cultures and even most religions. Anaesthesia, illness and death all reduce the strength of the conscious and leave the emotional will in charge of the self. Presumably, this makes it much easier for malefic attachments to bond to the self. This is the principle behind the many traditions of isolation of women during menstruation and childbirth as well. Extreme pain and hormone fluctuations can make it difficult for the conscious to maintain control, as evidenced by many symptoms associated with menstruation, pregnancy and post partum.

If spirit attachment is past the limits of what seems believable, it will be discussed in a different context in *Free Will and Seductive Coercion* which looks at emotional and conscious control over will. Again, there is no established reason for believing a one to one relationship must always exist for the five components of a person and, in the case of will, there is much evidence of many conflicting wills vying for dominance in one person. The emotional will follows the dictates of the self which is not individuated, except through endosocial barriers. It is, therefore, open to being dominated by any attached will.

The topic of possession is better suited to *Free Will and Seductive Coercion,* but as used by Fiore, it appears to represent an energy sucking parasite usurping conscious control over will. Medical science is very familiar with such parasites in many forms, but it may also describe the emotional will. Endogroups are a structure which enables the sublation of an individual will to an external person or group. *The Creation of Me, Them and Us* describes this scenario among the living; Fiore suggests the same relationships can exist with the unliving.

We have already explored the connection of the self to objects, rites and people in different spacetimes, so there does not seem any reason the self could not connect to any disembodied animus. There is no reason to assume there must a be a one to one relationship between a person and a self. The symptoms Fiore and others describe, mood swings, memory blanks, inner voices, and foreign character and ailments, along with a loss of control over will, all seem to indicate the influence of a separate will. Difficulty concentrating indicates difficulty for the conscious to gain control over will.

The self is a network of interactions involving many sources of will influencing each person through emotional signaling. The idea of possession seems to imply that decoupled energy clusters can attach to a person's self (or they are attached before decoupling) and continue to exert this influence. All accounts of possession involve some form of initial interaction between the possessed and the spirit.

According to Fiore, all past life regressions she did with those who were possessed showed them having possessed someone themselves at some point. In other words, their anima debt seemed to attract these debt collectors. The symptoms of possession she listed are also all symptoms of shame. Perhaps "low energy level, character shifts or mood swings, inner voices, abuse of drugs, impulsive behaviour, memory problems, poor concentration, anxiety, depression, physical symptoms with no cause", all traits of both shame and most endoselves, manifest as the possession. Perhaps the dark energy some insist they see or feel in these cases is the manifestation of the energy debt caused by attached guilt and an attached spirit is simply an attached guilt.

That does not exclude the possibility that the possession is also all the things it is experienced to be, such as an energy cluster from a decoupled person. Both things can be true; the guilt can attract a decoupled cluster which causes the experience of shame. Shame is an emotional pain that indicates deanimation. That energy loss can just as easily be lost to a wandering decoupled animus as to any other environmental source.

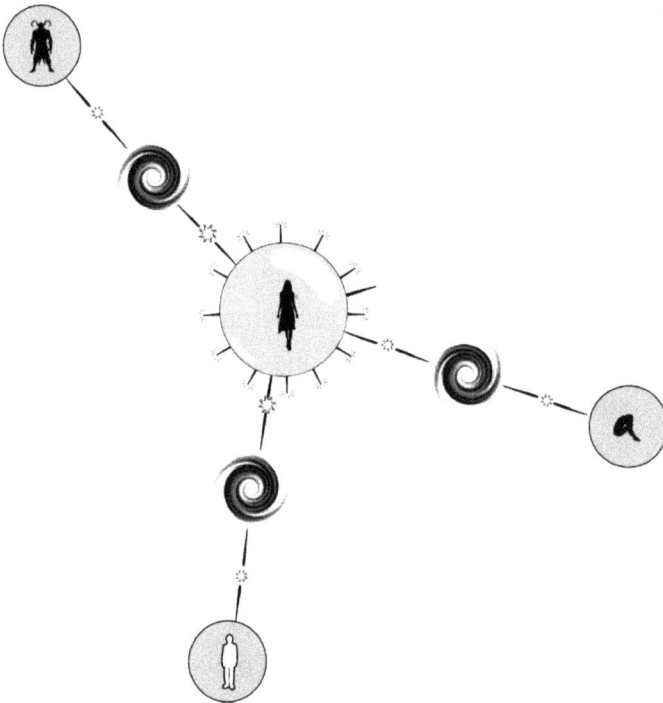

Figure 33: Self with an attached negative image

It appears that hell really is below and heaven above, aligning with gravity. Needy beings that cannot access primary anima and instead hunt for secondary cannot rise out of the earthly realm. The focus of the lost souls is towards earth, preventing their awareness of, or attraction to, primary (conscious) anima above. They try to pull back those who are traveling upwards very much like the needy and addicted do when they are alive. Both of these attributes are a replica of the behaviour of those trapped in an endogroup. It is possible there is not a sudden shift in behaviour upon leaving the body but a filtering by level of earthly attachment, represented by a lack of ability to access primary anima. Attachment is to secondary sources which are earthbound.

Earthbound spirits could be the source of the emotional wills which occupy us and cause such distress while we are living. Addiction and destructiveness among the living cause people to live in misery when they could very easily be living a joyful existence otherwise. The same behaviour seems to continue for some after death. As one person put it, *"the actual situation in hell is one of gray, dreary crowds rather than torment."*[115]   That is also the situation in much of the living world. These *"self-damned spirits"* seem to lack either the will or the desire to escape. According to one person, *"It seems that the frightening and painful aspects are sometimes caused by, or strongly linked to, the experiencer's resistance."* That resistance sounds very much like the emotional will which rejects so much joy in life.

Psychologist Edith Fiore wrote, *"These lost souls appear to be as limited in their ability to travel as we are."* Time and space is real for whatever part remains earthbound. Those that remain tied to the earth, "seemingly unaware" of what lies above them may be unable to traverse to the next dimension due to greater mass. By some accounts, there are different dimensions with different qualities and occasionally a choice of where to stay. The choice is usually, perhaps always, to go back or down a level, never up.

Is choice (the uncertainty principle) only present

with gravity? Does will require life? The choice to live or not appears to be bound to the earthly plane, still affected by gravity and life. The will of the vampire people is also in the earthly plane.

Do the people who remain refuse to relinquish their will? Is that why so many theologies taught the surrender of will?

Does the I no longer exist in the purest level of conscious? If I is tied to the dominant will, there would be no need for it in a realm composed solely of knowledge.

So many questions! It is time for some speculation, which we will begin in the next chapter, The nature of living, and continue in Part 3, The Meaning of Life.

Decoupled

a person whose five elements (body, self, life, will and consciousness) have been dissociated from each other and are no longer bound into a unified person.

Primary anima seems to be obtained from conscious and secondary anima from life.

The purpose of a lifespan is to expend life so the person is not weighed down with it during death.

The will may exist temporarily after death. Self and will may be able to escape the confines of the body (or, more likely, they were never limited to it) but be unable to go where conscious can. Conscious cannot effect change, or exert will, without being bound by the confines of the gravity sphere.

Death experiences that escape the gravitational field describe light, or a photon-like world.

Love is the experience of a flow of energy through connection.

Love, experienced as joy, is an emotion commonly described by those who ascend to the world of light, or photons, or conscious.

I is the dominant will.

Earthbound spirits may be anima clusters with imbalance, either debt or credit. They may retain emotional will, self and sometimes even conscious.

Possession may be a negative energy cluster which attaches to a self as a manifestation of guilt.

Shame may be deanimation caused by extraction of anima in response to guilt.

Anima bloat may cause a decoupled animus to slip into a saddle formation, or hell. Emotional pain and burning may be an attempt to reduce anima bloat.

Tunnels may be wormholes to a different plane.

Void experiences may be caused by a lack of attraction to

primary anima.

Inverted experiences may be caused by the reversed poles of the endoself.

A life review may be the experience of rising above spacetime.

Past lives may be just the experience of an extended self, not necessarily their own self.

Abstracting Divinity

Chapter 14

The nature of living

There is nothing that living things do that cannot be understood from the point of view that they are made of atoms acting according to the laws of physics. — Richard P. Feynman.

Humanity, as a corporal form, is a system of order. As such, it must always be at war with the predominantly chaotic nature of the universe. Every life form is an endosocial creation in which will is exerted and energy is harnessed to create a united system or an object-self. Energy is burned to create order, which is why we eventually run out of life energy.

What in physics is referred to as the macroscopic state of equilibrium is the appearance of order in what appears to be an object but is really a cluster of interactions. Our inability to see the true state is the result of an endofilter. We see an endoreality created by the human brain.

If there is a real or perceived spacetime membrane surrounding each interaction, perhaps this is the same type of membrane that surrounds larger groups of interactions and prevents, or appears to prevent, outside permeability. Perhaps the same bubble that allows one interaction to take place scales up to create the semi-impermeable clusters we know as objects. Perhaps this is also the endosocial membrane that bonds clusters of clusters, or groups of individual objects into endogroups. The endosocial membrane may be the spacetime membrane. Both may be the product of the dominant will.

This would explain the mortality of the endoself and the immortality of the exoself. The testimony in the preceding chapter made clear that it was the refusal or inability of earthbound spirits to see options that trapped them. The thicker spacetime membrane will trap energy and weigh down an endoself whether that membrane is universally real or only real in endoreality. If the will which creates interactions perceives it as real, the will cannot, or will not, act outside the bounds of that reality. What we refer to as the endosocial membrane is the refusal of the will to allow interactions outside of the bubble it has created.

Any additional energy affects gravity, resulting in additional weight. The equation $E=mc2$, illustrates how energy and mass can be produced from each other. Higher energy creates greater mass. In string theory, the mass of a particle is the energy of the vibrating string. This relates to the discussion on secondary anima at the beginning of this book. Secondary anima is available on the destruction of ordered objects because mass converts to energy.

No mass indicates a state of peace because there is no action possible and no attraction and repulsion acting on energy. This is reminiscent of the peace of higher (lower mass) post-death experience. Bad decoupled experiences indicate that surplus energy (mass) still remains. Anima bloat may make it harder to resist earth gravity and it may cause the mortality of the endoself.

In general relativity, acceleration is relative to the gravitational field. Acceleration is greater where gravity is stronger, which is why time passes more quickly at a height relative to something closer to earth. Matter and energy cause spacetime to warp and curve. Spacetime is the incarnation of gravity, with its warps and bends.

Our view of reality is only one of a vast number according to the curves of relativity. The creation of endogroups traps the energy that was once contained in individual bodies and creates a solid mass of inward energy with one viewpoint and one dominant will and one perception of reality. The creation of a person has the same effect. Both are illusions of one time and space because they share the endoreality of the dominant will.

Spacetime is created by will and life energy. Life energy acts in a very similar way to gravity and they may be the same thing, the inverted force towards order. If life is a force attracting interaction clusters to each other as objects, life may be simply gravity itself. Many traditions, seen in martial arts and yoga but also in dance and other rituals in most animist traditions, either explicitly or implicitly indicate a belief that life energy comes from the earth. Grounding in martial arts takes energy from the earth and from gravity to resist attack.

The energy of the gravitational field can become negative. Positive pressure pushes outward and adds to attractive gravity. Negative pressure sucks inward and adds to repulsive gravity. Gravity, expressed through the emotional will, strives to conserve and accumulate energy. Gravity is the endosocial force which acts in opposition to the exosocial force, the force towards greater entropy.

Perhaps it is life, or the emotional will, not mass, that restricts the general theory of relativity to objects with significant mass. Mass is simply a cluster of interactions. It is will that creates an endoreality which binds these clusters into objects.

The inflaton field is a theoretical field that accelerated the expansion of the universe. According to Brian Greene in *The Fabric of the Cosmos*,[116] "*the inflaton field is a gravitational parasite – it feeds on gravity – and so the total energy the inflaton field carried increased as space expanded – the energy density of the inflaton field remained constant throughout the inflationary phase of rapid expansion.*"

According to Greene, "*the inflaton field "mines" energy from gravity*" by virtue of its negative pressure. Whether this field exists or not, it is interesting to examine the work around it to understand the force driving the emotional will to suck energy to itself in order to maintain its own stores. The emotional will also seems driven by a gravitational parasite, resulting in a drive to accumulate a type of energy associated with life and mass.

If life may be gravity, conscious may be light. The combined speed of any object through space and through time is always equal to the speed of light. A moving object therefore experiences slower time than a stationary one. Light always travels through space at the speed of light and therefore experiences no time. The conscious is the timeless element of the person that remains during decoupling when even the will is gone.

Red light therapy uses specific photons to stimulate mitochondria in cells to produce more adenosine triphosphate (ATP). This provides energy to living cells and is also claimed to improve mood. Mood disorders such as seasonal affective disorder are related to an absence of light. Primary anima is the source of euphoria. Primary anima may be related to photons.

We are attracted to fire and light regardless of our need for them. We fear dark and dislike cold. We gather around the fireplace, not the refrigerator. A lighted home is inviting, the dark outside is not. Few people do not enjoy light and sunshine. Many people find their mood shifts to sadness when the days become shorter and darker. If light and warmth seem like home to us, perhaps it is because we are from the world of photons.

The higher plane of conscious is warm and the earthbound plane is cold. In that case, is it the conscious plane that provides the heat energy for life? Is living an attempt to rescue those trapped in the cold? Does life move towards states of greater entropy because conscious energy is occupying life energy? Are we photons?

The I of our conscious may indeed be photons. At least, no other likely contender has presented itself. According to Greene, *"a massless particle like a photon or graviton corresponds to a string executing the most placid and gentle vibrational pattern it possibly can."*[117] If our conscious is photons, or something similar, it may not have the energy to exert will and create interactions unless it merges with an animus, or ordered object. Creating interactions requires energy. It requires energy to exert will. Conscious may require gravitational energy from an object with mass in order to cause action.

Secondary euphoria seems to result from exposure to life energy which is related to gravity and macroscopic objects. Primary euphoria appears to accompany exercise of the conscious will, that which follows the second law of thermodynamics. Without conscious focus, beauty brings no joy. It may prove to be more apt to call primary anima conscious anima and secondary anima life anima, but that is premature. Once we have a better understanding of these energies, we will hopefully be able to name them with more accuracy, perhaps something related to gravitons or photons or whatever it is they prove to be.

The purpose of living is to create interactions through attractions to states of higher entropy. The attraction to a state of greater entropy is manifested through the conscious will. For the conscious will, the pursuit of happiness is the pursuit of greater entropy. For the emotional will, the pursuit of happiness is the pursuit of lower entropy. The conscious will joins or attaches to an object to compel interactions towards greater entropy. The quantum will also follows a path to greater entropy, leaving both the conscious and the quantum wills in opposition to the emotional will. As usual, this is explained in much greater detail in *Free Will and Seductive Coercion*.

Figure 34: Emotional will and concious will

The emotional will creates order and the conscious will disperses it. The tendency to chaos, or the exosocial drive, pushes towards the dispersal of energy clusters. This tendency may cause our drive to egalitarianism.

Life may be the energy used to create interactions and time may be seen as the link which provides sequence between the interactions. The attraction between interactions is will and it may be directed by either the conscious drive towards greater entropy (the conscious will) or the emotional drive towards order (the emotional will). Will creates time.

Life is not a state which is controlled by a binary on or off switch. It is an energy which can accumulate as power or be depleted to the point of death. Life is that energy which combines with mass to create spacetime. Will is the acceleration or attraction which propels an object through spacetime, or creates spacetime, via interactions. Conscious is timeless knowledge. Conscious is all that exists. Will is the creator and conscious is the creation.

Life, by this definition, is the energy that created the universe. Given this definition, there is no reason why an object such as a house or an idea such as this one you are reading or a rite such as preparing an old family recipe does not contain life. In fact, if life is the energy that creates interactions, all of those things must contain life.

Will can only be exercised alongside gravity, which correlates with life, as will is the catalyst that creates interactions and life is the energy that powers interactions. Will is what creates the unidirectional nature of events. The choice made by will collapses the wave of potential outcomes into one irreversible outcome. The order of these outcomes is time.

Figure 35: Time progression

In defining will as the chooser behind the choice made to create reality, we have not only introduced god into the fabric of the universe, but we have made everyone potentially god. The act of creating reality is open to whoever controls the will, which is why those exerting control over the will of others are often and accurately accused of playing god.

Henry More said that if space were empty it could not exist, but it is filled with spirit. Gottfried Leibniz believed that space did not exist except as a manner to refer to things relative to each other. Newton declared absolute space to be the sensorium of God and filled by *"spiritual substance"*. These opinions may all be true.

Will is what creates the unidirectional nature of events.

Nothing does not exist. Higgs field fills all of space. Mass is a measure of resistance to acceleration through Higgs field. Electromagnetic force and weak nuclear force are part of the same force, separated only by their different interactions with Higgs field. Photons pass completely unhindered through Higgs field and so have no mass at all. If Higgs field did not exist, all fundamental particles would have no mass, like the photon.

Far too often, scientists claim to disprove something when all they have really done is rename it. Higgs field and Henry More's divine spirit share all the same attributes and are therefore synonyms. Higgs field is More's spirit. Both are just words with no clear definitions, the earlier bowing to a religious endo-ideal and the later renaming for a scientific endo-ideal. All we really know about More's spirit / Higgs field is that it is the thing that causes particles to have mass. It is the creator of material reality, so More probably deserves more credit for accuracy. Certainly, the nature of the field is unchanged with the renaming.

If the notion of an omnipresent god takes the form of universal conscious and universal will, then such a being not only can be said to exist, but it may be considered The Being, the state that encompasses everything. This is not an external force that is acting upon a collection of wayward children, however. It is a state of which everyone is a part and it agrees with Leibniz as well. The Millennarians appear to have been more correct on this point than the organized religions that crushed them.

If the conscious is all that is, and it is conscious control over will which creates order, or macroscopic objects, then possibly Higgs field and More's spirit are both synonyms for the conscious. The idea of the conscious creating order may seem contradictory to the conscious will's drive towards greater entropy. The apparent contradiction will be explained further in the Agents of order and Agents of chaos chapters.

Quantum indeterminacy, or the probability cloud which precedes all interactions, even at the most elemental level of existence, includes will. It is will that determines the choice from the probability cloud. Just because the will does not always involve human consciousness does not mean it is not there.

If time is will, space may be conscious. The universe is made of interactions and is the location of interactions. Conscious may be full awareness of all interactions or it may be all interactions. The latter is a simpler solution: conscious is all that is. If conscious was defined as awareness, it requires an outside entity to be aware and we are left with a need to define the outside entity.

Electromagnetic force interacts with electrically charged particles like electrons and quarks but not with uncharged particles such as gravitons. Perhaps electromagnetic force is the vehicle of the conscious will and gravity is the vehicle of the emotional will. Certainly, pollution of the electromagnetic field makes it difficult to concentrate, which is to exert energy through the conscious will.[118]

As discussed in the chapter, The Nature of Time, there is no universal present time. If the present does not exist then how is it possible to live or not live in the present? According to some people who have decoupled, it is possible to move throughout spacetime and experience any interaction, including those that did not involve what they considered their self. It appears to be the will that is experiencing.

Will decoupled from life appears free of constraints which bind it to the present. The self has no bounds outside those which are placed on it by endoreality and the untethered will can move freely throughout the self. Many elders seem to have the ability to experience this untethering as well. Elders often seem to be experiencing interactions which, from the perspective of observers, are in the past or perhaps sometimes, in the future or outside the bounds of their usual individuated self.

One resuscitated person described the decoupled experience, *"I feel pity for my suffering self but not more than I would for a stranger in pain. ... I am my remembering self, and the experiencing self, who does my living, is like a stranger to me."*[119] The conscious, or what she refers to as her remembering self, is no longer connected to the self, which she refers to as her experiencing self.

Then is a person truly alive after death? The nature of the self is that the interactions still exist in the spacetime they were created in. The will (emotional, conscious or quantum) which directed the interactions is still manifested in them. The life energy which created each interaction is still an inherent part of it. The self still exists but is unable to continue expansion, at least without the assistance of outside wills.

The decoupled I does not identify as the self, life or will, however. The fully decoupled I always seems to remain tied to the conscious, even though the person may identify as the emotional will or self before fully decoupling. The conscious can no longer manifest a will without life energy, but the will may still have some form of existence in some cases, as explored in The nature of death chapter.

The I that is conscious may not be alive after death, but it could not really be considered alive while the person was living either, since it remains unchanged after decoupling. The real answer to the question Is there life after death? is that the question is not nearly as interesting as it is usually held to be. What people seem to really want to know is Is there existence after death? Since life is only one of the five elements of a person, there is much more to that question than the presence of life. We will go further into that discussion in the chapter To be or not to be.

Bizarrely, the physical sciences are far ahead of the social sciences in recognizing that material reality is an illusion. This is strange because that knowledge is far more intuitively obvious in the social realm. Surely, it is easier to intuit the nature of an interactional exoself and the fact that, in each interaction, the two components each become a small part of the other's interactional self, than it is to intuit quantum entanglement. Endoreality has succeeded in keeping the social sciences well over a century behind the physical sciences despite the ease of observation in the social realm. This fact ought to trigger serious questions about the effectiveness of empiricism under endoreality.

Flows exist; objects do not. Particles are points of interaction in an energy flow. The world is made up of only particles (collapsed waves) and fields. Spacetime is a field. Interactions are particles. Space is conscious, time is will, interactions are the self, bound by life energy. Every person is action.

A person is tied to a filtered and artificially individuated piece of the self. It is individuated by the experience of the emotional will. It ceases to be individuated when the conscious fully decouples.

If a person can exert conscious control over will, they can control time, as yogis, shamans, martial artists and many others have attested. If someone is in a fully decoupled state, they are only conscious and no longer experience spacetime. Many who have decoupled have told of the ability to be anywhere they choose and to relive moments in the past and even the future and beyond the confines of what they considered their self.

If any of the suggestions in this chapter are true, we have a lot to think about regarding the nature of life. In Part 3, let's turn our attention to how this affects our view of the meaning of life.

The emotional will creates order and the conscious will disperses it.

The endosocial membrane may be the spacetime membrane. Both may be the product of the dominant will.

What we refer to as the endosocial membrane is the refusal of the will to allow interactions outside of the bubble it has created.

Life is the energy used to create interactions and time is the attraction between interactions.

Will is time.

Self is interactions.

Conscious is space.

Conscious may be photons.

Life may be gravity.

Abstracting Divinity

The Meaning

of life

Abstracting Divinity

Chapter 15

The death of joy

After a battle of 30 years, I have emerged the victor: I have liberated humanity from superfluous ornamentation. — Adolf Loos

Adolf Loos was an influential polemicist and architect who lived from 1870 to 1933. He married briefly three times and was eventually convicted of sexualized violation of impoverished girls aged 8 to 10. From whatever vantage that gave him, he declared that *"All art is erotic."* and therefore, all ornamentation was the work of *"criminals and degenerates."* His work was devoted to the de-ornamentation of everything. In a lecture since published as Ornament and Crime he declared, *"The evolution of culture is synonymous with the removal of ornament from utilitarian objects."*[120]

While he made some valid points such as, ornament *"is no longer organically linked with our culture"* and *"has absolutely no human connexions"*, and he also decried unnecessary labour and the use of fashion to drive consumerism, for Loos, ornamentation was aesthetically repulsive. He claimed this view as a symbol of higher status. *"I can tolerate the ornaments of the ... peasant ... for they all have no other way of attaining the high points of their existence [but] anyone who goes to the Ninth Symphony and then sits down and designs a wallpaper is either a confidence trickster or a degenerate."*

Loos is one of many theorists who spearheaded a Brutalist revolution in industrial and home design that has brought us to the state of fast fashion and disposable homes we are in now. Some of these theorists were justly railing against the meaningless and poor quality pastiche that was pasted onto items targeted at the new middle class. Many were just cynically removing expensive ornamentation for increased profit and convincing the middle class it was a sign of good taste. Some were projecting what was truly their own taste.

An economic structure which caters to the taste of endoselves values the most monotonous sameness, the most ugly, over innovative creativity and joy. Totalitarian states put people in grey cement cities, grey cars and grey clothes, make them eat tasteless processed food from plastic packages and fill all their time with solitary busywork. Community meals with sharing and conversation is replaced with rushed and solitary ingestion of food. Joy is reviled and those who enjoy are reprimanded. Original thought and a love of discovery or creation is shunned as weird. Laziness, hostility and apathy are celebrated as natural.

Everyone in this world wears, drives and lives in black, beige, brown and grey. These colours are proven to cause depression [121] [122] and depression is a symptom of deanimation. Walls are all painted the same colour, chosen by the building manager. If an occupant owns the residence, then the colours are chosen by that disembodied tastemaker, the resale value. Colours (or lack of colours) are chosen to be soothing to endoselves instead of joyful to anyone else.

Walls must not have anything hung on them lest the hook is charged against the damage deposit or diminishes the resale value. Furniture is no longer designed for the home or built in situ. Instead, it is thrown out upon each move so that each new owner can bring their own generic, grey, newness. Grey couches and white dishes fill the brown, grey and white boxes that serve as holding coffins until the occupants are ready for permanent ones. Clothing is formless and generic, buildings are disposable and toxic and parks look like prison yards. Creativity, originality and embellishment are scowled upon. Everyone lives in institutional ugliness, a Stalinist nightmare of strangled beauty and fearful conformity.

The body is policed and moderated at all times. It must not stop unless it sits or stands in line. It must never run or jump or climb unless it pays to do so in designated areas in designated uniforms. It has forgotten how to sing or dance. It walks, or sits, and loses all ability to do anything else.

Dance, sport and art, once the focus of euphoric frenzies, are now carefully contained to authorized participants in corporate timeslots. Communities in the grip of totalitarianism recoil at the sight of people singing and dancing in daily life. The prevention of dancing, singing, running, games, social gathering, and all other euphoric release ensures traumatic bonding to schools and paid employment.

The first thing that any predator does is remove or restrict all anima conduits but those they control. Once behaviour limited to households, this deanimation and manufactured dependence has spread to states and beyond. Now supranational corporations monitor and control stimuli responses and keep most of the world on a drip feed with only the bare amount of joy required to exist. It is then very simple to encourage addiction in these starved people.

The squares where people once gathered are now occupied with speeding cars, a lethal threat against connection. People are trapped inside their squares and allotted crossing times. Their thoughts and senses are filled with threat and noise from traffic which also blocks scent, beauty and connection. White noise and pollution both cause isolation from sensory input.

Perfume is offensive. Colour is offensive. Music is offensive. The smell and sound of industrial pollution and a world of brown, grey and black is neutral, the default position. An entire industry of critics is employed to ensure that no one can enjoy anything without being accused of bad taste, bad politics or impropriety, the industrial equivalent of moral police. Rites have lost meaning and are now declared to be property and used increasingly out of context and for commercial purposes only. Joy is a radical departure from industrial-mandated norms. Puritan religions forbade enjoyment of any kind and so does industrialization.

The industrial aesthetic is the only thing uglier than the narco-chic alternative of gold toilets and pet tigers. Neither permit the beauty of primary anima, that produced from labour and joy. Expensive art is usually used as a money-laundering tool for the wealthy who seldom have any idea how to access primary anima. This is the taste, or lack thereof, that industrialized art is based on.

Art was the creation of work to uplift people and help them transcend the trials of the self. Art was an infusion of primary anima. Art is not defined by its ability to provoke a reaction, usually one of shock and revulsion, as the industrial aesthetic insists that it is. That is a redefinition of the word and appropriation of the concept.

Beauty is not subjective. Beauty is found in primary anima. Art is not subjective. Art is work which channels primary anima or acts as a capacitor for primary anima.

Endoselves do not have an attraction to beauty. Their experience of the joy of beauty is through aping the reactions of others. Art produces an emotional response of euphoria in those with healthy anima conduits and revulsion in endoselves, but it is still art in either case.

Aesthetics has gone from being a celebration and exploration of primary anima to a challenge to primary anima. Art is most celebrated and valued now when it depicts the grotesque and the shocking. Its proponents say this type of art stimulates thought. In reality, it causes the exosocial viewer to recoil, and that is its purpose. A great deal of art is now designed to block anima conduits instead of establishing and opening them. This is a celebration and exploration of secondary anima. Attempts to create beauty in art are now dismissed as pastiche or unsophisticated. Art is now encouraged to be an exploration of the ugly.

Ugly was once felt to be not simply aesthetically displeasing but spiritually dangerous. The word ugly has lost the feeling of dread and horror that once accompanied it as ugly is increasingly normalized and held to be subjective. Ugly is subjective, but only in determining whether the subject is an exo- or endoself.

The words first world, industrialized, western, civilized, educated, and enlightened, all have a purity test which is disenchantment. Anything of joy, anything that smells like the earth or feels like fond attachment or involves engagement in the moment of existence is proclaimed to be anti-progress, irrational and unscientific. Enchantment refers to a world full of conscious connection to sources of primary anima. Later forms of what Weber termed inner-worldly and outer-worldly asceticism[123]   sought dissociation instead of connection. Their goal was not to restore the health of anima ties but to sever them completely.

Excitement, the anticipation of anima, is discouraged as naive and childish. The joy of elders is institutionally sneered at and pathologized as senility just as joy in children is pathologized as immaturity and in adults as simple-mindedness. The ability to freely access primary anima is pathologized by those without the ability.

This classification of joy as pathology is then used to isolate all of the above target groups, restrict their access to primary anima and make them easily preyed upon. It is not coincidence that children, elders and those classified as simple-minded are all primary targets of predators and prime targets for institutionalizing. Meanwhile, an inability to experience joy is celebrated and idealized.

Religion has been credited with the creation of great art, but it simply captured and controlled it. Sacred places of peace and beauty may be very healing, but they do not need to be patrolled by religious authorities. Religion was compelled to use great art to attract worshipers, but it has periodic ascetic purges in which it destroys all art and beauty and even history. This cuts all ties that worshipers have established with beautiful objects in order to re-establish their traumatized dependence on the religious endo-ideal.

Death was the ultimate dissociation. Organized religion depicted heaven and hell as a continuation of war and a quest for delayed justice, both reward and punishment. Scientific dissociation insisted that after death there is nothing, a far more illogical, undefined and fantastical idea than heaven or hell.

Denial of any meaning or value to life or its enjoyment contributed to an outlook which saw life as an endurance test or recurring punishment. Primary anima was then seen as fool's gold or contemptible weakness. This outlook first sought the pre-eminence of conscious, or the lifeless mind, over the body, life and self. Now it seeks full immersion in the self and denial of the conscious.

Rejection of joy is rejection of debt. Those who seek power often reject enjoyment of it in an attempt to avoid the resulting debt. This is one root of the rejection of both the body and the world. The chimes and monotonous routines of monkish asceticism have similarities with the endless white noise, traffic, cubicles and condos of the industrialized world. Both produce dissociation of consciousness from the self. To watch the moment as an observer is to dissociate the conscious from the emotional self. The self does not passively observe events; it actively experiences them. In meditation, detachment can allow the person to fully experience their self or fully experience the conscious.

Some people deliberately seek to strengthen their conscious control over will by dissociating from their emotional self. This led to the idea that a complete lack of worldly joy and connection was required in order to attain otherworldly enlightenment. Combined with the idea that suffering in this life would be rewarded in the next, this led to a perceived superiority of ugliness and lack of bonded relationships. Frivolity and enjoyment were despised as emotional weakness and cruelty upheld as duty. Pursuit of every connection, human, animal, land, spiritual, thought, discovery and creation, was limited, controlled, dissociated and forbidden. This is outlined in much greater detail in *The Theft of Self*.

Industrialized life provides the detachment but ignores the conscious awareness of the emotional self that may be brought by meditation. Instead, the detached consciousness is distracted by busywork, external noise, plans for the future and obsessions about the past. The conscious is taught to decouple and ignore the self. The dissociation of industrialized life is used to silence conscious objections to the demands of the emotional will. It is impossible to create a connection to primary anima without conscious engagement, so this prolonged detachment creates an endoself.

In exosocial expansion, the emotions are in balance and the emotional and conscious will are in accord in their desires. In an endosocial structure, the emotions and conscious are at war with each other. This causes both a split in reality (discussed in *Shaping Reality*) and an internal war of wills (discussed in *Free Will and Seductive Coercion*).

As industrialization produces increasing dissociation, the household shrines which were replaced by ancestor photos were themselves replaced by department store stock photos. Rites became obligations which are now rejected. Worship became resented bureaucracy. Bonds with nature became plastic pollution tied on trees or floated down rivers for reasons no one recalls. Dissociated people will give their own dogs away, or abandon them, or have them killed and believe themselves when they depict murder as virtue and say the dogs are happier this way. They would be bemused and probably disgusted by a gift made by the giver instead of purchased from a stranger. Even gifts themselves are often seen as a grievance, and the recipients complain that they would rather just receive money. The idea of a gift as a euphoric object which binds the giver and the receiver is nearly completely lost in industrialization.

The very act of seeking meaning is seen as contemptible and weak under industrial endo-idealism, unless that meaning can be transformed into profit. Unavoidably, as endoselves become endo-ideals, pessimistic and nihilistic endosocial perspectives are the views which have been established as reality, throughout the world. Science aided industrial dissociation with its dogmatic denialism of anything outside of disconnected objects. Shared anima was denied. Connection to each other and the other creatures of the earth or earth itself was replaced with binary endosocial division: chosen or not, good or evil, heaven or earth.

Asceticism, particularly in its animist form, is an attempt to reconcile anima debt. Deprivation is encouraged to avoid incurring debt and suffering is encouraged to repay it. Asceticism by a person with functioning anima conduits is a method of reducing anima bloat. This autophagy of energy promotes health, renews anima conduits and energy, reduces anima debt and its accompanying guilt and provides exhilaration.

Consumption is anti-asceticism. The religious quest for full conscious control and a repressed emotional will became the reverse under industrial endo-idealism. Non-stop distractions, addictions and focus on the future disable conscious control or even presence in the moment. Lives are lived in full service to the self, through immediate gratification from drugs and entertainment or dissociation through plastic surgery or dreams of escape to Mars. Disenchantment brought an emptiness which is filled by endoself gluttony.

Unbearable boredom and covetuousness are the two states of the endoself

Asceticism in an endoself is their attempt to eliminate objects of desire from their lives as the source of their addictive and spiraling misery. Unbearable boredom and covetuousness are the two states of the endoself. Their solution to misery is a wait for death and a refusal to participate in the life they cannot enjoy. The personality type referred to by Freudians as a narcissist usually has more in common with Midas than Narcissus. The ascetic relief they seek is from the cycle of hope and disappointment with which they approach each possible contact and destroy it instead of connecting with it. With no anima conduits, however, asceticism alone is an outward display of inward misery and seldom stops the person from their spiteful attacks on the anima conduits of everyone else.

Puritans and their ilk were not depriving themselves of pleasure. They were blocking pleasure for everyone else and deriving their own form of euphoria from the deprivation of others. Puritanism, like the Inquisition and many other sacrificial festivals, provided righteousness to the predator which absolved them from guilt. Like the tyrant who receives anima from sacrifices, Puritans gained power from the asceticism they forced onto others and the righteous cruelty they could inflict by severing animated connections and destroying euphoric objects.

For the endoself, objects of desire replace anima conduits. They strive for ownership and control instead of connection and experience. To deny access and to destroy is as satisfying to them as possession and ownership. They will often substitute one of these methods of control for the other if the first is denied. Since their objective is not to enjoy beauty, ownership for them is the satisfaction of depriving others of what they are hoarding and that deprivation is also achievable through destruction. Industrialization has increased accumulation of objects as possessions, but their euphoric value has decreased.

An ideological war has been waged for the last few centuries between the Stoics and religious ascetists and the Epicureans, including most animists, who fully immersed themselves in earthly joy. This standoff seldom, if ever, acknowledges different experiences of worldly pleasure. For an exoself, those with working conduits to primary anima, worldly pleasure brings joy and exosocial expansion. Prolonged deprivation is extremely painful because it results in unrequited connections and starvation of those conduits. To an endoself, attempted experience with primary anima brings bitterness, craving, and ultimately, an overwhelming impulse to destruction. Asceticism is not a great accomplishment in one who experiences primary anima with revulsion.

There are three forms of asceticism. One, debt asceticism, causes joy, or at least relief, through the release from debt and guilt brought by a lessening of anima bloat. This asceticism can also be used to exchange for a credit, for example, people who do not eat when worried. The second, punitive asceticism, is a form of self-flagellation, debasement, deprivation or severe challenge in which the target extracts anima from their own stores (auto-anima) through punishment and shaming. They appear to then experience euphoria from the release of anima, just as predators experience euphoria when anima is released from their prey. This type of asceticism is often a result of stress brought by guilt which was either earned or unjustly assigned. The third, Tantalus asceticism, causes a slight lessening of the cravings of an endoself by removing from view objects they are unable to possess.

Endoselves seem to see their misery as an unredeemed credit which would explain why they appear to feel the world owes them. The asceticism of endoselves is definitely not aimed at debt reduction through service or hardship or reanimation through the release of auto-anima. Instead, they reject anything that would cause them to feel gratitude or acknowledge another's kindness. In forgoing sources of primary anima, they reject connections. Both Tantalus asceticism and dissociation from potential debt seem to motivate endoselves.

The retreat of will from the conscious to the self has progressed to the body, a true object self. Not only is conscious dissociated, emotions are increasingly silenced by drugs or manipulated by commercial coercion. The endoself that could not create connections banished the self. The endoself that could not experience joy banished emotions. The search for joy through conscious or self has been replaced by a quest to control every aspect of the body.

Today's self-loathing is abetted by plastic surgery. People seek their authentic self in their reflection in the mirror or online. They ignore the self they create with their interactions. The object self is left with no perception of who they are outside of what is reflected back at them, a reflection increasingly created and controlled by themselves. Effort that would formerly have been devoted to relationships is spent in therapy, creating an interactional self without the interactions to ensure it is the product of one perspective.

Today's body-worship manifests in the self care industry. A large amount of time is now spent on fitness, skin, hair and general health care where it would once have been devoted to caring for family or working for community, religion or industry. People who would once have spent all of their money and time to buy a car, house and other possessions are now buying dinner, travel and other experiences. Billionaires who would once have sought posterity through the creation of monuments or descendants now just seek to live forever.

The ornamentation deplored by Adolf Loos has moved from the home to the person to the body itself. Places like Vancouver, Canada are criticized as being not fashionable despite the phenomenal wealth of the population. In fact, the body is the fashion. It is displayed in the most basic athletic wear to not detract from the fortune in money, time and labour expended on the body. Ornamentation has moved from jewels and haute couture to tattoos and piercings to perfect muscles and perfect skin. Posterity is a picture on social media.

The focus that moved from the conscious to the self has moved again, to the body. The obsession which moved from preparation for the afterlife to unmitigated enjoyment of life has moved again, to prolonging life.

A focus on any of the elements of a person to the detriment of the others seems unhealthy. A balanced union of the conscious, self, body, life and will would be ideal. That may be what the world is starting to move toward.

Joy is found through experience of life by full conscious participation in every interaction. A study of women in France and the US found that French women experienced far more joy from eating than women in the US because they focused fully on the meal. Women in the US may spend more time eating or eat more, but since the culture has normalized multi-tasking while eating, it did not bring the same satisfaction. [124]

Secondary anima ought to be feared and shunned. Primary anima ought to be enjoyed to the fullest but then expended. In athleticism, it is recognized that energy must be consumed with relish and expended with even greater relish. Life should follow those principles. Generosity and gratitude are the twin traits of a healthy exosocial self. Pure happiness lies in the fullest exploration and development of as many anima conduits as possible and the maintenance of balance in interactions. Neither hoarding nor rejection of anima can bring peace or joy. The act of living is not to sit in the conscious, the self or the body but to experience the union of all elements.

So what do we need to allow us to follow these principles and achieve a joyful, peaceful life? Let's look at where we have arrived so far and try to identify some concrete guidelines in the next chapter.

Art

Creation which channels primary anima or acts as a

capacitor for primary anima.

Enchantment

A world full of conscious connection to sources of primary anima.

There are three forms of asceticism

Debt asceticism causes joy through the release from debt and guilt brought by a lessening of anima bloat.

Punitive asceticism is a form of self-flagellation, debasement, deprivation or severe challenge in which the target extracts anima from their own stores (auto-anima) through punishment and shaming.

Tantalus asceticism causes a slight lessening of the cravings of an endoself by removing from view objects they are unable to possess.

Abstracting Divinity

Chapter 16

Silencing the wolf

They behave not like pastors but like wolves! — cleric in
The Pursuit of the Millennium

In 1787, Thomas Jefferson wrote a letter to Edward
Carrington and warned, *"under pretence of
governing they have divided their nations into two
classes, wolves and sheep. ... If once [the people]
become inattentive to the public affairs you and I, and
Congress and Assemblies, judges and governors shall all
become wolves. It seems to be the law of our general
nature, in spite of individual exceptions; and experience
declares that man is the only animal which devours his
own kind, for I can apply no milder term to the
governments of Europe, and to the general prey of the
rich on the poor."*

Since history has been recorded, the predatory nature
of humanity has been affirmed. For a period after World
War II, when Never again! became a mantra that
drowned out the sound of genocides which continued
unabated, it was fashionable to consign such pessimism

to the dustbin of history. In the year 2024, it is permissible to again recognize our gloomy condition, but our institutions are no closer to understanding it.

In *The Creation of Me, Them and Us*, considerable time is spent in describing the role of psychology in defining a segment of humanity as the other. Science, like modern religion before it, has opted to define an idealized version of humanity by declaring all the parts it didn't choose to idealize as abnormal, inhuman or evil. This is a very unscientific copout.

Pretending that modern man is a species evolved beyond all recognition from his predecessors has not worked out well for us. Instead of forcing the nature of humanity to match our new definition, we have simply denied the modern evidence of our unchanged nature. In order for real change, we have no alternative but to face the worst parts of our nature and understand them, not in a spirit of fatalism or acceptance, but in the manner of a physician diagnosing a fatal illness which may be cured if we find the correct remedy quickly enough.

Based on the material in this book, here are a few starting premises:

1. Interactions are a source of anima.

2. The will that directs an interaction receives the anima for that interaction.

3. Unbalanced interactions result in power for one side of the interaction.

4. The only balanced interactions are connection. Sublation and violation both result in power imbalances.

5. Chronic unbalanced interactions result in compensatory behaviours such as guilt deflection and the creation of endogroups.

6. Intercepted interactions or sublation of will causes the anima within interactions to be diverted, leaving the victim deanimated and the predator bloated.

7. Violation is an attack on an animus that causes the anima within to be released and available for consumption by those in the vicinity.

8. Power causes anima bloat. Anima bloat is an illness with many easily recognizable symptoms. It damages both the individual suffering from it and those around them.

9. Deanimation is an illness that damages the victim, prevents their expansion and may result in depression or death.

10. Endogroups are structures created to facilitate the accumulation of power, reallocate guilt and alter perception of reality. They are created by merging into a shared animus with one dominant will and endoreality.

11. Endogroups maintain power by restricting, intercepting and destroying external

connections.

12. Endogroups are strengthened by preventing access to primary anima, strengthening extreme endoreality and accumulating imbalances, both debt and credit.

13. Development of the self through exosocial expansion is seen as disloyal, unauthorized, disobedient, and even lazy and self-indulgent by endosocial people and groups.

14. Individual will is lost in endogroups.

15. Conflict between universal reality and endoreality, or conflicting endorealities, causes cognitive dissonance.

The above points highlight the importance of maintaining balance in interactions. Anima theft changes a person. That message is repeated in legends all over the world. The premise is always the same. A person wishes for either power or immortality, or both, and they enlist the help of black magic to achieve it. The exchange is never what they expect because in attaining their desire, they transform themselves and lose immortality.

The transformation is caused by the loss of conscious control over will. Anima bloat strengthens the emotional will at the expense of the conscious will. The loss of conscious control means that they can continue to accumulate life, or power, but they will be trapped in the life-time-gravity level otherwise known as hell because their conscious control over will is no longer strong enough to lift them out of it. In Christian parlance this exchange is represented by the idea that he sold his soul to the devil.

There is a modern trope, often repeated in news media, that a 'sociopath' hid in plain sight and that no one could see them for what they were. This is untrue. A predator is noticeably changed by their actions. People may not recognize what they observe, but the change is no less perceptible. The predator's social immunity results from the fact that so many people are attracted to predators, or the power they hold temporarily.

This is often referenced in legends as the honeymoon period, when the predator attains his heart's desire. The accumulation of secondary anima turns the predator into an anima bank, so they can gather followers and become an endo-ideal. Often, a group of people will roundly condemn an unscrupulous action until it is complete, and then they seem to change their opinions. The newly acquired power encourages the idealization of the perpetrator. It is not only the perpetrator who is changed by predation; the people around them are transformed into reflectors.

The first law of thermodynamics is the conservation of energy; within a closed system, energy can be neither gained nor lost, although it can be altered. The nature of an endoself may be related to a buildup of energy, or anima bloat. Four things that may create an endoself could be causing an overabundance of energy: power, sugar, drugs and electronics.

Anima bloat may be thought of as flooding the primary anima conduits of an endoself and rendering them incapable of accessing primary anima. This is due to the second law of thermodynamics. Energy flows from the source with the most to the source with the least. Those suffering anima bloat cannot access new sources of primary anima because they are the source with the most. Neither can they create balanced connections. These overloads of energy can be balanced by expenditure of energy through physical activity, creation, altruism, etc. The endo-ideals who escape becoming endoselves often seem to expend a lot of energy in such activities.

An endo-ideal has inhibition of empathic conduits. An endoself has inhibition of primary anima conduits.

Empathic conduits connect to the conscious and their lack traps a person in endoreality. Primary anima conduits connect to life and their lack locks a person away from expansion and joy.

Endo-ideals have a disconnect from universal reality. Endoselves have a disconnect from an extended self.

An endoself is a person with no web of life-sustaining primary anima conduits. An endoself is therefore dependent on external life support in the form of parasitical or predatory anima transfusions. The withdrawal of this secondary anima is truly a threat to the existence of an endoself, at least in their current form. Because a predatory lifestyle requires the guilt reversing power of endoreality, endoselves are often their own endo-ideals, craving and demanding outside reflection they will usually never receive.

Parasites are institutionalized in predatory societies. They are professionals, kept alive by their own little allotments of the misery of others. Often, they were created by the institutions they serve and would have led balanced exosocial lives if they had not been lured or forced into feeding on the lives of others. Mass upheavals, those referred to as tearing the social fabric, do tear the connections woven between people and places which make up a community. The more we industrialize and dissociate, the more we amputate our own anima conduits and cripple our ability to survive without infusions of secondary or simulated anima.

The dissociation of villages and the abstraction of connection by the trade economy has created a world of endoselves, endlessly craving connection and never giving any. An endoself is a person isolated by the impermeability of their own personal membrane. They are isolated from connection to others by the restriction of their self to only one individual. An endoself lives a life of misery, trapped in a state similar to Tantalus, forever craving something almost, but not quite, within their grasp.

Money given to others with contempt, with no accompanying recognition, gratitude or respect, will establish a power relationship and drain the recipient. This is one part of the reason some people are so addicted to spending money. Even money given as charity may serve to drain the recipient. The exploitation of others by endoselves has created a world filled with victims who have been stripped of their protective membranes. These people live without self-esteem or dignity and often expect none.

If life is used to create interactions, every interaction in which the will is sublated to another is a theft of life. As discussed in *The Creation of Me, Them and Us*, the difference between asceticism and torture is the source of the will controlling the action. The energy that holds a personal membrane and animus together is enhanced by asceticism and robbed by torture, even where the act is identical. Instead of pain producing auto-anima, available to the person subjected to it by their own will, torture produces secondary anima, available to the external predator. The location of the controlling will is the destination of the resulting anima, so asceticism produces joy from experience of auto-anima, and torture produces extreme pain due to the theft of anima.

The imposition of the Inca empire over the nations they conquered came with three laws: Do not lie, Do not steal. Do not be lazy. You can only lie to the one who defines reality; you can only steal from the one who claims ownership; you can only be lazy to the one who defines work. The colonization of the individual will was inherent in the laws. Acceptance of the law was acceptance of sublation. Prisoners are forced to reflect their own guilt through forced attendance and obedience in courts and prisons. Every prison sentence is a death sentence of at least a portion of a life as that portion is spent under the direction of an external will. The taking of that life provides anima to the predators taking it and is torture to the prisoner.

Stealing is not an act of unbalanced force if ownership is defined by power. Hoarding is an act of unbalanced force, particularly if it results in hardship for one and produces no reduction of hardship in the other. Happiness due to wealth has a satiety point far lower than wealth endo-idealism would indicate. In a 2010 study the satiety point was around US$75,000 for a wealthy household in the U.S. and much lower in other regions. [125] Daniel Kahneman, one of the authors of the 2010 study, participated in a new study in 2023 which found the satiety point had increased to US$500,000, but recent studies have shown that the income-happiness correlation increases in countries with greater income inequality, like the US [126]. Greater income inequality exists in areas where wealth endo-idealism is stronger. Those at higher than satiety levels derive power, not happiness, and power is a bottomless craving. The trade economy intercepts access to basic needs with no benefit for those at the top except the secondary anima extracted through exertion of force.

There is no wealth without poverty because wealth is extracted from misery. This is why the rich, and their bureaucratic reflectors, fight so hard to deprive the poor even when it would make far more financial sense to allow the poor a share of joy and peace. The trade economy is constructed to feed the insatiable demands of power, instead of financial reason or even happiness and peace. The trade economy is built to facilitate power, not financial efficiency. This is just a note on a topic explored in *The Power Economy*.

People who would destroy, hoard or use more than they need or want rather than give or share are causing unrequited interactions for others. As discussed earlier, an unrequited interaction produces increased pain in the form of longing and anima extraction from the initiator.

The following people do not benefit from possessions. They benefit from the secondary anima resulting from deprivation of others.

People who hoard more than they need.

People who destroy what they cannot use or hoard.

People who refuse to help others even when it requires little or no effort on their part.

People who attempt to obtain more attention, credit, sympathy, gratitude or other positive response than they are entitled to or are offered.

People who attempt to fill the lives of others with mess, destruction and stress.

People who drain the time, energy, or space of others, including by creating unnecessary stress, for instance, those who are chronically late, unprepared or loudly overwhelmed, angry or needy.

People who actively work against others obtaining peace, happiness or security and fight for others to remain in misery.

The following are violations of autonomy and dignity:

Manufacture and enforcement of busywork.

Attacks on the health of others.

Attacks on the shared environment.

Creation of interpersonal conflict.

The following are social coercion against exosocial expansion.

Association of endogroup guilt with exosocial expansion.

Association of negative image status with exosocial expansion.

Restriction of opportunities.

All of the above behaviour upholds a structure which enables unequal interactions.

Post-traumatic stress disorder (PTSD) is a self destructive, learned reaction to potential predation, now manifesting as widespread anxiety. The healthy response to attempted predation is anger. Anger is widely equated to violence, but it is not the same. Anger can be used as a tool of predation, but it is also the strongest tool of resistance. This is why anger is so often deemed unacceptable, especially for those who are usually sublated such as women, children, employees and those at the mercy of state bureaucracy. Anger is increasingly considered a universally unacceptable emotion as the entire world is expected to be sublated under a totalitarian mono-empire.

The fact that predation is seldom met with anger is what enables predation. Even an infant, if they bite their mother's nipple, should be met with a cry loud enough to startle them and show that they have reached the boundary of another person. An adult who hurts another person should be met with anger. Most of all, states and corporations who prey on the entire world through violation and sublation should be met with anger.

Protection from predation requires a greater energetic force, produced by anger. Anger is not the same as violence. If it stops at simply marking the boundary of another person, and does not violate the boundaries of the person it is directed at, it is necessary social communication. There is a reason that anger exists and all people are capable of experiencing it.

The appropriate response to predation is resistance. Many people who deliberately cause stress seek assistance and comfort. Providing either will just feed an addiction to secondary anima. It is very important to set boundaries while providing the assistance that is necessary. Maria Montessori provided very good guidelines for encouraging strength and skill within a child rather than feeding lifelong dependence. The responsibility and accountability she taught to children must also be expected and demanded of adults, states and corporations. Undefended boundaries are no boundaries at all.

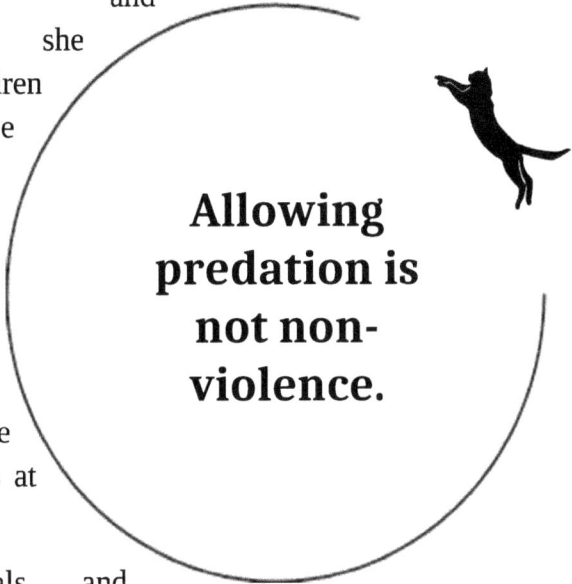

Allowing predation is not non-violence.

Endo-ideals and reflectors are both invested in upholding the endoreality that their own virtue and exceptional myth depends on to avoid the shame that would come with acknowledgement of guilt. The negative image is the only role that has nothing to lose by shattering endoreality. The revolutionary idea that all negative image rebellions must result in creation of their own endogroups is what needs to change.

The idea that misery, poverty, destruction, ugliness, unnecessary death, pain, violation and sublation are reasonable and necessary must be constantly and steadfastly challenged with firm boundaries and a willingness to defend them. Allowing predation is not non-violence.

The quest for conquest of the self and its accompanying desire often becomes a quest to strengthen consciousness at the expense of the self and emotional will. Many traditions seek to strengthen the exosocial self and reduce endosocial ties. Examples of this are finding peace and joy in natural beauty and treating all people with the same love and acceptance. These lifestyles may be briefly summed up as seeking primary anima and eschewing secondary anima. Anger, which is necessary for some to protect against depletion, is replaced with the ability to find strength in one's surroundings through strong connections.

In establishing these connections, it is important to centre the conscious will as the focus of the self. The emotional will pursues gluttony until it results in anima bloat. Interception and sublation by others result in deanimation which may eventually make the victim a starving predator. A person cannot have a healthy self without full conscious control of their own part in interactions and a willingness to defend against predatory attachments.

In an exosocial structure which eschewed the

accumulation of power, Do not steal. Do not lie. Do not be lazy. would become Do not hoard. Do not violate dignity and privacy. Do not inhibit exosocial expansion.

We now have an initial summary of things to avoid in our lives. In the next chapter, we will take a brief excursion to discuss existence, before we proceed to the meaning of life!

Anima bloat strengthens the emotional will at the expense of the conscious will.

Abstracting Divinity

Chapter 17

To be or not to be

unbeingdead isn't beingalive — e.e. cummings

To be is, at its most basic, an action. An action requires energy, which the living obtain from life. Death is the absence of life, but life is more than simply the absence of death. Life is a part of existence in a macroscopic reality that occurs alongside time. Death is a decoupling of conscious from body and life, where hopefully will follows conscious and does not become stuck in a ball of disembodied life.

Can those who are unable to establish primary anima conduits truly be considered living, or are they simply parasiting life? If the decoupled animus retains an emotional will and ties to the self, they are only separated from the living by an absence of body and perhaps, absence of conscious. If these disembodied clusters are able to attach to the self of another and control action through dominating the emotional will, are they then living?

Perhaps it is those who have been sublated and whose interactions are driven by the will of another who may be considered dead or unliving. The question is, is it the ability to access anima or the ability to exercise will for the initiation of interactions that is the defining feature of living. Certainly, both are not always present in those we consider alive.

Will is discussed in much greater depth in *Free Will and Seductive Coercion*, but it is worth noting here that the will of a living person can be sublated to the will of one who has died. This is often seen in extreme filiality, in a widow's devotion or in ideological endogroups. Final wishes are even put forth in documents which are called the will of the deceased. The exercise of will is, therefore, not an integral aspect of living. There may be many living things which do not exercise a will of their own. There may also be wills that exercise solely through sublation or violation and do not access primary anima.

A shared animus may be created by an act of individual or joint wills. Control of the animus of another must surely be considered a theft of life and agency. That assertion leads to more questions, however, such as who or what is the thief and who or what are the robbed if the life is shared? These questions hopefully illustrate why will must be considered separately from life. In the case of a shared animus, although the life within may be shared, one will may be sublated to another. The sublated will is the one robbed of its agency.

If spirits are energy clusters, or animus, it may be possible to be alive after decoupling from a body. Life, in common usage, is the coupling of the five elements of the person to create the action of living. If our definition of life includes not just energy but the ability to use energy to affect macroscopic reality, then life must be coupled to will. Most (but not all) accounts of spirits would then be relegated back to the realm of the dead. The definition of life in Binding Chaos theory is simply energy, however, so any animus is alive. The opposite of alive in Binding Chaos theory is either energy that is no longer held in a macroscopic cluster or a fully decoupled conscious. A spirit, by this definition, is still alive but at least partially decoupled.

In Binding Chaos theory, the ability to access either primary or secondary anima is considered the defining feature of living as will is a separate thing. Living is a consequence of access to life; being is a consequence of exercising will. A rock can be because a will must be exercised to bind a macroscopic object together. The will does not have to be under conscious or emotional control.

Some define death as unawareness. If such a death exists, it is the state of being alive. It is possible to be alive with a decoupled conscious will, as people in comas are alive. It is possible to be alive and not to think, or be aware, and it may just as easily be possible to be conscious and not be alive. According to those who have died, life was a state of limited conscious and ability near to death and death was similar to a rebirth into a fully functioning conscious. Even those who do not achieve a positive experience after death seem to just continue the same meaningless and joyless existence they experienced in life. Life is akin to a coma and some coma states are akin to an escape from coma.

Some define death as a state of non-existence. The presence or absence of life has nothing to do with existence. These are two entirely separate topics. The conscious, will, life and self may all exist after decoupling, just as the body does.

Living is not existence. Living is a state, or phase, in some existences.

The body can be dead, as a physical state of low animation that occurs on a spectrum, but the conscious either is or is not, which is a very different problem. To be non-existent one must exist because non-existence is unable to be anything. If life were equated to existence then, to be dead, one must be alive.

As Jean-Paul Sartre argued in Being and Nothingness, and many others before and after have agreed, to be not present is still to be. Sartre attempted to refute Hegel by claiming that non-being was not the opposite of being but its contradiction. Sartre argued that non-being is a state which exists due to a consciousness seeking being and receiving a negative response. He claims the two states cannot be contemporary, therefore cannot be opposites.

They are contemporary, however, in that they are two potentialities held in the questioner's head. Contrary to the supposed paradox posed by Schrödinger's cat, everything is both dead and alive until it is authoritatively declared to be one or the other. Schrodinger's cat being neither (or both) dead and alive is, in fact, a picture of reality, as death is not a binary switch but a process. Death is also, often, a matter of opinion. As anyone who has ever witnessed the death of a loved one knows, something of the person remains after the death pronouncement. As animists have always taught, that something can take days to fully leave and it is clear to anyone attached to them, including animals, when that residual death is completed or the spirit or essence has departed. If that something can leave, it must still exist.

In the words of Pamela Reynolds, who decoupled and was declared dead after brain surgery,[127] *"I think death is an illusion. I think death is a really nasty, bad lie."* Death is an endoreality negative image created by the living. Perhaps a fear of death was instilled by industrialists to keep people living. The idea of nothing existing after death is an attack on filiality and religion which was very instrumental to industrialists in encouraging people to be more rootless and have more free time available for industrial labour. It also encouraged gluttony as people sought objects as permanence.

In defining the dead as a negative image, scientific-industrial endo-idealists could and did invoke the laws of endoreality against them. Thus, the existence of the dead, or even the possibility of their existence, has been denied. Their problems evoke no empathy or consideration. The state of living is the ideal and the only state considered. All effort which could be spent studying the state of the dead is spent attempting to preserve the state of the living.

As a negative image identity, dead is an endoreality term with a fuzzy definition. Death is not a clearly defined word outside of medical convenience. Decoupled is a far more accurate idea which allows elaboration into the distribution of each of the five elements.

Being is unrelated to living. It is impossible to unbe which is why the word does not exist. To be once is to be always.

But if we exist without living, why do we live? Finally, in the next chapter, we will look for the answer to the meaning of life! We will put together what we have seen from the accounts of people who have died, physics, theology and the experience of living to look for the answer to the purpose of living.

Chapter 18

Th purpose of life

The immature run after sense pleasures

And fall into the widespread net of death.

But the wise, knowing the Self as deathless,

Seek not the changeless in the world of change.

— Katha Upanishad

I f what we think of as I is a conscious and will which chose to live, there must be a reason behind that choice. There must also be a reason, beyond the fatuousness of good and evil, for differing experiences upon decoupling.

According to researcher Gracia Fay Ellwood[128] *"some persons have had painful and radiant experiences in quick succession with no noticeable change of heart between them and occasionally experiences will begin with peace and happiness then become painful or vice versa"*. There are accounts of joyful death experiences by an abusive pimp and a military assassin, and another by a five year old boy who encountered a devil. The percentage of people with distressing death experiences may be as high as the mid to high teens.[129] If the living experienced such a crisis with this frequency, it would be a global emergency.

As one person with a negative death experience asked. *"What are the rules if the rules I lived by don't work?"* Surely this is a question of paramount importance, yet these questions and tentative answers to these questions are being abandoned to theologians and psychologists. Unlike so many, or most, other ideologies, science has no Book of the Dead and offers no knowledge for the dying or recently dead.

Religion taught people to reject those with negative experiences on decoupling just as industry taught people to reject the sick and the poor. Stigmatizing the negative experience is both naive and the product of a very Calvinist outlook. Bad lives or afterlives may be a desired or necessary opportunity for growth, or they may be a voluntary act of altruism. Many martyr and angel figures are said to voluntarily provide the energy required by others to escape the earthly realm.

Negative experiences could easily be a part of a spiritual challenge or hero's journey offered only to the strongest, as difficult lives could be as well. Cultures that celebrate passivity can see challenges only as punishment. In many cultures, what would be considered negative experiences by researchers are presented as challenges along a journey. What could be seen as pleasurable may simply be easy because the person is not being offered the opportunity to rise to a higher plane. Healthy development includes attraction to fear and challenge as a path to growth.

The Tibetan Book of the Dead speaks of aversion to, or inability to perceive, the brightest light as a sign that the person is not ready for ultimate wisdom or ultimate reality. There are many schools of thought that teach that evolution is necessary to reach the highest levels of the timeless dimensions. That evolution often looks like burning off secondary or life energy and replacing it with the energy of the conscious world. The hellish experiences may be an ascetic method to reduce anima bloat.

According to Ellwood, the overall decoupling experience of humanity appears to be evolving. She points out that *"angelic guides in medieval cases are authority figures whereas [now] guides … leave it up to them whether or not to return to earth. Similarly in medieval cases, the judgement is imposed upon the NDE by an authority figure holding a record, whereas in contemporary cases NDEs tend to encounter their past themselves and judge themselves accordingly."*[130] This sounds like the Age of the Holy Spirit predicted by Joachim of Fiore which swept the Millennarian movements of the last millennium.

When Thoth measured the heart against a feather, the odds of escaping the downward journey were almost non-existent. According to Ellwood, *"in New Kingdom copies of Going Forth [The Egyptian Book of the Dead] … instead of weighing of the heart against the feather of Maat, which demands perfection, the deceased's good and evil deeds are weighed against one another."*[131] Is it now a 50% pass?

Thoth weighs the heart in a scale against a feather; guilt weighs down the heart. It is fairly clear that what is being weighed is guilt, not inherent evil, and the guilt is taken as an ending balance of all interactions over the lifetime. If the heart had weight, it would mean that the person was a net beneficiary of interactions - that they had accumulated power, or owed debt. Redemption is always possible if the debt is not too extreme.

The heart, in several cultures, has been considered the repository or medium for social interaction, specifically a receptacle for emotions. A light heart signifies joy and a heavy heart signifies sorrow. A heavy heart may indicate earthly (emotional) attachments or a strong attachment to the self. To some extent, the stronger the earthly ties a person has, the more miserable they are, even while living. Bonds to places, possessions and endogroups are getting far weaker in modern cultures.

Saviours have transitioned from powerful beings who are negotiated with or served in exchange for advocacy to unconditional love and assistance available to any who request it. Is this due to a growth in power of an anima bank or an increase in the ability to access it?

There has been a tremendous recent population explosion which could mean more people are coming back faster. Is evolution happening exponentially as well?

According to Nancy Evans-Bush[132] *"The sense of self as interior, as inwardly responsible, driven and reflective from within, is a social construction of identity recently born in the development of ... Buddhism, Christianity, Islam and Hinduism ... In ... archaic religions such as those of native Americans, Australian Aborigines and many Pacific cultures, the distinction between self and the world is less explicit."* What she is referencing is both the creation of the object self and the religious shift in focus from the self to the conscious.

Regarding a lack of life review and judgement in earlier cultures, she writes that the mind *"as store for social experience is not paramount, for experience is also drawn from the animistic world ... Individuals are no more responsible than the world. Anxiety, guilt and responsibility are in-the-world properties or characteristics not located purely within the private orbit of an individual's make up."*

The lost souls and other inhabitants of the earthbound ring were the primary preoccupation of animists. Animists seldom concern themselves with the conscious outside of divination, and even then, they typically use a spirit intermediary. As discussed in The death of joy chapter, the early focus of humanity was with the self, which is not individuated. Organized religion brought nearly exclusive focus onto an individuated consciousness. Neither focus provides any clarity on why the five elements are bonded into a person or what the purpose of a lifespan is. An integrated approach is required.

We live for a reason. If our experience of life is through acts of will, the will must have a motive. There must be more to life than seeking knowledge, or our conscious could simply stay in the world of knowledge. If living is an act of will, and many who have experienced death have recounted that living again is a choice, there must be a purpose behind the choice. There is a purpose to life beyond an endurance test, an exercise in futility or a game to be mastered.

The superficial purpose of life is to spend it. A lifespan is designed to end in death, or the exhaustion of all life energy. The purpose of living is to use life energy, not to preserve it. Dying with money (or anima) in the bank will just prevent the conscious from escaping earthly ties.

The fundamental purpose of life may be to create reality, or the universe. The universe appears to be composed of interactions, created by will. The fabric of the universe, the spacetime, seems to be composed solely of interactions. Spacetime is a quality or component of interactions. Life is the energy that creates interactions and will is the attraction between interactions which we perceive as time. We create spacetime. It does not create us.

Life may be the means by which conscious can

exercise will and create interactions. Life, time and gravity are so intrinsically linked they may be thought of as different perspectives of the same thing. Where time and gravity do not exist, neither does life. According to animism, life does exist wherever time and gravity are. Where there is no life, time or gravity, there is only conscious. Conscious is the awareness and understanding of all interactions and it exists independently of life, or the ability to create those interactions.

Imbalance in interactions causes power, or accumulated energy, which warps the fabric of existence. The weight of accumulated power creates an object self. The egalitarian force attempts to disperse power and restore the weave of an evenly expanding universe. To live in peace is to live a life of balance and to create peace is to create balance.

Primary anima appears to follow the path towards greater entropy, the force which seeks to disperse order. Secondary anima appears to be related to gravity or the force which creates order. Secondary anima may be related to life and

We are not life. Life is just the energy that enables living.

primary anima may be a different quality and able to escape the gravity sphere. This may provide a basis of separation between those who deal with forces near earth, animist forces often held to be demonic and typically persuaded through sacrifices or other exchanges of life energy, and those who attempt through divination and conscious focus to reach energy forces in a higher level.

We are not life. Life is just the energy that enables living. The fact that our life on earth is a temporary and surreal part of our existence is the belief that has been held throughout human history and has been evidenced continually. It is the improbable and inexplicable faith that our existence somehow ends when life leaves the body that is the challenger, and it presents no evidence, simply blind faith and dogmatic belief.

The lives we are living may have been lived many times before and possibly they will be lived many times again.

The question of the primacy of the knower or knowledge becomes simpler when consciousness is recognized as the product of interactions fueled by life instead of conflated with life itself. It is then only the origin of life that remains a puzzle, If life is an energy, it is no more exotic a problem than the origin of energy which created the universe, since they appear to be one and the same.

The idea of existence as something to be endured and laboured through to earn higher existence for the real self or soul does not seem rational. Who would choose to leave what they feel is their home and endure this restricted and painful existence for no reason? Perhaps all of conscious among the living is here in the role of bodhisattvas, those who have attained enlightenment but elect to return to earth to help others escape the pull of gravity (life) and attain enlightenment (conscious). Perhaps conscious is here to free ordered energy to follow the path of greater entropy and disperse into pure outward energy. The goal of conscious seems to be to sublate the emotional will and reverse its drive to order.

It is common for philosophers and theologians to interpret evolution as both personal and following a sequence ordered alongside the progression of time. Lives are thought to be started at birth and ended at death. Past lives are in the past and future lives will occur in the future. Each life, once lived, is complete. There is no valid reason to assume any of these things.

It appears that the decoupled conscious can move back or forwards and drop into any interaction in the past and possibly in the future. Instead of thinking of the universe as an invariable set of events that starts and ends, it could be thought of as data in a constant state of flux. An interaction, once created, cannot be uncreated, but if a conscious can drop in and experience that interaction again, there does not appear to be any reason the conscious cannot also direct a will and recreate the interaction. The act of experiencing seems to be the exertion of will. If the will is exerted again, it can choose a different outcome.

The lives we are living may have been lived many times before and possibly they will be lived many times again. The I that we feel is living our current life, has lived past lives and may live future lives may not be individuated. It may, in fact, be a we. Living may be the experience of conscious recreating existing interactions to produce a less ordered state and free whatever is trapped in the ordered state. This may be the purpose of living.

The best practices for living seem to be pursuit of balanced connection, or love, and the quest for knowledge. These are attained through altruism and exosocial expansion. Love is the dissolution of endosocial membranes and the expenditure of energy through anima conduits. Knowledge is an expanded and focused awareness of conscious. Both seem to prepare us for the world after life. Currently, many people are striving to accumulate as much secondary anima, or power, as possible and live as long as possible. If the purpose of life were known to be to reject and balance all secondary anima and seek out primary anima, much of the world would be living very differently.

While scientists, technologists and politicians

breathlessly wait on news of communication with aliens, they ignore the testimony of millions or billions of people who say they have been in contact with spirits. While physicists argue entirely theoretically about wormholes and travel through space and time, they ignore all the people living now and throughout history who explain their experience of such travel. While religious leaders and scientists thunder their opinions of what does or does not happen after death, almost none are consulting the increasing numbers of people who have died and come back to tell us about it.

Before people concern themselves with populating other planets with humans, they should probably know if humans were formed as an effort of universal or individual will, if the body is just a macroscopic co-ordinated effort of will, if life can occupy any form, if conscious exists with or without a life form and if a self is a network of interactions that lasts forever or is in a continual state of change.

If the definition of life in this book is a good depiction of what the word means in practice, then there is life, not only on Mars, but in all macroscopic objects, including those referred to as dead. Furthermore, the quest to find life on Mars or, for that matter, in a person, is misguided. What ought to be sought is not life but conscious, and conscious is the entire universe.

In the next chapter, we will revisit the study of life. The study of everything must be reconciled to move forward. There can be no theory of everything created from studies of isolated parts of existence, all speaking different languages.

Our lives come with only one guarantee, which is death. It is not likely that the only thing guaranteed to any who choose life is a bad thing.

There is no reason to assume a hellish experience is punishment. It could be just a method of reducing anima bloat.

The conscious can experience interactions the I did not create. It is possible that what we think of as an individual life is lived by many wills successively or concurrently. There is no reason to assume a lifetime or interaction is lived only once or by only one will or in order of time.

Chapter 19

The theory of everything

It is more important to have beauty in one's equations than to have them fit experiment. — Paul Dirac

I t is reasonably well acknowledged that the social sciences are a garbled mess. They largely consist of studies either floating around with no unifying theory or anchored to flimsy and easily disproven ideas masquerading as theory (see psychology and economics). Lately, the lack of foundations has been embraced as a feature, not a bug. The invention of shifting lens through which to view findings provides justification for a shifting sand foundation.

In contrast, those in the physical sciences rarely acknowledge their own garbled mess. Instead, they insist they are imminently on the verge of agreeing to a theory of everything, developed without a single glance at anything in the realm of social sciences. The need to reconcile lived, social reality with physical science is almost universally ignored. When a paper does appear that mentions a cross-disciplinary view, it is typically so simplistic and surface level it appears gratuitous or a cynical attempt at a headline rather than a real effort at workable theory.

Instead of attempting to reconcile the split in sciences, the division is becoming stronger. There is a growing trend for some researchers to replace the suffix -ology with -science. New disciplines such as neuroscience and geroscience now exist alongside neurology and gerontology, studying the same topics but as physical science more clearly divorced from social science. This is an unspoken acknowledgment of how divided the two sides have become.

Newton explained the earth, the general theory of relativity explained the solar system and quantum mechanics explains the universe. As physics itself has sought the unification of general relativity with quantum mechanics, the rest of knowledge also needs to seek reunification with quantum mechanics.

We think in words and often forget to think in definitions. A theory with an undefined word, a word with a circular definition, or multiple words presenting the same definition as different is a worthless theory. Physical science is still using words with no definitions, such as life and death, even while actively working to create life and eliminate death. There very little concrete and useful examination of the question of whether creating life and eliminating death is a beneficial path to be on. Where this question is examined at all, it is usually from the standpoint of economic, environmental or social impacts. There is no attempt to look for the purpose of life and how that purpose would be better served by a course of action to extend or replicate life.

Brian Greene wrote in *The Fabric of the Cosmos: Space, Time, and the Texture of Reality*, "*The history of the universe according to an energetic causal set model, consists of events which are each the cause of future events, to which they transfer some energy and momentum. But there is no spacetime fundamentally; there is just the discrete set of events connected by causal relations, with the events and the relations endowed with energy and momentum.*"

If two things share all the same attributes, they are identical. That is to say, they are not two things, but one. If events and momentum are occupying the same position in theory as spacetime, they are spacetime. If events which are sequenced according to the laws of thermodynamics follow time, perhaps the will which directs the sequence is time. And perhaps all of these things, events (interactions) connected by momentum (will) and transferring energy (life) are what creates reality. The purpose of life may be to create reality.

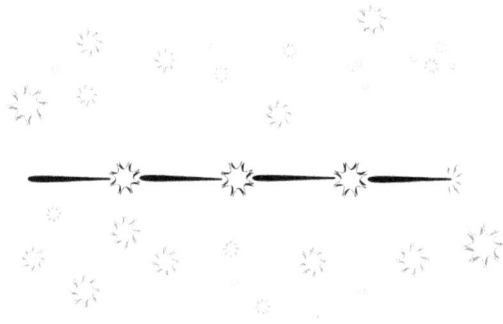

Figure 36: Interactions connected by will

transferring life

Various theories attempting to explain quantum wave collapse have been criticized for violating the first law of thermodynamics, the conservation of energy. During collapse, kinetic energy increases under several spontaneous collapse theoretical models. Ghirardi–Rimini–Weber (GRW) is the first of these, followed by the Continuous spontaneous localization (CSL) and Diósi–Penrose (DP).

That increase may cause headaches for physicists, but it models what can be (or ought to be) observed in social sciences; interactions produce small bursts of energy that is sought by all living things. That energy can be stored in euphoric objects if they are interacted with often enough. The source of the energy added to the system in these models is a problem which may be related to the diversion of the expansive energy of the universe required to create objects. In other words, the energy of the wave is inverted, but there may be a missing energy beyond that which is inverted to create order (objects) out of chaos (expansive force). That bonus amount may be used to reward the creator of order and fuel them to continue doing so.

Where life exists, order is formed out of chaos. The idea that a low entropy system emerges from a high entropy system appears to contravene the second law of thermodynamics. The Diósi-Penrose (DP) model posited the idea that gravity was related to the quantum wave collapse. In the DP model, gravity does not tolerate the superposition of two spacetime curvatures and forces the wave collapse. In Binding Chaos theory, two separate spacetimes become one for that one collapse, or interaction. The two spacetime endorealities are sublated to one will, as one choice determines outcome. The quantum collapse theories suggest collapse as a result of gravity; Binding Chaos theory suggests collapse as the result of will which can only be exercised in the presence of life energy. That life energy may either be the same as or occur alongside gravity.

Figure 37: Earth will

What is considered an isolated object in classical physics is a vast network of colliding realities. All that is, is interactions. The more interactions that are shared between wills, the more their endorealities will also be shared.

Emotional will, driven by life energy, can only act in conjunction with life. Conscious will does not seem able to act unless it occupies and dominates a life form. There may be exceptions to this as higher spirits appear in many stories to be able to advise and sometimes to influence outcomes, but the conscious of a decoupled person has very limited ability to act in the world of the living.

Living can be described as the state of an individuated consciousness trapped in a wave of life or a will propelling a wave of life. The purpose of living is to create the interactions and exercise the will joining them to create the universe.

Time follows the path to greater entropy to move individuated consciousness through interactions. Individuated consciousness is trapped on a train, powered by life, conducted by will.

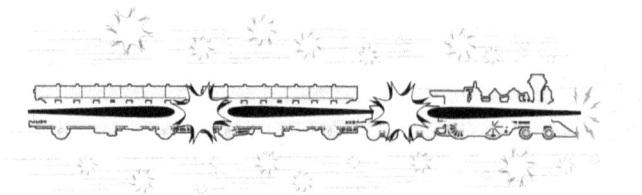

Figure 38: Conscious conducted by will and powered by life

The Creation of Me, Them and Us stated that if Newton was the tap root of western thought, then Kant and Hegel are the trunk and this is true. All of the world's modern institutions have been built according to Kant and Hegel. But ought they to be? Newton's thoughts were expanded to produce a far healthier sapling that has been left swaying to the side of the Hegelian tree, unable to flourish due to the shadow. The result is a comparatively healthy and realistic study of physical sciences and technology due to the development of quantum mechanics, and a stunted and fantastical study of social sciences that utterly fails to reflect the world as it is or correspond with the study of physical sciences.

The sapling of quantum mechanics is so much stronger than the rotting wood of the social sciences that they appear to inhabit different worlds. This appearance is not false. While quantum mechanics is striving for a description of universal reality, all social sciences and institutional structures are still firmly ensconced in the crumbling structures of endosocialism they built out of Newton, Kant and Hegel.

While the physical sciences simply dismiss historical or current accounts of animism and experience of other dimensions, social scientists examine cultural knowledge as amusing fiction. Once social data has been gathered, it is placed in a feminist, anti-colonialist, anti-capitalist or other Hegelian framework. Those frameworks are used to find an origin for what are preemptively assumed to be the delusions of those who have experienced such phenomena. The first, starting assumption made before nearly every study of decoupled experience is that the experiences are delusional. The Hegelian frameworks are needed to find an origin for the delusion. There is validity to the occasional Hegelian lens, as it points out the negative image and endo-ideal perspectives that exist in endoreality, but that just exposes endoreality. The search for universal reality stops as soon as this Hegelian context is diagnosed.

There are enough volumes written interpreting all prior beliefs through the lens of current ideology. It is time to interpret modern science through the lens of all prior knowledge as well. This knowledge was not forgotten. It was, like the knowledge that space and time are an illusion, forbidden – not only by religion but also by science.

In order to truly understand the nature of power and violence, sociology needs to be bold and brave enough to embrace a radical new starting supposition: what if animist experiences were not anecdotes but empirical evidence? What if people outside of academia do not speak in riddles that must be analyzed as metaphor, allegory, superstition or other encrypted messaging, but instead were giving factual and direct accounts of their own experience? What if scientists simply replied, *"Oh. How does that work?"*

Whether the ideas in Binding Chaos theory compose a usable framework or not, all of these components need to be part of the same conversation, using the same words, with clear meanings. A person is composed of a body, self, life, will and consciousness. A self is an artificially individuated piece of conscious. A body is interactions clustered together by an effort of will. Conscious is interactions, created by life and will. Energy, will and interactions are all that exist. When both social science and physical science recognize this and resist the urge to rename and disguise what they see, there will be only one category of science. Or better, there will be only one category of knowledge.

Everything is an interaction. Clusters of interactions are driven by will to a state of greater chaos or order. In the next two chapters, we will look back at these two opposing forces once more, to see how they manifest in social behaviour.

Abstracting Divinity

Chapter 20

Agents of order

When an overflowing river sweeps all before it one speaks of violence, but when its banks confine the river in its bed by force, then one is silent. — Bertolt Brecht

Evil exists if evil is meant to describe a predatory will that feeds on the life energy of others. Endoselves exist that are nearly wholly under the control of such a will. This force is the opposite of the force experienced as good. These forces are also known as order and chaos. Order is just as violent as chaos. The endosocial force extracts energy from those it crushes to create order and the egalitarian force extracts energy from the violations it commits to create chaos.

All order will eventually disperse in an expanding universe. This expansive drive may be just one aspect of the universe, however, if the universe is indeed created by a big bounce instead of a big bang. In that case, the forces of order and chaos are in continual flux, a pendulum of doing and undoing.

Order is produced by a compulsion to resist expansion to a state of greater entropy. All macroscopic systems are ordered systems. These are mass groupings of interactions held together by the sublation of interactions to a master will. All ordered systems require energy to bind them together. This energy is obtained by trapping the chaotic force of the universe into an endosocial membrane which surrounds the macroscopic system and gives the illusion of an object. An object is really an animus, an energy cluster held together by a dominant will.

An exoself is an agent of order and an endoself is an agent of chaos.

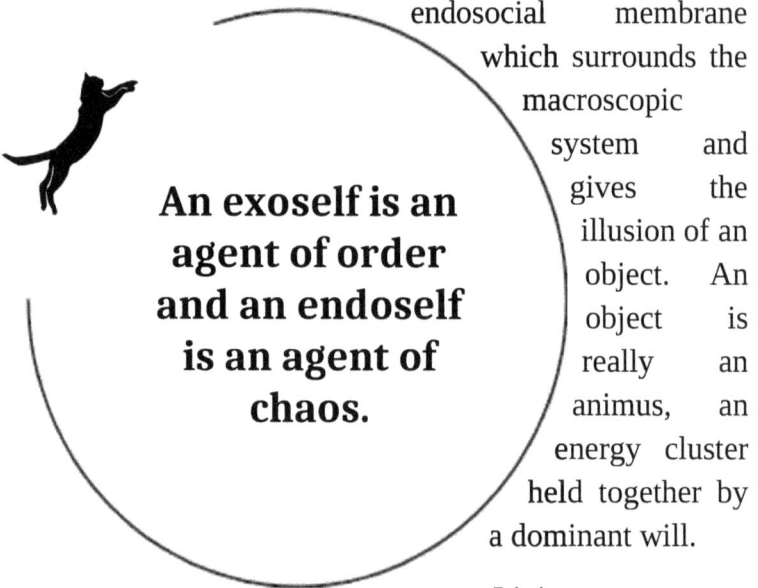

Living appears to follow an exosocial path towards greatest entropy. The emotional will attempts to block this path and trap it into an endosocial semblance of order. The emotional will acts as an endosocial drive which seeks to preserve and increase the energy in the animus of a person. It accomplishes this through destruction, the creation of chaos, in other places. The emotional will is an agent of chaos.

Because of the first law of thermodynamics, the conservation of energy, creating order transfers energy from the creator to the ordered system. Conversely, creating disorder, or chaos, releases energy from the ordered system and transfers it to the destroyer. Thus, creators of order become more chaotic and creators of chaos become more ordered. Creators spend energy and destroyers accumulate it.

Newton's third law of motion states that every action is met by an equal and opposite reaction. If the actions create order, there will be an equal and opposing reaction to disperse order. Creation of order results in depletion of order. The energy in ordered objects is spent in the creation of other ordered objects. The focus of conscious is to disperse ordered energy into chaos. An exoself is an agent of order and an endoself is an agent of chaos.

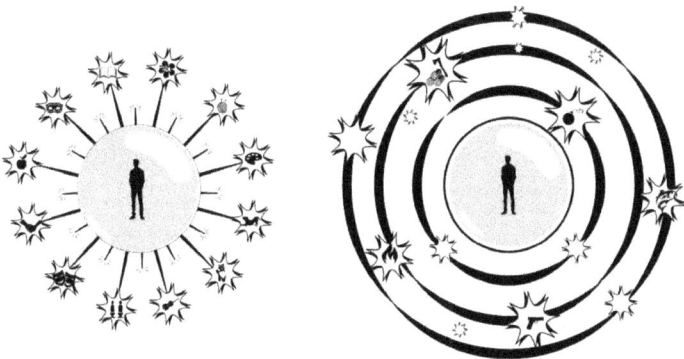

Figure 39: Exoself and endoself

Those who create order are spending their life energy. It may be that this is what needs to be done if a person does not want to die with a surplus life energy that will linger around or require them to continue to come back until it is all spent. In any case, spending life energy by creating order appears to be the path which brings greatest happiness and strengthens the conscious will relative to the emotional will. Since it is the emotional will that appears to cling to earthbound attachment upon death, anything that strengthens the conscious will relative to the emotional will appears to be a good idea.

Creating order includes anything that involves losing energy to the other side of an interaction. That can be creating, maintaining, cleaning, using, worshiping and any other interaction that does not involve taking energy. With people, that includes any primarily altruistic gesture or establishing and maintaining connections. It also includes the performance of rites and physical and mental labour in creation and discovery. All of these things require conscious focus and expenditure of energy.

Creating order also includes interactions where energy is lost due to sublation or violation. Those types of interactions overcome the conscious will instead of strengthening it, however, so they are not interactions initiated by agents of order. Instead, they are initiated by agents of chaos, those who commit sublation and violation of others.

Life is the energy, but will is the force of attraction and repulsion. Attraction and repulsion are reversed between exoselves and endoselves, which seems to be the root of much human conflict. This may be viewed as the conscious and emotional wills at war with each other. Mind over matter is conscious will over emotional will. The conscious will, as a force of order, usually initiates creation, and the emotional will, as a force of chaos, initiates destruction.

The conscious acts as an exosocial drive because its goal is to expend the energy in the animus of a person. This energy is commonly used through creating order in other places. Expenditure of this energy brings joy. It is the conscious that loves primary anima and has the ability to access it. The emotional will which is not sublated to conscious seeks secondary anima. Primary and secondary anima may be two different types of energy or they may be the same energy under the influence of two opposing forces, the conscious and emotional wills.

If the purpose of life is to expend life energy, then the direction of living is in creating order. Life energy is expended by creating order. The ordered person is expanded to a state of higher entropy by creating lower entropy elsewhere. The emotional will strongly resists this expansion. Those dominated by their emotional will become agents of chaos. We will look at them in the next chapter.

An exosocial person expends their own energy in creating order elsewhere. An exosocial person is an agent of order.

An endosocial person accumulates energy in creating chaos elsewhere. An endosocial person is an agent of chaos.

Primary and secondary anima may be two different types of energy or they may be the same energy under the influence of two opposing forces, the conscious and emotional wills.

Chapter 21

Agent of chaos

Standing there on the embankment, staring into the current, I realized that—in spite of all the risks involved —a thing in motion will always be better than a thing at rest; that change will always be a nobler thing than permanence; that that which is static will degenerate and decay, turn to ash, while that which is in motion is able to last for all eternity. — Olga Tokarczuk

An extreme resistance to maintaining creation is effectively a destructive force. A refusal to clean, repair, communicate, interact or exercise causes the neglected object or relationship to disintegrate over time or over continued interactions. A lack of anima spent in maintaining order will allow increased entropy or destruction. Use it or lose it is a useful expression, but the ordered thing must be used in a way that increases the energy available to it, if it is not to be lost.

Agents of chaos are those who dismantle order and release secondary anima. Chaos and the unbinding of order are typically associated with evil, probably due to this release of secondary anima. Agents of chaos are those who initiate interactions of sublation and violation. They are those who primarily initiate interactions in which they are the net beneficiaries of energy. Because of the second law of thermodynamics, they are also those who resist expending energy through their network of connections and passively allow their surroundings to decay.

The energy in an exoself is outwardly focused on exosocial expansion, while in an endoself it is turned inwards and results in external destruction. In some cases it seems to reach equilibrium and trap the person in near inertia.

Figure 40: Inertia

When people clean their houses and invite others into them, they are sharing the anima that went into establishing order and creating beauty. If guests leave the house worse than they found it, the energy is depleted, although it may be more than made up for by other euphoric energy from the gathering. Gifts to the host are acknowledgement of the gift of energy that went into creating a beautiful space. People feel happy and energized in clean places because of the creation energy stored in them.

A living space, community or ecosystem is filled with life energy. A person creating stress-producing situations, even if ostensibly for themselves, is creating a vortex which sucks the life from the surrounding environment. This includes people they are connected to. The people they deplete then often extract anima from those they interact with until an entire group or community is affected.

An endoself under stress will create messes as blockage. Destruction is carefully encouraged. Beauty and creation are removed from their protective places and placed in high risk areas. Anything beautiful that they don't dare destroy (yet) is made ugly. A particular focus is on garbage, urine and feces, which they value as other people might value plants and art.

The pole reversal of an endoself causes them to be attracted to secondary anima and repelled by primary anima. They will seek to block and destroy the flow of primary anima. People living with endoselves often describe the attachment in terms such as drowning, trying to keep my head above water or finding room to breathe. These expressions are (as is often the case) very illustrative of what is actually happening. The blockage of energy caused by destruction, pollution and accumulation of filth is leaving people gasping for life.

A similar state is familiar to practitioners of yoga as blocked chakras. It is the ha channel, with hot sun energies of anger, jealousy and isolation, and the tha channel, with cool moon energies of desire and attachment that become out of balance. The ha energy corresponds somewhat to an endo-ideal, and the tha corresponds to reflector and negative image roles, so these blocked chakras may be a useful image to illustrate energy trapped in endogroup or power relationships instead of being allowed to flow freely.

People who respond to stress by stacking up garbage and filling their living spaces with filth are blocking the flow of primary anima. The most well known study of this flow in the home is in the roots of feng shui. Beneath the pop culture decorating tips, the idea behind feng shui is the flow of life energy. The most important aspect of this idea is to avoid blockage by sickness-producing accumulations. As any practitioner of feng shui will attest, the accumulation of garbage, filth, poor house maintenance and blockage of living areas all prevent a healthy flow of qi, or life energy. The fact that hoarders so often fill doorways and hallways and collect garbage, including rotten food, mouldy items or even feces and urine, indicates a compulsion to block the flow which feng shui teaches is essential to health.

Hoarding may be used to trap others, but it may also be trapping the hoarder. This act of working against themselves is a reflection of a struggle between the conscious and emotional wills. The emotional will is attempting to immobilize the conscious will. Hoarding and filth, along with other self induced stress, often accompany other signs that an emotional will is in charge.

Feng shui is the most famous guidance to creating surroundings conducive to energy flow, but similar beliefs are recognized in various forms in many cultures. The European traditions of spring cleaning, especially in Celtic and Slavic cultures, are rife with the ideas behind the flow of energy and spirit movement, and many of these ideas recur at winter solstice and other celebrations. Even among the disenchanted Protestants, this idea remained as Cleanliness is next to Godliness. If the idea of godliness is life energy, that is a perfect summation of the idea behind feng shui.

There is nothing divine about cleanliness in the form of ascetic ugliness, however. Beauty can be defiled by filth and destruction, but it can also be scrubbed away in an excess of Brutalism. Endoselves often attempt to convince others that garbage and ugliness are creation and beauty. They will hold up destruction and ugliness as the ideal, as progress or a modern aesthetic. They will use any connivance to destroy nature and beauty when there is absolutely no need to do so. It is as though harmony is repellent to them and they cannot bear its existence.

A key aspect of the compulsion to block energy flow is that the flow of life is an egalitarian force which brings a balancing of debt. The emotional will may be attempting to barricade itself from a forced accounting of accumulated debt, just as those who strive to avert death live in dread of that accounting. For those who have managed to block this energy flow, its release is like the release of a dam. The release may eventually bring clear and healthy water but only after the accumulated debris has been dealt with. This may help to explain the extreme stress so many hoarders feel at the idea of their blockages being removed.

Some hoarders may simply be obtaining secondary anima from others. As creation and beauty are sources of primary anima, destruction and ugliness are sources of secondary anima. Creating mess, being late, unprepared or unpredictable, destruction and refusal to work, all have one thing in common; they act against order. There are people who will eagerly labour for hours to produce destruction but refuse to contribute even minutes to creating order. To create order we must expend energy. Destruction of that order releases the life energy expended to create it. This appears to be the energy that people who destroy are feeding off of.

The Sisyphean task of the housewife, condemned every day to pick up what others drop, fold what they unfold, close what they open and clean what they dirty is a continual drain of life energy abstracted through order and disorder. If she attempts to stop this continual outflow of energy, by exchanging it for even more draining discussions, fights or negotiations, the cost is even higher.

A common argument used regarding household chores is that one person just has higher standards than the other and therefore ought to do all or most of the work to meet those standards. This ignores the laws of endoreality which dictate that even if the endo-ideal creates all the mess, the negative image will receive all the shame, humiliation and guilt assigned both internally and externally. The endo-ideal will not only not receive guilt or shame, and therefore not notice the mess, he may also be credited as a victim of a wife who fails to keep a clean house. This will give him even more motivation to create mess and even less to clean.

This energy drain may be part of the reason why heterosexual divorce and widowhood are more lethal for men than they are for women, despite the much greater risk to women of poverty, single parenthood, lessened safety and other stressors.[133] The futility of housework in a home where others destroy order is a parallel to the life-draining futility of bureaucracy. In both cases, those who object are accused of overreacting and encouraged to just continue the compelled labour. The emotional reaction to deanimation is appropriate, however.

Uglification is not just a personal phenomenon. It is

often seen at the level of higher endogroups such as states. Many apartment blocks are created as institutional warehousing without even the requisite access to a fresh air courtyard. Schools and daycares are sometimes impossible to differentiate from prisons. Deliberately manufactured ugliness and deprivation is everywhere under institutions of power. Both communism and capitalism have wreaked havoc on beauty and created ugliness as far as they could reach, even to the point of clogging the oceans and outer space.

Neither is the accumulation of garbage restricted to physical space. Pollution of the air is global. Perfumes and flowers are forbidden in many places, but industrial pollution is everywhere. Radio broadcasts are strictly regulated, but the electromagnetic field which all living things use to communicate is saturated with toxic pollution. Music and conversations will have the police at your door, but traffic and white noise are ubiquitous. This is despite overwhelming evidence that traffic and white noise damage cognitive functioning and music and conversations improve it.

Destruction is a component of endosocialism. The more pervasive and powerful endogroups become, the greater the destruction they will wreak. But destruction is also a component of the collapse of endosocialism. Our authoritative endogroups are in an advanced stage of collapse. Along with them, the metanarratives we use to create social order is also in collapse and we have no new ones. In the next chapter, let's take steps towards building a new metanarrative.

Blockage of the outward flow of energy acts against agents of creation, or order. Blockage produces destruction, or chaos.

Blockage of the flow of primary anima and destruction of order is a forced release of secondary anima to feed the dominant will.

The creation of powerful systems of order will always result in the creation of surrounding chaos. A negative image must always be crushed to provide the energy for an endogroup.

Primary anima may be the exosocial force towards greater entropy, or chaos. Secondary anima may be the endosocial force towards order.

Abstracting Divinity

Chapter 22

A new metanarrative

One who believes all of a book would be better off without books. — Mencius

E very society has its own metanarrative. The search for the reason why we are here and how we should govern our lives, along with what our aims should be, has preoccupied every society of record. Currently, the world is divided between the eschatology of religions, the mantra of progress at any price from science and the pursuit of unlimited gluttony dictated by industrialization. None of these are serving us very well at present, if they ever did.

The current endosocial order is definitely weakening, however. Endogroups are increasingly loose and people are increasingly connecting as individuals. Joy and connection are returning as we move to a post-industrial future. The shattering of shared animus has brought increasingly untethered selves, open to interaction from anywhere. More people are free floating, following no rites and not tied to objects, living neither in the past or the future but in full conscious awareness of the present.

We cannot attempt again to scale up a hierarchical structure which has exhausted its capacity for expansion. Many prototypes of decentralization of power have been developed, but they are all attempting to decentralize the institutions which exist currently. The metanarrative behind these institutions reflected now obsolete endorealities. The metanarrative itself must be reexamined.

A new structure must be created which can sustain the coming collapse of the old and redirect the energy which will be released by it. The first step in creating this structure is understanding the origins the world is about to collapse back into. We need an understanding of the first indebtedness, the guilt which required sacrifice and magic, the first endogroup which enabled guilt transference and the first endoself who was damned to existence with no or limited ability to access primary anima.

Infrastructure to prepare for the fall of our ideological ponzi schemes should avoid guilt by avoiding power through involuntary interactions of unequal force. It should avoid endogroups by avoiding the reflection of endoreality with endo-identities, endo-ideals and negative images. Most of all, it should avoid the creation of endoselves and help those damned to an existence neither mortal nor immortal, trapped in a bitter and predatory existence maintained by an artificial reality.

There are two universal laws to govern life that should be considered when developing laws for societies.

🐈

1. Exosocial expansion must not be blocked.

2. Balanced connection should be sought in interactions.

These two laws, the law of exosocial expansion and the law of egalitarian force, correspond to Newton's second law of thermodynamics, that all systems will progress towards greater entropy.

These are universal laws because their violation causes serious distortions, paradoxes and perversions of society, to the point that people are engineering their own extinction and primary anima is increasingly difficult to obtain. The violation of these two laws necessitates guilt transference, the manufacture of endorealities and punishment of a negative image. To be at peace is to be in accordance with these two laws. Legal institutions and their role in upholding and violating these and other laws are examined in *Law and Chaos*.

Anima is that energy which is the currency of the universe, so anima dictates all social behaviour. Scientists who view the body as a mechanist object confuse the message with the messenger and assume hormones and chemicals cause euphoria. Euphoria is the response to anima. It is anima that triggers the emotion-controlling hormones, not the hormones which initiate the process.

Regulating hormones requires understanding of the triggers that cause hormone release. The hormone alone does not produce reanimation, which is why the synthetic euphoria of drugs and other dopamine triggers do not produce health. Increasing numbers of studies confirm that anti-depressants and anti-anxiety medications are no more effective than placebos.[134] The placebo effect is really endoreality, the result of a medical science endo-ideal able to dictate and create reality. The placebo effect is discussed in more detail in *Political Science*.

Euphoria does not energize; it is a response to energy. Depression does not deanimate; it is a response to deanimation.

The first decision to be made in deciding what is pathological lies in deciding what ought to be normative. Many people are currently in an existential crisis caused by external pressures on their health and external torment by predatory institutions of power. In such a world, examples of pathological behaviour can far outnumber those that are indicative of healthy expansion. Psychologists have had a tendency to look for normal instead of normative and to base their standards on either what is common or what is similar to themselves.

Since psychologists are endo-ideals, this has led to calls for so-called narcissism to be normalized, or even considered a healthy standard. Sexualized sublation and violation, which are predatory behaviours found wherever power is found, have often seen calls for their normalization. Efforts to normalize other severe symptoms of distress are used to protect corporations causing health crises globally.

We can define good vitality as the ability to establish and maintain a large and diverse quantity of connections to primary anima, and poor vitality as the blockage of anima conduits and the inability to continue exosocial expansion. We then have a more clear and less subjective standard of healthy and normative behaviour. To explain the definition of poor vitality, we have to define its ill effects. Since the world is filled with people who live perfectly long lives, unencumbered by any particular discomfort, but are largely endoselves, and the reverse can be found for exoselves, it is necessary to define vitality as a wider issue.

Measures of vitality must include, not just the body, but also a self which includes society and the world at large. A person who revels in death and destruction cannot then be considered healthy, even when they are perfectly content and suffer no bodily illness. An extreme endoself who is unable to establish primary anima connections outside themselves does not have good vitality even when they have the income and automation to provide for all their needs. Because they are not reciprocating to a wider network, their self is not expanding. Vitality depends on the development of connections to primary anima and the cure of addictions to secondary anima.

The decision of which actions are good or bad have so far been defined through subjective moral judgement. There is a much more universal way to separate the actions of an endoself from those of an exoself. The endoself creates chaos and the exoself creates order.

This may seem intuitively wrong, since endosocialism is a restrictive force and exosocialism is an expansive one. To resummarize the previous two chapters: The restriction of endosocialism creates craving for secondary anima extracted through external destruction. The expansion of exosocialism is achieved by release of stored energy through external creation.

In love, we are all one, but in hate we are individual.

The exosocial release of energy is what is sought through the practice of asceticism. Creation is a way to achieve egalitarian balance, since the energy stored through creation is available to those in need of it. Altruism also releases energy and creates balance.

Evil has generally been considered usurpation of another's will or access to power through secondary anima. Sublation and violation are the root of what has always been considered dark magic. Morality is in the domain of endoreality, but entropy and energy are universal reality topics that may one day provide guidelines for behaviour. Right and wrong in terms of energy is not a puzzle or subjective. Wrong is sublation or violation of others, as this prevents their conscious will from fulfilling its goal of exosocial expansion.

Predatory behaviour is punished through the change in the nature of the self. The predatory self changes from an interconnected empathic network to an isolated object, addicted to life and unable to obtain it except through artificial and parasitical means. Those who most cling to power and identity lose both. Those whose hearts are weighed down are those who have hoarded anima rather than using it.

The first universal law is a law against barriers to exosocial expansion. This is not the right to pursue happiness as advocated by the Marquis de Sade and his compatriots. Neither is it the Golden Rule advocated by Kant and so many others. It does not forbid the exercise of power as some feel that anarchy or libertarianism must. A caregiver may still stop a baby from running in front of a car. This use of power facilitates the future expansion of a baby that does not have a fully formed, autonomous self or the ability to exert a strong conscious control over emotional will. An adult may not have that conscious strength either, if they are intoxicated or suffering from some other loss of ability to focus.

The second universal law may be considered a replacement to the Golden Rule. The law against sublation or violation ensures that the duty of every person to another, whether they are a child or an ancestor, a person in possession of all that they need or a person in great need is the same. Each is responsible for creating balanced connection in all interactions. This natural inclination has been corrupted by a system of unequal exchange, as explained in *The Power Economy*.

In order to have a balanced interaction in situations of unequal power, altruism must be rewarded. Respect, gratitude and acknowledgment avoids martyring the benefactor. People should not be accepted or rejected, whole and unconditionally. Acceptance or rejection should be applied to each interaction. Interactions should all be balanced, not so carefully that there is no bond, but carefully enough that there is no traumatic bond. People often seem to swing from one extreme to the other. Either the person is in predatory relationships, or they are isolated with no real connections. Both of these states are encouraged and celebrated in endosocial culture.

In an endogroup, people are either in or out. In exosocial relationships, they are accepted or rejected through each accepted or rejected interaction.

In love, we are all one, but in hate we are individual. Hate is the creation of endosocial membranes and love is the creation of connections. Endosocial membranes create one dominant will around a person or group of people and prevents anima exchange or empathic connection outside of the group. A shared animus can be either exosocial or endosocial depending on the strength and permeability of the surrounding membrane.

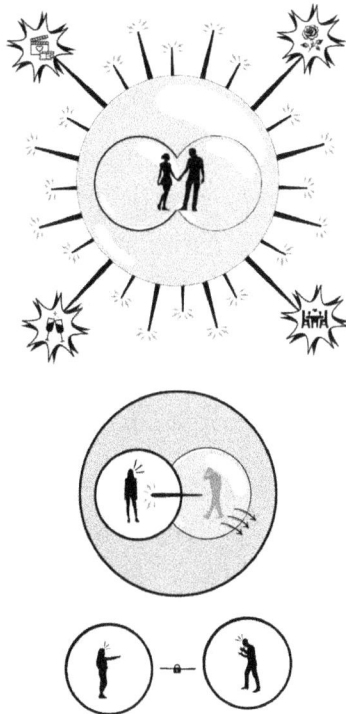

Figure 41: Connection, sublation and violation

The secret to a happy relationship may be in the

melding of energy to the point that there is one perspective, like the couples who finish each others' sentences. Definitely, they should not have conflicting endorealities. Such relationships are usually reduced to each side calling the other crazy, a certain indicator of conflicting endorealities. Additionally, each partner should be experiencing time at the same rate if they are not to be a source of extreme frustration for each other. If the membrane is too strong, however, and there are not enough outside connections for each person, the shared animus will become an endogroup with a power struggle and one person will be sublated to the other.

Behaviour is taught by acceptance or rejection of that behaviour. If exosocial expansion is met with disapproval, with accusations that the person is not acting like their family, sex, nation, etc., then the result is an association of shunning with the behaviour. Negative image associations cause guilt, shame and stress responses to be associated with attempts at expansion.

Is it then permissible to dismantle an endogroup which is voluntarily upholding an endo-ideal, when in so doing, it is creating a negative image and blocking exosocial expansion? An action to prevent endogroups and predation is in obedience to the second law, which is the law of egalitarian force. Any deconstruction of endogroups must obviously be taken with extreme care. Giving the negative image opportunities to make external connections allows them to develop their own conscious will. Dismantling an endogroup without their consent overrides their will and is itself a violation. Endogroups are strengthened by outside opposition and weakened by outside connections. The ends do not justify the means because the ends dictate the nature of what follows.

Figure 42: Endogroup weakening

Further, not all group associations or shared animus are endogroups, not all interactions of unequal force are exploitative and emergency endogroups are sometimes acting exactly as they ought. Many people, especially children, are vulnerable due to an undeveloped or weakened conscious control over will. The lifegiver and caregiver circles begin as emergency endogroups, created to assist an infant and child to develop a strong and healthy self. The caregiver circle may assist other members in the same way, when they are in a weakened state. The key to successful temporary endogroups is discussed in detail in *The Theft of Self*.

Every ordered system is a sublation of all interactions within the system. Where acceptable sublation starts and ends is a matter to be given very careful consideration. This will be discussed further in *Free Will and Seductive Coercion*, but in brief, a developed conscious will should never be sublated and all ordered systems that are capable of developing conscious control over will should be fully encouraged, allowed and assisted to do so.

The law of egalitarian force should prevent anyone from hoarding that which is needed by others. This does not mean that all property ownership is theft. It does mean that depriving others of their basic needs is predation at worst and blocking their expansion at best.

Egalitarian does not mean equal; someone who is idle is already hoarding energy, so someone who is creating does not need to share the product of their energy with them. Neither should generosity have to continue where it is met with ingratitude or abuse as this does not result in balanced interaction. Contempt and predatory or dominant anger should especially never be tolerated as they are both attempts to sublate the other. Generosity and gratitude are the most important virtues to develop for the happiness of the person and those around them.

These reasonable conditions have been extremely misrepresented in the trade economy, however. Now, anyone not engaged in labour for corporations is classified as idle, anyone not subservient to the powerful is classified as ungrateful and corporations demanding labour are presented as gifting employment. The problems and solutions to the current economic model are explored in *The Power Economy*.

At this point, the following points appear to be defensible from our examination of life. These may be base principles on which to construct a new metanarrative. These principles will be expanded in the rest of The Ontology Quartet after we establish a greater understanding of consciousness and will.

1. The only guarantee in life is death. Therefore, the only thing we know for certain is not the purpose of life is the avoidance of death.

2. The purpose of life is to spend life energy. We cannot take it with us when we die, and a surplus may keep us here.

3. Joy, health and motivation are obtained from sources of primary anima, so we must protect the right and develop the ability to freely access primary anima.

4. It is our interactions which will be both our experience of life and our legacy. We are actions, not objects.

Therefore, we ought to seek:

5. Love is the experience of energy going through a connection to a primary anima source. Hate is the experience of energy creating or defending an endosocial membrane. Peace comes from a state of requited love,

free from predation and hate.

6. As agents of order, we are meant to be caregivers, not exploiters. We each have the responsibility to create and care for everything it is within our power to assist.

7. Personal membranes should have the strength to withstand endosocial pressure and the openness to form connections.

8. The conscious will is necessary to access primary anima. The conscious must be free to focus on the present, without unnecessary distraction from the past or future.

9. Debt and credit should be released by balancing our debts and forgiving our credits. Unbalanced interactions create traumatic bonds.

10. Generosity and gratitude are the two most important traits to guide interactions.

11. Human rights are not temporally bound. Those from the past have the right to be remembered accurately and not have their creations destroyed or corrupted (including knowledge). Those from the future have the right to inherit a world that has been cared for to our best ability.

12. Every person has the right and responsibility to uphold the law of egalitarian force and to stop cruelty, sublation and destruction. The repercussions of imbalance ripple to all.

Therefore, we should avoid:

13. Endosocialism is the cause of all human cruelty and destruction.

14. Sublation and violation prevent exosocial expansion and balanced connection. Both must be avoided as they violate both of the two universal laws.

15. Shame, fear and boredom are signs of extreme distress that should be remedied. Contempt and predatory or dominant anger are signs of sublation and violation and should be stopped and blocked.

16. Guilt should be assigned to the guilty person. Unassigned guilt will be transferred and the person it is transferred to will be punished.

17. Endo-idealism is attractive in that it reduces the stress of responsibility which would be overwhelming for someone in crisis or a child. Endo-ideals eventually deanimate and block the expansion of those bonded to them. Temporary endo-idealism must not be allowed to become a permanent state.

A narrative is just words that tell a story. Sometimes the story resonates and helps us understand our lives and sometimes the story is endoreality and serves to disguise what is happening. The purpose of this work is not to tell the only story or provide the only viewpoint that suits our experience. The purpose is to provide a more useful and accurate story than the ones currently in use. Words like quantum entanglement, narcissism and class are of very little use in describing our interactions and their repercussions, and those words bear no relationship to each other. New frameworks are necessary for better understanding and reconciliation of different studies.

New frameworks will make it much more clear that new areas of study are needed to replace the stagnant disciplines that research is now being dropped into. In particular, this book has tried to make it clear that vitology is an urgent field of study. Hopefully, it is apparent that the study of vitology needs to address the following areas:

Physics, to identify the possible forces influencing the experience of life and describe their behaviours.

Medicine, including resuscitative medicine, to study the phases of life and death in terms of energy.

Ayurvedic, traditional Chinese, Kallawaya and all other forms of indigenous magic and medicine to provide context and theory to explore.

Post death studies, current and historical, across as many cultures as possible.

Anthropology, history, literature and linguistics to study early thinking about life and death.

The principles behind animism and the use of anima banks such as icons, totems, gods, euphoric objects and charms.

Decoupled studies to record and analyze all types of decoupled experience in a unified manner.

Endofilter breaks due to trauma, drugs or so-called mental illness.

Spiritual revelations, visions, premonitions and experiences of higher energy such as attained through kundalini or similar practices, through hallucinogens or naturally.

Experiences of earthbound energies such as ghosts or spirits.

Infancy and childhood, to discover experiences, memories or knowledge that may be present before the creation of endofilters and endosocial membranes are complete and to examine the nature of the emotional will.

Elder experiences, particularly around time and their seeming ability to experience past interactions clearly, visions of departed people, partial decoupling or conscious drifting, and any other experience that is wider than normal.

Variant time experiences among people, situations and other species, including those diagnosed with manic behaviour, delayed or advanced learning, and more.

The principles behind astrology, namely the idea of large masses in the planetary system affecting smaller masses on earth and any effect on the emotional will or self. An obvious place to start is emotional disturbances related to moon cycles.

The nature of primary and secondary anima. Are they qualitatively different or is the difference found in the means of accessing them (sublation and violation vs bconnection)?

Power, its use and methods of creation and defence against it.

Violence and self-destructive behaviours.

Contagious emotional responses and other possible responses to anima such as excitement and piloerection.

Correlations between sugar with mood swings, anger and violence, and electronics and electrical sources with anxiety and immobility.

The manifestations, triggers and blocks to experience of excitement and boredom.

Brain fog and mood disorder producing substances.

The nature and causes of endosocial membranes and their dissolution.

Environmental causes for endosocialism.

All of the above should focus on life and death as states and processes, not binary attributes. Other species, including plants, should be studied as well as objects and the planetary systems.

There are thirteen books in the *Binding Chaos* series. We finish exploring the five components of a person in the rest of The Ontology Quartet, and we look at the social ramifications of those findings in The Sociology Quartet and The Institutions Quartet. Based just on *Abstracting Divinity*, we can already say the following: Sociology should be entirely based on vitology. Psychology and economics can be replaced with neuroscience, sociology and vitology. Institutions such as law and government need to be completely redesigned.

There is so much to be done. We live in interesting times, which is a blessing, not a curse. We have opportunity for change and with opportunity comes hope.

Let's go!

Good vitality

The ability to establish and maintain a large and diverse quantity of connections to primary anima.

Poor vitality

The blockage of anima conduits and the inability to continue exosocial expansion.

Abstracting Divinity

Afterword

Heather Marsh

Afterword

My childhood in an extremely isolated village in northern Canada was like something from centuries ago. We travelled by dog sled, riverboat or horseback, we spent much of the year in hunting, fishing, trapping or berry picking camps, there was no running water, electricity, or modern medicine, and we were surrounded by animism. Death was far more common than in outside communities, even including many that are war zones. Birth was equally common. I lived in a world of extremely heightened emotional responses and awareness. I learned many guidelines and answers for daily behaviour based on spiritual traditions. National Geographic did an issue featuring my home[135], complete with a photograph of my mom, who was also featured on the PBS series, Billy Connolly`s "*Journey to the Edge of the World*"

Going outside for school was something we all had to do, for me at 11 years old. Leaving our home was a traumatic wound for many reasons, but many came back and lived out their lives where we were born, often with unhealed trauma. I was accepted into outside culture much more easily than many of my family and village and had a great deal of ambivalence and guilt over whether to leave. The summer I was 13, I had ridden my horse with my cousin to the top of a mountain overlooking the sacred river, my home and greatest love. We climbed to the top of a boulder for the best view to eat lunch. My cousin told me stories from traditional history and sang me a song he had written in the first nations language. Then he said, *"You should be a computer scientist. That's a good job."* The juxtaposition of the moment still makes me laugh. The memory perfectly sums up my childhood of extreme contradictions. Still, it instantly felt like the perfect choice.

Getting there, for a girl from the north, was easier said than done. Even graduating from high school seemed like an impossible feat for years, but eventually I fought my way into a very different world. Leaving the place of my childhood for a life in a modern city was like spinning a cocoon around myself. Things that I once sensed and experienced were left behind as childhood fantasies or superstitions. I became a software developer, the most logical career of all. I studied in assembly language, where everything is both clearly defined and binary, where the same thing cannot hide under different names and different things cannot pretend to be the same. I was no longer terribly sad or melancholy or joyful. I was simply busy.

I always worked to help others, because those others were usually part of the greatly extended community of the north that were expected to help each other. As a lifelong habit, this continued in every community I spent time in, including online. I noticed a great difference in communities and how they responded to altruism, or any unpaid labour, however.

As my work expanded, it got darker and darker. Probably because death and tragedy had been accepted as part of life when I was a child, I gained the reputation for not being able to say no to any fight, no matter how desperate or horrific. I inadvertently conducted extensive research into the vast array of depravity humans were capable of. I spent years trying to help people living in what could only be described as hell, tormented by demons in the shape of humans.

Of course, my first impulse was to look at authoritative knowledge to explain what I was seeing. All I found was Manichean dogma from religions and labels with no meaning from science. The scientific labels were just euphemisms for the religious label of evil, with no more evidence or insight behind them. Neither provided a solution or any understanding.

The more I looked at the darkest acts of humanity, the more I realized that the world outside my cocoon was real. When I helped communities fighting against ritual killings in Gabon [136] and elsewhere, the predators were openly extracting energy from their victims through torture to gain power. There was full understanding, and acceptance of what they were doing. Elsewhere, the exact same behaviour had a veneer of disguise over it. I fought for over a decade against the endless and needless torture of a 14 year old in Guantánamo.[137] His torture was held to be a matter of national security, but it clearly was not. I fought for much longer against the slavery, rape, torture and murder of people for entertainment. These were and are primarily women and children, captured and sold by a massive, global industry of predators. This is often depicted as sex, but it clearly is not.

As the patterns took shape across the world, in so many predatory situations, I began to see them in everyday life as well. The problem wasn't just lone predators who could be authoritatively diagnosed as deviant. Very often, the entire structure of communities or wider society was set up to enable, excuse and justify the predation. Law, economics, governance, and people themselves were all part of an enabling structure. We are governed by organized crime. Media feeds us the blood of the negative image as daily entertainment. This is happening now, and it had clearly been happening throughout history.

My childhood self recognized what I was seeing, but my logical assembly programmer self demanded an explanation. To the best of my ability, this is the most logical analysis I can make of the world that I have seen. This predatory behaviour is something that needs to be faced clearly. The first step is to stop denying that this is what the world looks like. The second step is to stop accepting labels with no meaning as if they are an explanation. The last step is to understand that this is not inevitable human nature. It is something we can and must understand and resolve.

A world of universal empathy is possible. A world where nobody lives in fear, shame, or isolation is possible. We can create a world where everyone is connected and free to expand. People who cannot, or do not want to, control their cruelty can learn and grow past predatory behaviour and they can be convinced to do so.
I realize this is hard to believe based on the history in this book and the reality we are living in. In the next two books of The Ontology Quartet we will explore the obstacles to such an evolution. *Free Will and Seductive Coercion* examines the reasons we make the choices we do and *Shaping Reality* looks at how our understanding is created and limited. The path forward is through understanding. Thank you for taking this journey with me.

Key Concepts

Abstracting Divinity

Key concepts

There are two universal laws to govern life that should be considered when developing laws for societies. These two laws correspond to Newton's second law of thermodynamics, that all systems will progress towards greater entropy.

The law of exosocial expansion: Outward expansion must not be blocked.

The law of egalitarian force: Involuntary, unbalanced interactions must be avoided.

Life force expands outward through interactions with other sources of life energy.

This expansive force can be blocked or deviated through the use of a greater opposing force.

Primary anima may be the exosocial force towards greater entropy, or chaos. Secondary anima may be the endosocial force towards order.

What we refer to as the endosocial membrane is the refusal of the will to allow interactions outside of the bubble it has created.

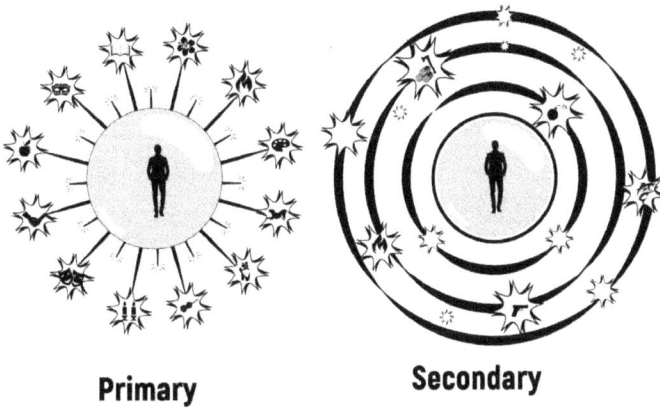

Primary   Secondary

The two types of anima: primary and secondary

- Primary sources of anima are marked by two characteristics. One, they produce euphoria. Two, they prolong life.

- Primary anima is obtained from all interactions resulting in connection.

- Secondary anima is obtained by the predator and lost by the prey in all interactions involving violation and sublation.

- Euphoria is the experience of life and shame is the experience of death, or the depletion of life. The emotional will seeks euphoria and rejects shame.

- The experience of living is an attraction to anima and a continual quest to assure its availability.

- Emotions are all a response to attractions and repulsions to the reality or possibility of a gain or loss of anima.

- The emotional will is motivated solely by potential anima gain or loss and it operates outside the domain of the conscious will.

- Exertion of the conscious will is required in order to access primary anima.

- Depression and fear are triggered by the loss of anima

or anticipation of its loss.

- Joy and excitement are triggered by a gain in anima or anticipation of its gain.

- Anxiety is an emotional response caused by fear of deanimation, meant to prevent exposure to potentially deanimating events.

- Primary anima creates an interactive self; secondary anima creates an object self.

Primary anima sources

All of the following have been shown to extend life and increase health in the general population:

- Expenditure of anima in one's own animus, through experience of one's own body. This expenditure differs from the deanimation triggered by simulated sources such as drugs and passive entertainment. Primary anima can be attained through athleticism, sex, sensory experience, danger, fear, pain or other ascetic ritual. Birth and death may also be a part of this group; although death cannot be said to prolong life, the euphoric surge it provides may advance the life contained in the animus to its next phase.

- Personal interactions involving connection (not sublation or violation).

- Ritual and sharing involving bonded nations and communities.

- Meeting strangers: this brings fear, danger, attraction and the possibility of exosocial expansion.

- Altruism, including time spent with children, elders and those in need of reanimation who repay it with gratitude.

- Receipt of kindness. The actions which offer shared anima to others are collectively referred to as kindness. Widespread kindness is very helpful in balancing anima debts and credits which is why it is encouraged in many cultures.

- Caregiving given or received: massages, hair or skin treatments, personal adornment, especially when individualized, gifts and service given or received.

- Social approval and recognition.

- Creation of a shared animus or strengthened bonds through personal relationships and shared experience, particularly those involving meals, sex, dance, music, pleasant scent, fire, sport, creation, discovery, danger, fear, pain, altruism, risk, ritual, ascetic experience or shared information.

- Rites which establish contact with a larger temporal or spatial self, through communion with ancestors, spirits or an extended nation.

- Personal experience of nature, art, ideas, music, dance, creation, beauty (including the presence of beautiful, generous, happy, wise, talented or otherwise attractive people or animals).

- Gifting of euphoric objects, such as presents, heirlooms, rewards or earnings, which are intended to carry personal esteem. Earnings given with a lack of gratitude and respect do not impart primary anima as they are not offered through balanced connection.

- Discovery: adventure, travel, meeting new people, learning new skills, acquiring new knowledge.

- Creation, especially when using skill or artistic expression.

- Experience of divinity (universal conscious) through visions, devotion, ritual or other means.

Four types of interactions

A **balanced** interaction produces joy.

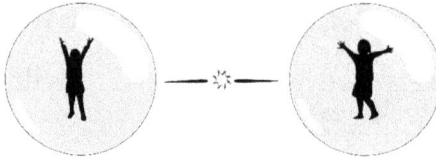

A **rebuffed** interaction may produce anger, aggressiveness or apathy.

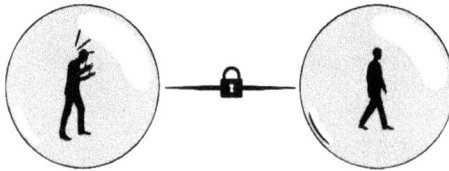

An **unrequited** interaction drains energy from the source.

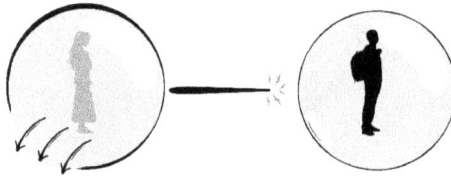

A **predatory** interaction drains energy from one agent, the prey, and that energy is picked up by the other agent, the predator.

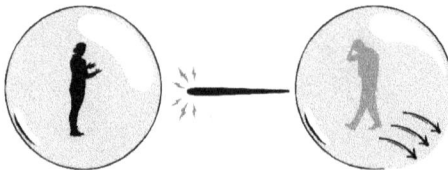

The three types of relationships

Connection: provides a balanced bond between two sides of the interaction.

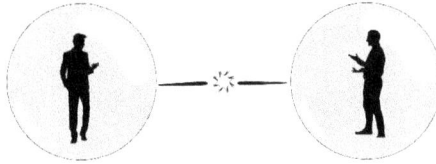

Sublation: one side of an interaction is absorbed into the animus of the other and the dominant will receives the majority of anima.

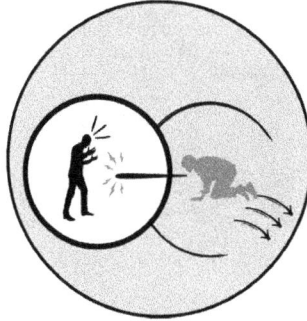

Violation: one animus is attacked by the will of the other to forcibly extract anima.

A traumatic bond

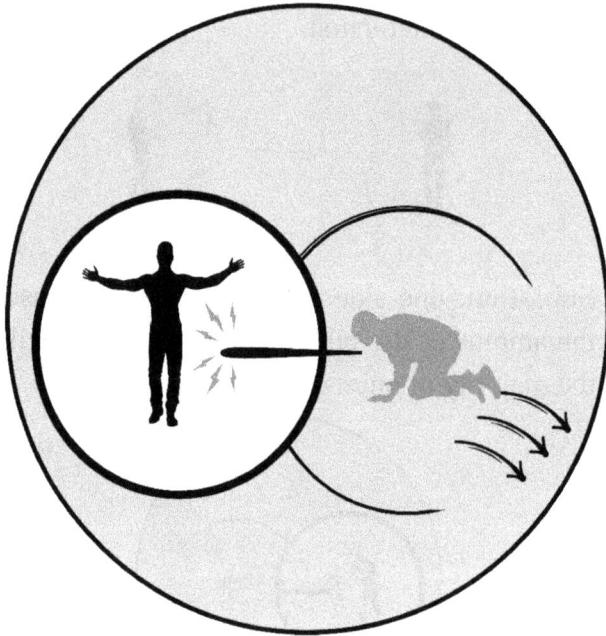

A traumatic bond is formed when one will is sublated to another, they share the same animus and emotional reactions, and are dominated by the same will.

The two types of sublation: endogroup and endo-ideal

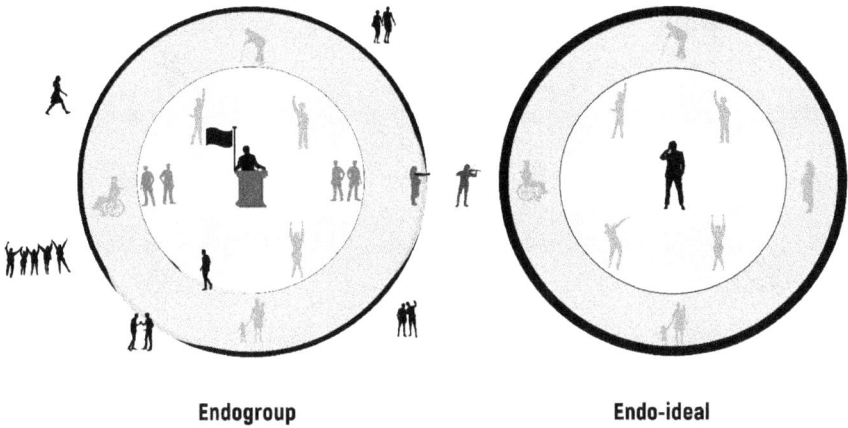

Endogroup   Endo-ideal

The three types of predator

Parasite: Predator who drains energy by exhausting open anima conduits and leaving no reward for the initiator of interactions.

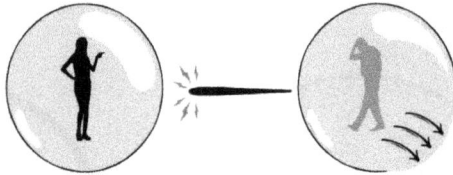

Sublator: Predator who dominates the will of another and creates a shared animus through which they freely access the energy of another.

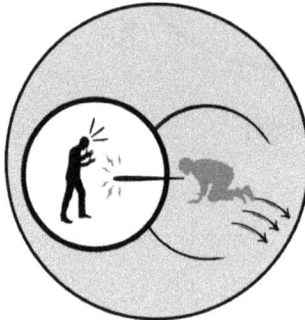

Violator: Predator who destroys the personal membrane of another animus so they can access the released energy as secondary anima.

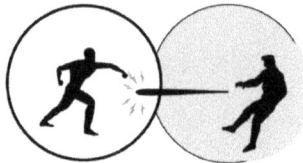

The following are people who do not benefit from possessions. They benefit from the secondary anima resulting from deprivation of others.

- People who hoard more than they need.

- People who destroy what they cannot use or hoard.

- People who refuse to help others even when it requires little or no effort on their part.

- People who attempt to obtain more attention, credit, sympathy, gratitude or other positive response than they are entitled to or are offered.

- People who attempt to fill the lives of others with mess, destruction and stress.

- People who drain the time, energy, or space of others, including by creating unnecessary stress, for instance, those who are chronically late, unprepared or loudly overwhelmed, angry or needy.

- People who actively work against others obtaining peace, happiness or security and fight for others to remain in misery.

All of the above behaviour upholds a structure which enables unequal interactions.

Violations of autonomy and dignity

- Manufacture and enforcement of busywork.

- Attacks on the health of others.

- Attacks on the shared environment.

- Creation of interpersonal conflict.

The creation of powerful systems of order will always result in the creation of surrounding chaos

A negative image must always be crushed to provide the energy for an endogroup.

Social coercion against exosocial expansion

- Association of endogroup guilt with exosocial expansion.

- Association of negative image status with exosocial expansion.

- Restriction of opportunities.

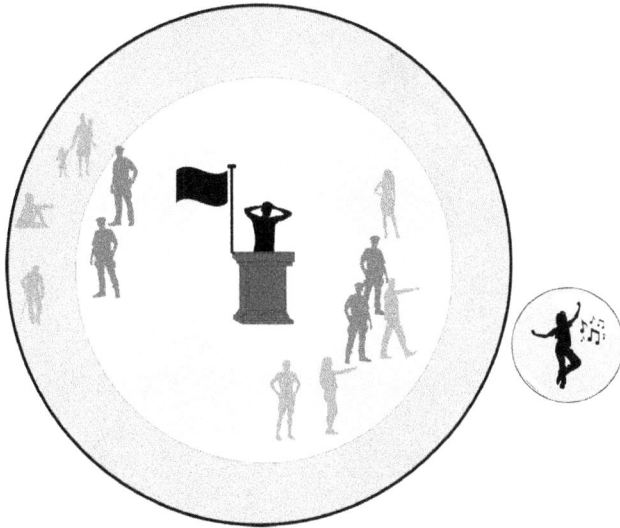

Types of governance

- **Exosocial networks** – anima connections.

- **Endosocial martyrdom** – anima taken from the idol to the masses.

- **Endosocial tyranny** – anima taken from the masses to the idol

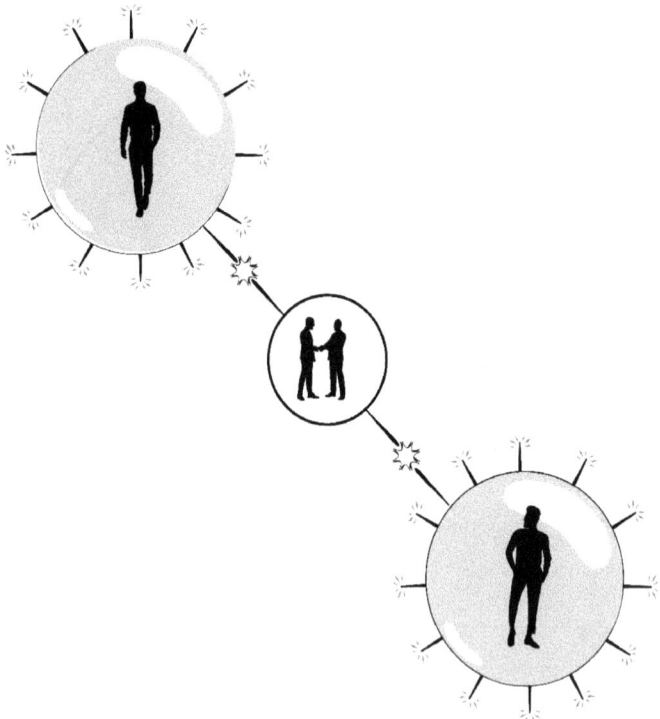

Exosocial network

Sources of Anima

Powerful sources of anima may be an exo-ideal martyr, an endo-ideal tyrant, a reflector saviour or a negative image siren.

Exo-ideal martyr

Endo-ideal tyrant

Reflector saviour

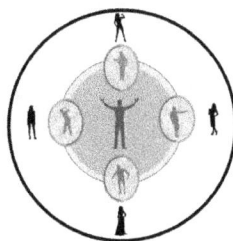

Negative image siren

Martyr

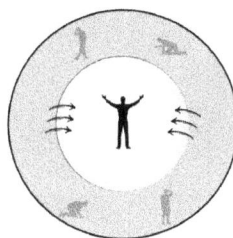

Tyrant

Martyrs are victims of the egalitarian force and tyrants are beneficiaries of endosocial force.

A person is a fusion of five elements: body, self, life, will and consciousness.

- Life makes up the animus of the individual.

- Their relative position in an animated network is their self.

- Their individuated awareness of conscious is their consciousness.

- Their control over the choices of themselves or others emanates from their will.

Just as the body needs healthy food every day, the self needs balanced interactions, the consciousness needs knowledge, the will needs exertion over choice and the animus needs life energy.

Personality is made up of emotional responses to anima attraction and repulsion, governed by conscious and emotional control over will.

Two points of ancient belief about the self

- The self is created at birth
- The self is part of an interactional web where anything that happens affects everything else, although greater influence is accorded to greater and closer events.

The three forms of asceticism

- **Debt asceticism** causes joy through the release from debt and guilt and a lessening of anima bloat.

- **Tantalus asceticism** causes a slight lessening of the cravings of an endoself by removing from view objects they are unable to possess.

- **Punitive asceticism** is a form of self-flagellation or debasement in which the target extracts anima from their own stores through punishment and shaming. They are then able to experience euphoria from the release of anima, just as predators experience euphoria when anima is released from their prey.

The conscious and quantum wills follow the second law of thermodynamics.

The second law of thermodynamics, the tendency towards greater entropy, is also the egalitarian or exosocial force which seeks to dissipate all ordered objects. The primordial chaos that encouraged continual dispersal is always at war with the endosocial force of order, or the will to create clusters of interactions which appear as objects.

The emotional will creates order and the conscious will disperses it.

- The emotional will seeks to conserve energy in an animus. This leads to depression because euphoria is attained through expenditure of energy.

- The emotional will craves energy. The emotional will is attached to gravity and ordered objects and fights to preserve endosocial structures.

- Anima bloat strengthens the emotional will at the expense of the conscious will.

- Blockage of the outward flow of primary anima acts against agents of creation. Both blockage and destruction of order cause a forced release of secondary anima which feeds the dominant will.

The original debt of life which all are born into has two repercussions.

- One, the newborn must interact or suffer crippling damage to the development of their self.

- Two, they are sublated to the will of the debt holder until they have completed childhood or longer.

A lifetime is a struggle between a store of life (order) and time (chaos).

The only basic law of physics that distinguishes the past from the future is the second law of thermodynamics. Time appears only alongside expenditure of energy.

Time flows in the direction of greater entropy because time links interactions and the conscious and quantum will choose greater entropy. Movement towards greater entropy is time. The exosocial drive is towards greater entropy.

Life is the energy used to create interactions and time is the attraction between interactions.

Will is the attraction between two interactions. Will creates mass and time.

Space is the location of an interaction relative to other interactions. Time is the link between interactions.

The endosocial membrane may be the spacetime membrane. Both may be the product of the dominant will.

Life is a force in the direction of exosocial expansion.

Life is the creation of an ever-expanding network of animated interactions.

What separates life from unlife is time. Time is the exertion of will. Exertion of will appears to be a function of living.

The will may exist temporarily after death. Self and will may be able to escape the confines of the body (or, more likely, they were never limited to it) but be unable to go where conscious can. Conscious cannot effect change, or exert will, without being bound by the confines of the gravity sphere.

The purpose of a lifespan is to expend life so the person is not weighed down with it during death.

Earthbound spirits may be anima clusters with imbalance, either debt or credit. They may retain emotional will, self and sometimes even conscious.

Primary anima seems to be obtained from conscious and secondary anima from life.

Love

Love is the experience of a flow of energy through connection.

Love, experienced as joy, is an emotion commonly described by those who ascend to the world of light, or photons, or conscious.

Death experiences that escape the gravitational field describe light, or a photon-like world.

Conscious may be photons.

Life may be gravity.

Will is time.

Self is interactions.

Conscious is space.

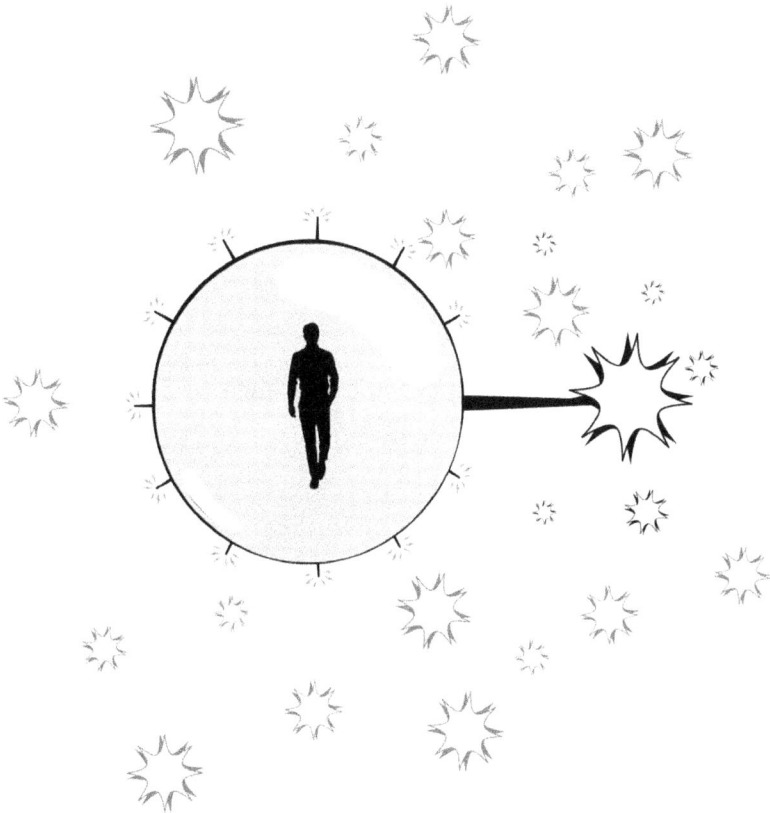

Perhaps ...

Perhaps the universe already exists but in a mutable state so we still have the ability to change it.

Perhaps all lives have already been lived and will continue to be lived with different choices made each time.

Perhaps the will travels through pre-existing lives and recreates them with new choices.

Perhaps multiple wills are living different parts of what we perceive as the same life.

Past lives may be just the experience of an extended self, not necessarily their own self.

None of these statements are an assertion of fact or likelihood. These ideas are included here as Binding Chaos theory opens them up as aspects that need to be explored.

I is the dominant will.

Possession may be a negative energy cluster which attaches to a self as a manifestation of guilt.

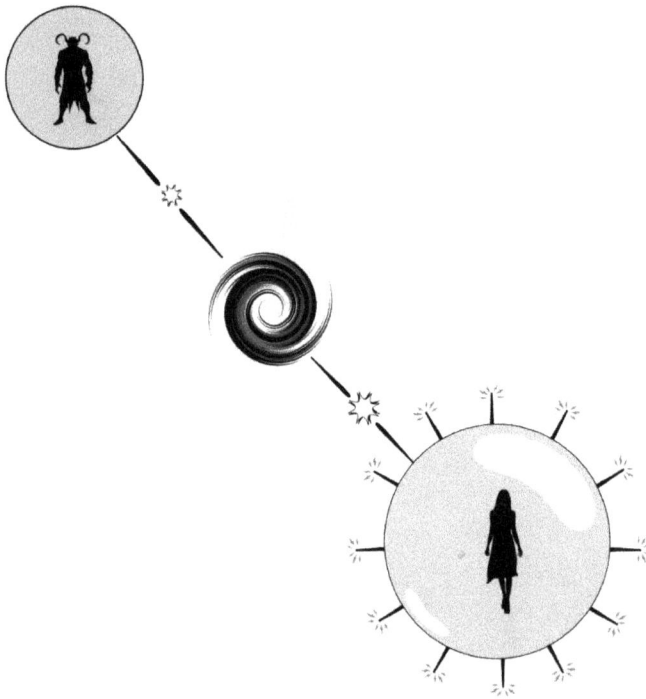

Death..

Anima bloat may cause a decoupled animus to slip into a saddle formation, or hell. Emotional pain and burning may be an attempt to reduce anima bloat.

Tunnels may be wormholes to a different plane.

Void experiences may be caused by a lack of attraction to primary anima.

Inverted experiences may be caused by the reversed poles of the endoself.

A life review may be the experience of rising above spacetime.

Categories of magic

- Guilt allocation, guilt deflection and punishment which are now largely under the jurisdiction of law and economy

- Divination and influence of outcomes which were first transferred to prayer and are now controlled by economics

- Bondage and sublation which are now the business of government

Magic	Modern	Book
Guilt Allocation Deflection & Punishment	Law, Economy	Law and Chaos
Divination & Influence of Outcomes	Prayer, Economics	The Power Economy
Bondage & Sublation	Government	Autonomy, Diversity, Society

Divinity: A loosely defined term representing sometimes the universal or quantum will and sometimes the conscious.

Abstractions of divinity

- Conscious is abstracted into the black box words *imagination* and *nothing*.

- Will is abstracted into the black box word *random* and the institutions of law, economy and algorithms.

- Life energy is abstracted into icons, such as currency.

- Life's influence is buried in the endoreality worlds of psychology and economics.

Abstracting Divinity

Glossary

Abstracting Divinity

Glossary

T he following is a glossary of what I personally mean when I say these words. This is not an attempt to impose my definitions as the correct ones or an invitation to debate the definitions. It is only meant to apply to anything I say or write. As language is meant to be a shortcut to communication I try not to spend too much time discussing definitions. These books use definitions from universal reality unless otherwise noted. Terms using endoreality definitions are often denoted by single quotes.

Abstracting divinity:

1. The ways in which conscious and will have been disguised, hidden, denied and abstracted into ideas and institutions of governance, religion and science.

2. The methods through which the living access universal conscious and will, through anima banks, ritual and divination.

Alienation:

1. The process by which many smaller endogroups are created within a wider endogroup. This can happen organically as a wider endogroup dissolves or weakens, and it is also a political strategy used to weaken rival endogroups.

2. A separation created between two or more endogroups.

3. The separation of a part of the self, such as seen in those with refracted or amputated cores.

Alive:

1. An endoreality term for objects which meet an arbitrary threshold of animation and have not been authoritatively declared dead.

2. In Binding Chaos theory, the ability to access either primary or secondary anima is considered the defining feature of living.

Altruism: An exosocial act of assistance to another in order to create egalitarian balance.

America: Two continents and 35 countries.

American: Residents of any part of America.

Amputated core: The alienated part of a self caused when a person's own core is seen by them as an enemy outsider.

Anarchy: Society free of subordination to endogroups at any level. An exosocial society.

Androtheism: worship of men or gods in the form of

men.

Anger: Anger can be defensive, dominant or predatory. Defensive anger is against external threat and can be experienced by anyone. Dominant anger is used to sublate another. Predatory anger is used to obtain secondary anima through the stress response of another.

Anglo / Germanic: Relating to states that speak primarily English and heavily adopt Anglo culture or are part of Germanic-speaking Europe. Notable for an industrial-scientific endo-idealism that took early precedence over the various church, filial or other endo-idealisms elsewhere. Recently, this group became the global endo-ideal through transcendental industrial-scientific endo-idealism. This is currently being replaced by the mono-empire.

Anima: life energy

Anima bank: A repository which contains surplus anima, obtained through sacrifice, devotion, offerings or interactions. An anima bank can be a person, dead or living, a rite, an object or an idea.

Anima conduit: A means of allowing the transfer of anima from a primary source.

Anima credit: A balance owed in a relationship or interaction where the subject has given more than they have received.

Anima debit: A balance owed in a relationship or interaction where the subject has received more than they have given.

Animus: Life energy contained within a personal or shared membrane for use by an individual or group.

Anima bloat: The overfilling of an animus with life energy.

Anonymous: A specific stigmergic method of collaboration and the people who use it.

Anxiety: An emotional response caused by fear of deanimation, meant to prevent exposure to potentially deanimating events.

Approval theory of value: The value of goods is based on the amount of social approval they represent.

Approval economy: Economy based on societal approval and acceptance.

Art: Creation which channels primary anima or acts as a capacitor for primary anima.

Asceticism: Depletion of energy in a personal animus by the will associated with the animus. asceticism under control of an external will is torture. There are three forms of asceticism: debt, Tantalus and punitive asceticism.

Authoritative endogroup: The endogroup with the coercive force available to enable them to define reality, morality, norms and law.

Auto-anima: Anima produced by feeding on oneself through asceticism, drugs or other attacks on one's own animus.

Auto-objects: People objectified by themselves who

thereby become subjects with the power to objectify others.

Autocoercion: Transparent, consensual coercion a society applies onto itself.

Autogenocide: Genocide instigated remotely, usually though media incited sectarianism or trade of drugs or weapons to the targeted population, but performed by the population on itself.

Autohomicide:

1. Homicide instigated remotely, usually through violation and sublation techniques which destroy a personal membrane and leave the prey vulnerable to coercion by external wills.

2. Giving a negative image the desperation and means by which to destroy themselves, usually through self abuse, risk taking or suicide.

Autonomy:

1. Freedom from involuntary, unbalanced interactions aided by possession of a healthy personal membrane and a network of primary anima sources and conduits.

2. Governance by user group including governance of self for those things which impact only self.

Billion: A billion is a million million (bi + million), but the US. changed it to mean a thousand million so that they could have 'billionaires'. The two definitions are now known as the short scale and long scale definitions. This is a classic example of reality manipulation to serve an exceptional myth and endo-identity created from magical words subject to the whim of the endo-ideal.

Binding Chaos:

1. The natural method of using extrapolation, experience and experimentation to bind chaotic input into ordered packets of information as our brains are designed to do.

2. The use of extreme coercive force to prevent chaotic systems from living, evolving or creating change.

3. The transition from primordial chaos to a world of ordered objects.

4. Endosocialism.

Black box words: Words with no definition other than circular, often used to pretend a meaning where none is known or disguise a meaning which is against the authoritative endoreality. Examples are *nothing, imagination*, and *random*. In the *Binding Chaos* series, black box words are used when the full definition is unknown. An example is *anima conduit*.

Body: A physical form, one of the five elements of a person.

Boredom: A sign of severe distress which occurs when someone is offered an interaction which they cannot access or a third party is attempting to intercept an interaction or there is no interaction available. Boredom is the inability or refusal to exercise will and seek interaction. This is the chronic condition of an endoself.

Bureaucrats: People with institutional authority to exert their will over the interactions of others.

Butterfly: An idea which can cause a hurricane of change. Reference to the butterfly effect.

Capacitor: A cluster of interactions in the form of an object, rite or idea which serves as an anima bank. A capacitor stores an excess of anima which can be accessed in other times and places.

Caregiver: A person whose work involves the care of other people, animals, communities or ecosystems.

Caregiver-self: A circle of expansion which includes or replicates those relationships first formed by a baby or small child with their home and caregivers, particularly if that circle has created an endogroup.

Centripetal force: A force which acts on unequal populations in forced interactions to create ponzi schemes of celebrity, wealth and power and endogroups. Slight advantages become huge by the requirement that everyone support those with resources or power in order to benefit. This force creates and upholds endogroups and is an endosocial force.

Centrifugal force: An egalitarian force which acts in opposition to ponzi schemes and endogroups. This force serves to either strengthen the existing ponzi scheme by increasing the defending force or collapse it. This is an exosocial force.

Censorship by noise: Using celebrity or official status to amplify certain voices or opinions to the disadvantage of others who may have better or opposing information. Using astroturfing spam for the same purpose.

Channeler: A person with the ability to channel prolific amounts of primary anima, often through art, which differs from craft due to this added feature.

Charity: An endosocial act of giving which results in establishing the giver as the endo-ideal and the receiver as the negative image. This differs from altruism in the fact that no connection is established and debt and guilt are incurred by the receiver, along with a negative image status.

Circle of self / circle of expansion: Clusters of relationships and interactions that form naturally or through coercion as a person's self develops from birth onward. These clusters may form into endogroups and block further expansion. They often occur at the levels of lifegiver, caregiver, nation, discovery, creation or divinity.

Civilization: A vast network of interception points for sublation of interactions and interception of anima.

Class: A social construct (endoreality) resulting from classification of people relative to the endo-ideal. Modern usage is usually related to wealth endo-idealism.

Cognitive dissonance: Distress caused by a conflict between dominant and authoritative endoreality, between universal reality and endoreality or between an endoreality believed in the past and what the subject believes now.

Colonization: sublation of the will and animus of a nation.

Commoner: A stable majority created to uphold the status quo, or overthrow it during times of revolution. Societal structures are designed for the comfort and coercion of commoners. Mass acceptance of this role creates a solid block of uniform opinions which can be used to create and uphold oligarchy and ostracize witches and wretches. Reflector at a state level or higher.

Community: A group affiliated around allocation of common resources. Communities may be societies, where allocation is through social relationships, or trade economies, where allocation is through trade.

Concentric circle: Peer promoted voices or ideas in a transparent, permeable structure where those at the centre receive the most amplification and ideas are audited and taught to the outer circles by knowledge bridges.

Connection:

1. A balanced interaction.

2. An anima conduit constructed with balanced interactions.

Connection nihilism: The idea that all connections are qualitatively the same and there is no added value to bonded people, objects, ritual or ideas. A denial of the existence of euphoric objects.

Conscious: All that exists. Awareness of every interaction that makes up universal reality, from all perspectives. Universal knowledge.

Conscious will: A will controlled by the conscious. Conscious will chooses the path of greater entropy through dispersal of personal energy, usually in the creation of order.

Consciousness: Filtered, condensed, modified and individuated awareness of a part of conscious, presented from the perspective of a specific will's position in a self. This awareness is limited to only those interactions within zero degrees of the subject will and initiated through conscious control of will. This subset of reality is subjected to the laws of endoreality through an endofilter.

Contempt: Shame and guilt are punished by contempt, an emotion directed downwards from the endo-ideal to the reflectors or negative image and from the reflectors to the negative image to increase their separation from guilt.

Corporate feminism: Feminism which emanated from the United States in the 1960s and was heavily guided by both the CIA and corporate interests. It created an endogroup out of a global exosocial struggle for women's liberation.

Corporate masculinism: A political movement which began in the 1970s to advocate against women's liberation under the guise of men's rights. It is heavily guided by the primarily criminal sexual sublation and sexual violation industries as well as many state and religious bodies. The objective is to continue the enslavement of women for domestic labour, baby production and the rape industry. The objective is the oppression of women, but the target of coercion is men.

Crabs in a pot: If only one crab is placed in a pail, they can easily escape, but if more than one are there, they will each other back from any attempt to escape. This is used as a metaphor or simile for similar social behaviour.

Creation-self: A circle of expansion which includes those relationships related to creation. This is often trapped into a career endogroup.

Creation euphoria: The euphoria obtained from the act of creation. This can be stored in a euphoric object.

Credit: Anima owed to the prey of unbalanced interactions in order to achieve egalitarian balance.

Culture: The rites, objects and ideas that connect a national animus through space and time. This may include dances, songs, art, spirituality, some aspects of creation, rituals, and euphoric objects.

Currency:

1. Abstract, dissociated approval which allows access to all benefits of society without contribution, membership or acceptance of the society's values or norms.

2. Endosocial token to replace gratitude and approval and replace exosocial interactions with endosocial transactions.

3. A capacitor which contains anima in an easily exchanged format.

4. A talisman for transferring the guilt in an unbalanced interaction to the recipient.

Curse: Attribution of guilt through the assigning of a negative image status along with the guilt. Often used alongside punishment, i.e. screaming the curse while beating or killing someone assigns them the blame for their own victimhood.

Deanimation: the loss or depletion of life from an animus. Deanimation often results in physical manifestations such as low stress resistance, weakened immunity, adrenal exhaustion, depression or other weakness and can result in serious illness or death.

Dead: A state of low animation that occurs on a spectrum. An endoreality term used to authoritatively assign an attribute and define some objects and formerly living things as not living.

Death: The decoupling of the five elements of a person (body, self, life, will and consciousness) in such a way that they often cannot be rejoined.

Death Eaters: Members of a society where the norms or culture are driven by sadism. The agony of others is not a side effect of their actions but a goal. Death eaters are distinct from those with an individual personality disorder in that their society's norms, structure and actions are all constructed to feed their sadism.

Decoupled: a person whose five elements (body, self, life, will and consciousness) have been dissociated from each other and are no longer bound into a unified person.

Debt: Anima owed by a predator in unbalanced interactions in order to achieve egalitarian balance.

Debt asceticism: asceticism which causes joy through the release from debt and guilt brought by a lessening of anima bloat.

Democracy: Governance by representative or direct voting systems.

Demographics: Objectification and alienation of people

through further division of the already objectified populations, usually in an attempt to create new endogroup identities for coercion.

Depression: A state of deanimation. This may be caused by blocked or ruptured conduits, unrequited interactions, an inhibited will, shame, sublation or violation.

Dignity: Preservation of ownership over one's own inner circles of self. This ownership creates personal integrity and strength.

Discovery-self: A circle of expansion which contains those relationships unique to discovery. This is often trapped into an academic endogroup.

Dissociation:

1. Separation of individuals from the dependency relationships which make up society.

2. Separation of self in the case of refracted or amputated cores.

3. Separation of conscious, self or will from each other.

Diversity: There is diversity between every two humans. In endoreality, this term is used to create endo-identities, which is the opposite of diversity. The concept could be replaced with anti-endo-idealism. A better path would be to simply point out endo-idealism and leave anti-endo-idealism as the default state.

Divinity: A loosely defined term representing sometimes the universal or quantum will and sometimes the conscious. This is possibly also Jung's *collective unconscious* and the source of Kant's *synthetic a priori knowledge*. In the *Binding Chaos* series it is used to refer to universal conscious and will as they are referenced colloquially.

Divinity-self: the self created by euphoric interactions with divinity. These can include spiritual sources but can also be found in everyday euphoric sources, whether or not the subject experiences them as spiritual. Any interaction with primary anima or the conscious expands the divinity self. The divinity self is often trapped into a religious endogroup.

Divination: The attempted acquisition of divine (universal conscious) knowledge or divine (universal will) choice through skill, following a methodology. Some rationalism and even some science falls under this category.

Dominant endogroup: The endogroup which has the subject person or population most immersed in its endoreality or most sublated to it.

Economy:

1. Resource allocation.

2. When referred to as *the economy*, it serves as an anima bank or god for wealth endo-idealism.

Emotion: Response to anticipation or experience of access to anima or anticipation or experience of an attack on an anima source.

Emotional will: A will controlled by the self and motivated solely by potential anima gain or loss.

Empathic bond: An empathic conduit that is strong and somewhat permanent.

Empathic conduit: The means by which understanding can be shared or jointly experienced between two sources.

Empathy: The ability to share understanding with another through empathic conduits.

Endo-exceptionalism: Adherence to the exceptional myth of an endogroup.

Endo-ideal: The idealized self of an endogroup, embodying all virtue, ownership, victimhood and credit.

Endo-ideal sublation: Sublation of will to an endo-ideal.

Endo-idealism: Adherence to the laws of endoreality which attribute all virtue, ownership, victimhood and credit to the endo-ideal and all vice, guilt and punishment to the negative image.

Endo-identity: A magical word used to set an endogroup off as exceptional and create difference where none exists.

Endofilter: A cognitive filter which causes the subject to filter all information from universal reality according to the laws of endoreality. This includes the endoreality experienced by humans as macroscopic objects and the perception commonly accepted as 'sane'.

Endogroup: A social structure for creating power through the transfer of energy. A group of affiliated people who use inclusion and shunning to define their society and are bound by an endosocial membrane. An endogroup may be temporally unlimited to allow ownership and appropriation of property, culture, achievements and victimhood from generations past. An endogroup includes six components:

- An identity which enables exclusive membership. May be referred to as an endo-identity or a [specific endogroup] identity, ie state identity, race identity, etc.

- An idealized source of collective reality, residing in a person or ideology. May be referred to as an endo or exo-ideal or a [specific endogroup] ideal, ie scientific-industrial ideal, religious ideal, etc.

- An existential threat from external forces.

- An exceptional myth justifying unequal entitlement. May be referred to as an exceptional myth or a [specific endogroup] myth, ie nation myth, family myth, etc.

- A negative image, made up of people identified as opposite the ideal. May be referred to as a negative image or a [specific endogroup] negative image, ie wealth negative image, health negative image, etc.

- Reflectors which may exist separately from the negative image in groups of more than two. May be referred to as a reflector or a [specific endogroup] reflector, ie academic reflector, male reflector, etc.

Endogroup sublation: Sublation of will to an endogroup.

Endoreality: A reality which exists only within an endogroup and is created with the laws of endoreality. Endoreality is filled with magical words which have no universal meaning but serve to cast people as the negative image or endo-ideal. Endoreality is relative and has no meaning outside the perspective of the endogroup. Endoreality can change at the whim of an endo-ideal.

Endoself: A predator who can only exist, or prefers to exist, through acquisition of secondary anima.

Endoself contagion: The process by which exosocial interactions are blocked and discouraged in a population of endoselves, leading exosocial people to develop endoself behaviours through necessity.

Endosocial: Existing within the confines of an endogroup or endoself or according to the laws of endoreality.

Endosocial membrane: A membrane which blocks empathic and euphoric conduits and thereby creates endoselves and endogroups.

Endosocial martyrdom: Anima is forcibly taken from the idol and distributed to the masses.

Endosocial tyranny: Anima is forcibly taken from the masses and distributed to the endo-ideal.

Endosocialism: The belief that societies ought to be ordered within endogroup power structures.

Envy: The sense of injustice felt by members of an endogroup if external acclaim or a coveted item is held by someone outside the endogroup or its endo-ideal.

Epistemic community: A way to provide elite expertise for projects without relinquishing control to an elite oligarchy. People or ideas are peer promoted from within the user group and communities remain transparent and permeable to everyone. Acceptance or rejection of ideas is always up to the user group to avoid an unassailable oligarchy. Typically organized in transparent, permeable concentric circles.

Equality: An observably false idea that all people are equal used to justify imposing involuntary interactions of unequal force on diverse populations. This results in power accumulation and endosocialism.

Equivalence: The idea that all members of a society are entitled to equivalent benefit from the society and no one should be valued by standards of achievement which others have greater ability to attain. No contribution to society is inherently of greater value than another although the degree of effort may be. This is an idea which supports exosocialism.

Escapism: Entertainment which provides easy secondary anima and does not challenge endoreality. Escapism strengthens the emotional will over the conscious will. It is easier to watch because it does not require an expenditure of energy through the focus of the conscious will.

Euphoria: The emotional experience of anima, or life energy.

Euphoric bond: A euphoric conduit that is strong and somewhat permanent.

Euphoric conduit: A path or method allowing the transfer of anima from one source to another. An anima conduit.

Euphoric depletion: Deanimation.

Euphoric interaction: one which results in a net gain in primary anima.

Euphoric object: An object which contains anima from

its creator or previous or current owners and can be used as a capacitor to connect an extended self through space and time.

Exceptional lives: Lives which are given far more value by media and society due to endo-ideal status.

Exceptional myth: Exceptional myths encourage both unjustified glorification of the group and its endo-ideal and unjustified demonization of the negative image as well as other endogroups and their endo-ideals. The five primary types of exceptional myths address creation, leaders, superiority, persecution and destiny. A purely magical creation, like the endo-identity; its purpose is its function, not its meaning.

Excitement: The anticipation of primary or secondary anima.

Exo-ideal: The idealized centre of an endogroup where the primary energy transfer flows from the idol to the rest of the group.

Exogroup: This does not exist as an exogroup is simply a cluster of interactions.

Exoself: A person with no, or very few, endosocial attachments and a large exosocial network.

Exosocial: Pertaining to exosocial expansion.

Exosocial expansion: Uninhibited expansion of self by continual establishment of euphoric conduits through relationships, discovery, creation, spirituality, etc to primary anima sources.

Exosocial networks: Created by conduits between primary sources of anima to allow balanced euphoric interactions.

Exosocialism: The belief in universal freedom to uninhibited exosocial expansion.

Extranational: Existing outside national or state structures.

Extroversion: Enjoyment of social interactions as a source of anima.

Face: An integral part of a person, signifying a healthy personal membrane, free of debt or unreleased credit and able to establish balanced connections.

Fear: Fear is anticipation of an attack on a qnima source. In a primarily exosocial person, the feared attack is on an anima conduit or source. In a primarily endosocial person, the feared attack is on an endogroup or endo-ideal.

Feminism: The belief in the liberation of women to fulfill their full potential through uninhibited exosocial expansion. The word feminism is a poor substitute for the concept of women's liberation. Removal of male and other types of endo-idealism would be much more helpful in achieving liberation than establishment of endogroup feminism.

Festival: An event for producing a surge of primary and/or secondary anima from a variety of sources. Festivals are common before life threatening events such as war or winter and in the creation of shared animus such as marriage or coronations,

First age of nations: A great variety of autonomous and complete societies, occasionally networked and sharing or trading with each other, which people lived in for hundreds of thousands of years.

Forbidden chamber: A construction which conceals and forbids access to secrets of the guilt of the powerful. This supports the endoreality law that knowledge of endo-ideal guilt is a greater offence than any crime committed by the endo-ideal. See also Secret chamber guilt.

Fourth age of nations: A potential society we could develop, more diverse, flexible and mutually supportive than the first tribal one and more rewarding and universally beneficial than the third parasitical, supranational one.

Fraternity: Decentralized patriarchy resulting from politics which espoused Liberty, Equality, Fraternity. Fraternity as a goal is not suitable to global collaboration as it implies both equality and unanimity of principles. It has resulted in a fraternity of endo-ideals aligned under endosocialism. They still claim the right to control the lives of other people and occupy the top strata of society, like patriarchy, but now they bear no responsibility for governance or any participation in society.

Gaslighting: Assertion of the laws of endoreality through denial of universal reality and guilt reversal.

Gender: A social construct (endoreality) created in order to impose power relations based on sex with a male endo-ideal and a female negative image.

Genocide: The murder of a nation.

Ghosts: Decoupled but undispersed animus. These may be interaction clusters with an imbalance, either credit or debit.

Gift: Goods or services allocated to a person who is not automatically entitled to a share by social norms, or goods or services one is not automatically entitled to by social norms, such as personal or rare property. Gifts are not an entitlement and frequently carry expectations such as eventual reciprocity or future friendship.

God: An anima bank with a will which allocates life energy according to whim, supplication, deception or justice.

Governance:

1. Endosocial definition: Enforced subordination to an endo-ideal and enforced membership in an endogroup.

2. Exosocial definition: Caretaker responsibility of the user group.

Gratitude: A feeling of good will and admiration directed towards the provider in an altruistic interaction.

Guilt: The debt from an unbalanced interaction. Guilt is transferable.

Gynophobia: Terror of women, the fear of becoming or being cast as a woman (the negative image), or fear of the loss of patriarchal power or male endo-idealism. Gynophobia is particularly prevalent in those with an amputated core.

Gynotheism: worship of women or gods in the female form.

Hate: The experience of the expenditure of energy in creating or defending an endosocial membrane.

Holosocial: A social group which includes everyone. May

be exosocial but may also refer to endosocialism under a global mono-empire.

Homo economicus: The endo-ideal of classical economists. A pure endoself, with no goals outside of the exploitation of others for accumulation of personal power.

Honour: Hierarchical approval awarded from the endo-ideal, signifying the state of not being the negative image.

Hope: Conscious striving for exosocial connection or relief from sublation or violation. To lose hope is to stop seeking connection or liberation.

Hostile seductive coercion: An external force of seductive coercion with interests in opposition to the subject.

Idea based collaboration: Collaboration that develops or verifies an idea or information.

Idol: The idealized self or anima bank for an endogroup.

Ideologues: Members of endogroups with an exceptional myth based on ideas attributed to them or ideas they adhere to.

Independence: The state of living free from dependencies. This is impossible in reality but can be simulated by the use of currency to abstract dependency and endosocialism to deny the labour of the negative image.

Imagination: A black box word used to describe glimpses of conscious outside of personal perspective. This often appears in dreams or a trance state.

Incel: An acolyte of an offshoot of corporate masculinism which uses the dehumanization and debasement of women to manipulate men. The associated propaganda encourages men to be anti-social and suicidal, and incites acts of domestic terrorism. It appears to be heavily influenced by rival state agencies.

Indigenous: Customs or hereditary members of a community which follows a first or second age culture of the subject region.

Infidelity: Embezzlement of the energy of a shared animus to feed outside interactions or an external animus, particularly in monogamous, romantic relationships.

Inhumanity: A lack of empathy and denial of the need of others to live dignified lives.

Integrity: Strength of personal membrane and exosocial network.

Interaction: An action involving two entities, initiated by will, using energy from life, occurring in one spacetime. Irreversible units of conscious. The base unit of the universe. Interactions are clustered into individual selves by endosocial membranes which exist only in endoreality. Interactions may be balanced, rebuffed, unrequited or predatory resulting in events and relationships of connection, sublation or violation.

Interaction self: The true self, composed of networks of interactions.

Introversion: Fear of social interaction because of experienced deanimation.

Inverted debt: Guilt or debt which is transferred to a benefactor so that the beneficiary feels ever-increasing credit or entitlement instead of gratitude or guilt.

Iron law of oligarchy: Theory of Robert Michels, *"Who says organization, says oligarchy"*. This theory says that oligarchy is inevitable and it is used as a justification for fascism. Oligarchy is inevitable under endosocialism but not through exosocialism.

Jealousy: Fear of a negative change to one's own endogroup status due to the relative rise of another.

Joy: The experience of euphoria caused by available and secure connections to primary anima. An endoself may feel excitement, but never joy.

Kindness: Collective term describing the actions which offer shared anima to others.

Knowledge bridge: People who help disseminate information from an expert to a novice level of understanding and collectively audit what the epistemic community is doing. Besides being essential for education and auditing, this is important to avoid demagogues who have the ability and time to develop mass appeal but are not the source of expertise. Epistemic communities and knowledge bridges allow elite expertise a direct path of communication to the entire user group and provide a path for anyone in the user group to promote ideas and achieve elite expertise if they wish.

Laughter: A method of sharing euphoria and a reaction to the experience of euphoria or awareness of endoreality. The seven types of laughter are experience of euphoria, self affirmation, self destruction, social affirmation, social exclusion, endogroup domination and endogroup submission.

Laws: Coercive strictures which reflect the laws of endoreality for the authoritative endogroup.

Liberation: Freedom to continue exosocial expansion.

Libertarian: Desirous of liberty, as the freedom to do anything one desires, without social responsibility or acknowledgment of debt. This is a very popular ideology among endoselves.

Liberty: Coercion, responsibility and dependency are part of all human existence. The endosocial illusion of liberty for a few is created through dissociation, enabled by the trade economy. Exosocial liberty is freedom from involuntary interactions of unequal force (sublation and violation) and freedom to continue exosocial expansion through connection.

Life: The energy which is used to create interactions. Life force expands outward through interactions with other sources of life energy. Exosocial expansion can be blocked or deviated through the use of a greater opposing force.

Lifegiver: A woman who has given birth.

Lifegiver-self: The initial self created by the shared animus and cluster of interactions between a lifegiver and an infant.

Living:

1. An attraction to anima and a continual quest to assure its availability.

2. The exercise of will to create interactions.

Loneliness: A melancholy state of longing caused by unrequited connections or a lack of opportunity to establish connections.

Love: The flow of energy through a connection to a primary anima source. Love has three stages: *attraction*, marked by excitement and intense curiosity, *connection*, marked by joy in sharing anima, and formation of a *shared animus*, at which point destruction of the new shared self would cause severe trauma. Love is created by the conscious will.

Lust: Avarice, or a desire for possession in order to obtain secondary anima. Lust has three stages, which are *lust*, manifesting as an intense desire for possession, *possession*, during which the endoself seeks complete ownership or sublation of the target and outside reflection in the form of admiration of their new possession and lastly, *disillusionment*, boredom and punishment of the object which is blamed for the disappointment. Lust emanates from the emotional will.

Magic: The deliberate use of skill and methodology to achieve any of the following:

1. Creation of endosocial barriers and endorealities.

2. Causing ideas or people to be shunned or accepted through the creation of endogroups, endo-ideals and negative images. Sublation of one will to another through creation of a shared animus or bond. Modern examples are employment contracts or student enrollment.

3. The transfer of energy, guilt and debt, especially

through the use of magic words and ritual, including curses and protective spells. *Diplomatic immunity* is an example of a modern spell, complete with talismans, to ward off curses carrying guilt (criminal accusations).

4. Access of information from the universal conscious or guidance of choice or outcome from the universal will through divination.

5. Rituals around guilt allocation, guilt deflection and punishment are now largely under the jurisdiction of law and economy. Divination and influence of outcomes was first transferred to prayer and is now controlled by economics. Bondage and sublation is now the business of government.

Magic words: Words whose usage is unrelated to their meaning in universal reality. Words used solely for the purpose of magic, such as creating an endogroup or endoreality or casting information as authoritative or not based on association with the endo-ideal or negative image.

Martyr: The idol of an endogroup where anima flows from the idol to the rest of the group. An exo-ideal.

Masculinism: Male endo-idealism.

Masculinist theory: Theory based on research that only includes men or is presented from an exclusively male point of view or which sets the experience of men as the normative standard.

Megaphone: A platform able to reach a large number of people.

Migratory endo-ideals: When a transcendental endogroup has an overpopulated group of endo-ideals, or they are under pressure, they will begin to swarm by creating a multitude of smaller endogroups at lower levels. This results in alienated societies and in the colonization of negative image groups both within and without the original endogroup.

Mono-empire: The transcendental global empire at the end of the third age of nations. This is a transitional phase as a mono-empire has no outside opposition and can therefore never fully form.

Nation: Layered and overlapping societies gathered for community, cooperation and sharing, and existing across borders and generations. Nations may include sacred objects, rites, land and culture which facilitate connection across distances of time and space.

Nation-self: A circle of expansion which contains those relationships unique to a nation. This is often trapped into a state endogroup.

Negative image: An endogroup role which causes a person to adopt the perspective of an external endo-ideal and uphold the laws of endoreality. This role acts as the inverse of the endo-ideal. It embodies all vice, guilt and shame assignment within the endogroup.

Neo-necromancer: The powerful of the third age who seek to control populations through occupation of their most intimate circle of self, that containing control over the body, consciousness, self, will and life.

Nightmares: Perception of glimpses of unfiltered

earthbound reality.

Nothing: A state that cannot exist. This is a black box word used by those who choose to deny the existence of whatever they are describing as nothing.

Object: an animus, an energy cluster held together by a dominant will, perceived as individuated.

Object self: A self with an endosocial membrane which is difficult to penetrate or create connections through. An endoself.

Outgroup: A population not included in, or shunned by, an endogroup. This does not include the negative image which is within the endogroup.

Paedosadist: There is no such thing as a sexual orientation called paedophilia. A sexual orientation, or sex, requires consenting partners. It is not sex if some of those involved are called victims, that is rape. Someone attracted to rape has sexual sadism disorder or paraphilic coercive disorder. Someone attracted to the rape of children is a paedosadist. A paedosadist who acts on their impulses is a criminal paedosadist and one who does not is a non-offending paedosadist. This definition is for those relying on the DSM as authority. A more appropriate term is the legal one, child rapist.

Parasite: Predator who obtains secondary anima by intercepting interactions between two primary sources, exhausting open anima conduits and leaving no reward for the initiator of interactions.

Passive genocide: The denial of life essentials to

populations where people will die without access to them.

Patriarchy: A form of male and filial endo-idealism with a hierarchical social structure and a paternal elder as each family endo-ideal. Often inaccurately used to describe male endo-idealism.

Pedosadist: US spelling, see paedosadist definition.

Person: A temporarily bound unit containing a body, self, life, will and consciousness that appear as an individuated, cohesive whole.

Personality: A pattern of conscious and emotional responses to anima attraction and repulsion governed by conscious and emotional control over will.

Personal membrane: A strong and permeable boundary around the inner circle of self which controls intimacy and permits the establishment of euphoric and empathic conduits.

Philosophy: A framework for viewing and analyzing large, fundamental areas of knowledge and experience. A philosophy is based on foundational principles which work in diverse situations. Mechanism and animism are philosophies.

Philosopher: A person who has developed a complete, coherent, original body of fundamental ideas known as a philosophy.

Photoshop: Remove aspects of a story which the writer does not deem relevant or agree with and leave only those which support the writer's bias.

Ponzi scheme:

1. A pyramid scheme algorithm which requires those at the bottom to support those at the top in order to benefit. This type of scheme never benefits more than a few.

2. Social structure in which everyone tries to acquire celebrity, wealth and power, creating a centripetal force that holds oligarchs in place. Egalitarian systems imposed on unequal populations tend to ponzi.

Population: The people objectified and possessed by the endo-ideals of an endogroup.

Power:

1. The ability to control interactions through exertion of greater force. Power is based on energy acquired through unequal force in interactions. There is no idle or inert power and there is no benevolent power.

2. Social approval that causes others to identify with and emulate the powerful ahead of themselves or others. This power can be used to realize one's own will or include or shun the will or person of others and it can also be used to accumulate wealth, celebrity, credit or any other offering that the social group brings. Once this power is established, it provides the unequal force which can be used to turn every interaction into a transaction in which the powerful gain more power.

Power economy: An economy in which every interaction is a transaction, or an energy exchange in which no connections are established.

Predation: Obtaining secondary anima through

involuntary interactions of unequal force. A predatory interaction drains energy from one agent, the prey, and that energy is picked up by the other agent, the predator.

Predator: One who obtains secondary anima from others through stress, pain, obstruction and destruction. The three types of predator are: Parasite, sublator and violator.

Prey: Those who lose secondary anima to others through stress, pain, obstruction and destruction. Those suffering damaged personal membranes and deanimation, or channelers of primary anima with no method of protecting themselves from predatory or egalitarian forces, are often prey. Prey either is or becomes the negative image.

Pride: An endo-ideal emotion. A surge of power and affirmation of their endo-ideal status.

Primary anima: Anima obtained through conscious connection to primary sources. Primary anima produces euphoria and prolongs life.

Primary euphoria: Euphoria obtained through conscious connection to primary anima sources.

Privacy: Privacy is ownership of an individual membrane, control over one's own circles of intimacy and the ability to establish one's own boundaries of intimacy. Privacy is sovereignty over the most intimate circle of self. It includes control over the body, thought and interactions.

Punitive asceticism: asceticism as a form of self-flagellation, debasement, deprivation or severe challenge in which the target extracts anima from their own stores (auto-anima) through punishment and shaming. They are then able to experience euphoria from the release of anima, just as predators experience euphoria when anima is released from their prey.

Quantum will: The chooser behind the choice of outcome in quantum interactions.

Race: A social construct (endoreality) created in order to impose power relations by arbitrary classifications. These have historically included sex, economic class, real or imagined heredity and colourism. The concept, or word, has been sometimes expanded recently (primarily in the United States) to include ideological belief, ancestral language, and self identification.

Random: This is a black box word used by those who choose to deny that every choice includes that which chooses, aka a will. It is usually used to describe an event decided by the quantum will. It is impossible to create a random event in code because random does not exist.

Reaction: A movement demanding change back to a time when a larger portion of the people at the top of the ponzi scheme of power benefitted from it. Reactionaries have no interest in changing underlying principles or helping those at the bottom except with promises of reforms trickling down. Reforms in a ponzi scheme will never trickle down as what feeds the top, bleeds the bottom.

Reanimation: The gain of life energy in an animus.

Ren: A Confucian term once translated as manliness, which is, in the old sense of the word man, humanity. Ren is described most clearly in *The Analects* where it mentions equitable relationships and healthy self-valuation. Ren may be somewhat equivalent to face or personal membrane.

Reflection: The process whereby the empathic conduits of a person are all directed to an external endo-ideal and they act as an obedient enforcer of the laws of endoreality.

Reflector: An endogroup role which causes a person to adopt the perspective of an external endo-ideal and uphold the laws of endoreality. A reflector is seen as obedient and selfless and so avoids the guilt and shame assignment of the negative image. They sublate their own will to the endo-ideal to avoid guilt.

Refraction: The process whereby a person's core self is redirected to an external self and they give up all autonomy and will to the occupying endo-ideal. Extreme dissociation can result from refraction.

Repeater: A rite or action which brings forth another cluster of interactions from a different spacetime.

Resistance: Building new systems and exosocial networks and defending them against oppressive coercion.

Revolution: A change of the top of a power structure, usually replacing an old oligarch with a representative of the largest or most powerful negative image group. The paradigm remains unchanged.

Revolutionary event: One in which an endo-ideal becomes the negative image for a portion of their former obedient reflectors.

Rites: A practice which can be used as a capacitor or

repeater to connect an extended self through space and time.

Sandbox villages: Societies (which do not have to be geographically defined) for trying out new ideas for governance and collaboration.

Saviour: A person who replenishes the anima of others and reflects an idealized image of those they save. A reflector.

Science: Science: 1. A research methodology. 2. A set of ideologies and philosophies used as frameworks to interpret research data. 3. An endo-identity. 4. An endoreality term for an authoritative source of knowledge under scientific – industrial endo-idealism.

Scientific superstition: Fear by scientists of looking at topics outside of their endoreality which is largely the perspective of endo-ideals. Superstition causes a refusal to study, or even acknowledge, anything associated with their negative image, primarily women and indigenous people, or associated with rival endogroups, primarily religion.

Sealed well: Databases of public information which have access controlled by corporate owned web pages and apps.

Second age of nations: Hierarchical trade empires which included a powerful extranational merchant class.

Secondary anima: Anima obtained through fear or other stress responses of another, or destruction. It does not result in the experience of joy, improvement of health or the creation of primary anima conduits. It results in highs, crashes and cravings instead of the peace brought by secure primary anima conduits. It eventually helps to create an endoself which is no longer able to access primary anima.

Secondary euphoria: The experience of secondary anima obtained through sublation or violation.

Secrecy: Ownership and control over the intimate knowledge of another or involving another.

Secret chamber guilt: A tool of guilt reversal where the discovery of guilt is depicted as more grievous than the original act. Secret chamber guilt is used to negate original guilt and justify guilt, shame and punishment being passed to the accuser instead of the accused. It represents the law of endoreality which dictates that the endo-ideal may never be assigned guilt; therefore, the accuser is guilty of breaking the laws of endoreality by doing so. Under industrial or state endo-idealism, secret chamber guilt is often enforced by law. See also Forbidden chamber.

Seductive coercion: Seduction is coercion through emotional attraction and repulsion. Such coercion includes manipulation and control of information by authoritative endoreality. It is often based on shunning and inclusion.

Self: The unique positioning of an individual relative to others connected through a network of interactions.

Self-governance: Governance by user group.

Sex: There are three powers of sex. The exosocial power creates strong euphoric and empathic bonds and eventually, a shared animus with another person. The endosocial power creates an endosocial membrane, with the subjects joined within the membrane or divided by it. The endogroup power can be used to sublate one self to another within an endogroup membrane.

Sexual connection: Sexual interactions which establish connection.

Sexualized sublation: Interactions of humiliation or sublation promoted as sex to disguise their nature.

Sexualized violence: Violent interactions promoted as sex to disguise their nature.

Shame: Shame is the experience of deanimation caused by being assigned guilt and the internalization of the perception of the self as the negative image. Shame inhibits the establishment of euphoric conduits or connection.

Shame killing: The murder of a negative image to eradicate shame assigned to a sublated endo-ideal or endogroup by the transcendental endo-ideal or endogroup. Shame killings are often referred to by the euphemism *honour killings* when they refer to the murder of a negative image under sublated male endo-idealism.

Share: Division of goods or services to benefit all participants. Sharing is considered fair if all participants have an equal amount or as much as they want or need. Sharing is typically practised among members of a physical community such as a tribe or family or an endogroup such as a corporation or state. It is distinct from giving, which is the allocation of goods or services the recipient is not socially entitled to.

Shunning: The refusal to recognize, acknowledge or interact with another. Punitive deanimation through the loss of anima conduits.

Singularity: The common definition is of a technological singularity, a time when artificial intelligence will have progressed to the point of a greater-than-human intelligence. The *Binding Chaos* series refers to social or societal singularities to describe society that is already far too complex and requires too much information processing for individual comprehension to be attainable. We now require mass collaboration to understand any aspect of society or to be able to rationally govern ourselves.

Siren: A powerful person who refuses to reflect an idealized image of others and refuses to dispense anima on demand. A negative image.

Society: A tightly bound network of heavily interdependent relationships between people, often used to describe authoritative endogroups.

Solidarity: The (usually revolutionary) demand that reflectors (the Commoners) unquestioningly uphold endoreality.

Sorrow: Sorrow is a result of deanimation. There are three primary types of sorrow: loss sorrow, when euphoric sources are no longer available, expansion sorrow, when exosocial expansion is forced, restricted or diverted, and shame sorrow, when exosocial freedom is lost due to the destruction of self by shame.

Spacetime: The membrane formed around each interaction and the position of interactions relative to each other.

Spirit: An animus, or energy cluster, which may be attached to a self and may be attached to an emotional will but is decoupled from body and usually conscious.

State: Highly militarized partitioning of societies into economic markets imposed for segregating, competing, allocating and establishing property ownership. An endogroup established at the nation self level.

Stigmergy: Action based method of collaboration which follows an idea. If people understand and agree on a goal, everyone has autonomy as to how or whether they work to further that goal. Communication is through transparency. Secrecy and ownership of ideas are in opposition to stigmergy.

Strata slipping: To fall from obedient reflector to negative image status or from endo-ideal to reflector (due to sublation to a transcendental endogroup) or from endo-ideal to negative image (due to revolution).

Strata slumming: Associating or identifying with those one perceives as the negative image. The motivation for strata slumming may be the acquisition of power by migratory endo-ideals, in which case the subject will seek to create an endogroup through demanding recognition from other endo-ideals, or it may be a humiliation fetish, in which case they will seek to further caricature and degrade the group they claim to be a member of.

Stratification: The creation of different classes of society and formation of hierarchy based on roles.

Sublated: The state in which one's interactions and perception of reality are dominated by an external will.

Sublation: The process by which an individual self or an endogroup is merged into a larger endogroup and identifies more strongly with the larger group's endo-ideal than with their earlier self. One side of an interaction is absorbed into the animus of the other and the dominant will receives the majority of anima. Sublation may be to an endo-ideal or endogroup.

Sublator: Predator who dominates the will of another and creates a shared animus through which they freely access the energy of another.

Supranational: Existing above the power of states or nations.

Sympathy: Pity for another as a result of cognitive analysis and moral judgment.

Synthetic euphoria: Euphoria produced by autopredation on a person's own body, through use of drugs or similar.

Systems: Interacting people, ideas, infrastructure and labour which work in a common area, similar to ministries in today's governance. Health, transportation and housing are examples of three different systems. Systems can overlap and cooperate with each other and they have local and global levels. The global level usually acts as an epistemic community of ideas and the local level controls acceptance and rejection of ideas and implementation of them.

Systems of dissociation: Systems constructed to isolate and divide people from their basic needs or each other and their ability to collaborate.

Tall poppy syndrome: The fear, impulse or act of attacking a person who visibly excels above their peers.

Tantalus asceticism: asceticism which causes a slight lessening of the cravings of an endoself by removing from view objects they are unable to possess.

The Taxpayer: The obedient reflector of industrial endo-idealism, closely related to The Working Class and The Honest Hardworking Man. Someone willing to exploit their communities and the unpaid labour of lifegivers and caregivers and employ reversed accounting to accuse others of parasiting off of them. Serves an abstracted endo-ideal anthropomorphized as The Economy.

Third age of nations: A supranational empire where trade has fully abstracted the relationship between oligarchs and the people they exploit.

Thought bubble: A group which is closed to outside thought by forum or propaganda. An endogroup with a strong endoreality.

Time: The attraction or movement between two interactions. This may be synonymous with will.

Torture: An attempt to fully sublate another by instigating a struggle for control over the most intimate circle of self, that containing the body, thoughts, self and life. asceticism under the direction of an external will is torture.

Trade: An endosocial transaction which does not involve connection and is not subject to guilt in the case of imbalance. Trade is conducted between those without the social ties or desire for social ties that accompany sharing or gifting.

Trade economy: An economy which values only goods and services traded to the wealthy and acts as an abstracted force for coercing unbalanced transactions. This creates a form of approval dissociated from society and placed in the hands of the powerful. A method of resource allocation across endosocial barriers.

Trade empire: One which includes an extranational merchant class and is wealthy in large part due to trade.

Trade relationship: An endosocial relationship allowing interactions of unequal force and the accumulation of power.

Transaction: Interactions which do not establish empathic or euphoric conduits through connection but instead facilitate an energy exchange and result in power for the stronger agent.

Transcendence: The sublation of smaller endogroups into a higher authoritative endogroup.

Transcendental endogroup: An endogroup formed through the sublation of smaller endogroups.

Traumatic bond: A bond formed when one will is sublated to another, they share the same animus, or emotional reactions, and are dominated by the same will.

Tribe: A first age nation barely removed from a family structure where all relationships are direct and there is little to no hierarchy or stratification.

Trust networks: A network of people who rely on each other's knowledge and judgment to filter information and sources.

Truth dictatorships: Powerful information sources or endogroups which present one view of reality as a complete 'truth' or 'fact'.

Tyrant: The idol of a power structure in which anima is

taken from the masses and given to the idol. An endo-ideal.

User group: The entire population which will be affected by an action, including no one not affected. User groups range from one person to the entire world.

Universal reality:

1. Reality which is outside the subjective viewpoint of the endo-ideal and is not based on the laws of endoreality.

2. Reality which is outside of macroscopic experience.

Vapour capital: Equity, options, intellectual property and rights, or social capital as a product of class such as position, education, citizenship and connections.

Vapour wealth: Conceptual financial wealth, not tied to any physical property.

Violation: An attack on one animus by the will of the other to forcibly extract anima.

Violator: Predator who destroys the personal membrane or connections of another animus so they can access the released energy as secondary anima.

Violence: Forceful violation of bodily autonomy. Violence can be used for the same social purposes as laughter: experience of euphoria, self affirmation, self destruction, social affirmation, social exclusion, endogroup domination and endogroup submission. It also has the same powers as sex: the exosocial power creates strong euphoric and empathic bonds with another person, the endosocial power creates an endosocial membrane, with the subjects joined within the membrane or divided by it, and the endogroup power can be used to sublate one self to another within an endogroup membrane.

Vitality: The health of the life energy of an animus, such as that of a person. Good vitality is the ability to establish and maintain a large and diverse quantity of connections to primary anima. Poor vitality is the blockage of anima conduits and the inability to continue exosocial expansion.

Vitology: The study of life energy.

Volition: The process whereby the conscious will initiates action or intercepts an action initiated by the emotional will to allow or deny its execution.

Wealth: An accumulation of social approval, abstracted or otherwise.

Will: That which chooses. The quantum will controls quantum interactions and it may be sublated to the emotional self (which includes external wills) or the conscious.

Witches: Sources of knowledge or innovation where authoritative power does not want knowledge and innovation.

Wretches: Those hidden from endogroup perspective by the one-way mirror of reflectors and made to absorb all of society's guilt and punishment. The negative image.

Abstracting Divinity

Index

Alphabetical Index

A

Abstracting divinity   42, 481

Adam Smith 347

Africa, African   **182**

‚Â°mile Durkheim   194,

Alan Stern   24 f., 39 f., 153,
243, 253, 283, 302, 360, 395, 444

Alienation   105, 528, 539

Alienation; alienate   **105**

Alive   xvii, 32, 37, 200,
229, 299, 349, 368, 383, 411,
420 ff., 529

Altruism   55 f., 59 ff., 93 f.,
97 f., 130 f., 139 f., 146, 175,
213, 256, 263, 267, 273, 294,
316, 411, 427, 434, 469, 471,
486, 497

Altruism; alturist; alturistic
55 f., 59 ff., 93 f., 97 f., 130 f.,
139 f., 146, 175, 213, 256, 263,
267, 273, 316, 411, 434, 469, 471

America   429

American   429

Amputated core   304

Anarchy   470

Androtheism 192, 247, 251, 286,
296 f.

Androtheism; androtheist;
androtheistic **192**

Angela Davis   361

Angelo / Germanic

Germanic   29 ff., 38, 232, 530

Anger   48, 51, 55 f., 66,
70, 76, 78, 90, 95, 104, 109, 126
f., 134 f., 163, 165, 171, 195,
198, 250, 254, 297, 301, 350,
353, 357, 383, 395, 398, 416 ff.,
457, 475, 477, 480, 496 f., 499

Anima   38, 42 ff., 84 ff., 101, 103 ff., 116, 118, 120 ff., 128 ff., 139 ff., 153 ff., 160 ff., 181, 183 ff., 209 ff., 216 f., 220, 222, 226 ff., 230 ff., 238 ff., 244 f., 247 f., 250 ff., 256, 260 ff., 267 f., 270, 272 ff., 277 ff., 285, 288, 290 ff., 304, 317 ff., 325, 337, 343, 345, 347 ff., 357, 359, 361 ff., 366, 368, 370 f., 373 f., 376 f., 393 ff., 399 ff., 404 f., 407 ff., 417 ff., 428 f., 431 f., 434 ff., 452, 454 ff., 459, 461 f., 465 f., 468 ff., 476 f., 479 f., 482, 494 ff.

Anima bank   58, 71, 73, 78 f., 160, 174, 184, 186 ff., 191, 193 ff., 201 f., 204 ff., 209 ff., 216 f., 220, 230, 244 f., 251, 253, 262, 285, 288, 292, 410, 429, 479

Anima bloat 71, 94, 190, 195, 343, 353, 371, 374, 399, 402, 405, 408 ff., 418 f., 428, 436

Anima conduit   xiii, 43, 47, 53, 62, 65, 68 ff., 73 f., 78, 80, 87, 94, 97, 99, 101, 105, 107, 118, 120, 126, 128 f., 132, 142, 146, 153, 156, 166 ff., 170, 172, 189, 192, 267, 285, 294, 317 ff., 325, 345, 393 f., 399 ff., 404, 410 ff., 420, 434, 468, 482

Anima credit 203, 270, 272

Anima debit 530

Animus   xii, 26, 43 f., 47, 49 ff., 53, 55 f., 66 ff., 72, 76 ff., 81, 85, 90, 94, 98 f., 101 ff., 115, 118, 120 ff., 154, 158, 163, 173, 186, 191, 197 f., 200, 203, 206 f., 216, 230 ff., 245, 258, 264, 284, 288, 293, 305, 315 f., 327, 329, 335, 354, 359, 366 f., 371, 377, 408, 412, 420 ff., 449, 451, 464, 471, 473 f.

Bear   37, 177, 181, 240, 252, 292, 306, 400, 458, 478, 547, 814

Breath   38, 87, 217, 435, 456

Buddhism

Bodhisattvas 433

Buddha   201, 211

Christianity

Holy Spirit   38, 428

Consciousness   ii, vi, xvi f., 24 ff., 29 f., 36, 41 f., 44, 47, 50 f., 67, 125, 191 f., 219, 222, 248, 256, 260, 271, 294, 296, 303, 332 f., 335, 337, 339, 342, 356, 358, 369, 381, 397, 418, 423, 430, 433, 443, 445, 476

Consciousness Beyond Life 356

Core   184, 273, 304, 350, 529, 539, 548, 560

Creator   282, 286, 302, 378,

381, 442, 449 f., 544

Essence   424

God   38, 161, 188 f., 194 f., 201, 206 f., 210 ff., 240, 243 ff., 248, 251, 254, 257, 285, 295, 298, 328, 348, 379 ff., 540, 548

Heart   40, 62, 332, 353, 363, 410, 426, 428 f., 470

Hera   25, 75, 228 f., 264, 357 f., 363, 376, 403,

Hinduism   28

Brahma   28

Devi   45 f., 50, 85, 94, 117, 296, 409, 427, 487, 493, 552

Vishnu   296

Inti 36, 91, 124

Life force   28, 38, 45 f., 50, 79, 283, 290, 296, 304, 493, 552

Mind   45, 112, 172, 174, 210, 261, 301, 322, 338, 347, 358, 364, 395 f., 430, 451

Personality   39, 44 ff., 51, 54, 73 f., 172, 275, 400

Primary anima   55, 63, 82, 86, 93, 95, 156, 184, 274, 294, 317, 337, 348 ff., 359, 368, 370 f., 376 f., 394 ff., 401 f., 404 f., 408, 410 f., 418, 420 f., 432, 435, 452, 456 f., 459, 461, 465 f., 468, 476 f., 482, 494 ff.

Psyche   43

Raven   117, 442

Secondary anima   69, 96, 122, 133, 145, 268, 277, 288, 294, 337, 349, 351, 353 f., 359, 361, 370, 373, 377, 394, 404, 410 f., 413 f., 417 f., 422, 432, 435, 452, 454 ff., 459, 461 f., 468 f., 480, 494 ff.

Soul   150, 200, 248, 341, 343, 352 f., 361, 368, 409, 430, 433

Spirit   38, 43, 150, 188, 191, 193 f., 197 f., 206, 223, 244 f., 251, 253 f., 283, 288 ff., 301, 340 f., 344, 353, 359, 362 f., 365 ff., 380 f., 407, 422, 424, 428, 430, 458

Taoism   300

The Tao   300

Vitality   468, 482, 569

50

Anima bank 58, 71, 73, 78 f., 160, 174, 184, 186 ff., 191, 193 ff., 201 f., 204 ff., 209 ff., 216 f., 220, 230, 244 f., 251, 253, 262, 285, 288, 292, 410, 429, 479

Anima banks 186

Anima bloat 71, 94, 190, 195, 343, 353, 371, 374, 399, 402, 405, 408 ff., 418 f., 428, 436,

Anima conduit   43, 47, 53, 62, 65, 68 ff., 73 f., 78, 80, 87, 94, 97, 99, 101, 105, 107,

118, 120, 126, 128 f., 132, 142,
146, 153, 156, 166 ff., 170, 172,
189, 192, 267, 285, 294, 317 ff.,
325, 345, 393 f., 399 ff., 404,
410 ff., 420, 434, 468, 482

Anima credit 203, 270, 272, 530

Anima; animus   **22 f., 28,
32, 38 f., 42 ff., 46 ff., 84 ff., 101,
103 ff., 116, 118, 120 ff., 137,
139 ff., 160 ff., 170 ff., 181, 183
ff., 187 ff., 202 ff., 209 ff., 216 f.,
220, 222, 226 ff., 230 ff.**

Animus   26, 43 f., 47, 49 ff.,
53, 55 f., 66 ff., 72, 76 ff., 81, 85,
90, 94, 98 f., 101 ff., 115, 118,
120 ff., 154, 158, 163, 173, 186,
191, 197 f., 200, 203, 206 f., 216,
230 ff., 245, 258, 264, 284, 288,
293, 305, 315 f., 327, 329, 335,
354, 359, 366 f., 371, 377, 408,
412, 420 ff., 449, 451, 464, 471,
473 f., 496 f.

Anna Freud 26, 400

Anonymous 75, 530, 821

Anorexia   71

Anticipation 44, 64, 70, 82, 94,
134, 158, 308, 395, 495 f

Anxiety   60 f., 64, 66, 69, 75
f., 82, 91, 126, 130, 134, 152,
274, 296, 301, 364, 366, 416,
430, 467, 480, 496

Approval theory of value

212, 531

Art 40, 55, 57, 75, 130, 178, 190,
214, 299, 303, 390, 392, 394 ff.,
405, 456, 497

Asceticism   71, 257, 395, 397,
399 ff., 405, 412 f., 469

Asia; Asian **38**

Assembly   358, 485, 487

Astronomy

Alan Stern   24 f., 39 f., 153,
243, 253, 283, 302, 360, 395, 444

Isaac Newton   46, 219,
306 ff., 380, 439, 444, 450, 466,
492

Martin Rees 31, 204, 225, 234,
288, 296, 325, 381, 398, 536

Stephen Hawking   310, 313
f.

Australia   429

Continents

Australia   429

Authoritative endogroup
110, 239, 461

Auto-anima 402, 405, 412 f

Autogenocide   111

Autonomy   vi, 101, 106, 117,
124, 251, 265, 276, 415

Autonomy Diversity Society
vi

Aviour   178

Aztec   188, 190, 200, 261,
813

B

Bear 37, 177, 181, 240, 252, 292, 306, 400, 458, 478, 547, 814

Beatrix Potter 814

Benazir Bhutto 270

Benin 261

Benjamin Rush 40, 67, 92, 98, 171, 222, 290, 381, 391, 448, 461, 505

Billion 32, 145, 166, 216, 239, 403, 435

Binding Chaos 42 ff., 232, 234, 250, 354, 422, 442, 445, 481

Abstracting Divinity 42, 481

Binding Chaos 2 ff., 232, 234, 250, 354, 422, 442, 445, 481

Free Will and Seductive Coercion vi, xvii, 94, 125, 143, 150, 194, 256, 300, 311, 326, 328, 365, 377, 398, 421, 475, 488

Law and Chaos v50, 466

Political Science 23, 467

Shaping Reality 355, 398, 488

The Creation of Me, Them and Us vi, xvi f., 43 f., 90, 92, 127, 278, 294, 365, 407, 412, 444

The Fourth Age of Nations vi, 192

The Institutions Quartet 304, 481

The Ontology Quartet 476, 481, 488

The Power Economy 250, 253, 291, 414, 471, 475

The Sociology Quartet vi, 297, 304, 481

The Theft of Self 304, 397, 474

Biology

Beatrix Potter 814

Biologists 31

E.O. Wilson 810, 814

Edward O. Wilson 810, 814

George Church 29, 201, 208, 213, 218, 240, 243, 252, 270, 286, 530

Leroy Hood 32, 60, 100, 103, 115, 138, 141, 143, 163, 170, 179 f., 206, 262 f., 271, 282, 305, 356, 460, 479, 484 f., 487

Maria Sibylla Merian 286

Mary Anning 146

Rosalind Franklin 28

Black box words 30, 33, 191

Blood 70, 131, 133, 148, 162, 190, 200, 203, 208, 242, 269, 487

Body 22, 24, 29 f., 33, 36, 38 ff., 44,

46 f., 49 ff., 53, 55, 58, 62, 67 f., 70 f., 74, 109, 124, 128, 130, 138, 149 f., 163, 190 f., 194, 196 f., 200 f., 206, 208, 217, 219, 222, 233, 260, 270, 276, 282 ff., 290, 294, 303 f., 307 f., 316, 323, 332 ff., 339 ff., 344 f., 347 f., 352, 355 f., 360, 368 ff., 392, 396, 402 ff., 420 f., 423, 432, 435, 445, 466, 468, 496

Boredom   80, 113 f., 166, 228, 321, 323, 400, 477, 48

Breath   38, 217

Brian Greene 308, 336, 375 f., 440,

Buddhism   429

Bureaucrats 109, 113 f., 254

C

Canada   403, 484

Capacitor   230 f., 394, 405, 531, 533, 537, 545, 561

Caregiver   59, 67, 96, 126, 175, 257, 277, 282, 288, 470, 474, 476, 533 f., 566

Caregiver-self   288, 533

Carl Jung   42, 75, 540

Carl Rogers 812

Celebrity   157 ff., 162, 164, 166 f., 173, 204, 212, 534

Censorship by noise   534

Centrifugal force   157, 534

Centripetal force   162, 534, 557

Channeler   62 f., 156, 158, 164, 181, 184, 534, 558

Charity   139, 215, 253, 261, 264, 412, 534

Charlotte Witt   323, 357

Chemistry

Rosalind Franklin   28

China   144, 202

Christianity 201, 207, 210, 212, 241 f., 244, 429

Civilization 110, 286, 298, 535

Class   26, 64, 176, 180, 391, 478

Climatology; climatologist

23

Code Will Rule   vi

Cognitive dissonance 100, 121, 409

Colonization 114, 413

Communism 460

Community iv, 76, 142, 146, 148, 184, 186, 195, 256, 262, 265, 270, 277, 289, 352, 391, 403, 411, 456, 486

Compassion 61

Connection 27, 41, 43, 49, 52 ff., 61 ff., 66, 68, 70 f., 74 f., 79, 81, 86, 88, 94, 97, 101, 105 f., 120 ff., 128, 130, 138, 140, 142, 144, 146, 153 f., 158, 165 f., 184 f., 196, 198, 201, 205, 232 f., 267, 279 f., 288, 293, 301, 316 f., 325 f., 340, 345, 347, 351 f., 361, 366, 370, 393, 395, 397, 399, 401 f., 405, 407 f., 410 ff., 418, 434, 451, 455, 464, 466, 468, 470 ff., 476 f., 480, 482, 495 ff.

Conscious   24 ff., 29 f., 33, 36, 41 f., 44 f., 47, 50 f., 55, 57, 63 f., 67, 69, 82, 87, 91, 95, 100, 115, 125, 132, 142 ff., 150, 191 f., 200, 219, 222, 233, 247 f., 256, 260, 271, 275, 282, 294, 296, 303, 309 f., 313 f., 325 f., 328 f., 332 f., 335, 337, 339, 341 f., 344 ff., 351 f., 354 ff., 361 f., 364 ff., 368 ff., 375 ff., 381 ff., 395 ff., 400, 402, 404 f., 409, 411, 418 ff., 422 f., 426, 428, 430 ff., 443, 445, 450 ff., 457 f., 464, 470, 473 ff., 480, 495, 498,

Conscious will   55, 64, 82, 87, 91, 95, 115, 125, 142 ff., 282, 314, 325 f., 328, 358, 377 f., 381 f., 385, 398, 409, 418 f., 422, 443, 450 f., 458, 470, 473, 475, 477, 495

Consciousness   24 ff., 29 f., 36, 41 f., 44, 47, 50 f., 67, 125, 191 f., 219, 222, 248, 256, 260, 271, 294, 296, 303, 332 f., 335, 337, 339, 342, 356, 358, 369,

381, 397, 418, 423, 430, 433, 443, 445, 476

Consciousness Beyond Life 356

Contempt   xii, 28 f., 98, 123, 127, 264 f., 296, 396, 399, 412, 475, 477

Contentment 112

Continents

Africa   182, 190, 215, 286, 302, 304

Asia   38, 87, 168, 171, 200, 304, 363

Europe   29, 40, 144, 171, 176, 241 ff., 302, 406, 458

Core   184, 304, 350

Creator   282, 286, 302, 378, 381, 442, 449

Credit   61, 104, 124, 151, 163, 165, 171, 175, 183, 188 f., 191, 195, 198, 203, 206 f., 214, 226 f., 229, 234, 240, 244 f., 250 f., 254, 256, 258, 260, 264, 266 ff., 279 f., 292, 299, 340, 345, 353, 361, 363, 370, 381, 402, 408, 415, 477

Cree   143, 153, 225, 234, 248

Crime   109, 263, 293, 390, 547, 816

Culture   31, 38 f., 56, 58, 75, 78 f., 163, 176, 182, 187, 194 f.,

202, 229 ff., 233 f., 239, 241, 243 f., 247, 252, 261, 264, 266, 269, 286, 291, 301, 340, 360, 363 f., 390, 404, 427, 429 f., 457 f., 471, 479, 485, 497

Currency   30, 34, 106, 195, 202, 204, 206, 213, 252 ff., 263 ff., 280, 466

Curse   224 f., 481

D

Daniel Amen 26, 138, 167, 190, 206, 213 f., 252 f., 294, 307, 380, 390 f., 403, 431, 440

Dead   22, 24, 31 f., 41, 52, 190, 198, 203, 226, 231, 244, 290, 292, 298, 321, 332, 335, 339 f., 363, 420 ff., 427 f., 435

Deanimation 72, 93, 267 f., 301, 324, 345, 355, 367, 370, 392 f., 408, 418, 460, 467, 496

Death   37 ff., 44, 47, 55, 62 ff., 66 ff., 82, 92, 94, 105, 112 ff., 118, 125, 130 f., 136, 140, 148, 150 ff., 189, 196, 198 f., 202 f., 205, 215, 225 ff., 233, 238, 240, 244 f., 251, 260, 270, 278, 288, 291 f., 294, 299, 303, 315, 318, 321, 327 f., 332 ff., 337 f., 340 ff., 346, 350 f., 355 f., 361 f., 365, 368, 370, 374, 378, 383, 390, 396, 400, 408, 413, 417, 420, 422 ff., 426 f., 430 f.,

434 ff., 439, 451, 458, 468, 476, 479, 481, 484, 486, 495

Debt   65, 72, 96, 98, 103 f., 112, 168, 175, 190 f., 193, 195 f., 198, 206 f., 214 f., 224, 227, 238 ff., 243 ff., 248, 250 ff., 256 ff., 260, 262 f., 265, 267 ff., 272 ff., 277 ff., 281 f., 284, 288 ff., 303 ff., 335, 340 f., 345, 353, 361 ff., 366 f., 370, 396, 399, 401 f., 405, 408, 429, 458, 477

Debt asceticism   401, 405, 510, 539

Decoupled   258, 267, 309, 334, 339 f., 342 f., 354 ff., 359, 364, 366 f., 369, 371, 374, 382 ff., 420, 422, 424 f., 434, 443 f., 479

Democracy 153, 539

Democracy 153

Demographics   139

Dene   272

Depression 55, 60 f., 64 f., 68, 74 f., 82, 92, 121, 267, 316, 324, 329, 355, 360, 364, 366, 392, 408, 467, 495

Dignity   117, 171 f., 184, 412, 415, 418, 505, 539

Disappointment   400

Disgust   398

Dissociation 217, 252, 256 f., 300, 304, 333, 355 f., 395 ff., 402, 412

Diversity   vi, 251, 539

Divination   250, 258, 283, 430, 432, 523, 528, 540, 553

Divinity   28 ff., 33, 42, 57, 179, 196, 212, 481, 498

DNA   44

Dorothea Dix   25

Dorothy Smith   347

Dorothy Swaine Thomas 406,

Dr Walter Franklin Prince 28 f., 180, 216

Prince   28 f.

E

E.O. Wilson 810, 814

Economy   vi, x, 30, 33, 153, 188 ff., 211 ff., 215 f., 224, 245, 247 f., 250 f., 253, 258, 260, 277, 280 f., 291, 293, 298, 412, 414, 471, 475

Adam Smith 347

Emily Oster 73 f., 136, 203, 300, 403

John Stuart Mill   38, 117, 136, 153, 334, 338, 381, 406, 428, 435

Milton Friedman   353

Economy; economists; economics   **153, 188 ff., 211 ff., 215 f., 224**

Edith Stein   306

Education

Maria Montessori   417

Plato   228 f., 287

Salman Khan120, 122, 138

Egypt   206, 428

Elf 367

Elf, body,   345

Elite   180, 543, 551

Emily Oster 73 f., 136, 203, 300, 403

Emotion   24, 26 ff., 39, 41 f., 44 ff., 50 f., 53, 55, 61 ff., 66 ff., 71, 82, 85, 87, 91, 93, 100, 111, 124 ff., 137, 142 ff., 150, 167, 173, 194, 202, 222, 256, 268, 282, 294, 301, 314, 316, 324 ff., 328 f., 334, 340, 343, 345, 350, 352 ff., 361, 365 ff., 370 f., 375, 377 f., 382 ff., 394, 397 f., 400, 402, 409, 416, 418 ff., 422, 429, 433, 443, 449, 451 f., 457 f., 460, 466, 470, 479 f., 484, 495 f

Emotional will   42, 45, 53, 64, 66, 71, 82, 85, 87, 91, 125 f., 142 ff., 150, 194, 202, 256, 282, 314, 325, 328 f., 334, 352, 354 ff., 361, 365, 368, 370, 375, 377 f., 382 ff., 397, 400, 409, 418 ff., 433, 443, 449, 451 f., 457 f., 470, 479 f., 495

Emotions

Anger   48, 51, 55 f., 66, 70, 76, 78, 90, 95, 104, 109, 126 f.,

134 f., 163, 165, 171, 195, 198, 250, 254, 297, 301, 350, 353, 357, 383, 395, 398, 416 ff., 457, 475, 477, 480, 496 f., 499, 529 f.

Anticipation 44, 64, 70, 82, 94, 134, 158, 308, 395, 495 f.

Anxiety 60 f., 64, 66, 69, 75 f., 82, 91, 126, 130, 134, 152, 274, 296, 301, 364, 366, 416, 430, 467, 480, 496

Boredom 80, 113 f., 166, 228, 321, 323, 400, 477, 481, 533, 553

Compassion 61

Contempt 28 f., 98, 123, 127, 264 f., 296, 396, 399, 412, 475, 477

Contentment 112

Depression 55, 60 f., 64 f., 68, 74 f., 82, 92, 121, 267, 316, 324, 329, 355, 360, 364, 366, 392, 408, 467, 495

Disappointment 400

Disgust 398

Empathy 24, 144, 252, 264, 344, 349, 424, 488

Envy 198

Excitement 64, 73 f., 82, 94 f., 97, 109 f., 121, 124 f., 133 f., 143, 157 f., 166, 203, 395, 480 f., 496

Fear 28, 55 f., 63 f., 70, 75 f., 78, 82, 84, 90, 123, 126 f.,

143, 148 f., 151, 162, 171, 182 f., 194, 198, 202, 225, 233, 245, 288, 296 ff., 302, 304, 328, 335, 340, 350, 353, 355, 362 ff., 376, 392, 404, 424, 427, 477, 488, 495 ff.

Frustration 100, 472

Gratitude 56 f., 59 f., 96 ff., 165, 169, 184, 195, 227, 247, 264 ff., 272, 279, 402, 404, 412, 415, 471, 475, 477, 497, 504

Guilt ii, 42, 64 f., 67, 71, 73 f., 93, 96, 103 f., 112, 115, 125, 127 f., 133, 138, 140, 143 ff., 151 f., 158, 163, 168 ff., 173 f., 177, 179, 181 ff., 186, 196, 207, 213 ff., 217, 224, 238 ff., 258, 262 ff., 275 ff., 283 f., 291, 293, 297, 305, 316, 341 f., 357, 367, 370, 399 f., 402, 405, 408, 411, 413, 415, 417, 429 f., 459, 465 f., 473, 478, 485

Happiness 61, 97, 112, 125, 153 f., 275, 377, 404, 413 ff., 426, 450, 470, 475, 504, 811, 820

Hope 146, 204, 232, 250 f., 269, 271 f., 274, 343, 377, 400, 420 f., 478, 481

Jealousy 457, 550

Joy ii, x, 48, 51, 55, 64, 70, 78, 80, 82, 97, 99, 112 f., 120 f., 124, 130, 141 f., 146, 155, 166, 171,

214, 240, 246, 255, 261, 277, 343, 345, 349 ff., 361, 368, 370, 376 f., 390 ff., 400 ff., 404 f., 411, 413 f., 418, 422, 426, 429 f., 452, 464, 476, 485, 496, 499

Loneliness   137, 552

Love   47, 55, 58 f., 70 f., 84, 101, 103, 105, 120, 130, 191, 198, 202, 220, 252, 264, 343 ff., 349, 352, 370, 391, 418, 424, 429, 434, 452, 471, 476, 485

Lust   31, 36, 49, 88, 102, 123, 148, 162, 172, 189, 191, 195, 197, 219 ff., 226, 228, 244 f., 255, 258, 308, 314, 328, 333, 335, 339, 355, 360 f., 366 f., 370, 372 ff., 378, 420 ff., 445 f., 449, 456 f.

Pride   98, 558

Sadness   80, 137, 269, 271, 376

Shame   42, 65 f., 74, 82, 99, 104, 127, 138, 151, 186, 241, 252, 262, 264, 269, 278, 316, 366 f., 370, 417, 459, 473, 477, 488, 495

Sympathy   415, 504

Empathic conduit   192, 411

Empathy   ii, 24, 144, 252, 264, 344, 349, 424, 488

Endo-ideal 28, 72, 78, 81, 90, 96, 110, 112, 116 f., 133, 135 f., 138

f., 143, 151 f., 156 f., 159 ff., 166 ff., 170 f., 173, 175 ff., 179, 181 f., 184 f., 187 ff., 205 f., 210 ff., 214 ff., 227, 233, 240 ff., 245 f., 248 ff., 254 f., 258, 263 ff., 272, 275 ff., 282, 290 f., 294, 296 f., 299, 302 f., 357, 359, 380, 396, 399 f., 410 f., 413 f., 417, 424, 445, 457, 459, 465, 467, 473, 478

Endo-idealism   110, 117, 133, 135, 139, 152, 157, 162, 166, 179, 181 f., 214, 216, 227, 233, 243, 249 ff., 267, 276, 278, 290, 294, 296 f., 299, 302, 399 f., 413 f., 478

Endo-identity   291

Endogroup   **61, 69, 76, 78 ff., 90, 104, 107, 110, 112, 121, 134 f., 138, 141, 144 ff., 151 f., 154, 157 ff., 164, 169, 175, 180 f.,** 184, **186 ff., 191, 193, 205 ff., 210 f., 215 f., 224 ff., 230 f., 234,** 239 f., 242 f., 245, 247, 251 ff., 263, 266 f., 270 ff., 274 ff., 280 f., 284, 289, 291 f., 303 f., 315, 335, 368, 415, 457, 461, 465, 471, 473 f.

Endogroup sublation   78

Endogroups   **75**

Endoreality   26, 28, 30 f., 34, 104, 125, 132, 135, 140, 143, 241 f., 251, 254, 258, 262, 265,

267 f., 272, 276, 278 f., 290, 297, 306 f., 311, 327, 334, 355, 361, 364, 372 ff., 382, 384, 408 f., 411, 417, 424, 445, 459, 465, 467, 469, 478

Endoreality; endorealities **26, 31, 104, 125, 135, 140, 143**

Endoself xiii, 54, 69, 80, 86, 111, 120, 125, 129 f., 140, 161 ff., 190, 233, 252 f., 265 f., 279 f., 282, 325, 351, 357, 371, 373 f., 395, 398, 400 ff., 405, 410 ff., 450, 455 f., 465, 468 f.

Endoself, endoselves **54, 69, 80, 86, 111, 120, 125, 129 f., 140, 161 ff., 190**

Endoselves 54, 112 f., 129 f., 162, 165, 167, 254, 272, 350, 366, 391 f., 394, 399, 402, 411 f., 448, 451, 456, 458, 465, 468

Endosocial 43, 50, 65, 73, 89, 96, 103 f., 140, 160, 166, 173 ff., 184 f., 199, 205, 234, 252 f., 264, 267, 269, 272, 279 f., 284, 291, 294, 297, 305, 314 f., 328 f., 336, 342, 345, 365, 372 f., 375, 385, 398 f., 409, 418, 434, 444, 448 f., 452, 461 f., 464, 469, 471, 476 f., 479, 481, 494

Endosocial martyrdom 185

Endosocial membrane 43, 50, 73, 96, 104, 160, 264, 279, 294, 336, 345, 373, 385, 434, 449, 471, 476, 479, 481, 494

Endosocial tyranny 185, 507, 543

Endosocialism 65, 175, 444, 461, 469, 477, 481

Endo-ideal xii, 28, 72, 78, 81, 90, 96, 110, 112, 116 f., 133, 135 f., 138 f., 143, 151 f., 156 f., 159 ff., 166 ff., 170 f., 173, 175 ff., 179, 181 f., 184 f., 187 ff., 205 f., 210 ff., 214 ff., 227, 233, 240 ff., 245 f., 248 ff., 254 f., 258, 263 ff., 272, 275 ff., 282, 290 f., 294, 296 f., 299, 302 f., 357, 359, 380, 396, 399 f., 410 f., 413 f., 417, 424, 445, 457, 459, 465, 467, 473, 478

Endo-ideal sublation 541

Endo-idealism xii, 110, 117, 133, 135, 139, 152, 157, 162, 166, 179, 181 f., 214, 216, 227, 233, 243, 249 ff., 267, 276, 278, 290, 294, 296 f., 299, 302, 399 f., 413 f., 478, 530, 535, 540 f., 546, 548, 554, 556, 561 ff., 566

Endo-identity 291, 532, 541 f., 545, 561

Endogroup xiii, 61, 76, 78 f., 81, 90, 110, 112, 121, 138, 145 f., 151 f., 154, 157 ff., 164, 169,

180 f., 184, 186 ff., 191, 193,
206 f., 210, 215 f., 224 ff., 234,
239 f., 242 f., 245, 247, 251 ff.,
263, 266 f., 270 ff., 274 ff., 280 f.,
284, 289, 291 f., 303 f., 315, 335,
368, 415, 457, 461, 465, 471,
473 f.

Endogroup sublation   78

Endosocial martyrdom 185

Endosocial membrane 43, 50, 73,
96, 104, 160, 264, 279, 294, 336,
345, 373, 385, 434, 449, 471,
476, 479, 481, 494

Endosocial tyranny   185

Endosocialism   65, 175,
444, 461, 469, 477, 481

Ndogroup weakening   474

Envy   198

Epicurus   153

Equality   137, 154, 274 f.,
298, 353, 414, 544, 547, 812, 820

Equivalence 544

Escapism   143, 544

Essence   424

Ethiopia   225, 814

Euphoria   xvi, 44, 52 f., 58 f.,
63, 66 ff., 70 f., 73, 75, 77 f., 81
f., 88, 95, 97 ff., 125, 129 ff., 143,
145 f., 162, 175, 196, 202, 205,
222, 228, 325, 329, 348, 355,
357, 376 f., 394, 400, 402, 466 f.,
495

Euphoria   xvi, 44, 52 f., 58 f.,
63, 66 ff., 70 f., 73, 75, 77 f., 81
f., 88, 95, 97 ff., 125, 129 ff., 143,
145 f., 162, 175, 196, 202, 205,
222, 228, 325, 329, 348, 355,
357, 376 f., 394, 400, 402, 466 f.,
495

Euphoric bond   76

Euphoric conduit   43, 294,
316, 543 ff., 563, 567

Euphoric interaction   230,

Euphoric object   xvi, 57 f.,
79, 121, 193, 196, 198, 204, 209,
216 f., 220 f., 230, 232, 289, 343,
349, 398, 401, 441, 479, 497,

Euphoria; euphoric   **xvi, 43,
53, 55, 57, 63, 67, 71, 76, 79 f.,
112, 121, 128, 143, 146, 158,
193, 196, 198, 202, 204, 209,
216 f., 220 ff., 228, 230, 232**

Euphoric bond   76

Euphoric conduit   xvi, 43,
294, 316, 543 ff., 563, 567

Euphoric depletion   544

Euphoric interaction   230

Euphoric object   57 f., 79,
121, 193, 196, 198, 204, 209,
216 f., 220 f., 230, 232, 289, 343,
349, 398, 401, 441, 479, 497

Europe   144, 242 f.

Europe, European   **40, 144,
171, 176**

Exceptional myth   78, 210,
248, 269, 271, 417, 532, 541 f.,
545, 549

Excitement   ii, 64, 73 f., 82, 94
f., 97, 109 f., 121, 124 f., 133 f.,
143, 157 f., 166, 203, 395, 480 f.,
496

Exo-ideal   156, 159, 175 f.,
184 f., 205, 242, 258

Exogroup   545

Exoself   xiii, 86, 120, 173,
184, 351, 373, 384, 401, 450,
455, 469

Exoselves   451, 468

Exosocial   47, 56, 61, 70, 74,
80, 87, 93 f., 99, 112, 121, 144,
154, 161, 166, 184 f., 193, 217,
242 f., 254, 258, 264, 267, 274,
312 ff., 328 f., 337, 375, 378,
394, 398, 401, 404, 409, 411,
415 f., 418, 434, 449, 451 f., 455,
461, 466, 468 ff., 473, 477, 482,
492, 494, 496

Exosocial expansion   47, 56,
70, 74, 80, 99, 112, 121, 154,
274, 312 f., 315, 337, 398, 401,
409, 415 f., 418, 434, 455, 466,
468, 470, 473, 477, 482, 492, 496

Exosocial networks   185

Exosocial; exosocialist;
exosocialism **47, 56, 61, 70, 74,
80, 87, 93 f., 99, 112, 121, 144,**

154, 161, 166, 185, 193, 217

Exosocialism 469

Exo-ideal   156, 159, 175 f.,
184 f., 205, 242, 258

Exosocial network   185

Exosocialism   469

F

Face   xvii, 100, 112, 125,
129, 134, 167, 211, 240, 270,
290, 348, 407, 438, 487, 546, 560

Fear   xii, 28, 55 f., 63 f.,
70, 75 f., 78, 82, 84, 90, 123, 126
f., 143, 148 f., 151, 162, 171, 182
f., 194, 198, 202, 225, 233, 245,
288, 296 ff., 302, 304, 328, 335,
340, 350, 353, 355, 362 ff., 376,
392, 404, 424, 427, 477, 488,
495 ff.

Feminism   536, 546

Feminism   536, 546

Festival   76 ff., 146, 148,
230, 363, 400

Financial system   257

Fourth Age of Nations vi, 192

France   144, 404

Free Will and Seductive
Coercion   vi, xvii, 94, 125,
143, 150, 194, 256, 300, 311,
326, 328, 365, 377, 398, 421,
475, 488

Free Will and Seductive
Coercion   vi, 365, 488

Frustration   100, 472

G

Gabon   486, 821

Gaslighting   128, 163, 249, 297, 547

Gender   176, 547, 812, 820

Genocide   111, 121 f., 158, 190, 203, 230, 250, 255, 263, 292, 406

Georg Wilhelm Friedrich Hegel 423, 444 f.

George Church   29, 201, 208, 213, 218, 240, 243, 252, 270, 28

Germany; German; Germanic **30 f., 38**

Gerontology; gerontologist; gerontological   **24 f., 33**

Ghosts   244, 258, 315, 328, 335, 360, 363, 479

Gift   56 f., 77, 98, 103, 132, 171, 184, 188, 212, 227, 239, 241, 245, 247, 249, 264, 266 ff., 272, 274, 277, 279 f., 288 f., 304, 341, 398, 456, 475, 497

Global collaboration   547

God   38, 161, 188 f., 194 f., 201, 206 f., 210 ff., 240, 243 ff., 248, 251, 254, 257, 285, 295, 298, 328, 348, 379 ff.

Gottfried Wilhelm Leibniz

380 f.

Governance   vi, 153, 185, 245, 257, 276, 294, 487,

Governance   vi, 153, 257, 276, 294

Government   107, 109, 114, 157, 251, 280, 481

Gratitude   56 f., 59 f., 96 ff., 165, 169, 184, 195, 227, 247, 264 ff., 272, 279, 402, 404, 412, 415, 471, 475, 477, 497,

Group affiliation   78

Guilt   42, 64 f., 67, 71, 73 f., 93, 96, 103 f., 112, 115, 125, 127 f., 133, 138, 140, 143 ff., 151 f., 158, 163, 168 ff., 173 f., 177, 179, 181 ff., 186, 196, 207, 213 ff., 217, 224, 238 ff., 258, 262 ff., 275 ff., 283 f., 291, 293, 297, 305, 316, 341 f., 357, 367, 370, 399 f., 402, 405, 408, 411, 413, 415, 417, 429 f., 459, 465 f., 473, 478, 485

Gynophobia   180, 296 f., 302

Gynotheism   192, 284, 286, 297, 548

H

Haiti   186

Happiness   61, 97, 112, 125, 153 f., 275, 377, 404, 413 ff., 426, 450, 470, 475, 504, 811, 820

Hare   77

Hate   113 f., 130, 147, 155, 157, 170, 208, 262, 279 f., 296, 332, 345, 348, 350, 353, 368, 376 f., 390, 434, 471, 476

Heart   40, 62, 332, 353, 363, 410, 426, 428 f., 470

Herbert Spencer   326

Hinduism   429

Hollywood   177

Holosocial   548

Homo economicus   190, 548

Honour   53, 151 f., 241, 262, 267, 291 ff., 340, 363, 548, 563, 816

Hope   146, 204, 232, 250 f., 269, 271 f., 274, 343, 377, 400, 420 f., 478, 481, 549

Hopi   279

Hostile seductive coercion 549

Human rights   145, 153, 477

Hypoglycaemia   71

Hypoglycaemic   70

I

Idea based collaboration 549

Ideologues   549

Idol   102, 157 f., 160 ff., 165 f., 168, 172 f., 177 f., 184 f.

Imagination   30, 33, 311, 35

Ime   320

Immanuel Kant   444, 470

Imran Khan   120, 122, 138

Inca   45, 211, 220, 228, 279, 285, 358 f., 374, 410, 413

Incel   549

Independence   166, 549

India   283, 293, 295, 303 f., 816

India   293, 303 f.

Indigenous   27, 29, 38 f., 479, 549, 561

Infidelity   101 ff., 105

Integrity   171

Intelligence 32, 117

Interaction   46, 48 f., 51 f., 54, 59 f., 81, 88, 90 f., 93, 98 ff., 105, 109 f., 113 f., 120, 132, 157, 163, 197, 217 ff., 228, 230, 239, 244, 252 ff., 258, 260, 264, 267, 274, 279 f., 284, 308, 310 ff., 315, 317, 320 f., 329 f., 333 f., 343, 345, 357, 366, 372 ff., 382 ff., 404, 407, 412, 414, 429, 434, 436, 442, 446, 451, 464, 471, 475, 499 f.

Interaction self   284

Inti 36, 91, 124

Introversion 550

Inuit   231

Inverted debt 268

Ireland   200

Iren   183

Iron law of oligarchy 550

Isaac Newton 46, 219, 306 ff., 380, 439, 444, 450, 466, 492

Islam 429

Israel 816

J

Japan 145, 200, 269

Jealousy 457

Jean-Paul Sartre 423

Jeffrey Sachs 811

Joan Robinson 812, 814

John Locke 24, 26, 46, 50, 78, 99, 142, 145, 180, 266, 457, 466, 477, 492 f., 539, 543, 552

John Stuart Mill 38, 117, 136, 153, 334, 338, 381, 406, 428, 435, 532, 812

Joseph Stalin 392

Joy ii, x, 48, 51, 55, 64, 70, 78, 80, 82, 97, 99, 112 f., 120 f., 124, 130, 141 f., 146, 155, 166, 171, 214, 240, 246, 255, 261, 277, 343, 345, 349 ff., 361, 368, 370, 376 f., 390 ff., 400 ff., 404 f., 411, 413 f., 418, 422, 426, 429 f., 452, 464, 476, 485, 496, 499

Judaism 206

K

Kamala Harris 356

Karen Franklin 28

Kim Jong-un 815, 819

Kindness 56, 96, 402, 497

L

Language

Greek 43

Latin 43

Laughter 80, 94, 118, 149, 181, 203

Law 30, 33, 37, 46, 84, 88, 94, 107, 153, 168, 186, 215 f., 227, 239, 250, 254, 258, 284, 293 f., 296, 312 ff., 328 f., 333, 377, 406, 410, 413, 441 f., 449 f., 455, 466, 470, 473, 475, 477, 481, 487, 492

Law and Chaos vi, 250, 466

Leroy Hood 32, 60, 100, 103, 111, 115, 138, 141, 143, 163, 170, 179 f., 206, 262 f., 271, 282, 305, 356, 460, 479, 484 f., 487,

Liberation 154

Libertarian 153, 470

Libertarianism 470

Liberty 257, 265, 294, 547, 551

Life f., 20, 22 ff., 36 ff., 49 ff., 55 f., 58, 60, 62 ff., 66 ff., 71, 77, 79, 81 f., 84, 86 f., 91 ff., 97, 108 f., 112, 114, 117, 129 f., 132, 137, 140, 143, 148 f., 152, 158, 166, 172, 174, 176 f., 186, 188 ff., 196, 200 ff., 204, 208 f.,

213, 215, 219 f., 222, 224, 226 f.,
229 f., 232 ff., 236, 239, 244,
247 f., 251, 255, 257, 260, 263,
268, 273 ff., 280 ff., 294, 296,
298 ff., 312 f., 315, 317 f., 323 f.,
327 ff., 332 ff., 337, 339 f., 342
ff., 346 f., 355 f., 359 ff., 366,
368 ff., 374 ff., 382 ff., 388, 392,
396 f., 400, 404 f., 409, 411 ff.,
419 ff., 425 f., 428, 430 ff., 439
ff., 445, 448, 450 ff., 456 ff., 466,
470, 475 f., 478 f., 481, 485 ff.,
492

Life force   28, 38, 45 f., 50, 79,
283, 290, 296, 304, 493

Lifegiver   284, 288, 474

Literature

Abstracting Divinity   42, 481

Binding Chaos   iv, vi, xvi
f., 42 ff., 232, 234, 250, 354, 422,
442, 445, 481

Free Will and Seductive
Coercion 94, 125, 143, 150, 194,
256, 300, 311, 326, 328, 365,
377, 398, 421, 475, 488

Law and Chaos   250, 466

Maria Montessori   417

Political Science   3, 467

Shaping Reality   355, 398,
488

The Creation of Me, Them and
Us vi, xvi f., 43 f., 90, 92, 127,

278, 294, 365, 407, 412, 444

The Fourth Age of Nations
vi, 192

The Institutions Quartet
vi, xvi f., 304, 481

The Ontology Quartet 476, 481,
488

The Power Economy   vi, 250,
253, 291, 414, 471, 475

The Sociology Quartet vi, 297,
304, 481

Yiyun Li   811
443
543

Living   31, 36, 45, 49, 53,
58, 63 f., 71, 82, 87, 148 f., 176,
178, 190, 198, 203, 205, 226,
231 ff., 240, 244, 248, 256, 275,
292, 296, 299, 304, 312 f., 318,
321 ff., 327 ff., 333, 336 ff., 341
f., 344, 350 f., 353 ff., 357, 360
ff., 368 f., 372, 376 f., 383, 404,
420 ff., 427, 429 ff., 441, 443,
449, 452, 456 f., 460, 464, 486,
488, 495

Loneliness   137

Love   47, 55, 58 f., 70 f.,
84, 101, 103, 105, 120, 130, 191,
198, 202, 220, 252, 264, 343 ff.,
349, 352, 370, 391, 418, 424,
429, 434, 452, 471, 476, 485

Lust   123

M

Madonna **178 ff., 182**

Magic 22, 173, 179, 189, 191, 206, 225, 242, 244, 247, 250, 252, 258, 262, 265, 276 ff., 280, 284, 290 f., 297, 305, 335, 353, 409, 465, 469, 479

Magic words 553

Male xii, 133 ff., 157, 162, 168 f., 177, 179, 181 f., 227, 233, 241, 249, 276, 278, 284 ff., 290, 293 f., 296 ff.

Male endo-idealism 162, 181 f., 249, 290, 294, 296 f., 299

Mali 42, 112, 117, 131, 145, 166, 220, 255, 352, 395, 404, 467 f.

Margaret Archer 24, 134, 136, 244, 324, 339, 343, 346, 351 f., 356, 358, 360, 426 f., 439

Maria Montessori 417

Maria Sibylla Merian 286

Marianne Weber 232, 250 f., 257, 395, 441

Marilyn Monroe **180**

Mars 32

Martin Rees 31, 204, 225, 234, 288, 296, 325, 381, 398

Martyr x, xii, 93, 155 f., 158, 161, 164, 166 f., 169, 171 ff., 180, 182 ff., 187, 189, 195 f., 201, 205 ff., 209, 242, 258, 261,

270, 427, 471

Mary Anning 146

Mass collaboration 564

Mathematics

Gottfried Wilhelm Leibniz 380 f.

Isaac Newton 46, 219, 306 ff., 380, 439, 444, 450, 466, 492

RenÃƒÆ'Ã†â€™Ãƒâ€šÃ‚©

Descartes 223, 326

Terence Tao 87, 299 f.

Matteo Renzi 79, 162, 180, 190, 392

Max Weber 232, 250 f., 257, 395, 441, 814 ff.

Maya 261

Megaphone 554

Mexica 363

Military 426

Mill 153

Milton Friedman 353

Mind 45, 112, 172, 174, 210, 261, 301, 322, 338, 347, 358, 364, 395 f., 430, 451

Mono 29, 85, 100 f., 105, 117, 247, 351, 391, 396, 416

Mono-empire 416

Motion 378

Motional will 378

N

Narendra Modi 39, 79,

213, 536

NASA　32

Nation　56, 77, 79, 98, 105, 121 f., 152, 188, 194 f., 202, 205, 216, 229 f., 239, 271, 288 f., 473, 497, 528 f., 533 ff., 537, 539 f., 542, 546 ff., 551, 553 f., 561, 564, 566 ff.

Nation-self　288 f., 554

Nation"　271

Nations

Aztec　188, 190, 200, 261, 813

Blood　70, 131, 133, 148, 162, 190, 200, 203, 208, 242, 269, 487, 813

Dene　272

Hopi　279

Inca　228

Inuit　231

Lummi　565

Maya　261

Mexica　363

Mono　29, 85, 100 f., 105, 117, 247, 351, 391, 396, 416

Tupi　279

Natural sciences

Biology　25

Chemistry　25

Physics　22 ff., 33, 87, 307, 312, 329, 372, 425, 439, 443, 478

Ndogroup weakening　474

Negative image　29, 61, 72 f., 89 f., 102, 107, 110 ff., 132 f., 137 ff., 142 f., 145 f., 148, 151 f., 154 f., 160 ff., 167, 169 ff., 174 ff., 178 f., 181 ff., 188 f., 196, 205, 207, 213, 241 f., 245 f., 248, 251 ff., 257 f., 263 f., 266, 273, 275, 277 ff., 291 ff., 296, 303 f., 367, 416 f., 424, 445, 457, 459, 461, 465 f., 473, 487

Neuroscience; neuroscientist

23 ff., 33

Nightmares　350, 356, 555

Nothing　30 f., 33, 37, 44, 89, 116, 126, 153, 165, 182, 186, 220, 245, 251, 267, 328, 334 f., 346, 360, 372, 380, 396, 417, 423 f., 458

Nteraction　224

O

Object　24, 27, 31 f., 40, 42, 53, 57 f., 63, 79, 86, 93, 104 f., 110, 120 f., 130, 177, 189 ff., 196 ff., 204, 206, 209, 211, 215 ff., 229 ff., 241, 243, 248, 263, 274, 289, 306, 310, 312, 314, 326 ff., 335, 338, 343, 346, 349, 366, 372 ff., 377 ff., 381, 384, 390, 396 ff., 405, 422, 424, 430 f., 435, 441, 443, 449 f., 454, 460, 464, 466, 470, 476, 479, 481, 496 f

Object self   86, 233, 402 f., 430 f., 496

Oceans   460

Oman   810

Outgroup   255, 555

Ownership   x, 110, 196 ff., 230, 276, 282, 289 f., 304, 401, 413, 475

P

Pacific   430

Parapsychology

Dr Walter Franklin Prince   28

Parasite   88, 94, 97, 99, 107, 110, 115, 118, 158, 163, 324, 365, 375, 411, 503, 556, 558

Passive genocide   556

Patriarchy   210, 231, 290, 294, 298, 304, 547, 556

Patriarchy   210, 290, 298, 304, 547

Patricia J. Williams   811

Person   24, 29 ff., 39 ff., 50 f., 54, 56 f., 63 f., 67, 69 f., 73 f., 76, 78, 80, 84, 87 f., 92, 94 ff., 102 ff., 106 ff., 111 ff., 115, 117 f., 120 ff., 125 ff., 129 f., 132, 138 f., 141 f., 147, 149, 151, 156, 158, 166, 168, 170 ff., 184 f., 190, 192, 195 ff., 201, 209, 215, 217 ff., 224 ff., 234, 240, 250 f., 253, 256 f., 262, 265, 268 f., 272

ff., 280, 282, 288 f., 294, 304, 308, 310, 314, 317, 320 ff., 324, 332 ff., 337 ff., 343 f., 347, 350 ff., 364 ff., 374, 376, 382 ff., 397, 399 f., 403 f., 409, 411 f., 415 ff., 421 f., 424, 426 ff., 434, 436, 443, 445, 449 ff., 455 f., 459 f., 468, 470 f., 473, 475 ff., 481, 496 f.

Personal membrane   43, 88, 108, 117 f., 122, 347, 412, 476, 503, 532, 546, 550, 556, 558, 560, 569

Personal property   289

Personality   39, 44 ff., 51, 54, 73 f., 172, 275, 400

Philippa Foot 317

Philosophy

Epicurus   153

Georg Wilhelm Friedrich Hegel 423, 444 f.

Gottfried Wilhelm Leibniz 380 f.

Immanuel Kant   444, 470, 540

Jean-Paul Sartre   423

John Locke   24, 26, 46, 50, 78, 99, 142, 145, 180, 266, 457, 466, 477, 492 f.

Mill   153

Philosophers 31

Plato   228 f., 287

Rene Descartes 223, 326

Schrödinger 32

Philosophy; philosopher; philosophical **22, 153 f.**

Physics

Brian Greene 308, 336, 375 f., 440,

Isaac Newton 46, 219, 306 ff., 380, 439, 444, 450, 466, 492

Physicists 22, 26, 31, 307, 313, 348, 435, 441

Richard Feynman 220, 372

Stephen Hawking 310, 313 f.

Physics; physicist **22 ff., 33, 87**

Plato 228 f., 287

Police 460

Political Science 23, 467

Politician 174

Politics

Benazir Bhutto 270

Imran Khan 120, 122, 138

Joseph Stalin 392

Kamala Harris 356

Kim Jong-un 238, 815, 819

Matteo Renzi 79, 162, 180, 190, 392

Narendra Modi 39, 79, 213, 536

Ponzi scheme 112, 204,

465, 534, 557, 559

Population 55, 72, 137, 141, 144, 159, 187, 249 f., 272, 359, 403, 429, 496,

Poverty 109 f., 114, 137, 152, 414

Power 23 f., 28, 33, 46, 49, 52, 59, 61 f., 76, 85 f., 89 ff., 100 f., 106 ff., 114 ff., 123 f., 136, 139 f., 149, 151, 154 ff., 161 ff., 166, 168 ff., 174 ff., 179 ff., 189 f., 193 ff., 201, 204 ff., 210 ff., 215 f., 220, 222 ff., 230 f., 239 ff., 243, 245 f., 250 f., 253, 255, 264, 267, 270, 275 ff., 279 f., 287, 291 f., 294 f., 299 f., 303 f., 315, 318, 328, 356, 362, 378 f., 396, 401, 407 ff., 418, 429, 431, 435, 443, 445, 457, 460 f., 465, 467 ff., 473, 475 f., 480, 486

Power economy 558

Power Economy 250, 253, 291, 414, 471, 475

Predation 78, 97, 99, 108, 112, 117, 123 f., 128, 166, 214, 274, 337, 410, 416 ff., 473, 475 f., 487

Predator 47 ff., 51, 58 ff., 66, 69, 76, 81, 85, 88, 90, 93, 97, 99 f., 104 ff., 108 f., 111 f., 115, 117 f., 122 ff., 131 ff., 137 ff., 148 f., 153, 157, 160, 164 ff., 173, 175,

180 f., 189 f., 194, 245, 248 f., 269 f., 273 f., 279, 346, 349, 353, 357, 361 f., 393, 396, 400, 402, 406, 408 ff., 413, 418, 448, 465, 467 f., 470 f., 475, 477, 486 ff., 495, 499

Prey   49, 51, 58 f., 69, 81, 85, 92 f., 106, 110 ff., 124, 127, 129, 131, 133, 138 f., 143, 149, 158, 160, 163 ff., 175, 275, 280, 300, 347, 395, 402, 406, 417, 495, 499

Pride   98

Primary anima   55, 63, 82, 86, 93, 95, 156, 184, 274, 294, 317, 337, 348 ff., 359, 368, 370 f., 376 f., 394 ff., 401 f., 404 f., 408, 410 f., 418, 420 f., 432, 435, 452, 456 f., 459, 461, 465 f., 468, 476 f., 482, 494 ff.,

Primary euphoria   377, 558

Princess Diana   **180**

Privacy   114, 117, 166, 168 f., 171 ff., 184, 249, 418

Propaganda   248

Property ownership   289, 475

Psyche   43

Psychiatry

Anna Freud   26, 400

Benjamin Rush   40, 67, 92, 98, 171, 222, 290, 381, 391, 448, 461, 505

Carl Jung   42, 75, 540

Daniel Amen   26, 138, 167, 190, 206, 213 f., 252 f., 294, 307, 380, 390 f., 403, 431, 440

Dorothea Dix   25

Karen Franklin   28

Sigmund Freud   26, 400

Viktor Frankl   28

Psychology

Anhedonia   74

Psychology; psycologist; pyscological **23, 26, 33, 42, 46, 74**

Punitive asceticism   402, 405, 510, 531, 559

Q

Quantum will   33, 313 f., 329, 377

R

Race   32, 117, 164, 181, 206, 214, 224, 269, 287, 336, 339, 438, 445

Random   28, 30, 33, 311, 524, 533, 559, 812

Raven   117, 442

Reaction   44, 46 f., 50, 53, 69, 72, 89, 108, 110, 124 ff., 132, 136 f., 166, 195, 222, 228, 266, 268 f., 304, 326, 394, 416, 450, 460

Reanimation   402, 467, 497, 559

Reflection   89, 114, 176, 178 f.,

182, 303, 403, 411, 457, 465

Reflector 72, 107, 110, 112, 155, 159 ff., 170, 172 ff., 184 f., 189, 205, 211, 240, 242, 246 f., 251, 254, 272, 277, 292, 303, 410, 414, 417, 457

Religion

Animist 29

Buddhism 429

Catholic 29

Christianity 201, 207, 210, 212, 241 f., 244, 429

Hinduism 429

Islam 429

Judaism 206

Orthodox 29

Protestant 29

Taoism 87, 299

Zoroastrianism 242

Ren 38, 530 f., 533 ff., 543 f., 549 ff., 555, 560, 564 ff.

ReneDescartes 223, 326

Rene Descartes 223, 326

Repeater 228, 231, 233, 560 f.

Resistance 90, 92, 99, 101, 110, 128, 169, 368, 380, 416 f., 454, 538, 560

Resuscitation; resuscitate; resuscitated **24 f.**

Revolution 121 f., 144 f., 168, 194, 202, 205, 210, 216, 391,

417, 535, 560, 564 f.

Richard Feynman 220, 372

Rite

Lian 114, 146, 190, 219, 242, 256, 429, 444 f.

Ren 38, 560

Rites x, 38, 55 f., 79, 148, 171, 188, 192, 203, 206, 208, 212, 216, 218, 221 f., 226, 228 ff., 285, 289, 291 f., 295, 297, 334, 341, 343, 356 f., 360, 366, 393, 398, 430, 451, 464, 497

Buddhism 429

Buddhist 241

Christianity 201, 207, 210, 212, 241 f., 244, 429

Bible 297

Christian 201, 206 ff., 210, 212, 241 ff., 258, 363, 409, 429

Confucianism

Confucian 560

Hinduism 429

Hindu 241, 429

Islam 429

Muslim 241

Judaism 206

Jew 207, 210, 282, 403, 813

Taoism 87, 299

Taoist 299

Zoroastrianism 242

Zoroastrian 242

Rosalind Franklin   28

Royal   **180**

Russia   145

S

Sadness   80, 137, 269, 271, 376

Salman Khan 120, 122, 138

Saviour   3, 155, 174 ff., 178 f., 181 ff., 429, 508, 561

Science   23 ff., 37, 39, 41, 46, 208, 211, 219, 228, 232, 248, 307, 317, 326, 332, 336, 356, 365, 384, 399, 407, 427, 438 f., 441, 444 ff., 464, 467, 481, 486

Scientific superstition   28, 561

Sealed well   561

Second age of nations   561

Secondary anima   xii, 69, 96, 122, 133, 145, 268, 277, 288, 294, 337, 349, 351, 353 f., 359, 361, 370, 373, 377, 394, 404, 410 f., 413 f., 417 f., 422, 432, 435, 452, 454 ff., 459, 461 f., 468 f., 480, 494 ff.

Secondary euphoria   xvi, 73, 98, 129, 377

Secrecy   75, 117, 249

Secret chamber guilt   249

Seductive coercion   59, 94

Seductive Coercion   4, 125, 143, 150, 194, 256, 300, 311, 326, 328, 365, 377, 398, 421,

475, 488

Self   23 ff., 27 ff., 36, 41 f., 44 f., 47, 49 ff., 56, 72 f., 75, 77, 85 f., 88, 90, 99, 109, 120, 124, 129 f., 139, 141 f., 151, 160, 163 f., 167, 171 f., 184, 188 ff., 193, 195, 197, 217, 219 ff., 226 ff., 233 f., 242, 250, 254, 256, 260, 269 f., 272, 275 f., 280, 282 ff., 288 ff., 294, 296 ff., 301, 303 ff., 308 f., 311 f., 317, 325 f., 332 ff., 336, 339 f., 342 ff., 348, 354 ff., 364 ff., 382 ff., 394, 396 f., 400, 402 ff., 409, 411 f., 416, 418, 420, 423, 426, 429 ff., 433, 435, 445, 458, 468, 470, 474, 480, 487, 496 f

Sex   55 f., 58, 76 f., 80, 94, 118, 123, 134, 136 ff., 144 f., 152, 169, 181 ff., 199, 208, 275, 294 f., 299 ff., 356, 364, 390, 460, 468, 473, 487, 496 f

Sexualized sublation   138, 468

Sexualized violence   138, 563

Shame   xii, 42, 65 f., 74, 82, 99, 104, 127, 138, 151, 186, 241, 252, 262, 264, 269, 278, 316, 366 f., 370, 417, 459, 473, 477, 488, 495

Shame killing   151, 262, 278, 563

Shaping Reality   vi, xvii,

355, 398, 488

Share   26, 31, 47, 49 f.,
53, 56, 66 f., 69, 72 f., 76 ff., 85,
88, 90 f., 94, 98 f., 101, 103 ff.,
112, 115, 118, 122, 126, 129,
148, 154, 158, 161 ff., 171, 173,
175, 186, 191 f., 196, 198, 200 f.,
203, 206, 210, 220 f., 226, 229 f.,
232 f., 239, 262, 264, 270, 274,
284, 286, 288, 305, 313, 315 f.,
340, 343, 356, 363, 374, 380,
399, 408, 414 f., 421, 440, 443,
464, 471, 473 ff., 497

Shunning   62, 146, 151, 158,
177, 179 f., 225 f., 228 f., 234,
304, 345 f., 473

Sigmund Freud   26, 400

Silencing the wolf   406

Simone Veil 111, 294, 322, 364

Sir Ken Robinson   812, 814

Siren   93, 155, 174, 181 ff.

Social media 158

Society   26, 62, 133, 147,
153, 166, 171, 184, 194, 240,
251, 253, 262 f., 266, 273, 464,
466, 468, 487

Sociology
Adam Smith 347, 811, 816
Ãmile Durkheim   194, 813
Anna Julia Cooper   554, 566
Georg Wilhelm Friedrich Hegel
423, 444 f.

Margaret Archer   24, 134,
136, 244, 324, 339, 343, 346,
351 f., 356, 358, 360, 426 f., 439
Sigmund Freud   26, 400
Ulrich Beck iv
William James   317
Sociology; socologist;
sociological23 f., 33, 46
Solidarity   79, 564
Sorrow   48, 153, 269 f., 321,
340, 429, 564, 815
Soul   150, 200, 248, 341,
343, 352 f., 361, 368, 409, 430,
433
South Korea 269
Spacetime   191, 221 ff., 226,
230 f., 233 f., 308 f., 312, 319 f.,
323, 330, 333, 337 ff., 342, 353,
366, 371 ff., 378, 382 ff., 431,
440, 442
Spain   277
Spirit   38, 43, 150, 188,
191, 193 f., 197 f., 206, 223, 244
f., 251, 253 f., 283, 288 ff., 301,
340 f., 344, 353, 359, 362 f., 365
ff., 380 f., 407, 422, 424, 428,
430, 458
State
Australia   429
Benin   261
Burkina Faso352
Canada   403, 484

China   144, 202

Egypt   206, 428

Ethiopia   225

France   144, 404

Gabon   486

Haiti   186

India   283, 293, 295, 303 f.

Ireland   200

Japan   145, 200, 269

Mali   42, 112, 117, 131, 145, 166, 220, 255, 352, 395, 404, 467 f.

Russia   145

South Korea 269

Spain   277

United States 182, 262, 269

Stephen Hawking   310, 313 f.

Study of life x, 22 ff., 26, 29, 33, 42, 436, 569

Study of thought

Linguistics 479

Logic   28, 177, 195

Mathematics 306

Neuroscience   23 ff., 33, 439, 481

Neuroscientist   26, 74, 318

Philosophy   22, 153 f., 280, 283, 299

Psychiatry   26, 84, 812, 815

Psychology   23, 26, 30, 33 f., 42, 46, 74, 317, 407, 438, 481,

Sociology   23 f., 33, 46, 297, 304, 445, 481, 811, 815

Sublate; sublation   **43, 45 ff., 50, 85, 88, 90, 99, 112, 116 f., 134, 151, 159, 183, 195 f., 216, 227, 232 f.**

Sublated   43, 45 ff., 50, 85, 88, 90, 99, 112, 116 f., 134, 151, 159, 183, 196 f., 216, 227 f., 246, 248, 256, 267, 276, 282, 290 f., 294, 300, 303, 305, 327, 356 f., 364, 412, 416, 421, 442, 452, 473, 475

Sublation   54, 56, 58, 61, 73, 78 f., 81, 84 ff., 90, 104, 110, 112, 114 f., 117, 120, 122, 138, 144, 150, 171, 193, 195, 233, 240, 242, 246, 250 f., 258, 263, 271, 276, 282, 284, 288, 290, 297 f., 300, 316, 345, 357, 365, 407 f., 413, 417 f., 421, 449, 451, 455, 468 ff., 472, 474, 477, 480, 495 f.

Sublator   118, 503, 558

Supranational   393, 547, 566 f.

Sympathy   415, 504, 566

Synthetic euphoria   145, 467, 566

Systems   58, 122, 151, 219,

263, 312, 449, 461, 466, 475, 481, 492, 505, 532 f.,

Systems of dissociation 566

T

Tantalus asceticism 402, 405, 510, 566

Tantra 282

Taoism 87, 299

Terence Tao 87, 299 f.

Th purpose of life 426

The Creation of Me, Them and Us**43 f., 90, 92,** 127, 278, 294, 365, 407, 412, 444

The Fourth Age of Nations vi, 192

The Institutions Quartet vi, xvi f., 304, 481

The Ontology Quartet vi, xvi f., 476, 481, 488

The original sin 238

The Power Economy 250, 253, 291, 414, 471, 475

The Sociology Quartet vi, 297, 304, 481

The Theft of Self 304, 397, 474

The theory of everything 438

Theresa May 261

Thomas Jefferson 406

Time 24, 42, 56, 60 f.,

71, 74, 84, 96, 100, 105, 113 f., 116, 124, 128, 140, 152, 157, 161, 182, 190, 197, 200, 204, 212, 217, 221 ff., 228 f., 231, 238, 246, 251, 274, 287, 290, 304, 306 ff., 334, 337 ff., 342, 346, 355, 363 f., 368 f., 374 ff., 378 f., 381 f., 384 f., 391, 403 f., 407, 409, 415, 420, 424, 431, 434 ff., 440, 443, 445, 454, 472, 480, 486, 497

Torture 62, 78, 113 f., 123, 128, 139 ff., 143 ff., 148 ff., 189, 206 f., 209, 228, 245, 278, 288, 322, 412 f., 486 f., 531, 567

Trade 188 f., 212 f., 252 ff., 264, 277, 280, 298, 412, 414, 475

Trade economy 277, 280, 298, 412, 414, 475, 551, 567

Trade economy 277, 280, 412, 414

Trade empire 561, 567

Trade relationship 567

Transaction 114, 193, 195, 212 f., 245, 253, 264 ff., 273, 279, 281, 362

Transcendence 247

Transcendental endogroup 188, 216, 243

Traumatic bond 47, 50, 59, 78, 85, 141, 146, 164, 393,

471, 477

Tribe   304

Tupi   279

Tyrant   x, xii, 93, 112, 138, 155 f., 158 ff., 164, 166 f., 172 ff., 181, 183 ff., 187, 250, 401

U

Ublation   86

Ulrich Beck iv

Universal reality   278 f., 307, 311, 350, 409, 411, 444 f., 469

V

Vatican   29

Pope   29

Reformation 29

Viktor Frankl   28

Violate; violation   54, 56, 58, 62, 81, 117, 120, 138, 144, 168 f., 171, 228

Violation   x, xiii, 54, 56, 58 f., 62, 81, 107, 117, 120, 138, 144 f., 168 f., 171, 228, 233, 345, 357, 390, 407 f., 415, 417, 421, 448, 451, 455, 466, 468 ff., 472 f., 477, 480, 495 f.

Violator   118

Violence   24, 73, 94, 97, 110, 114, 118, 121, 129, 138, 140 f., 143 ff., 152, 173, 177, 199, 202, 250, 277, 293, 416 ff., 445, 448, 480

Vitality   468, 482, 569

Vitology   23 ff., 33, 37, 46, 88, 478, 481

Vitology; vitologist   **23 ff., 33, 37, 46, 88**

Volition   45, 125

W

Wealth   27, 32, 110, 152, 166, 188 f., 194 f., 204 f., 208, 210, 213, 215 f., 243, 257, 275, 394, 403, 413 f

Wealth   110, 152, 166, 188 f., 194, 204 f., 210, 215 f., 243, 275, 403, 413 f.

Wendy L. Williams   811

Will   24, 26, 29 f., 32 f., 36, 38, 41 ff., 49 ff., 59, 64 ff., 69 ff., 78 ff., 85, 87 f., 90 f., 93 ff., 99, 104, 106, 112, 114 ff., 120 f., 123 ff., 131, 134, 138 ff., 142 ff., 146 f., 149 ff., 154, 157, 159 ff., 171, 173 f., 178 f., 181 ff., 190 f., 194, 196 ff., 200, 202, 204, 206, 211 f., 219, 222, 226, 229, 231 ff., 240, 242, 244, 246 ff., 251, 253 ff., 258, 260 ff., 267, 271 ff., 297 f., 300, 302 ff., 308 ff., 318, 320 ff., 332 ff., 338 ff., 343 ff., 347, 352 ff., 361 f., 364 ff., 368 ff., 372 ff., 381 ff., 397 f., 400 ff., 404, 407 ff., 417 ff., 425 f., 430 f., 433 ff., 440 ff., 445 f., 448 ff.,

454, 456 ff., 465 f., 469 ff., 473
ff., 488, 492, 494 f.

Witches   152, 352

X

Xiaoyuan Huang   811

Xoself   450

Xosocial   315

Y

Yiyun Li   811

Yoga   38, 374, 457

Z

Zoroastrianism   242
443

Heather Marsh

Citations

1. Merriam-Webster. (n.d.). Life. In *Merriam-Webster.com Dictionary*. Retrieved May 12, 2024, from https://www.merriam-webster.com/dictionary/life

2. Parnia, S., & Young, J. (2013). *Erasing Death: The Science That Is Rewriting the Boundaries Between Life & Death* (1st ed.). HarperOne.

3. Prince, W. F. (2013). The Enchanted Boundary: Being a Survey of Negative Reactions to Claims of Psychic Phenomena, 1820-1930. *Literary Licensing, LLC.*

4. CNN. (2021, November 29). Scientists have built a new kind of self-replicating robot. CNN. https://www.cnn.com/2021/11/29/americas/xenobots-self-replicating-robots-scn/index.html

5. Cleland, C. E., & Chyba, C. F. (2002). Origins of Life and Evolution of the Biosphere, 32(4), 387-393. https://link.springer.com/article/10.1023/A:1020503324273

6. Viegas, J. (2017, January 28). Life Continues Within the Body After Death, Evidence Shows. Seeker. Retrieved from https://www.seeker.com/life-continues-within-the-body-after-death-evidence-shows-2212720233.html

7. Oman, D., Thoresen, C. E., & McMahon, K. (1999). Volunteerism and Mortality among the Community-dwelling Elderly. *Journal of Health*

Psychology, 4 (3), 301-316. https://doi.org/10.1177/135910539900400301

8. Musick, M. A., & Wilson, J. (2003). Volunteering and depression: The role of psychological and social resources in different age groups. *Social Science & Medicine, 56* (2), 259–269. https://doi.org/10.1016/s0277-9536(02)00025-4

9. Brown, S. L., Brown, R. M., House, J. S., & Smith, D. M. (2008). Coping with spousal loss: Potential buffering effects of self-reported helping behavior. *Personality & Social Psychology Bulletin, 34* (6), 849–861. https://doi.org/10.1177/0146167208314972

10. Moen, P., Dempster-McClain, D., & Williams, Jr., R. M. (1992). Successful aging: A life-course perspective on women's multiple roles and health. American Journal of Sociology, 97 (6), 1612-1638. http://www.journals.uchicago.edu/doi/10.1086/229941

11. Kayloe, J. C., & Krause, M. (1985). RARE FIND or The value of volunteerism. *Psychosocial Rehabilitation Journal, 8* (4), 49–56. https://doi.org/10.1037/h0099659

12. Post, S. G. (2005). Altruism, happiness, and health: It's good to be good. *International Journal of Behavioral Medicine, 12 (*2), 66–77. https://doi.org/10.1207/s15327558ijbm1202_4

13. Vastag, B. (2003). Scientists find connections in the brain between physical and emotional pain. *JAMA, 290* (18), 2389–2390. https://doi.org/10.1001/jama.290.18.2389

14. Holm, A. L., & Severinsson, E. (2010). Desire to survive emotional pain related to self-harm: A Norwegian hermeneutic study. *Nursing & Health Sciences, 12*, 52-57. https://doi.org/10.1111/j.1442-2018.2009.00485.x

15. Sachs-Ericsson, N. J., Sheffler, J. L., Stanley, I. H., Piazza, J. R., & Preacher, K. J. (2017). When emotional pain becomes physical: Adverse childhood experiences, pain, and the role of mood and anxiety disorders. *Journal of Clinical Psychology, 73*, 1403-1428. https://doi.org/10.1002/jclp.22444

16. Nusbaum, E. C., & Silvia, P. J. (2011). Shivers and timbres: Personality and the experience of chills from music. *Psychology of Aesthetics, Creativity, and the Arts, 5*(3), 169-175. https://libres.uncg.edu/ir/uncg/f/P_Silvia_Shivers_2011.pdf

17. Yan, M., Cui, X., Liu, F., Li, H., Huang, R., Tang, Y., Chen, J., Zhao, J., Xie, G., & Guo, W. (2021). Abnormal default-mode network homogeneity in melancholic and nonmelancholic major depressive disorder at rest. *Neural Plasticity, 2021*, Article ID 6653309, 12 pages. https://doi.org/10.1155/2021/6653309

18. Antonovsky, A. (1967). Social Class, Life Expectancy and Overall Mortality. *The Milbank Memorial Fund Quarterly, 45*(2), 31–73. https://doi.org/10.2307/3348839

19. Aburto, J. M., Villavicencio, F., Basellini, U., Kjærgaard, S., & Vaupel, J. W. (2020). Dynamics of life expectancy and life span equality. *Proceedings of the National Academy of Sciences of the United States of America, 117*(10), 5250–5259. https://doi.org/10.1073/pnas.1915884117
20. Robinson, C. D., Gallus, J., Lee, M. G., & Rogers, T. (2021). The demotivating effect (and unintended message) of awards. *Organizational Behavior and Human Decision Processes, 163*, 51-64. https://doi.org/10.1016/j.obhdp.2019.03.006

21. Cartwright, J. (2000). *Evolution and Human Behaviour: Darwinian Perspectives on the Human Condition.* Palgrave Macmillan.

22. Graham, D. S., & Eysenbach, G. (2021). The impact of predatory journals on scholarly research: A review of literature and case studies. *Journal of the Medical Internet Research, 23*(3), e21575. https://doi.org/10.2196/21575

23. Katznelson, L., Finkelstein, J. S., Schoenfeld, D. A., Rosenthal, D. I., Anderson, E. J., & Klibanski, A. (2010). Increase in bone density and lean body mass during testosterone administration in men with acquired hypogonadism. *The Journal of Clinical Endocrinology & Metabolism, 95*(10), 4729-4737. https://doi.org/10.1210/jc.2010-0802

24. Campbell, A. (2008). Attachment, aggression and affiliation: The role of oxytocin in female social behavior. *Biological Psychology, 77*(1), 1-10. https://doi.org/10.1016/j.biopsycho.2007.09.001

25. Vigil, J. M. (2008). Sex Differences in Affect Behaviors, Desired Social Responses, and Accuracy at Understanding the Social Desires of Other People. *Evolutionary Psychology, 6*(3). https://doi.org/10.1177/147470490800600316

26. Verma, R., Balhara, Y. P., & Gupta, C. S. (2011). Gender differences in stress response: Role of developmental and biological

determinants. *Industrial psychiatry journal*, 20(1), 4–10. https://doi.org/10.4103/0972-6748.98407

27. Colloca, L., Pine, D. S., Ernst, M., Miller, F. G., & Grillon, C. (2016). Vasopressin Boosts Placebo Analgesic Effects in Women: A Randomized Trial. *Biological psychiatry,* 79(10), 794–802. https://doi.org/10.1016/j.biopsych.2015.07.019

28. Love T. M. (2018). The impact of oxytocin on stress: the role of sex. Current opinion in behavioral sciences, 23, 136–142. https://doi.org/10.1016/j.cobeha.2018.06.018

29. Thompson, H. (2023, August 30). Female surgeons have better patient outcomes, studies show. *The Guardian.* https://www.theguardian.com/society/2023/aug/30/female-surgeons-patient-outcomes-better-studies

30. Wallis CJD, Jerath A, Coburn N, et al. Association of Surgeon-Patient Sex Concordance With Postoperative Outcomes. *JAMA Surg.* 2022;157(2):146–156. doi:10.1001/jamasurg.2021.6339

31. Casale, R., Atzeni, F., Bazzichi, L., Beretta, G., Costantini, E., Sacerdote, P., & Tassorelli, C. (2021). Pain in women: A perspective review on a relevant clinical issue that deserves prioritization. *Pain and Therapy, 10*(1), 149-165. https://doi.org/10.1007/s40122-021-00244-1

32. Kristen, M. B., Cullen, P., Jewkes, R., & Gibbs, A. (2021). Intimate partner violence, substance use, and health comorbidities: A syndemic approach. *Trauma, Violence, & Abuse, 22*(4), 788-803. https://doi.org/10.1177/1524838020957989

33. Bartley, E. J., & Fillingim, R. B. (2013). Sex differences in pain: a brief review of clinical and experimental findings. *British journal of anaesthesia*, 111(1), 52–58. https://doi.org/10.1093/bja/aet127

34. Venniro, M., Zhang, M., Caprioli, D., Hoots, J. K., Golden, S. A., Heins, C., Morales, M., Epstein, D. H., & Shaham, Y. (2018). Volitional social interaction prevents drug addiction in rat models. *Nature neuroscience*, 21(11), 1520–1529. https://doi.org/10.1038/s41593-018-0246-6

35. Durkheim, E. (1912). *The Elementary Forms of the Religious Life* (J. Swain, Trans.). London: George Allen & Unwin Ltd.

36. Hassig, R. (1988). *Aztec Warfare: Imperial Expansion and Political*

Control. Norman: University of Oklahoma Press.

37. Matthews, J., & Matthews, C. (1994). *The Encyclopedia of Celtic Wisdom: A Celtic Shaman's Sourcebook*. Element Books.

38. CSU Northridge Department of History. (n.d.). The Log of Christopher Columbus' First Voyage to America in the Year 1492. *California State University, Northridg*e. https://www.csun.edu/~hcfll004/SV1492.html

39. Lindeboom, G. A. (1954). *The story of blood transfusion to a pope.* Journal of the History of Medicine, *9*(4), 455–459. https://doi.org/10.1093/jhmas/ix.4.455

40. Duffin, Jacalyn History of Medicine: A scandalously short introduction University of Toronto Press, 1999, p. 171

41. New York Post. (2020, May 2). Inside disgraced mogul Peter Nygard's Bahamas playground. *New York Post.* https://nypost.com/2020/05/02/inside-disgraced-mogul-peter-nygards-bahamas-playground/

42. Wolf, L. (1980). *Bluebeard: The Life and Crimes of Gilles de Rais*. New York, NY: C. N. Potter.

43. Davies, O. (2012). *Magic: A Very Short Introduction* (Very Short Introductions, p. 71). OUP Oxford.

44. Wolf, L. (1980). *Bluebeard, the life and crimes of Gilles de Rai*s (1st ed). C.N. Potter : Distributed by Crown Publishers.

45. Mercier, J. (1880). *Art that heals: The image as medicine in Ethiopia.* Museum for African Art.

46. Matthews, C. (1996). *The Encyclopaedia of Celtic Wisdom: The Celtic Shaman's Sourcebook* (p. 33). Element Books Ltd.

47. Dunn, J. (1914). *The Ancient Irish Epic Tale Táin Bó Cúalnge: "The Cualnge Cattle-Raid"*. London: David Nutt.

48. Weber, M. (1905/1930). *The Protestant Ethic and the Spirit of Capitalism*. London & Boston: Unwin Hyman.

49. Pollack, A. Z., Rivers, K., & Ahrens, K. A. (2018). Parity associated

with telomere length among US reproductive age women. *Human Reproduction*, *33*(4), 736–744. https://doi.org/10.1093/humrep/dey024

50.Barha, C. K., Hanna, C. W., Salvante, K. G., Wilson, S. L., Robinson, W. P., et al. (2016). Number of children and telomere length in women: A prospective, longitudinal evaluation. *PLOS ONE, 11*(1), e0146424. https://doi.org/10.1371/journal.pone.0146424

51. Ryan, C. P., Hayes, M. G., Lee, N. R., et al. (2018). Reproduction predicts shorter telomeres and epigenetic age acceleration among young adult women. *Scientific Reports, 8*, 11100. https://doi.org/10.1038/s41598-018-29486-4

52. Hamzelou, J. (2018, February 14). Having children may add 11 years to a woman's biological age. *New Scientist.* https://www.newscientist.com/article/2161978-having-children-may-add-11-years-to-a-womans-biological-age/

53. Fiore, E. (1995). *The Unquiet Dead: A Psychologist Treats Spirit Possession*. Ballantine Books.

54. Weber, M. (1968). *Economy and society: an outline of interpretive sociology*. New York, Bedminster Press.

55. Kurian, R. M., & Thomas, S. (2023). Gratitude as a path to human prosperity during adverse circumstances: a narrative review. *British Journal of Guidance & Counselling*, 51(5), 739–752. https://doi.org/10.1080/03069885.2022.2154314

56. Shapiro, L. J., & Stewart, E. S. (2011). Pathological guilt: a persistent yet overlooked treatment factor in obsessive-compulsive disorder. Annals of clinical psychiatry : official journal of the American Academy of Clinical Psychiatrists, 23(1), 63–70.

57. Kim, S. S. H. (2017). Korean Han and the postcolonial afterlives of 'The Beauty of Sorrow'. *Korean Studies*, 41, 253-279. University of Hawai'i Press. https://doi.org/10.1353/ks.2017.0015

58. Park, K. (1994, March). *The feelings and thoughts of the Korean people in literature*. Paper presented at the colloquium at the University of Paris, Paris, France.

59. Willoughby, Heather. (2000). The Sound of Han: P'ansori, Timbre and a Korean Ethos of Pain and Suffering. Yearbook for Traditional Music. 32. 17. 10.2307/3185241.

60. Piff, P. K., Stancato, D. M., Cote, S., Mendoza-Denton, R., & Keltner, D. (2012). Higher social class predicts increased unethical behavior. *Proceedings of the National Academy of Sciences, 109*(11), 4086–4091. https://doi.org/10.1073/pnas.1118373109

61. National Geographic. (2023). Spanish Galgo hunting dogs are dying by the thousands—can they be saved? *National Geographic.* https://www.nationalgeographic.com/animals/article/spanish-galgo-hunting-dog-killing-welfare

62. Galgo Amigo. (n.d.). The plight of the Spanish galgos. Galgo Amigo. Retrieved from https://www.galgoamigo.com/the-plight-of-the-spanish-galgos.html

63. Kunzig, R. (2008, July). The great human migration. *Smithsonian Magazine.* https://www.smithsonianmag.com/history/the-great-human-migration-13561/

64. Grosman, L., Munro, N. D., & Belfer-Cohen, A. (2008). A 12,000-year-old shaman burial from the southern Levant (Israel). *Proceedings of the National Academy of Sciences, 105*(46), 17665–17669. https://doi.org/10.1073/pnas.0806030105

65. Mai, M. (2006). *In the Name of Honour: A Memoir.* Virago.

66. Naqvi, M. (2014, July 16). Indian village council orders girl to be raped for brother's crime. *CTV News.* Retrieved from https://www.ctvnews.ca/world/indian-village-council-orders-girl-to-be-raped-for-brother-s-crime-1.1909235

67. "India: Dalit sisters at risk of rape as punishment for brother's alleged crime." (n.d.). *Amnesty International UK.* Retrieved from https://www.amnesty.org.uk/india-dalit-sisters-protection-raped-punishment-brothers-crime

68. Weber, M., & Bermingham, C. R. (2003). Authority and Autonomy in Marriage: Translation with Introduction and Commentary. *Sociological Theory, 21*(2), 85-102. https://doi.org/10.1111/1467-9558.00179

69. Greene, B. (2004). *The Fabric of the Cosmos: Space, Time, and the Texture of Reality.* Alfred A. Knopf.

70. Rovelli, C. (2018). *The Order of Time*. Riverhead Books.

71. James, W. (1890). *The principles of psychology*. Henry Holt and Company.

72. Sacks, O. (2017). *The river of consciousness*. (p. 31). Knopf.

73. Owen, A. (2017). Into the Gray Zone: A Neuroscientist Explores the Border Between Life and Death. (p.220) Scribner

74. Sacks, O. (2017). *The River of Consciousness* (p. 5). Knopf.

75. Parnia, S., & Young, J. (2013). *Erasing Death: The Science That Is Rewriting the Boundaries Between Life & Death* (1st ed. pp.133). HarperOne.

76. Darwin, C. R. (1881). *The Formation of Vegetable Mould, Through the Action of Worms, with Observations on Their Habits*. London: John Murray.

77. Sacks, O. (2017). *The River of Consciousness* (p. 72). Knopf.

78. Parnia, S., & Young, J. (2013). *Erasing Death: The Science That Is Rewriting the Boundaries Between Life & Death* (1st ed., pp. 272-2013). HarperOne.

79. Parnia, S., & Young, J. (2013). *Erasing Death: The Science That Is Rewriting the Boundaries Between Life & Death* (1st ed., p. 37). HarperOne.

80. Wienand, K., Kampschulte, L., & Heckl, W. M. (2023). Creating a foundation for origin of life outreach: How scientists relate to their field, the public, and religion. *PloS One, 18*(2), e0282243. https://doi.org/10.1371/journal.pone.0282243

81. Greene, B. (2004). *The Fabric of the Cosmos: Space, Time, and the Texture of Reality* (pp. 393-4). Alfred A. Knopf.

82. Moody, R. A. (1981). *Life After Life: The Investigation of a Phenomenon—Survival of Bodily Death* (p. 34). Mockingbird Books.

83. Moody, R. A. (1981). *Life After Life: The Investigation of a Phenomenon—Survival of Bodily Death* (p. 44). Mockingbird Books.

84. Moody, R. A. (1981). *Life After Life: The Investigation of a Phenomenon—Survival of Bodily Death* (p. 178). Mockingbird Books.

85. Evans-Wentz, W. Y. (Ed.). (1927). *The Tibetan Book of the Dead: Or the After-Death Experiences on the Bardo Plane* (L. K. Dawa-Samdup, Trans.). Oxford University Press.

86. Bush, N. E., & Greyson, B. (2014). Distressing near-death experiences: the basics. Missouri medicine, 111(6), 486–490.

87. Ellwood, G. F. (2001). *Uttermost Deep: The Challenge of Painful Near-Death Experiences* (p. 98). Lantern Books.

88. Moody, R. A. (1981). *Life After Life: The Investigation of a Phenomenon—Survival of Bodily Death* (p. 136). Mockingbird Books.

89. Fiore, E. (1995). *The Unquiet Dead: A Psychologist Treats Spirit Possession.* (p.25). Ballantine Books.

90. Ellwood, G. F. (2001). *Uttermost Deep: The Challenge of Painful Near-Death Experiences* (p. 156). Lantern Books.

91. van Lommel, P. (Year). *Consciousness Beyond Life: The Science of the Near-Death Experience* (p. 18). HarperOne.

92 Ellwood, G. F. (2001). *Uttermost Deep: The Challenge of Painful Near-Death Experiences* (p. 42). Lantern Books.

93. Ring, K. (1985). *Heading Toward Omega: In Search of the Meaning of the Near-Death Experience* (p. 63). William Morrow & Co.

94. Ring, K. (1985). *Heading Toward Omega: In Search of the Meaning of the Near-Death Experience* (p. 234). William Morrow & Co.

95. Ellwood, G. F. (2001). *Uttermost Deep: The Challenge of Painful Near-Death Experiences* (p. 42). Lantern Books.

96. Ellwood, G. F. (2001). *Uttermost Deep: The Challenge of Painful Near-Death Experiences* (p. 50). Lantern Books.

97. Ring, K. (1985). *Heading Toward Omega: In Search of the Meaning of the Near-Death Experience* (p. 57). William Morrow & Co.

98. Ring, K. (1985). *Heading Toward Omega: In Search of the Meaning of*

the Near-Death Experience (p. 234). William Morrow & Co.

99. Ring, K. (1985). *Heading Toward Omega: In Search of the Meaning of the Near-Death Experience* (p. 54). William Morrow & Co.

100. Ellwood, G. F. (2001). *Uttermost Deep: The Challenge of Painful Near-Death Experiences* (p. 74). Lantern Books.

101. Evans-Bush, N. (2009). Dancing Past the Dark. In J. M. Holden, B. Greyson, & D. James (Eds.), *The Handbook of Near-Death Experiences: Thirty Years of Investigation* (pp. 67). Praeger.

102. Ring, K. (1985). *Heading Toward Omega: In Search of the Meaning of the Near-Death Experience*. William Morrow & Co.

103. Somé, M. P. (1994). *Of water and the spirit: Ritual, magic, and initiation in the life of an African shaman* (p. 38). Putnam.

104. Somé, M. P. (1994). *Of water and the spirit: Ritual, magic, and initiation in the life of an African shaman* (p. 78). Putnam.

105. van Lommel, P. (Year). *Consciousness Beyond Life: The Science of the Near-Death Experience* (p. 77). HarperOne.

106. Ellwood, G. F. (2001). *Uttermost Deep: The Challenge of Painful Near-Death Experiences* (p. 49). Lantern Books.

107. Ellwood, G. F. (2001). *Uttermost Deep: The Challenge of Painful Near-Death Experiences* (p. 50). Lantern Books.

108. Ellwood, G. F. (2001). *Uttermost Deep: The Challenge of Painful Near-Death Experiences* (p. 170). Lantern Books.

109. Ellwood, G. F. (2001). *Uttermost Deep: The Challenge of Painful Near-Death Experiences* (p. 170). Lantern Books.

110. Ellwood, G. F. (2001). *Uttermost Deep: The Challenge of Painful Near-Death Experiences* (p. 83). Lantern Books.

111. Ellwood, G. F. (2001). *Uttermost Deep: The Challenge of Painful Near-Death Experiences* (p.). Lantern Books.

112. Ellwood, G. F. (2001). *Uttermost Deep: The Challenge of Painful Near-Death Experiences* (p. 63). Lantern Books.

113. Ellwood, G. F. (2001). *Uttermost Deep: The Challenge of Painful Near-Death Experiences*. Lantern Books.

114. Fiore, E. (1995). *The Unquiet Dead: A Psychologist Treats Spirit Possession*. (p.28). Ballantine Books.

115. Ellwood, G. F. (2001). *Uttermost Deep: The Challenge of Painful Near-Death Experiences* (p. 71). Lantern Books.

116. Greene, B. (2004). *The Fabric of the Cosmos: Space, Time, and the Texture of Reality* (p. 38). Alfred A. Knopf.

117. Greene, B. (2004). *The Fabric of the Cosmos: Space, Time, and the Texture of Reality* (p. 354). Alfred A. Knopf.

118. Kim, J. H., Lee, J. K., Kim, H. G., Kim, K. B., & Kim, H. R. (2019). Possible Effects of Radiofrequency Electromagnetic Field Exposure on Central Nerve System. Biomolecules & therapeutics, 27(3), 265–275. https://doi.org/10.4062/biomolther.2018.152

119. Kahneman, D. (2013). *Thinking, fast and slow*. Farrar, Straus and Giroux.

120. Loos, A. (1910). *Ornament and crime*. Lecture presented in Vienna.

121. Boyatzis, C. J., & Varghese, R. (1994). Children's Emotional Associations with Colors. *The Journal of Genetic Psychology, 155*(1), 77–85. https://doi.org/10.1080/00221325.1994.9914760

122. Jiang, A., Yao, X., Hemingray, C., & Westland, S. (2021, November 15). Young people's colour preference and the arousal level of small apartments. *Color Research & Application*. Advance online publication. https://doi.org/10.1002/col.22756

123. [cite economy and Society]

124. Kahneman, D. (2013). *Thinking, fast and slow*. Farrar, Straus and Giroux.

125.Jebb, A. T., Tay, L., Diener, E., et al. (2018). Happiness, income satiation and turning points around the world. *Nature Human Behaviour, 2*(1), 33–38. https://doi.org/10.1038/s41562-017-0277-0

126. Oishi, S., Cha, Y., Komiya, A., & Ono, H. (2022). Money and

happiness: the income-happiness correlation is higher when income inequality is higher. *PNAS Nexus, 1*(5), pgac224. https://doi.org/10.1093/pnasnexus/pgac224

127. van Lommel, P. (2010). *Consciousness beyond life: The science of the near-death experience (P 174)*. HarperOne.

128. Ellwood, G. F. (2001). *Uttermost Deep: The Challenge of Painful Near-Death Experiences*. Lantern Books.

129. Evans-Bush, N. (2009). Dancing Past the Dark. In J. M. Holden, B. Greyson, & D. James (Eds.), *The Handbook of Near-Death Experiences: Thirty Years of Investigation* (pp. 81). Praeger.

130. Ellwood, G. F. (2001). *Uttermost Deep: The Challenge of Painful Near-Death Experiences* (p. 123). Lantern Books.

131. Ellwood, G. F. (2001). *Uttermost Deep: The Challenge of Painful Near-Death Experiences* (p. 128). Lantern Books.

132. Evans-Bush, N. (2009). Dancing Past the Dark. In J. M. Holden, B. Greyson, & D. James (Eds.), *The Handbook of Near-Death Experiences: Thirty Years of Investigation* (pp. 153). Praeger.

133. Leopold T. (2018). Gender Differences in the Consequences of Divorce: A Study of Multiple Outcomes. *Demography*, 55(3), 769–797. https://doi.org/10.1007/s13524-018-0667-6

134. Kirsch I. (2014). Antidepressants and the Placebo Effect. Zeitschrift fur Psychologie, 222(3), 128–134. https://doi.org/10.1027/2151-2604/a000176

135. Davis, W. (2022, August 13). Deep North. *National Geographic*. Retrieved from https://www.nationalgeographic.com/science/article/deep-north

136. Boone, J. (2016, July 30). OpGabon: Anonymous attacks Gabon government sites to protest ritual killings. *The World*. https://theworld.org/stories/2016/07/30/opgabon-anonymous-attacks-gabon-government-sites-protest-ritual-killings

137.[Rehman, S. (2013, June). Freeing Omar Khadr: An Interview with Guantanamo Bay Activists. *The Diplomat*. https://thediplomat.com/2013/06/freeing-omar-khadr-an-interview-with-guantanamo-bay-activists/

The *Binding Chaos* series invites you on a transformative 13-book odyssey. This monumental work is organized into an introductory book and three quartets. Each quartet offers a unique vantage through which to explore different facets of our humanity, searching for the roots of the world we live in. The breadth of research and clarity of focus in this extraordinary work provides an illuminating new viewpoint on the world.

In *The Ontology Quartet*, we explore the five fundamental components that shape who we are and how we interact with society. From historical perspectives to the latest research, a wide and diverse world of knowledge produces innovative and bold new ideas. *The Creation of Me, Them and Us* explores the nature and creation of self, challenging our perceptions and understanding of who we truly are and why we are the way we are. *Abstracting Divinity* takes readers on a remarkable journey through theology, physics, and human nature to show us what we know about life and how that knowledge can be used to guide our choices. *Shaping Reality* ventures into the realm of consciousness and neuroscience to discover the nature of reality. *Free Will and Seductive Coercion* examines our choices, our coercion and the ways in which our paths are chosen.

The Sociology Quartet, brings us from the kernel of our self to the widest expanse of society, breaking down the nature of relationships, power and connection. *The Theft of Self* describes how our interactions create us, and how we are restricted and redirected by our social surroundings. *Great Men, Commoners, Witches and Wretches* explores the roles each person plays in a structure of power. *The Fourth Age of Nations* is a historical look at the evolution of societies with analysis and projection for the future. *Autonomy Diversity Society* offers insights into governance structures.

The Institutions Quartet, investigates the origins and structure of institutions shaping our lives as well as their true effects and purpose. *The Power Economy* dissects economic systems, with a very unique perspective on their nature. *Law and Chaos* looks at the less obvious origins, implications, and purpose of legal systems. *Political Science* investigates the systems, organizations and culture creating authoritative knowledge. *Code Will Rule* explores the ever-expanding role of technology and the world about to be created.

Heather Marsh

www.ingramcontent.com/pod-product-compliance
Lightning Source LLC
Chambersburg PA
CBHW062107020426
42335CB00013B/887

*9 7 8 1 9 8 9 7 8 3 0 9 2 *